The Economies of the Balkan and Eastern Europe Countries in the Changed World

The Economies of the Balkan and Eastern Europe Countries in the Changed World

Edited by

Anastasios G. Karasavvoglou

CAMBRIDGE
SCHOLARS
PUBLISHING

The Economies of the Balkan and Eastern Europe Countries in the Changed World,
Edited by Anastasios G. Karasavvoglou

This book first published 2011

Cambridge Scholars Publishing

12 Back Chapman Street, Newcastle upon Tyne, NE6 2XX, UK

British Library Cataloguing in Publication Data
A catalogue record for this book is available from the British Library

ISBN (10): 1-4438-2689-8, ISBN (13): 978-1-4438-2689-1

TABLE OF CONTENTS

Introductory Note

The fundamental economic and political changes that took place in the central, southeastern and eastern European countries at the end of the 80s shaped new data in Europe and in the world that were marked by positive aspirations regarding the development prospective of their economies and their integration in the global financial environment.

In the last two decades that have gone by, the countries, some more than others, have adopted open market policies, privatized previously government run businesses and supported the development of the private sector of the economy, made the work relations more flexible, intensified the economic relations with the rest of the world, put into place plans to attract foreign investments and in general they have implemented measures to boost the competitiveness of their economies emphasizing an extrovert orientation. In the meantime, they sought new alliances and cooperations in Europe as well as in the rest of the world and they have moved towards their integration in international economic-political organizations with absolute priority their full accession in the European Union.

The results were not streamlined, nor were they of the same intensity and magnitude nor were their effects of the same importance for the countries of the region. Thus, despite the expansion rate of the economies, the increase of the volume of the foreign trade, the progress of investments and infrastructures and the restructure of production, the course of the economies of the central and eastern European countries were hampered by significant problems in the area of competitiveness, high unemployment rates, unbearable loan burden and expansion of the percentage of poor people and the social exclusion of a part of the population.

After two decades one can claim that these countries have moved on to a new level with different characteristics and challenges compared to the ones they confronted in the initial phase of their transition from the old to the new status.

The initial adaptation period gave its place to a deep crisis. During the global economic crisis of 2007 the developing Europe initially showed significant resilience, but later on the exporting performance of the economies faced deceleration, the influx of funds were cut down and the countries became more vulnerable. Moreover, it seems that the accession of the ten new countries in the European Union is now the most defining stabilization factor of their economies and simultaneously constitutes the landmark for their transition to the market economy, given that the increased access to western markets can lead to a rapid development of exports and improved access to foreign investment funds.

In any case, the basic issues which are emerged in a financial policy level are:

- The acceleration of the growth rate of the economies
- The attraction of funds for the finance of investment plans
- The improvement of competitiveness and the increase of exports in Europe and the rest of the world
- The development and modernization of the infrastructures
- The effective participation of the countries in the European economy

In conjunction with the grave importance economic matters, arise certain sobering thoughts regarding the effects of implemented economic policies in a social level. Therefore, the social cohesion, the disintegration of the social fabric, the expanded unemployment and the disorganization of work relations and the social security system ought to be considered as the point of reference of the politics, and their treatment should accompany the applied measures in the financial level.

The second international conference 'The Economies of Balkan and Eastern Europe Countries in the Changed world', EBEEC 2010, that was held in May, in Kavala, Hellas, under the auspices of the Accountancy Department of Kavala Institute of Technology, aimed at approaching relative thoughts. The presentations that were performed refer to matters related to macroeconomic issues, such as the economic relations of the countries in the region with the European Union or the importance of the FDI in the development, and also to the factors which have an effect on the economic developments in the countries, for instance business practices and their role in the development process.

The papers of this Volume are classified in the following units:

1. European Union and economical developments in Balkan and Eastern Europe countries
2. Regional development
3. FDI, enterprise finance and banking
4. Rural developments in specific countries
5. Supreme Audit Institution and IFRS
6. Labor market, enterprises and entrepreneurship

In the first subject unit, Kekenovski and Cvetkoska mention the role of globalization during the formulation of the Integration policy in the European Union and highlight important factors which can shape a successful Public policy of the European Union. Fessel features significant parameters of the integration of trade relations of the Balkan countries in the E.U. putting emphasis on the free trade agreements among the immersed countries. Malkidis describes and elaborates on the role of the Stability pact in South Eastern Europe, taking into consideration the latest social, economical and political changes which took part in this region. Trifonova focuses on the significance of the exchange rate policy with regard to the Bulgarian economy. Pochaleev and Todorova evaluate the repercussions of the common agricultural policy on the agricultural sector of the Bulgarian economy.

In the second subject unit, Bejko, Combi and Qiqi examine the issues of the regional development in Albania and make recommendations for the regional development strategies in Albania for the confrontation of the difficulties. Mantatzis underlines important aspects of regional disparities in Greece, while Rova and Zyberi make reference to the especially interesting issue of the effects that the Greek economic crisis has on the economic development of Albania, taking into consideration the close economic relations of the two countries in addition to the existence of around one million Albanian immigrants in the Greek economy. Nikolaidis, Batzios, Mandilas, Nikolaidis and Polychronidou place emphasis on the significance of the manufacturing sector for the development of the Eastern Macedonia and Thrace region, and define those factors which are considerable for the effectiveness of the manufacturing sector in the regional development.

In the next subject unit, Maditinos, Kousenidis and Chatzoudes present the role of the Greek economy in the Balkans with specific reference to the importance, as well as to the effects of the Greek FDI. Makogon, Orekhova, Ryabchyn analyze the framework for the attraction of investments in the area of Black Sea emphasising the Synergetic approach, while Voutsa describes the significance of the International Financial Institutions in the Transition countries. What is more, Polychronidou, Kazanidis, Eleftheriadou and Valsamidis evaluate the webpages of Greek banks, concerning e-banking in Greece and Bulgaria.

In chapter four the two papers are developed on the basis of rural development; the first one is written by Belletti and Leksinaj rates that the micro credit system reinforces the sustainable development dynamic in Albania and the second one, which is written by Bitsani and Kavoura, looks into the contribution of rural tour methodology in the tourism development.

Chapter five presents two special issues in the sector of Financial Economic and Accounting. Bonic and Mladenovic examine the role of Reporting of supreme audit institution (SAI) in the Fiscal stabilization and in the stimulated investment and Baboukardos focuses on IFRS disclosure requirements for goodwill and goes through the Greek listed companies.

The labor market issues are discussed in the next unit. Pignatti makes reference to the position of women in the Ukrainian labor market and specifies the factors that lead to the discrimination against women. Karabchuk analyses the magnitude together with the importance of standard and non standard employment in Russia; Boga-Karteri, Stalidis and Papanicolas study the organisational practices in relation to communication and in the end, Roman and Ignatescu make a comparative analysis on the impact of financial crisis of SMEs in central and Eastern European countries.

We believe that the authors of this Volume contribute substantially to further investigation relatively to the past, the present but mainly to the future of the economies of the countries in the region, and promote major issues for scientific research.

Thus, we leave these papers to the academic community of economic and social sciences, the researchers and the policy makers with the hope that they can collect grave information, draw useful conclusions and form political proposals which will contribute to the amelioration of the economic and social conditions in a special region of our planet.

Finally, I would like to thank the authors for their participation at the conference EBEEC 2010 and their assent to publish their papers in this collective Volume. I am greatly indebted to Dr. Persefoni Polychronidou, adjoined assistant professor of Kavala Institute of Technology, as she undertook to accomplish all the necessary procedures from the conference until the publication of this Volume. During this effort she was supported by PhD Candidate Dimitrios Chatzoudes, Dr. Theodosios Theodosiou, Dr. Ioannis Kazanidis, M.A. Christi Christodoulidou and Dr. Eftichia Vraimaki. This volume substantially composes the result of these people's hard work.

Kavala, July 2010
Professor Anastasios G. Karasavvoglou

PART ONE:

THE EUROPEAN UNION AND ECONOMIC DEVELOPMENTS IN THE BALKAN AND EASTERN EUROPEAN COUNTRIES

GLOBALIZATION AND POLICY-MAKING IN THE EUROPEAN UNION

LJUBOMIR KEKENOVSKI
AND VIOLETA CVETKOSKA

Abstract

This paper sets out the foundations of how globalization, and more generally techno-economic forces, can be integrated into public policy and EU policy making. It seeks to contrast a perspective on globalization and EU policy-making in which techno-economic forces have a primacy with rival perspectives which stress the primacy of institutions and ideas. The prominence of globalization is based on the impression that many aspects of political, economical, social and cultural life have shifted from the national level towards the international and global levels. The anatomy of globalization can be thought of in terms of interconnectedness between all levels of societies and the extent, intensity and speed of interconnectedness mark out globalization from other forms of international connection. It is also pointed out the relationship between globalization and European integration. In this paper significant place is given to globalization and public policy. The strong perspective on globalization stresses its techno-economic roots and the reduction in state autonomy and the techno-economic context has a clear primacy in public policy. Public policy analysis reveals a number of perspectives which contrast with techno-economic. Two of the most important are: a perspective which stresses the primacy of institutions in which institutions have an independent impact on policy outcomes; and the primacy of ideas in which ideas, ideologies and belief systems have independent impact. Nevertheless, the techno-economic perspectives enable the globalization hypothesis to be spelt out clearly, while the other two enable critical analysis of hypothesis. This paper focuses on the relationship between globalization and EU policy-making through the lenses of three competitive approaches while recognizing the important division between supernationalism and intergovernmentalism that cuts through all of them.

Introduction

> "A day will come when all the nations of this continent, without losing their distinct qualities or their glorious individuality, will fuse together in a higher unity and from the European brotherhood. A day will come when the only battlefield will be the marketplace for competing ideas. A day will come when bullets and bombs will be replaced by votes"
> —Victor Hugo, 1849

Victor Hugo spoke those prophetic words in 1849, but it took more than a century for these utopian predictions to start coming true. During that time, two world wars and countless other conflicts on European soil caused millions of deaths and there were times when all hopes seemed lost.

In 1945, just after the Second World War, Winston Churchill described Europe as "rubble heap, a charnel house, a breeding ground for pestilence and hate". A year later, on 19 September 1946, in his famous Zurich speech, he proposed as a remedy:

> "to recreate the European Family… and to provide it with a structure under which it can dwell in peace, in safety and in freedom… a kind of United States of Europe".

Half a century later, realizing and exceeding Churchill's vision, the western part of the "European Family" had become an island of peace and prosperity in a world ravaged by hatred, conflicts, civil wars and misery. The successful formula that European nations had invented to overcome their depression was the integration to the formerly antagonistic nation-states into a union of peacefully interacting and competing nations. The multinational integration formula involves the gradual creation of imperceptible albeit innumerable links between the nations taking part in the process. Those links consist of common laws and common policies, which govern the Member States' economic activities and influence the day-to-day lives and occupations of their citizens.

This paper presents globalization and regional integration as two of the most salient international trends of our time. Their relationship, however, is not straightforward: on the one hand, a world of regional blocs appears to contradict a single globalization world, while on the other hand regions can be perceived as manifestations of globalization and building blocks of global integration. In an 'outside-in' view of this relationship globalization is the primary driving force. In this view regionalization might represent a stronger defense against globalization than the nation state or add to the existing global trends. Conversely in an 'inside-out' view, regional trends and policies to promote regionalization are important causes of globalization (Bartle, 2005).

The European Union (EU) is the most developed instance of regional integration and since the 1990s its relationship with globalization has increasingly become the subject of interest. A commonly held view is that globalization is the key variable which has driven European integration. Many political elites and policy-makers hold this 'outside-in' view.

Chris Patten, a former European Commissioner, wrote that it is

> "more widely accepted than ever that in the modern world [European] nations need to pool their sovereignty if only in response to the process of globalization".
> —Patten, 2002

What distinguishes the EU from other examples of regional integration is that it has a highly developed and institutionalized system of policy-making which involves legislation over a wide range of sectors.

This paper is organized in 6 sections together with the introductory one. Globalization and European integration are presented in section 2. Globalization and public policy are described in section 3. Enlargement of European Union is overviewed in section 4, while nota bene is given in section 5. Bibliography is presented in the final section.

Globalization and European integration

The prominence of globalization is based on the impression that many aspects of political, economic, social and cultural life have shifted from the national level towards the international and global levels. Studies of globalization are often introduced with an impression such as 'political processes, events and activities nowadays appear increasingly to have a global or international dimension' (McGrew, 1992, p. 2) and 'the world is rapidly being moulded into a shared social space by economic and technological forces and… developments on the region of the world can have profound consequences for the life chances of individuals or communities on the other side of a globe' (Held et al., 1999, p. 1). Technological change and the internationalization of trade, production and finance are prominent aspects of contemporary globalization (McGrew, 1992, pp. 24-25).

There is no consensus on the nature and the extent of globalization. Although there is a wide range of perspectives and subtleties, broadly two key schools of thought can be identified and termed 'strong' and 'weak' globalization (Jones, 2000) whose protagonists can respectively be labeled 'hyperglobalists' and 'sceptics' (Held et. al., 1999). Key aspects of globalization in contention are the extent of globalization, the importance of technology and markets and the role and autonomy of the state and policy-makers (Bartle, 2005).

In the notion of strong globalization, global interconnectedness is both extensive and intensive. We have witnessed the dawn of the borderless global age in which technology and markets are the main driving forces (Held et. al., 1999, pp. 3-5) Financial markets, trade and production are distributed across the world and becoming evenly spread (Jones, 2000, pp. 13-16). A process of 'denationalization' is also at the heart of the hyperglobalist challenge and being replaced by markets and regional and global forms of governance. Markets are much more dominant: ' where states were once the masters over markets, now it is the markets which, on many crucial issues are the masters over the governments of states' (Strange, 1996, p. 4), and the rise of the multinational corporation (MNC) has changed the nature of international relations (Stopford and Strange, 1991). As the state retreats and markets become more dominant, governments are compelled to implement market-friendly policies such as liberalizing the economy and developing policies which are congenial to MNCs (Ohmae, 1990, pp. 11-13). Details for strong globalization can be found in (Jones, 2000; Held et. al, 1999; Strange, 1996; Stopford and Strange, 1991; Ohmae, 1990).

The 'sceptics' and the proponents of 'weak' globalization take issue with the extent of globalization depicted by hyperglobalists, the decline of the state and its monocausal nature. The skeptics recognize increasing internationalization but the processes are uneven and not historically unprecedented (Held et al., 1999, pp. 5; Jones, 2000, pp. 16). For weak globalization see (Jones, 2000; Held et al., 1999; Hirst and Thompson, 1996; McGrew, 1992).

A combination of the hyperglobalist conviction that globalization is one of the most important forces shaping the modern world with a skeptical view which perceives 'global stratification' and new forms of division seems more plausible (Held et al., 1999, pp. 7-9).

Globalization and European integration appear prima facie to be different or even contradictory processes and debates have often been conducted as if they occupy separate spheres (Wallace, 2000). They appear to symbolize economic integration over very different geographical areas, a process limited to Western Europe which can even be a barrier to globalization, the other extending across the whole world. In Europe in the 1980s the stress was on completing the 'internal' market by eliminating internal barriers to trade which appeared to herald a closed 'fortress Europe' (Harrop, 1992; Tsoukalis, 1997, pp. 237).

The development of a single market and globalization since the 1980s indicate that the two phenomena are inextricably linked: they are complementary and possibly different manifestations of the same process. The single market of the 1990s, for example, represents a more open and globalised Europe than the fortress Europe imagined in the 1980s (Bartle, 2005).

The complementary nature of globalization and European integration is often noted: there are 'strong interconnections between regionalism and globalization that cover a variety of issues and draw similar motivational forces' (Bartle, 2005; Dent, 1997, p. 12) and 'ragionalisation can create the necessary kinds of economic, social and physical infrastructures which facilitate and complement the deepening of globalization' (Bartle, 2005; Held et al., 1999, p. 16). Cross-border connections are seen as a key aspect of globalization and their management is more intensive in Europe than at other global levels (Bartle, 2005; Wallace, 2000).

Addressing the relationship between globalization and European integration, Ross (1998) refutes the unilateral view and its predominantly strong notion of globalization. He argues that globalization as currently conceived – a global interconnected economy, high financial and trade flows – is very different from the external factors that influenced Europe prior to the 1990s.

A bidirectional view of globalization and European integration can be consistent with techno-economic perspectives on public policy: policy is a response to and reinforces technical and economic processes. However, emphasis on the policy sources of globalization is more likely to correlate with perspectives which stress the internal sources of policy change, such as those which give primacy to European institutions or ideas held by key actors. Bartle (2005) pointed out that in order to understand whether the relationship between globalization and European integration can be understood in terms of the primacy of techno-economic forces, of institutions or of ideas, various theories and approaches of European integration policy-making and how globalization figures in them need to be examined.

In 1972, Donald Puchala likened theorists of EU integration to blind men touching an elephant, each one feeling a different part of the elephant and purporting to describe a very different animal. Today, theories of the EU are even more diverse. Excellent introduction to European integration theories can be found in Rosamond's (2000), and in the essays in Wiener and Diez (2004).

Globalization and public policy

The idea that technological and economic factors such as globalization can influence politics and public policy is related to well established debates on technology and politics (Street, 1992) as well as to debates on the socio-economic context and public policy (John, 1998). The strong perspective on globalization stresses its techno-economic roots and the reduction in state autonomy and the techno-economic context has a clear primacy in public policy. The weak perspective takes a more complex view of the sources of globalization, particularly the policy sources and the autonomy of policy-makers. While the weak perspective is not necessarily incompatible with the primacy of techno-economic forces in public policy, other perspectives which stress the importance of endogenous political processes appear more appropriate (Bartle, 2005).

Public policy analysis reveals a number of perspectives which contrast with the techno-economic. Two of the most important are: a perspective which stresses the primacy of institutions in which institutions have an independent impact on policy outcomes; and the primacy of ideas in which ideas, ideologies and belief systems have an independent impact. There are of course other perspectives, some of which overlap with these two, and there are many variants and subtleties in each perspective (John, 1998).

Therefore, the following sections focus on the relationship between globalization and EU policy-making through the lenses of these three perspectives.

The primacy of techno-economic forces

Within this perspective policy change is understood primarily as an expression of the technological and economic context. In times of rapid techno-economic change, policy outputs are expected to respond likewise after a lag for legislation. In an extreme version of this perspective labeled 'autonomous technology' the dominance of technological logic is manifested in the illumination of difference, as everything, including the state, is brought under its influence (Street, 1992, p. 24). In a weaker version 'technology sets the conditions for the operation of the political system, including the political agenda, even if it does not determine the policy output' (Street, 1992, p. 30). The techno-economic perspective is also related to socio-economic and rational choice approaches to public policy (John, 1998). In socio-economic approaches, institutions, group dynamics and ideas are expressions of socio-economic forces and external context such as economic structures are the primary determinants of policy preferences. While socio-economic approaches also include class-based analysis of politics and policy, a techno-economic approach is more individualist and draws from rational choice. Preferences of actors are based on their judgment of their self-interest in response to changing material context (Bartle, 2005; John, 1998).

The primacy of techno-economic context in public policy has enjoyed a revival in the era of globalization. One variant of socio-economic approaches notes, for example, that when capital is mobile 'differentiation and political choice are not possible' and 'as a result, the market reigns' (John, 1998, p. 104). Policy and politics are clearly subordinate to globalization and there are strong impulses towards adopting policies of liberalization. Governments are advised, to 'concentrate on essentials', 'enforce competition', 'give up national champions', 'liberalize in stages' and 'watch the competition' (Stopford and Strange, 1991, p. 218-223). The result is a move to the 'competition state' in which state policies shift towards the promotion of competitiveness and marketiation (Cerny, 1997). The 'paradigm shift' from Keynesian to neo-liberal policies adopted in most European countries (Wright, 1995, p. 337) can be explained in these terms (Bartle, 2005).

This perspective is clearly linked with strong globalization, though the policy sources of globalization can also be important, as in weak globalization. Whether the initial source of policy changes or not, techno-economic forces become dominant and globalization and liberalization are reciprocal and elements of a single mutually reinforcing process (Bartle, 2005). As the process gathers momentum, a 'ratchet effect' ensues in which, 'in a process of competitive deregulation and creeping liberalization', the state gives away more and more powers which it finds difficult to recover (Bartle, 2005; Cerny, 1997, p. 273).

In European integration, despite the bitter rivalry between intergovernmentalism and neo-functionalism, the primacy of techno-economic forces, particularly globalization, can be perceived in both theories. Neither theory necessarily excludes the possibility of political choice (Verdier and Breen, 2001), but both theories are founded on an 'interest group' model in which national or transnational actors' preferences formed from contexts are at the roof of step changes in European integration and policy (Parsons, 2000, p. 46). However, the techno-economic processes and how they impinge on actors, the role of national and supranational institutions and the way in which preferences are transmitted into EU policy vary considerably (Bartle, 2005).

Techno-economic forces and state centrism: liberal intergovernmentalism

In these perspective techno-economic forces, resulting from globalization, economic interdependence and sectoral contexts, have primacy and are transmitted into EU policy through national and intergovernmental political and institutional processes. If external forces are strong, national policy preferences are expected to converge and intergovernmental agreements for common EU policies can be easily achieved. Conversely, if external forces are weak and national sectoral contexts are divergent, European-level agreements are more difficult to achieve. At the EU level intergovernmental bargaining is the dominant mode of decision-making and EU institutions, law and procedures are subordinate and their impact is secondary. In liberal intergovernmentalism, which is close to this perspective, European integration is likely to increase when global forces impact on domestic interests leading to a convergence of policy preferences and a logic for European states to agree common policy responses (Moravcsik, 1993; 1998). Moravcsik (1993; 1998) pointed out that there are three key stages in liberal intergovernmentalism. In the first stage, the demand for policy outcomes, national preferences are established from domestic interests which are shaped within socio-economic environments, including globalization and national and international sectoral context. In the second stage, policies are agreed in intergovernmental negotiations and can be understood from the strategic behavior of states within the inter-state system of the EU, relative state powers, the intercity of domestic preferences and the linkage of issues (Moravcsik, 1993, pp. 496-507). The third stage is a process of 'institutional choice' in which the pooling and delegation of sovereignty to supranational institutions take place (Bartle, 2005; Moravcsik, 1998, pp. 67-77).

Techno-economic forces and supranationalism: neo-functionalism

This perspective argues that the impetus for policy change can come from transnational business interests and European decision-making is characterized by supranationalism. Economic globalization is the crucial techno-economic process which has led to many large MNCs with substantial global and regional operations and to problems which transcend the nation state. Organized transnationally and sometimes globally, transnational interests prefer European level policy solutions and, in alliance with supranational institutions, are primary drivers of EU policy. Again the rationality assumption pervades this perspective, with the primacy of societal interests shaped in techno-economic contexts. Political and institutional processes are essentially reactive and secondary (Bartle, 2005).

Globalization, however, was not at the heart of neo-functionalism, the main supranational theory of integration. Rosamond (2000) pointed out that the main force is 'economic spillover', a geographically limited process in which economic and technical forces act between interconnected areas of the economy. Although many recent explanations of European integration stress EU political and institutional processes, they draw from the neo-functional tradition and emphasize global markets, business and communications, which militate towards supranational policies (Sandholtz and Zysman, 1989; Cowles, 1995; Sweet and Sandholtz, 1998). Figure 1, presents primacy of techno-economic forces.

Figure 1. Perspective on policy-making in the EU: Primacy of techno-economic forces

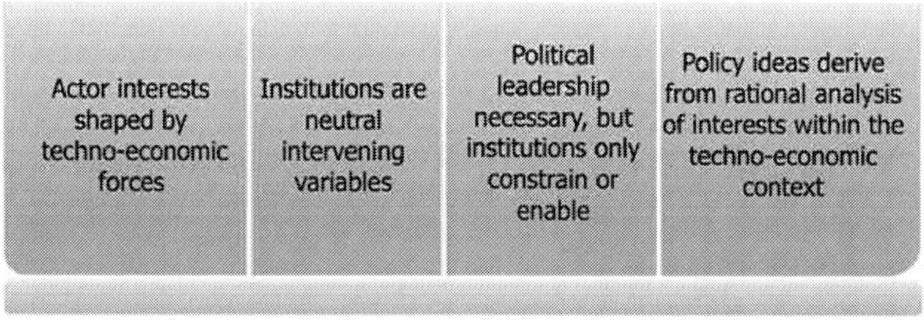

The primacy of institutions

> "First the engine was key individuals with vision. Then the Commission became the motor for Europe, a common institution helped along by the Franco-German alliance, particularly in the 1980s, when Delors, special relation with European leaders brought in the Single Market and EMU. But since Maastricht the Community has run down hill. Nice was a caricature of what should have happened"
> —Alain Lamassoure, 2000

The idea that institutions can have an independent impact on policy has undergone a revival since the 1980s under the guise of 'new institutionalism' (March and Olsen, 1989; Peters, 1999). New institutionalism moves beyond a limited functional view of institutions as:

> "a neutral transmission belt for political actions that begin in society, transmit to the executive and legislature, and are applied by bureaucracies to return to society again in the form of policy outcomes"
> —John, 1998

Institutions rather have 'standard operating procedures' which routinise the values of the political system (John, 1998, p. 41). Political and societal actors are constrained in their actions and are unable or unwilling to follow unconstrained self-interested preferences. Institutions do more than constrain, they define the norms of a political system and actors' preferences are shaped by these norms instead of, or in addition to, rationally formed responses to social, economic and technological contexts (Bartle, 2005). Institutional theory, however, does not repudiate the context per se, but the primacy attached to it: 'political democracy depends not only on economic and social conditions but also on the design of political institutions'

(March and Olsen, 1989, p. 17) and 'causation can go in both directions' (Peters, 1999, p. 15). Exogenous forces such as globalization and technical change therefore can provide stimuli for policy change but the actual response is shaped by institutional factors. Stronger versions of new institutionalism, namely the historical and sociological variants, ascribe a primacy to institutions in policy change and globalization becomes secondary. A weak concept of globalization is more appropriate: globalization is more than a monocausal techno-economic process and policy preferences and decisions have significant endogenous sources.

Understanding the EU means understanding the inter-institutional cooperation and competition that occurs as the EU's institutions perform their three core functions:

1. providing political direction,
2. managing the Union, and
3. integrating interests.

If institutions matter in determining politics in any political society, they may matter even more in the European Union than in other systems. Why? We can think of at least six reasons (Peterson and Shackleton, 2002).

First, the EU's institutions remain young. Second, the EU's institutions matter because they are the vehicles used by the Union's member governments to enforce the terms of the bargains they make with each other (see, Moravcsik, 1998). Moreover, as a third observation, the EU's institutions do not simply manage. Fourth, the EU's institutions fascinate because they are powerful yet mostly unloved by European citizens. Fifth, the EU's institutions not only link Brussels to national EU capitals. They also link Europe to the wider world of international politics. Sixth and somewhat paradoxically, EU politics are largely a product of competition between its institutions – each of which has its own identity and interests – but the Union's institutions are profoundly and inescapably interdependent.

In European integration, analysis focuses mainly on EU-level institutions rather than national institutions, though the two levels are sometimes integrated (Rosamond, 2000, pp. 113-22; Hooghe and Marks, 2001). Nugent (2002) gives a thorough catalogue of the EU institutions, while Dinan (2004) sets them into their historical context. Among the many studies of the Commission, Edwards and Spence (1997), and Page (1997) provide a valuable explanation and insights. For the Council and European

Council, see Hayes-Renshaw and Wallace (1997; 2005), and Westlake and Galloway (2005). Jacobs, Corbett, and Shackleton (2000), provide a comprehensive account of the European Parliament. The ECJ and the European legal system are covered by Dehousse (1998), and Mattli and Slaughter (1998). On the national dimension, see Maurer and Wessels (2003), Cowles, Caporaso, and Risse (2001), and Bulmer and Lequesne (2005). Figure 2, presents the primacy of institutions.

Figure 2. Perspective on policy-making in the EU: Primacy of institutions

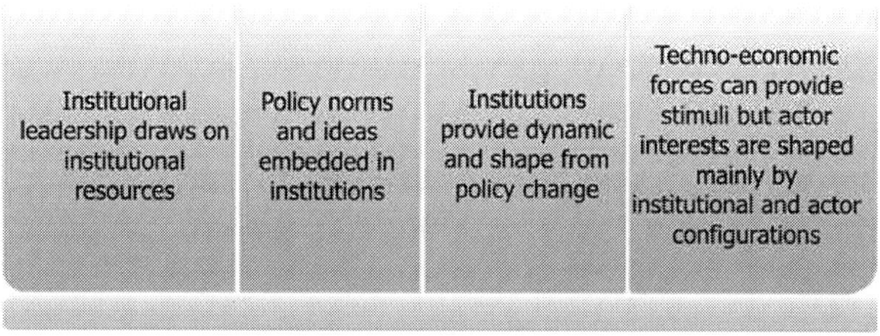

The primacy of ideas

In a third perspective idea, belief systems and ideologies play a central role in policy change. Ideas, of course, are central in any perspective on politics and policy; they form the basis of policy and provide a framework in which decision-makers think and act (John, 1998, p. 144). In an idea's perspective, ideas are not simply 'out there' waiting to emerge from rational analysis of material reality or embedded within institutions but derive from, and are elements of, belief systems and ideologies held by actors. Ideas held by actors thus condition and interpret external forces. In this way ideas can have an independent impact 'by being the way in which people frame questions, give meaning to the world and propose solutions, ideas have a life of their own' (John, 1998, p. 157). Ideas have a primacy in 'social constructivist' perspectives on politics, which involve attempts to understand how ideas are formed from individuals' perceptions and relations with society (Bartle, 2005;).

In European integration, perspectives which stress the primacy of ideas have not been prominent but have increased since the late 1990s. Christiansen et al. (2001, p. 2) argue that:

> "European integration has had a transformative impact on the European state system' which has changed 'agents' identity and subsequently their interests and behavior have equally changed"

The ideas held by key actors in the Commission are important for EU policy-making and arise from a variety of sources, primarily the national and political backgrounds but also from the transnational community of actors in the Commission (Hooghe, 2001). The ideas held by key actors at national level which are not directly connected with domestic interest groups or with economic conditions can also be decisive in European integration (Parsons, 2000; 2003). Figure 3, presents the primacy of ideas.

Figure 3. Perspective on policy-making in the EU: Primacy of ideas

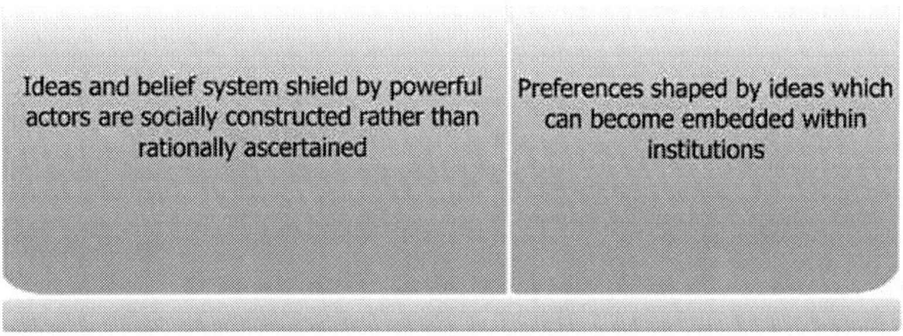

Enlargement of the European Union

In his historic declaration of May 1950, Robert Schuman, Minister for Foreign Affairs of France, stated that:

> "Europe will not be made all at once, or according to a single plan. It will be built through concrete achievements which first create a de facto solidarity"

Enlargement was always an integral part of the integration process and policy-making in the EU (Wallace, 2000, p. 150). The EU enlargement policy has very particular characteristics. These characteristics affect both the policy process through which it is produced and the shape of substantive policy outcomes. Enlargement is a 'composite policy', that is, a broad policy framework that draws on policies in a broad range of issue areas. EU membership has grown from six to twenty seven nations, bringing the EU's population to nearly half a billion. The successive enlargements have strengthened democracy, made Europe more secure and increased its potential for trade and economic growth.

Is the EU membership a good or bad thing? The majority of citizens in all EU countries believe membership is a good thing for their country, see Figure 4 and Figure 5. The level of support varies across the Union and fluctuates over time. A 2007 Eurobarometer survey showed that the strongest supporters are still some of the oldest member states (Ireland and the Benelux countries).

Figure 4. Support for EU membership, as a percentage of persons surveyed, EU-27 (autumn 2007)

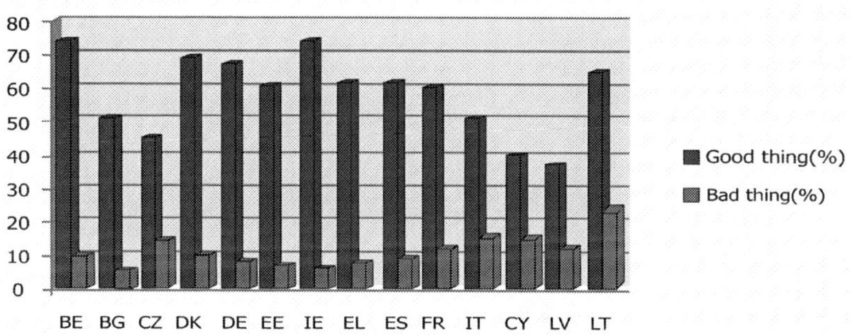

Figure 5. Support for EU membership, as a percentage of persons surveyed, EU-27 (autumn 2007)

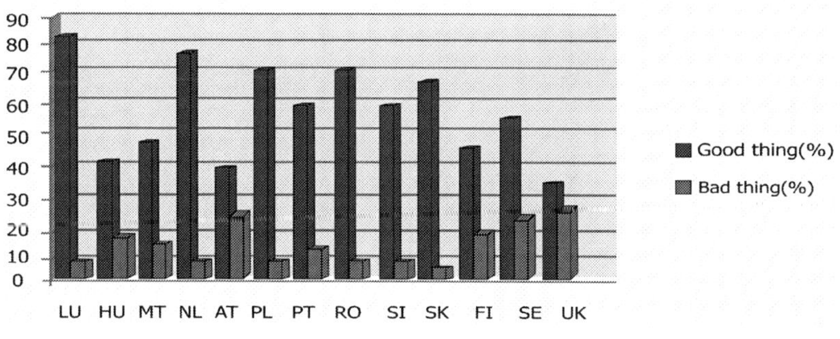

Source: Eurobarometer.

Not all European countries are, or wish to be, EU members - but the Union is open to any European country that fulfils the democratic, political and economic criteria for membership.

Nota bene

> "The EU is a unique experiment embedding the national in the European, and the European in the national"
> —Laffan, 2000

Europe's history mainly relates to the wars for the domination of some nations over the others and the battles of those others for their liberation from their oppressor or oppressors. Right after the Second World War, some inspired politicians, like Schuman, Adenauer, De Gasperi and Spaak, realized that the European nations, which had just ruined each other in a nonsensical war for the enlargement of their economic space, were in fact parts of a single geographic, economic and political entity, that could guarantee the prosperity of all in a single market. The famous declaration of Robert Schuman of the 9th May 1950, inspired by Jean Monnet, was clear as to the step by step approach to be followed by European integration. The realization of a customs union would fulfill the requirements for building a large common market and this would in turn establish the conditions and exert the pressures needed for the attainment of an economic and monetary union. This close economic integration would eventually necessitate a common foreign policy. Thus, political integration would follow the economic one.

Common policies, as all other public policies, are there to answer societal needs which arise in a defined community at a certain time. Therefore, not only the objectives that the member states set for each common policy, but also the means that they give to the common institutions to attain them and the measures that the latter adopt in order to implement them change in accordance with the economic, political and social needs that the states, which take part in the process, experience at a certain time.

Today it may be said with confidence that the experiment was largely successful. We agree with Diamandouros (2004) that multinational integration has established peace in Western Europe, has turned the former enemies into good partners, has secured the equality of all participating nations under common laws, and has ensured development opportunities and thus the relative prosperity of all. In short, the European Union has become an island of peace and prosperity in a world that is still suffering from skillfully cultivated ethnic, racial, religious and other differences, battles for the glory of warmongers, slaughters and displacements of populations for ethnic and/or economic reasons and finally, the exploitation of the vast majority of mankind by an unscrupulous minority, equally distributed among various nations.

Not all European countries are, or wish to be, EU members - but the Union welcomes membership applications from any democratic European country.

References

Bartle, I., 2005, *Globalization and EU policy-making*, Manchester University Press.

Bulmer, S. and Lequesne, C., 2005, *Member States and the European Union,* Oxford, Oxford University Press.

Cerny, P.G., 1997, Paradoxes of the competition state: the dynamics of political globalization', *Government and Opposition*, 32, 2, pp. 251-74.

Christiansen, T., Jorgensen, K. E. and Wiener A., 2001, *The Social Construction of Europe.* London, Sage.

Cowles, M. G., Caporaso, J. A., and Rise, T., 2001, *Transforming Europe: Europeanization and Domestic Change*, Ithaca, Cornell University Press.

—. 1995, Setting the agenda for a new Europe: the ERT and EC, 1992, *Journal of Common Market Studies*, 33, 4, pp. 502-26.

Dehousse, R., 1998, *The European Court of Justice*, London, Macmillan.

Dent, C.M., 1997, *The European Economy: The Global Context*, London: Routledge.

Diamanadouros, N., 2004, *Access to European Union: law, economics, policies*, 13th revised edition, European Study Service.

Dinan, D., 2004, *Europe Recast: A History of European Union*, London, Palgrave Macmillan.

Edwards , G., and Spence, D., 1997, *The European Commision*, 2nd ed., London, Longman.

Harrop, J., 1992, *The Political Economy of Integration in the European Community*, 2nd ed., Aldershot, Elgar.

Hayes-Renshaw, F. and Wallace, H., 1997, *The Council of Ministers*, London, Macmillan.

Hayes-Renshaw, F. and Wallace, H., 2005, *The Council of Ministers*, 2nd ed., London, Palgrave Macmillan.

Held, D., McGrew, A., Goldblatt, D. and Perraton, J., 1999, *Global Transformations: Politics, Economics and Culture*, Cambridge, Polity Press.

Hirst, P. and Thompson, G., 1996, *Globalization in Question: The international Economy and the Possibilities of Governance,* Cambridge, Polity Press.
Hooghe, L. and Marks, G., 2001, *Multi-level Governance and European Integration*, New York and Oxford, Rowman & Littlefield.
Jacobs, F., Corbett, R., and Shackleton, M., 2000, *The European Parliament*, 3rd ed. London, John Harper.
John, P., 1998, *Analyzing Public Policy*, London and New York, Pinter.
Jones, R.J.B., 2000, *The World turned Upside Down? Globalization and the Future of the State*, Manchester, Manchester University Press.
March, J.G. and Olsen, J., 1989, *Rediscovering Institutions: The Organizational Basis of Politics*, New York, Free Press.
Mattli, W. and Slaughter, A.M., 1998, The ECJ Governments and Legal Integration in the EU, *International Organisation*, 52, 1, pp. 177-210.
Mauer, A. and Wessels, W., 2003, *Fifteen into One? The European Union and its Member States*. Manchester, Manchester University Press.
McGrew, A.G.,1992, *Concepttualizing global politics*, McGrew A.G., Lewis P. et al., *Global Politics: Globalization and the Nation State*, Cambridge, Polity Press, pp. 1-28.
Moravcsik, A., 1993, Preferences and power in the European Community: a liberal intergovernmentalist – approach, *Journal of Common Market Studies*, 31, 4, pp. 473-524.
—. 1998, *The Choice for Europe: Social Purpose and state Power from Messina to Maastricht*, London, UCL Press.
Nugent, N., 2002, *The government and Politics of the European Union*, 5th ed. London, Palgrave Macmillan.
Ohmae, K., 1990. *The Borderless World: Power and Strategy in the Global Market Place*. London: Fontana.
Page, E., 1997, *People who Run Europe*. Oxford, Clarendon Press.
Parsons, C., 2000, Domestic interests, ideas and integration: lessons from the French case, *Journal of Common Market Studies*, 38, 1, pp. 45-70.
Patten, C., 2002, *Foreword*, in Arnull A. and Wincott D. (ed), *Accountability and Legitimacy in the European Union*, Oxford, Oxford University Press.
Peters, B.G., 1999, *Institutionat Theory in Political Science: The 'New Institutionalism*, London, Pinter.
Peterson, J. and Schackleton, M.M., 2002, *The Institutions of the European Union*, Oxford Union Press.
Rosamond, B., 2000, *Theories of European Integration*, London, Palgrave.

Ross, G., 1998, *European integration and globalization*, R. Axtmann (ed.), *Globalization and Europe: Theoretical and Empirical Investigations*, London and Washington DC, Pinter, pp. 164-183.

Sandholtz, W. and Zysman, J., 1989, 1992: recasting the European bargain, *World Politics*, 42, 1, pp. 95-12.

Stopford, J. and Strange, S., 1991, *Rival States, Rival Firms: Competition for World Market Shares*, Cambridge, Cambridge University Press.

Strange, S., 1996, *The Retreat of the State: The Diffusion of Power in the World Economy*, Cambridge, Cambridge University Press.

Street, J., 1992, *Politics and Technology*, Basingstoke, Macmillan.

Sandholtz, W. and Stone Sweet, A., 1998, *European Integration and Supranational Governance*, Oxford, Oxford University Press.

Tsoukalis, L., 1997, *The New European Economy Revisited*, Oxford, Oxford University Press.

Verdier, D. and Breen, R., 2001, Europeanization and globalization: politics against markets in the European Union, *Comparative Political Studies*, 34, 3, pp. 227-62.

Wallace, H., 2000, Europeanisation and globalization: complementary or contradictory trends?, *New Political Economy*, 5, 3, pp. 369-82.

Westlake, M. and Galloway, D., 2005, *The Council of the European Union*, 3rd ed., London, John Harper.

Wiener, A. and Diez, T., 2004, *European Integration Theory*, Oxford, Oxford University Press.

Wright, V., 1995, *Conclusion: the state and major enterprises in Western Europe: enduring complexities*, Hayward J. (ed.), *Industrial Enterprise and European Integration: From National to International Champions in Western Europe*, Oxford, Oxford University Press, pp. 334-59.

THE INTEGRATION PROCESS OF WESTERN BALKANS TO THE EUROPEAN UNION

MARIETTA FESSEL HARSÁNYI

Abstract

The focus of this paper is the trade integration of the Balkans to the EU with special consideration to the free trade agreements between the named parties. The European Union offered membership with full rights to the Western Balkan countries; however, this process will require a long time and will be accomplished gradually.

The European Union made free trade agreements with the Western Balkan countries after the end of the Balkan wars. The basic purposes of the EU were not only to integrate these countries to the European Community, but also to induce these countries to strengthen the trade cooperation with each other. Consequently within the framework of the Stabilization and Association Agreements, the Balkan countries made several bilateral contracts. The extension of the CEFTA was accepted on the summit meeting of the Southeast European prime ministers in Bucharest on the 6th April 2006.

With the accession to the EU, Bulgaria and Romania resigned from the CEFTA, but till the end of 2007 all the other countries (Albania, Bosnia and Herzegovina, Kosovo, FYROM, Moldova, Montenegro and Serbia) became already members of this cooperation. The main object of the extended agreement was to develop a regional free trade zone by the end of 2010. This step was needed as the bilateral free trade agreements made by some Balkans countries had not been successful before, neither had the mutual customs preferences given to each other, nor the acceptance of the rules of origin stipulated in these agreements.

The main commercial measures of these agreements made by European Union with the Balkan countries were basically the same, mutual customs preferences and the rules of origin could support the trade integration. Some agreements were symmetrical, however others were asymmetrical which meant that only the European Union granted one-sided preferences to the products arriving from the member countries signed the agreements.

These agreements have to be consistent to reach the aim of the trade integration. So the asymmetrical ones have to be modified and the rules of origin have to be unified in order that these rules suit the Pan-European ones. Once the unification of the agreements made between the EU and the Balkan countries and among each other are signed, the Western Balkan countries could be the integrated part of the Pan-European area. However, it would be desirable that the integration to the Pan-European zone will be realized in a different way compared to the earlier enlargement. Instead of bilateral agreements with the eight Western Balkan countries individually, the EU and the other Pan-European countries will make a multilateral one with the CEFTA to make the cooperation much more efficient. During the same time forty countries will create a unified free trade zone based on one free trade agreement. Parallel to this, the Western Balkan countries will become the part of the extended Pan-Euro-Mediterranean zone as well. This situation will significantly accelerate the development of the free trade zone based on the common diagonal accumulation.

The aim of this research is to analyze how common diagonal accumulation functions and promotes the trade development among the member countries of the common free trade zone.

Introduction

In connection with the accession to the European Union of the Czech Republic, Estonia, Cyprus, Latvia, Lithuania, Malta, Hungary, Poland, Slovenia and Slovakia in 2004 then Bulgaria and Romania in 2007, an important change was followed not only in the European economic landscape, but for the countries of the Southeast Europe (SEE) (Novák, 2005). After the end of the Balkan wars, the European Union realized that it is necessary to integrate the former Yugoslavian countries to the European Union (Juhász, 1999). The question was how to make it. The final decision of the EU was to promise full membership to the SEE countries. So the European Union created its Western Balkan policy (Gyökös, 2006; Marján, 2006). The matter of which countries belong to the Western Balkans is raised.

The political notion of the Western Balkans came into being after 2000, the technical term of EU and NATO: actually and in geographical aspect it marks the eastern member republics of the former Yugoslavia and Albania, so the south-eastern part of the area qualified the "eastern question" in the 21st century (Füzes, 2006). Bulgaria, Romania, Turkey, Moldova, Croatia and Slovenia are not the parts of the former "eastern question". Bulgaria and Romania have already been the members of European Union as well as NATO, Turkey has got a totally different geopolitical area, Moldova is in the geostrategic "field of no one".

Croatia was part of, for a historically short time only seventy years, the former Yugoslavia and belongs to the attraction sphere of the EU and Slovenia is the member of the EU (Füzes, 2006). In 2004 it was considered that Croatia might prove to be capable of catching up with Bulgaria and Romania and would most likely finish negotiations on full EU membership at the same time, probably in 2008 (Jurlin, 2004). Croatia did not become the member of the EU with Bulgaria and Romania, so in the political aspect the countries which will get the membership of the EU are the parts of Western Balkans (except for Turkey) (Jurlin, 2004; Iliev, 2004).

The purpose of EU was not only to integrate these countries to European Community (Vincze, 2008), but also to induce them to make free trade agreements with each other. CEFTA gives a suitable framework for these countries to create a regional free trade area (Totev, 2006). In this paper Western Balkans are used for the countries taking part in CEFTA: Albania, Bosnia and Herzegovina, Croatia, Kosovo, FYROM, Moldova, Montenegro and Serbia. The accession process is based not only on the CEFTA, but the contracts of free trade and accession made by European Union with the Western Balkan Countries (WBC) at several dates.

This paper focuses on the economic position of the WBC. Its main purpose is to introduce the process of the integration to European Union taken place by the free trade agreements (Krugman and Obstfeld, 2010; Palánkai, 2004). European Union offered membership with full rights to WBC. It lasts a long time and the integration takes place in more steps. The aim of this paper is to introduce how the common diagonal accumulation works and how it promotes the trade development among the countries being part of a common free trade zone.

Integration of the western Balkans

Stabilization and Association Agreement

According to the plan of the EU the Stabilization and Association Process (SAP) was initiated to integrate the Western Balkans to the European Union and it was realized through the Stabilization and Association Agreement (SAA) (Jurlin, 2004). The SAP is a long-term process to give general frameworks to the WBC to create closer economic links with the EU and to become members of the EU (Novák 1999a, 1999b, 2003). However, the EU made bilateral agreements with the WBC giving one-sided, autonomous preferences or offering mutual ones, the important element of the SAP is to insist and to back the regional co-operation between the WBC. After the Balkan-EU summit meeting held in Zagreb in 2000, the SAP was strengthened by Thessaloniki section of the European Council in 2003. In Vértesy (2009, p. 88) it is written that at this meeting the EU prescribed certain undertakings and preconditions for the WBC to join the Union in the future The European Union emphasized the conditions which are needed to be fulfilled by the WBC on account of becoming EU members. It means that the EU expected that the membership of the EU would become the priority of the foreign, economic and internal politics of the WBC.

European Union signed the SAA at first; with FYROM in April 2001 then with Croatia in October 2001 (Jurlin, 2004). The present valid other SAAs with Bosnia and Herzegovina, Moldova, Montenegro and Serbia entered into force in 2008 and the one with Albania in 2009 (Vám- és Pénzügyőrség, 2010).

CEFTA

Central European Free Trade Agreement (CEFTA) was signed by Czechoslovakia (later the Czech Republic and Slovakia), Hungary and Poland in 1992. Four countries became its members later: Slovenia (1996), Romania (1997), Bulgaria (1999) and Croatia (2003).

Within the framework of the Stabilization and Association Agreements the Balkan countries made several bilateral contracts (Table 1). This process accelerated after 1st of May 2004 when only three countries (Bulgaria, Croatia, Romania) remained in CEFTA (Samardzija, 2004). Just before the EU accession of Bulgaria and Romania, it had been decided to extend CEFTA to all the other Balkan countries. It was accepted on the summit meeting of the Southeast European prime ministers in Bucharest on the 6th of April 2006. With the accession to the EU Bulgaria and Romania resigned from CEFTA, but till the end of that year (2007) all the present members (FYROM in 2006, the others: Albania, Bosnia and Herzegovina, Kosovo, Moldova, Montenegro and Serbia in 2007) had already joined it.

The main object of it was to create a regional free trade zone come into existence till 31st of December 2010. It was needed because the bilateral free trade agreements made by the WBC had not been unified (Table 1). Neither have the mutual customs preferences given to each other, nor the rules of origin stipulated in the agreements. These contracts were bilateral free trade agreements, so the mutual preferences given to one another by the countries worked only on bilateral basis. The agreements (Table 1) contained bilateral accumulation of the rules of origin. This bilateral character existed because the countries of this area did not think of a common region. The European Union wanted to change these agreements into multilateral contracts. It means that the free trade agreements have to contain the same preferences and the same rules of origin. The aim was to change the bilateral accumulation into diagonal accumulation in each agreement (Table 2). This would lead to creating a regional free trade area in the Western Balkans.

In order to understand the difference between the bilateral and diagonal accumulation the rules of origin are introduced.

Table 1. Free trade agreements between the CEFTA-countries

Countries	Albania	Bosnia and Herzegovina	Croatia	Kosovo	FYROM	Moldova	Montenegro	Serbia
Albania		01.12.04	01.06.03	01.10.03	15.07.02	01.11.04	01.08.04	01.08.04
Bosnia and Herzegovina	01.12.04		01.01.05		01.07.02	01.05.04	01.06.02	01.06.02
Croatia	01.06.03	01.01.05			11.07.02	01.10.04	01.07.04	01.07.04
Kosovo	01.10.03							
F.Y.R.O.M.	15.07.02	01.07.02	11.07.02			01.01.05		
Moldova	01.11.04	01.05.04	01.10.04		01.01.05		01.09.04	01.09.04
Montenegro	01.08.04	01.06.02	01.07.04			01.09.04		
Serbia	01.08.04	01.06.02	01.07.04			01.09.04		

Source: Inotai, 2006

Rules of origin

The confirmation of the origin of the exported product has a great importance in the international trade. Sometimes it is needed only for administrative reasons. In case of preferential rules of origin, it is significant to get a certificate of origin, because the importer can get preference of customs duty for the imported goods. The exporter is only allowed to give certificate of origin to the importer if the strict rules of origin are observed.

The types of the rules of origin

There are two types of the rules of origin in international trade. One of them is the general rule of origin. The products confirmed by this rule do not get customs preference in the importing country. It is needed only for administrative reasons. The other type of rules of origin is the preferential one. The rules of it have two parts. One of them is the rules of origin of the GSP (Generalized System of Preferences). In the framework of this system, the products of the developing countries get one-sided, autonomous customs preferences in developed countries.

The other one is the rules of origin in free trade agreements made by the countries giving mutual customs preferences to one another. There are two types of mutual preferences; the accumulation of products and the accumulation of labor. The accumulation of products may be bilateral or diagonal. The accumulation of labor is total accumulation. I do not deal with it, because free trade agreements regarding the WBC do not contain this accumulation.

In connection with this paper it is not needed to deal with the general rules of origin and the rules of origin regarding developing countries (GSP) either. This paper focuses on the rules of origin in free trade agreements.

Accumulation

Accumulation means that a company producing export goods can take the imported articles into consideration as an originating material and can add it to its own material without paying customs duties. The question is which products are allowed to be taken into consideration as originating ones.

Bilateral accumulation

If a free trade agreement contains bilateral accumulation, it means that the contracted partners are allowed to take only the products of the two contracted countries into consideration as a product of origin. The bilateral accumulation assures customs free position for only the products of the partner country. If the exporter imports from any other countries, the confirmation of the originating status of the final products is more difficult and the exporter has to pay customs duty for the imported goods.

Diagonal accumulation

If a free trade agreement contains diagonal accumulation, it means that several countries are named in connection with this rule of origin. Each country is allowed to take the products of the other ones into consideration as originating import material. The free trade agreements containing diagonal accumulation are exactly the same, they contain the same rules of origin and each country is named in the agreements as the country belonging to diagonal accumulation.

Diagonal accumulation works between the Pan-European countries: EU-27, EFTA and Turkey. If a company of the Pan-European area exports to another country of this zone and imports only from the countries of the zone, the export product will have the originating status. The question is which of the countries. In order to decide this question, the so-called accumulation rule has to be applied. If the export product is worked satisfactorily, it can get the status of origin of the country where the final working was done. If the working was unsatisfactory but the product is exported in an unchanged condition, the product keeps the original status of origin. If the working was unsatisfactory but the product is not exported in an unchanged condition, the product can get the status of origin of the country which the raw material with the highest value was imported from.

Sufficient working

If the export product contains only one raw material with non-originating status, so it was imported from a country outside of the Pan-European zone, or the seller did not send a certificate of origin, another rule of origin has to be applied. It is true for free trade agreements containing either bilateral or diagonal accumulation.

First, it has to be decided whether the export product is worked satisfactorily. If not, the export article does not get the status of origin. If yes, the rule of sufficient working applicable for the given export product must be looked up. The cases of sufficient working are in Appendix II of the minutes of the rules of origin in the free trade agreement. There are four types of rules: the value percentage rule, the rule of the change of customs code, the rule of processing and the rule when it is prescribed to use only the raw material produced in full in the given exporting country. In the respect of this paper it is not important to give full particulars of these rules. I only wanted to demonstrate how complex the rules are.

The system to certify the status of origin of the export goods is really complicated, but very important. The reason for this is the rule of "draw back".

The rule of "draw back"

The rule of "draw back" means that the accumulation customs duty has to be paid and it is not allowed to claim it back on the non-originating raw material when it is mounted into the product that is being exported with the status of origin (own definition). So companies have financial advantages if they import and use raw material with the status of origin, because in this case it does not have to pay accumulation customs duty which would result in higher export prices. To avoid paying this duty, companies producing for abroad, exporting to the countries of the common zone have to import from a country being the member of the common zone which diagonal accumulation exists in. So, the aim of this rule is to reach a significant increase in trade between the countries being in the common accumulation.

Joining the common zones

As it was mentioned, the purpose of EU was not only to integrate these countries to European Community, but also to induce them to make free trade agreements with each other. It happened because these countries had already made free trade agreements (Table 1) before their foreign trade started to run in the framework of CEFTA from 2007.

Free trade agreements between the WBC

For the accession to European Union, as the first step, WBC countries had to change their mutual bilateral accumulation of free trade agreements into diagonal accumulation. The plan was to change the agreements containing bilateral accumulation into new agreements with diagonal accumulation which contain the same rules of origin as the ones in the agreements made by the countries of the Pan-European zone. It is important because by using diagonal accumulation, each WBC can use the raw material imported from any other CEFTA-country as an originating one. The advantage of it for the export companies is to avoid the payment of accumulation customs duty (the rule of "draw back"). In this case the exporter can send its products at a better, i.e. lower price or can realize higher profits. According to my conception the countries being in a common free trade zone will increase the export-import turnover with the other countries of the common zone.

The creation of the free trade zone in the Western Balkans is important not only because of the trade integration and the higher export-import turnover between each other, but for the sake of joining the Pan-European zone. Table 2 shows that the European Union began to change its SAAs with the WBC from bilateral accumulation into diagonal. The WBC made free trade agreements with diagonal accumulation not only with the EU and with each other, but they began to make the same contract with Turkey as well. It is a large step to integrate the Western Balkans into the

Pan-European area. Croatia's agreement with EU has still contained bilateral accumulation. However, EU signed the SAA with Moldova in 2008, this agreement contains autonomous trade preferences, so Moldova is not in the diagonal accumulation. There is no official SAA with Kosovo, so this CEFTA-country is not in the diagonal accumulation either. It has to be mentioned that this diagonal accumulation works only between the countries that made the new agreement.

The WBC joining to the Pan-European area

The bilateral free trade agreements made by the WBC were not unified, and it was true for the agreements made by European Union with the WBC as well. Some agreements were symmetrical; the others were asymmetrical which meant that only the European Union gave one-sided preferences to the products arriving in the EU from the countries which signed the agreement. These agreements have to be the same, so they have to be modified; the asymmetrical ones have to be changed into symmetrical ones. It means that these agreements have to contain preferences given to each other on a mutual basis. It happened with Albania, Croatia and FYROM. However this type of agreement has not entered into force with Serbia, it began to give the mutual customs preferences to the products coming from EU in 2009. The aim is to continue this process with Bosnia and Herzegovina and Montenegro, to make the same agreement with Kosovo and to change the autonomous trade preferences into mutual ones with Moldova.

If all the CEFTA-countries have the same agreement with EU and with each other, every agreement will have to be the same and comply with the rules of origin in order that these rules of origin suit the Pan-European ones. Once the unification of the agreements made between EU and the WBC and by the WBC with each other is realized, the WBC would be ready for being the integrated part of the Pan-European area. So the CEFTA-countries will have to make the new agreement not only with the EU, but with the EFTA-countries and Turkey as well. (It has to be mentioned that this process has already partly begun with Turkey.) At the end of this process forty countries will create the unified free trade zone based on free trade agreements and containing equivalent rules of origin.

Table 2. Date of the minutes of the rules of origin using diagonal accumulation between EU, WBC and Turkey

Countries	EU	Albania (AL)	Bosnia and Herzegovina (BA)	Croatia (HR)	FYROM (MK)	Montenegro (ME)	Serbia (RS)	Turkey (TR)
EU		01.01.07	01.07.08		01.01.07	01.01.08	08.12.09	27.07.06
AL	01.01.07		22.11.07	22.08.07	26.07.07	26.07.07	24.10.07	
BA	01.07.08	22.11.07		22.11.07	22.11.07	22.11.07	22.11.07	
HR		22.08.07	22.11.07		22.08.07	22.08.07	24.10.07	
MK	01.01.07	26.07.07	22.11.07	22.08.07		26.07.07	24.10.07	01.07.09
ME	01.01.08	26.07.07	22.11.07	22.08.07	26.07.07		24.10.07	01.03.10
RS	08.12.09	24.10.07	22.11.07	24.10.07	24.10.07	24.10.07		
TR	27.07.06				01.07.09	01.03.10		

Source: Vám- és Pénzügyőrség (accessed 24 February 2010)

The extended Pan-Euro-Mediterranean zone

Becoming the members of the Pan-European zone, the WBC, CEFTA will become the part of the extended Pan-Euro-Mediterranean zone too. At the same time the WBC will have the possibility to make free trade agreements with the other countries belonging to the extended Pan-Euro-Mediterranean zone. Now the members of this zone are the Pan-European countries, Algeria, Cisjordania and the Gaza-area, Egypt, Israel, Jordanian, Lebanon, Morocco, Syria, Tunisia and the Ferrier-Islands (they are the parts of Denmark, but they are not parts of the customs area of the Community).

In accordance with the agreement containing the Pan-European rules of origin made between EU and CEFTA, the countries of the present extended zone will make new agreements containing the rules of origin of the extended zone as well. The plan of EU is not to make these new agreements with the eight WBC individually, but with the CEFTA as a single partner. As a result, not 276 new agreements will be made but only 136. This situation will make the development of the extended free trade zone based on the common diagonal accumulation significantly easier and will also accelerate it. The new contracts will denominate all the countries, so the new common diagonal accumulation will be extended for fifty members of the zone. It has to be mentioned that not all the countries being in the present extended zone have already signed the new free trade agreement with the other countries.

Trade development of the Western Balkans

According to the concept of this paper that free trade agreements made by the WBC with EU promote trade integration to European Union, the foreign trade between the WBC and EU is examined.

The growth and the share of the export-import trade of the WBC with the EU

Considering that Kosovo, Montenegro and Serbia belonged to Yugoslavia, the turnover data were together (Yugoslavia) before 2004 and separately after it. There were not data in Eurostat for 2004 either for Yugoslavia or for the countries separately. Therefore, a comparison can only be made between the five years before 2004 and the five years after it.

We can see that both the export and the import increased in a rapid pace. The growth of the import was higher (with nearly 10%) than that of the export. If the export in 1999 (11 118 mill EUR) is compared with the export in 2009 (26 707 mill. EUR), it can be stated that the increase was nearly 2.5 times bigger. The import growth showed the same development (4 740 mill EUR in 1999 and 11 690 mill EUR in 2009). So, the agreements made from 2002 (Table 1) had positive influence on the export-import trade between EU and the CEFTA-countries.

Table 3. Foreign trade of EU with WBC (M EUR)

Countries	EU export to WBC			EU import from WBC		
	1999-2003	2005-2009	Index (%)	1999-2003	2005-2009	Index (%)
Albania	5 142	8 697	169,14	1 544	2 882	186,66
Bosnia and Herzegovina	10 036	15 554	154,98	3 325	8 353	251,22
Croatia	35 416	61 414	173,41	14 933	23 501	157,38
Moldova	3 147	6 694	212,71	1 560	2 942	188,59
FYROM	7 485	10 087	134,76	3 541	7 134	201,47
Kosovo		2 005			253	
Montenegro		2 878			1 120	
Serbia		32 046			14 890	
Yugoslavia	16 669	(36 929)*	221,54	6 229	(16 263)*	261,09
Total	77 895	139 375	178,93	31 132	61 075	196,18

*There were no data of Kosovo, Montenegro and Serbia separately before 2004, so in order to compare the data of Yugoslavia between 1999-2003 with the data of the three countries between 2005-2009, the data of these three countries were added.
Source: Eurostat, (2010)

In spite of the fact that the growth of both EU's export and import was the highest with Yugoslavia, so with Kosovo, Montenegro and Serbia, the turnover with Croatia was the greatest, nearly the half of both the export and the import trade (Table 4). We can suppose that the reason of it was that in 2004 the European Union strengthened the candidate status of the EU membership of Croatia and the SAA came into operation in the beginning of 2005. Croatia was close to the accession to the EU in 2006. Of course Croatia has the largest and the most developed economy among the WBC.

Table 4. Share of each WBC -countries in the total export-import turnover of the region towards the EU countries, 1999-2009 (%)

Countries	EU export to WBC		EU import from WBC	
	1999-2003	2005-2009	1999-2003	2005-2009
Albania	6,60	6,24	4,96	4,72
Bosnia and Herzegovina	12,88	11,16	10,68	13,68
Croatia	45,47	44,06	47,97	38,48
Moldova	4,04	4,80	5,01	4,82
FYROM	9,61	7,24	11,37	11,68
Kosovo		1,44		0,41
Montenegro		2,06		1,83
Serbia		22,99		24,38
Yugoslavia	21,40	(26,49)*	20,01	(26,62)*
Total	100,00	100,00	100,00	100,00

*There were no data of Kosovo, Montenegro and Serbia separately before 2004, so in order to compare the data of Yugoslavia between 1999-2003 with the data of the three countries between 2005-2009, the data of these three countries were added.
Source: Own calculation based on Table 3.

While the share of the import trade of EU from Croatia decreased with nearly 10% in the period of 2005-2009, the share of both the export and the import of Serbia reached nearly the quarter of the total turnover. It can be said that Serbia made all the efforts to sign the SAA.

Bosnia and Herzegovina were on the third place of the export-import trade with European Union. However, Yugoslavia showed the greatest growth of export to the EU in the period of 2005-2009 (Table 3), in the same period the export turnover to the EU of Bosnia and Herzegovina was more than 2.5 times of the former period (1999-2003), so it was the second greatest growth. Table 5 shows that the export turnover of European Union was much higher than the import one in both periods, but the index of the export/import of Bosnia and Herzegovina decreased significantly in the second period (from 301,83% to 186,21%). It seems that the beginning of the negotiations about the SAA between EU and Bosnia and Herzegovina in 2005 inspired the integration process of the country.

Albania, FYROM and Serbia could diminish the share of the import from the EU as well, but the share of the export to EU decreased in Croatia and Moldova.

Foreign trade of the region before and after the accession to the EU by twelve countries

Considering that in 2004 European Union was enlarged with ten new countries and since 2007 with two more, five of the ten countries (the Czech Republic, Hungary, Poland, Slovakia and Slovenia), Bulgaria and Romania had considerable trade with the WBC before their accession as well, it is interesting to examine the trade development from 1999 to 2009 biannually. From the 1st of May 2004 these five countries and from the 1st of January 2007 Bulgaria and Romania give the same customs preferences to the products of the WBC than the EU, so it may be supposed that the greatest growth occurred from 2003 to 2005 and from 2005 to 2007.

It can be stated that the accession to EU of Bulgaria and Romania had greater influence on the trade development of the WBC than the accession of the other mentioned countries. The export trade of almost all the WBC to EU-27 increased in the greatest pace from 2005 to 2007. The export growth in Bosnia and Herzegovina was the highest from 1999 to 2001 and it was greater from 2003 to 2005 than from 2005 to 2007. It is interesting that the export growth in Croatia was the highest from 1999 to 2001, because Croatia became the member of CEFTA in 2003. The export growth in Moldova was greater from 1999 to 2001 and from 2001 to 2003 than from 2003 to 2005. There were large differences in the export growth of the periods in Yugoslavia, so in Kosovo, Montenegro and Serbia. There was a decrease from 2003 to 2005 only in Yugoslavia, but then its growth was more than three times larger from 2005 to 2007 and the increase from 1999 to 2001 was the highest among the countries. It is interesting, because the EU signed the SAA with Serbia only in 2008. Except for Albania and Kosovo export trade decreased from 2007 to 2009. The reason of this is possibly the world economic crisis. Examining the total export turnover of the WBC to European Union it can be seen that the growth from 1999 to 2001 was higher than from 2003 to 2005. Therefore, the influence of the SAP, the Zagreb summit in 2000 on the export trade can be considered greater than the accession of the ten countries, but the influence of the Bulgarian and Romanian accession was the greatest.

Table 5. Index of export and import values of the EU foreign trade (M EUR and %)

Countries	EU export to WBC	EU import from WBC	Index: Export/Import (%)	EU export to WBC	EU import from WBC	Index: Export/Import (%)
	1999-2003	1999-2003		2005-2009	2005-2009	
Albania	5 142	1 544	333,03	8 697	2 882	301,77
Bosnia and Herzegovina	10 036	3 325	301,83	15 554	8 353	186,21
Croatia	35 416	14 933	237,17	61 414	23 501	261,33
Moldova	3 147	1 560	201,73	6 694	2 942	227,53
FYROM	7 485	3 541	211,38	10 087	7 134	141,39
Kosovo				2 005	253	792,49
Montenegro				2 878	1 120	256,96
Serbia				32 046	14 890	215,22
Yugoslavia	16 669	6 229	267,60	(36 929)*	(16 263)*	227,07
Total	77 895	31 132	250,02	139 375	61 075	228,20

*There were not data of Kosovo, Montenegro and Serbia separately before 2004, so in order to compare the data of Yugoslavia between 1999-2003 with the data of the three countries between 2005-2009, the data of these three countries were added.

Source: Own calculation based on Table 3.

Table 6. EU import from CEFTA-countries (M EUR) and the growth of it (%)

Countries	1999	2001	'01/'99	2003	'03/'01	2005	**'05/'03**	2007	**'07/'05**	2009	'09/'07
Albania	232	337	145,26	360	106,82	417	**115,83**	627	**150,36**	654	104,31
Bosnia&H	426	706	165,73	848	120,11	1 332	**157,08**	1 832	**137,54**	1 527	83,35
Croatia	2 472	3 135	126,82	3 347	106,76	4 077	**121,81**	4 980	**122,15**	4 385	88,05
Moldova	212	304	143,40	430	141,45	435	**101,16**	727	**167,13**	516	70,98
FYROM	668	717	107,34	701	97,77	1 018	**145,22**	1 858	**182,51**	1 189	63,99
Kosovo						12		47	**391,67**	80	170,21
Montenegro						85		341	**401,18**	130	38,12
Serbia						1 177		3 656	**310,62**	3 209	87,77
Yugoslavia	728	1 327	182,28	1 528	115,15	(1274)*	**83,38**	(4044)*	**317,43**	(3419)*	84,55
Total	4 738	6 526	137,74	7 214	110,54	8 553	**118,56**	14 068	**164,48**	11 690	83,10

*There were not data of Kosovo, Montenegro and Serbia separately before 2004, so in order to compare the data of Yugoslavia between 1999-2003 with the data of the three countries between 2005-2009, the data of these three countries were added.
Source: Own calculation based on Eurostat on-line

Conclusion

Considering that more than half of the agreements containing diagonal accumulation have already been made between EU and CEFTA-countries, it seems that it is true that this type of agreements with the EU and the bilateral free trade agreements among WBC make the EU-integration of the WBC faster. However, because of the world crisis both the export and the import trade with EU decreased in 2009, the mutual turnover will possibly increase in the next decade. Though probably the accession to EU of the WBC will take place individually, it is important to integrate the WBC by the agreements with diagonal accumulation in order that they become the parts of the Pan-European area and the extended Pan-Euro-Mediterranean zone as well. In this case the accession to the European Union of the WBC which will still be outside of the EU at that time will be easier.

Acknowledgement

I am grateful to the management of the College for Modern Business Studies for the possibility to participate in this conference in Kavala.

References

Eurostat, 2010, http://epp.eurostat.ec.europa.eu, (accessed 21 March 2010).

Füzes, O., 2006, Nyugat, Balkán, Nyugat-Balkán, (West, Balkan, Western Balkans), *Európai Tükör*, 11, 5, pp. 26-39.

Gyökös, P., 2006, Az Európai Unió bővítés után, közben és előtt (The European Union after, during and before enlargement), *Európai Tükör,* 11, 1, pp. 96-102.

Iliev, G., 2004, Regional Cooperation in Southeast Europe: A Bulgarian Perspective, *Europe beyond the first wave of Eastern enlargemet, Papers of the first regional scientific seminar,* Pécs, Hungary.

Inotai, A., 2006, Fordulóponton a délkelet-európai gazdaságok? (Are the south-eastern economies at a turning-point?), *Műhelytanulmányok* 70, pp. 34-44.

Juhász, J., 1999, *Volt egyszer egy Jugoszlávia. A délszláv állam története (Once upon a time there was a Yugoslavia. The history of the southern Slavian state),* Budapest, Aula Kiadó.

Jurlin, K., 2004, The Scope of Regional Cooperation in Southeast Europe after 2004, *Europe beyond the first wave of Eastern enlargement,*

Papers of the first regional scientific seminar, Pécs, Hungary.

Krugman, P.R. and Obstfeld, M., 2010, *Nemzetközi gazdaságtan elmélet és gazdaságpolitika (International economics. Theory and Policy)*, 5th ed. Budapest, Panem Könyvkiadó Kft.

Marján, A., 2006, EU-bővítés: vissza- és előretekintés (EU expansion: Review and Preview), *Európai Tükör*, 11, 11, pp. 3-28.

Novák, T., 1999, A rendezés lehetőségei a Balkánon I. Az EU Balkán politikája (The settlement of disputes in the Balkans I. The Balkans Policy of the EU), *VKI*, 120, pp. 1-12.

—. 1999, A rendezés lehetőségei a Balkánon II. A lehetséges jövő a CEPS tervezete alapján és annak kritikája (The settlement of disputes in Balkans II. The potential future on the basis of the CEPS scheme and its critics), *VKI*, 121, pp. 1-12.

—. 2003, Some Issues of Regional Cooperation in the Balkans, *Europe beyond the first wave of Eastern enlargement. Papers of the first regional scientific seminar,* Pécs, Hungary.

—. 2005, Economic Transformation and Regional Cooperation in Southeast Europe, *Facing Challenges: Selected Key Issues of Economic Transformation and European Cooperation, Hungarian-Bulgarian Bilateral Workshop,* Budapest, Hungary.

Palánkai, T., 2004, *Az európai integráció gazdaságtana (Economics of the European Integration)*, Budapest, Aula Kiadó.

Samardzija, V., 2004, After Enlargement: A Croatian View. *Europe beyond the first wave of Eastern enlargement*, *Papers of the first regional scientific seminar,* Pécs, Hungary.

Totev, S., 2006, Balkan Countries' Cross-border Economic Cooperation in an Integrating Europe, *Facing Challenges: Selected Key Issues of Economic Transformation and European Cooperation,* Hungarian-Bulgarian Bilateral Workshop, Budapest, Hungary.

Vám-és Pénzügyőrség, http://vam.gov.hu/viewBase.do?elementId, (accessed 24 February 2010).

Vértesy, L., 2009, Az Európai Unió és a Nyugat-Balkán (The European Union and the Western Balkans), *Európai Tükör*, 14, 9, pp. 83-101.

Vincze, D., 2008, Az európai Unió, mint a demokratikus normák exportőre a Balkánon (The European Union as the exporter of the democratic norms on the Balkan), *Három éve az ötven éves EU-ban. Conference*, Budapest, Hungary.

THE STABILITY PACT AND THE SOUTHEASTERN EUROPE

THEOFANIS MALKIDIS

Abstract

The Stability Pact for South-eastern Europe was a reaction of European Union to crisis and wars in this part of Europe, precisely in the territory of Former Yugoslavia. It is established during the German Presidency over European Union in June 1999, and it was a result of their strong efforts to finally build common EU policy towards Balkans. The intention of the Stability Pact founders was to design a comprehensive initiative which will have the task to prevent future conflicts and to include not only Balkan countries, but also relevant international organizations and donor countries. This frame was finished successfully gathering; 38 countries and 15 international organizations on the Foreign Ministers meeting in Cologne (on 10 June 1999), when the Stability Pact Charter was adopted and then at a summit meeting on 30 July 1999 in Sarajevo, the Pact was officially inaugurated. The paper analyzes the role of Stability Pact in South Eastern Europe after the changes in South-Eastern Europe from the end of Cold War until today.

Introduction

The Stability Pact for South-eastern Europe was a reaction of European Union to crisis and wars in this part of Europe, precisely in the territory of Former Yugoslavia. It is established during the German Presidency over European Union in June 1999, and it was a result of their strong efforts to finally build common EU policy towards Balkans. The intention of the Stability Pact founders was to design one comprehensive initiative which will have the task to prevent future conflicts and to include not only Balkan countries, but also relevant international organizations and donor countries.

This frame was finished successfully gathering; 38 countries and 15 international organizations on the Foreign Ministers meeting in Cologne (on 10 June 1999), when the Stability Pact Charter was adopted and then at a summit meeting on 30 July 1999 in Sarajevo, the Pact was officially inaugurated. The predecessors of the Stability Pact were numerous and generally perceived as unsuccessful efforts to bring stability and moreover prosperity. The period immediately after the ending of Cold War is characterized with establishing different initiatives also supported by different organizations or institutions. The first among them are Central European Initiative (CEI), an Austro- Italian initiative with secretariat in Trieste and Black Sea Economic Co-operation (BSEC) which was originally Turkish initiative and has its secretariat in Istanbul (Salavrakos, 1999; Valinakis et al., 1997-1998).

The Royaumont Process was founded in 1995 to provide better implementation of Dayton Accord, following the end of war in Bosnia and Herzegovina, but its aims were changing, and it is planned that it should be integrated into OSCE. United States initiated in 1996 Southeast Cooperation Initiative (SECI), following with the Stability Pact. Also, the first summit of Foreign Ministers of Southeast European countries (SFMSEE) was held for the first time in 1988 in Belgrade and renewed again in 1996 (Budway, 1997-1998; Clement, 1997-1998). The common evaluation of all these initiatives and organizations done utill now, by a lot of scholars, is that they are usually overlapping in regards to their objectives which are numerous and covering different areas. All of them have as goals "regional co-operation and integration", "co-operation in fight against organized crime", "incentives for improving economic co-operation and foreign investments" etc. Furthermore, most of them (except for SECI), have very small budgets, with very few implemented projects and concentrated on holding meetings on mostly diplomatic level. And as Joschka Fischer, the German Foreign Minister said in his speech at meeting in Cologne concerning Yugoslav conflict, it can also be applied for these regional initiatives generally: "The previous policy of the international community vis-à-vis former Yugoslavia has two severe disadvantages: it concentrated on the consequences instead of the sources of conflicts, and it tackled the problems of the region individually and separately from the ones in other parts of Europe" (Bierman , 1999).

When the Stability Pact was launched, there was a lot of scepticism that this is one more initiative in crowded environment of organizations, which is going to overtake the work of smaller ones. But what makes the

Stability Pact different from other initiatives, is not only that it was launched in such a spectacular way, but it was supported practically by all significant factors of international community and it is determinate in fulfilling ambitious aims which were set in front of it.

The Stability Pact

The Pact is considered to be an inter-governmental and inter-institutional body, the organization of which is based on the model of Conference for Security and Co-operation in Europe (CSCE), and it cannot be perceived as a pure international organization. Accordingly, it is placed under the auspices of OSCE and fully relies on the OSCE to attain compliance with the provision of the Pact by participating states. It is political commitment and agreement of all participants to develop regional co-operation and to foster it in order to achieve lasting stability and growth.

Its principal goals are also to promote good neighbourly relations, establish common and flexible market, securing peace, democracy, multicultural and civil society, and as a final one, to integrate the countries of South East Europe in European and Atlantic organizations, namely European Union and NATO, as the most important. In the Stability Pact Charter, the countries of the region made a commitment to work together on "bilateral and regional co-operation amongst them to advance their integration, on an individual basis, into Euro-Atlantic structures" (European Stability Initiative, 1999, 2000).

Moreover, one of the conditions set in front of South-eastern European countries for opening negotiations on a Stabilization and Association Agreement was that countries have to enhance co-operation among the countries of the region and conclude free-trade agreements with its neighbours. This has been raised from the common opinion within the Europe that the problems of Southeast European countries can not be solved separately, but as a part of a wider strategy (Weidenfeld, 1995).

Its main body is Southeast European Regional Table, which includes governments and international institutions taking part in the Stability Pact. The Special Coordinator chairs over Regional Table and his office of 28 experts review progress under the Stability Pact, but do not have direct influence on planning or implementing specific projects, or influence donors and the usage of their funds. Staff from the Office of Special

Coordinator is responsible for one or more sub-tables or initiatives, while the Special Coordinator represents the Pact in public and providing his good offices in various kinds of agreements. The Regional Table coordinates activities among its three Working Tables that exist on expertise, institutions and initiatives, and could be further divided into sub-tables. Working Tables establish priorities within their respective areas of competence and they can also create a limited number of priority initiatives to be addressed by each of the Tables. Coordination of activities among the Working Tables is very important since many of the objectives are complementary and dependable on each other.

1. Working Table on Democratization and Human Rights is dealing with minority's rights, refugees and displaced people, rule of law and law enforcement, good governance and institution building, border questions, strengthening civil society, parliamentary co-operation and other related issues.

2. Working Table on Economic Reconstruction, Development and Co-operation has as its main objectives to enhance economic co-operation among the countries of the region and with European Union, to integrate this region in World Trade Organization and other economic institution, to achieve free flow of goods and capital, remove trade barriers, improve infrastructure, fight corruption and crime, support privatization and foreign investments.

3. Working Table on Security Issues is focused on creating good neighbourly relations and climate of security in the region, implementing arms control, promoting civilian control over military forces, fighting against terrorism, small arms proliferation, stabilizing population movements etc. It is divided in two Sub-Tables: Security and Defence and Justice and Home Affairs (Bierman, 1999).

One of the events which are important in strengthening Stability Pact as a main regional initiative was the beginning of the Quick Start Package Projects, initiated on the Regional Funding Conference in March 2000 in Brussels. It was a quick reaction on calling upon for fast help to the region, especially after the results of the wars in Former Yugoslavia, which were extremely devastating. The targets of the Quick-Start Package were projects and initiatives that will quickly make visible difference in the ordinary peoples' lives and lift the expectations of the local communities. This Package included 244 different projects with value of

2, 4 billion Euros (Stability Pact, 2004) and this number is also including Near Term projects, which were supposed to start later than one year after the conference. These projects included economic reconstruction, security and democratization, as well as combined projects. This was to be the first instalment of 12 billion Euros for the six-year period of time. According to some analysts, the Quick Start Package is characterized by the funding which was already allocated to the region and the Office of the Special Coordinator did not have the time to make a comprehensive strategy, neither the countries and agencies had the time to propose a lot of new projects ideas (European Stability Initiative Paper, 2001).

These projects should have some common features, such as: "quick start" capacity, refer to the region of South-eastern Europe, be attractive to donors etc. Most of the projects referred to infrastructure programs in the area (approximately 75%), under the Working Table II (Economic reconstruction). The biggest donor was European Union with 530 million Euros donation, which was to be matched by contributions of individual member states. Furthermore, some of financial institutions (e.g. Black Sea Trade and Development Bank, Council of Europe Development Bank) pledged 1.085 billion Euros. The biggest individual donations by country were from Germany, Italy and Netherlands, with sums of 149.60, 148.58 and 67.75 million Euros, respectively. On the second Regional Conference in Bucharest in October 2001, donors pledged another package of 2, 4 billion Euros for 27 infrastructure projects and return of refugees was to be supported with more than 500 million Euros.

But what was perceived as a major shortcoming is that Quick Start Package did not have strategic plan behind, and following that, programs considering democratization, development of civil society and institutional building were just one small piece of it, what should be the long-term goal of the Pact.

Initiatives

Within the Stability Pact exist plenty of taskforces and regional initiatives with different range of activities. Only Working Table I has six taskforces, but not all of them are very active and successful. They can have various roles-from sharing information on QSP projects to developing regional initiatives. The two most active are Education and Gender Taskforce. The former one primarily existed through Graz Process, with a strong network in the region, which gave it ability for quickly organizing projects in its field. The later was based on "Central East European Network for Gender Issues" with high activity in the region. Also, Stability Pact did not serve only as a base for co-operation, but as a catalyst for democratic changes in the political life of the region. The best example is so-called Szeged Process, founded in September 1999, in order to support oppositional municipalities and independent media in Serbia in their fight against the Milosevic's regime.

As it was mentioned, "The basic idea was to facilitate the isolation of these groups by connecting them with European partners. At the height of oppression under the Milosevic regime, more then 2 million euros were mobilized at short notice through a flash appeal in support of the free media in Serbia in June 2000, allowing them to buy newsprint materials and get legal protection. Out of the Szeged Process the European support program "Energy for Democracy" was developed. Following the democratic changes in Belgrade, the Stability Pact was the first multilateral body to accept the FRY, on 26 October 2000, as a full and equal participant."

It can be seen that most other taskforces are duplication of similar ones working under the auspices of different organizations. For instance, Parliamentary Co-operation Taskforce, which is supposed to strengthen the parliamentary ties throughout the region, has almost the same goals as parliamentary co-operation within the OSCE and Council of Europe. The same thing is with taskforces dealing with minorities and human rights issues and those referring to local administrations.

A lot of various regional initiatives are characteristic for the working of Stability Pact. Each of them represents agreement on regional level and some of them are: Anti-Corruption Initiative (SPAI), Anti-organized Crime Initiative (SPOC), Migration, Asylum, Refugee Regional Initiative (MARRI), the Stability Pact Investment Compact etc. SPAI, for instance, has as its aims to review national legislation related to transparency in government procurement, to review effectiveness of measures against corruption related to foreign development assistance and to provide public access to government information in order to expose corruption. On the other side, MARRI is dealing with asylum, legal and illegal migration, border management, visa and entry policies, return and settlement of refugees and displaces persons. Another initiative, Anti-trafficking Taskforce is initiated in 2000, under the Justice and Home Affairs Sub-Table, to fight with one of the most significant problems in Europe-human trafficking. It has to be developed in several different fields, such as-training programs, victim protection, and legislative reform, law enforcement co-operation, preventing social and economic causes of trafficking. However, all these initiatives are established in the period when some other international efforts already existed on same or similar issues, and made these actions to reduce their resources, to move slowly from the idea to the paper implementation, and with all these overlapping initiatives, countries cannot see any positive results. Most of them are based on numerous meetings, summits, seminars and similar events which are diluting their effectiveness.

Obstacles in working: Weakness of state institutions

The most significant problem in the role of the Stability Pact in the development of the South-eastern European countries, which is always emphasized in literature, is the weakness of state institutions. Weak state institutions are the main barrier for stronger and further regional co-operation because of their inability to enforce decisions within the Stability Pact. It is more than obvious that without effective institutional reform within all the countries of the region, there will not be any long-term results in achieving prosperity and lasting stability.

The scope of the different conditions of public institutions varies from country to country, and it is specific for each of them. On one side, we have countries or entities, such as Bosnia and Herzegovina and Kosovo which are considered as international protectorates and they are governed by international administration. And while the building institutions in Bosnia move on, the status of Kosovo is still unresolved and international UNMIK forces are still not replaced with internal ones (World Bank, 2000).

Serbia is still dealing with enormous number of public employees from the communist and Milosevic period, and the problem is going to become even greater after the split with Montenegro, and Serbia is going to inherit huge of federal administration in Belgrade.

Montenegro, although without duplication of functions, will have in immediate future to solve the problem of over-employment in public sector, especially in police forces. In last decade Albania was faced with complete failure of its internal institutions, when the international forces were called to intervene (Albanian institute for international studies,

2000). Except from these main features of each state, the common result for all of them is that they are suffering from insecure and unreliable public administration, influenced from corruption, and consequently, unable to enforce legal reforms, protect human rights and respond on the international obligations in order to achieve European integrations. This is also emphasized in United Nation Development Program Report:

"At present South-eastern Europe faces proliferation of protectorates and 'weak states"-states that are unable or unwilling to create and enforce rules in a democratic context. In particular, they are unable to maintain rule of law. In at least three cases, Kosovo, Albania and Bosnia and Herzegovina, the majority security provider is not the national state but the international community. Weak states are the major source of political, economic, social and cultural insecurity." (UNDP, 1999).

And according to the same report, human security should be the underlying principle of reconstruction and development of the region. These kind of states lead to "creation of illiberal democracies" and "if the Stability Pact is to succeed, it must therefore help each of these societies refashion its state and re-invent its democracies" what will demand paying attention on electoral processes, media, human rights, non-governmental organizations, corruption (UNDP, 1999). And what is concluded in some other research, "Balkan societies show little understanding for the necessity of linking economic assistance with certain political developments aiming at a successful transformation of the post communist societies in the region. The impatience is a widespread phenomenon in the Balkans; people tend to see the causes of their problems outside of their own communities or ethnic groups, and very often they try to commission others, whether the Great Powers in the past, or international community and the Stability Pact now, to solve them. Nevertheless, despite the mixed feelings, no one in the region doubts the significance of the Stability Pact." It is Stability Pact's responsibility to discover how institutional development within the states of SEE can be supported from outside. It is certain that there will be no success without the improvements in the working of state structures.

International donors

International donors, who are allocating funds for projects throughout South-eastern Europe, although cooperating among themselves and with beneficiary countries, are likely to emphasize their own contribution to specific problem, especially when particular donor country is concerned. The other problem is that this international assistance is not showing as good results as it was expected. This is because some countries are unsatisfied with unitary approach, knowing that each of them is facing problems with different range as regards institutional conditions, legislation and level of enforced reforms. On the other hand, in the same projects countries are invited to participate without being consulted, or in some of them they have a passive role, while the main part of the activities are in the hands of the "leading" states.

What is recommended for resolving this problem is that donors, separately or together, should give advantage to the inter-state projects, in which all included states will take part on the same basis. Furthermore, there was a fear that the Stability Pact is going to be the new "Marshall Plan" for South-eastern Europe (European Commission, 2003). But differences between South-eastern Europe and Western Europe are in few directions and show that no comparison is possible. As it is pointed out in UN Development Program Report, firstly, Southeastern European countries have less strong institutions and there is no common external threat, as it was in Western Europe, when the fear of Soviet communism was present.

Also, Marshall Plan had only one donor, United States, while it is not the case with Southeastern Europe, where numerous donors are involved, and not only central governments are playing important role, but also non-governmental organizations and the private sector too. The last difference is that while the German regime was destroyed at the end of World War II the sources of instability in the area of Southeast Europe still exist.

Regionalism

The establishment of the Stability Pact was driven also with the idea that problems of the region can not be resolved individually, but through one common, international initiative. The idea was that the regional co-operation will help the countries to achieve political stability and fulfill the conditions set by European Union, and they can do that much easier through a wider network of activities. Better connections and contacts among them have been seen as the guarantee for future conflict-prevention. Hence, the example of European Union was constantly given to show the good consequences of integration and as a step further to globalization and market economy. Furthermore, the policy of regional co-operation has not been defined yet, but it was largely perceived among some of the states as a barrier for their faster advancement to European Union. The condition for opening negotiations on a Stabilization and Association Agreement was also that each state must improve co-operation and conclude free-trade agreements with its neighbours. This was the reason for some of the candidates for membership to express their wariness that regional integration will throw them out from European Union, like for example Bulgaria and Croatia.

Slogans and political rhetoric characterized the 90's in almost all Balkan countries, which were strongly aiming to show their European nature and culture. And while on one side, Albania with its pro-American attitudes was likely to mark its neighbours as more backward, distinguishing themselves because of its relatively unique identity, on the other side, Croatia and Slovenia (not only in the period after the fall of communism) were trying to show that they belong to European culture and that they do not have any connections with eastern inheritance of Ottoman Empire. Even President Tudjman enacted an amendment which forbids Croatia to enter South-eastern initiatives. Bulgaria, wanted to distinguish itself from the area of conflicts, so it was presented as a factor which can play an important role in resolving these problems. Furthermore, it was emphasized that less developed countries of South-eastern Europe can postpone the integration of those more advanced in reforms.

Therefore, being part of one regional initiative, such as the Stability Pact, was not accepted with willingness, and the creation of the Pact brought about inside struggles among their main actors, too. Knowing that Pact does not have its own funds makes them dependant on the wishes and attitudes of their donors (i.e. mostly countries), a fact that can easily create reluctance among the beneficiary countries. The types of this regional co-operation can be diverse, from building regional infrastructure, trade agreements to stronger parliamentary actions. Through Quick Start Package, most of the projects included infrastructure, transport construction, road building, what can help to improve intra-regional trade, but does not do a lot for it in the long run. The example of postwar Bosnia and Herzegovina is more than enough. Today, the whole region is not more integrated in the economic sense than it was before the changes in 90s. And while in communism period we can enumerate lot of different factors for non-cooperation (from historical, geostrategic, ideological aspect, etc.), today the recent war conflicts and international sanctions can be added as well.

All indicators show that the level of trade of each SEE country is higher with European Union states than with other states of the area. (Uvalic, 2001) Promotion of intra-regional trade for greater use of financial and economic resources of Southeast Europe is one of the key answers for achieving long-lasting stability. And as it is pointed out "there is no doubt that trade liberalization would be quite hopeful. It would increase trade and decrease the importance of smuggling, corruption and of the attendant culture of criminality." (Gligorov, Kaldor, Tsoukalis, 1999).

The same authors are further proposing three circles of liberalization, which will first include the regional one (through bilateral and multilateral free-trade agreements), second the liberalization involving trade with European Union and third, the integration of the region into the world system of trade (i.e. World Trade Organization) should be achieved. Generally, the regionalization brought about a lot of discussions and perceptions that it will lead countries back to "mud of Balkans", especially in the eyes of the West, as a result of historical background. For them, even the name "the Balkans" was always associated as an area of constant conflicts, wars, marking this region as undeveloped and source of instability. For this reason, to some extent, it is normal why most of the South-eastern European countries want "to run away" and hurry to integrate into Europe, fearing that regional initiatives, and the Stability Pact as well, can be substitution for integration with the other parts of Europe. But, on the other side, regional and European integration can be considered as contradictory to each other, knowing that accession to EU membership is a bilateral act, concentrated on the reform of national regulations and systems, in order to be accustomed to EU criteria (European Commision, 2002).

It is perceived that "Stability Pact should avoid the policies of the exclusiveness as they damage the regional co-operation." (Yusufi, 1999). This refers mainly on exclusion of FR Yugoslavia from participation in projects under the auspices of the Stability Pact till the fall of Milosevic regime in October 2000, when not only FR Yugoslavia was damaged but the neighbouring countries as well as regards programs which referred to all of them.

Implementation

Recovery of the South-eastern Europe will require a significant effort, commitment, and the vision on the part of the international community, particularly the European Union. Nevertheless, any program of recovery and development will be unsuccessful without the full participation and effort of the South-eastern European countries themselves, and that will require one comprehensive strategic approach.

Till present days, the European Union offered broadly duty-free access of SEE exports to the EU market. In general, the region's economies are lagging behind in the process of integration into the larger European economy. Only two countries, Bulgaria and Romania, have managed to conclude association agreements with the European Union; the others, because of various reasons, have been left behind. However, aid, preferential trade policies and sporadic association agreements will not be enough to revitalize the economies of the region. The South-eastern Europe region needs strategy and vision. To date, several strategies have been proposed by different institutions and "think thanks". One of them was and from World Bank which made a following observation:

> "The World Bank paper rests on the assumption that a major factor underlying the poor economic performance of the SEE region as a whole is a lack of progress in the transition towards a market-based economy. Moreover, the problem of transition is largely considered an orthodox one; e.g. the key to macroeconomic stabilization and microeconomic restructuring lies in privatization. In addition, it repeats the now standard stress on public and private governance. It argues that the strengthening of civil society is a necessary concomitant to reconstruction."
> —World Bank, 2000.

The same paper proposed a two-phase process of trade integration. The first one should liberalize and eliminate all administrative barriers for trade. The European Union was supposed to conclude agreements with Albania, Bosnia and Herzegovina, Croatia, FR Yugoslavia and FYROM and they would be in the form of free-trade agreements or autonomous trade preferences. In the second stage, those countries would establish full free trade area with European Union and each other. They should also implement a convergence of their external tariffs to that of the European Union and to make progress in reforming of their economic systems. The paper suggested that this process could start its second phase in period 2004-05, but it is obvious that it is still far behind. In the same time, the countries of the region must implement their strategies of transition reforms, mainly as for the institutional building and regional co-operation. Without being able to absorb aid provided by the international community and to develop institutions conducive to change, the Stability Pact will become a failure. The institutional situation in Southeast Europe that was present in Western Europe after the World War II is missing now.

For that reason, the Stability Pact seems to be an even more ambitious project than the Marshall Plan was. And while economic development is a basic component of overall development, it is not its only aspect. This is because development must ultimately address more than to the economic and financial needs of the people. In essence, economic growth results not only from growth in the quantity or quality of resources and improved technology, but also from the social and political development of one society as a whole. Economic growth demands a stable and flexible social framework capable of accustoming on reforms. It also requires an environment capable of resolving conflicts that always follow huge changes in the society. And at present time, the institutions and organizations of the Southeastern European countries are still not on that level. It is evident that all of them lack or have very little capacity to effectively absorb international aid and implement the Stability Pact.

Evaluation

The last years brought significant attention to the international community regarding the Southeast Europe and the Stability Pact is its direct product. It is a result of wide recognition for active policy in the region. This is now evident in the number of governmental and nongovernmental organizations engaged in the area as well as in different types of international assistance programs. The Pact is serving as a powerful instrument for creating and maintaining the incentives for reconstruction in the region. Despite the fact that the Pact did not, till present days, succeed in all its missions, it was a good initial effort for the future tasks. Moreover, the success or failure of the Pact depends on its capability to reunite and gather international efforts, particularly those of European Union. Furthermore, the perception of success is very important, but the success will be possible if the Pact keeps going on with its promises.

It is essential and extremely important to get the assistance program off the ground. The Stability Pact provides political framework for cooperation throughout the region, making the countries to consider some other options for it. It is pointed out that: "European approximation and regional co-operation are complementary and mutually reinforcing approaches towards the region. The Stability Pact, through its many initiatives, has made it clear, that regional co-operation is a building block, not a stumbling block for European integration. It is indeed true that, in the early days, there was sometimes reluctance towards the regional approach as one of the founding principles of the Pact. Nonetheless, this attitude has quickly changed once it became evident that good neighbourly relations are not only an indispensable condition for European Union membership, but that they also serve the self-interest of the countries concerned." (Bierman, 1999, p. 45).

The Pact also has its preventive approach as regards migration and elimination of ethnic tensions in the area, and generally prevents long term conflicts. Its multidimensional approach refers to its activity in spheres of democratization, security issues and economic reconstruction.

One of the biggest problems of the Pact has been discrepancy between pledged money and its implementation and actual delivery, what is slowing the operation of the Pact. The European Union's support has been significant primarily in the rhetoric of EU and EC officials, but its rhetoric is not always supported by their concrete actions. The major difficulty and shortcoming in implementation of projects in the past years has been the way in which the assistance was provided. Because the Stability Pact itself does not possess its own fund, the current aid depends on the bilateral or multilateral sources. As a result, large gap exists between promises to provide assistance and its actual delivery. In many cases, projects do not reflect the interests of the South-eastern European countries, but of the donors.

This fragmented approach to assistance may be important for final success of the Pact, if the international donors start to perceive the region as sufficiently stabilized or without big inflow of refugees. Such a perspective could undermine the prospects for long-term development. Moreover, such an approach has significant psychological consequences, as postponing in action can endanger expectations in the region. Furthermore, after the initiating years of international enthusiasm and partial solutions of Balkan problems the interests of international donors is shifted on other parts of the world ad it is expected that it will fall down even more in the next years, what will leave a lot of projects in the phase of planning and the tasks, among them and those of the Stability Pact, uncompleted.

Conclusions

The Stability Pact is a much smaller response to the difficulties of the Southeast Europe than what was the Marshall Plan, as the response of the United States to the Western Europe problems after the World War II. The Stability Pact is mainly a framework for coordinating assistance to the region of Southeast Europe. As such, the Pact is aiming to be a type of comprehensive and long-term oriented strategy. Actions of the Western participants, in spite of their rhetoric and promises connected with Stabilization and Association Process show that their orientations for development in this part of the Europe are still uncertain. Meanwhile, the region is making small steps towards Euro-Atlantic structures.

The current policy of the European Union, as it was in past decade and a half, lacks its own clear vision for reconstruction, development and integration of the Southeast Europe. Consequently, the whole Europe will barely maintain the region stabilized, with fragmented and unresponsive assistance and a lot of uncompleted projects. The fact is that the Stability Pact did a lot in drawing attention to the region and in creating essential incentives for the recovery and stabilization, as well as for connecting broken ties throughout the region. However, it continuously fails to deliver its promises and to act promptly in the important moments for the region. As a result, many participating parties have mixed emotions about the Pact. Furthermore, the Pact and its creators have to decide about its priorities, because it is practically impossible to maintain all these numerous initiatives, taskforces and projects and to expect all of them to give significant and quick results.

Present experience of the Stability Pact shows that only the people of the Southeast Europe hold that power to break with the past and to contribute to their own economic and democratic development that will benefit all the people in the region. Nevertheless, the efforts of the countries in the region will require significant assistance from an international community with a clear vision and a clear strategy.

References

Albanian institute for international studies, 2000, Stability Pact, Tirana.

Bierman, R., 1999, *The Stability Pact for South Eastern Europe- Potential, Problems and Perspectives,* London.

Budway, V., 1998-1999, The role of SECI in a Post-conflict Reconstruction Strategy for Southeastern Europe, *The Southeast European Yearbook,* 1, pp. 9-22.

Clement, S., 1997-1998, Sub- Regional Cooperation in the Balkans, *The Southeast European Yearbook,* pp. 214-236.

Christopher, P., 1997, *Enlargement and Integration in the European Union*, London Routledge.

European Stability Initiative, 1999, *The Stability Pact and the Lessons from a Decade of Regional Initiatives*, Brussels.

—. 2000, *Stability, Institutions and European Integrations*, Brussels.

European Commission, 2003, *Regular Report from the Commission on Progress toward Accession by each of the Candidate Countries,* Brussels.

—. 1999, *Impact of the enlargement of the European Union towards the associated central and eastern European Countries on RTD. – Innovation and structural policies science research development,* Brussels.

—. 2002, *Enlargement Papers. Report on macroeconomic and financial sector developments in candidate countries*, Brussels Directorate General for Economic and Financial Affairs.

—. 1999, *ESDP-European Spatial Development Perspective,* Luxembourg Office for Official Publications of the European Communities.

Hombach, B., 2004, T*he Stability Pact-Lessons for the Future*, Essay on 5th anniversary of Stability Pact, available at: http://www.stabilitypact.org/special

International Monetary Fund, 1998, Working Paper 98/53, Washington, D.C..

Gligorov, V., Kaldor M., and Tsoukalis L., 1999, *Balkan Reconstruction and European Integration*, The Hellenic Observatory, The European Institute, LSE, The Centre for the Study of Global Governance, LSE and The Vienna Institute for International Economic Studies.

Jeffries, J. and Smith, A., 1996, *Problems of economic and political transformation in the Balkans. Problems of the transition to a market economy in Romania, Bulgaria and Albania: Why has the transition proved to be so difficult?*, London -New York.

Lavigne, M., 1995, *The Economics of Transition, From Socialist Economy to Market Economy*, London MacMillan Press.

Petrakos, G., 1996, *The New Geography of the Balkans: Cross-Border Cooperation Between Albania, Bulgaria and Greece*, University of Thessaly Department of Planning and Regional Development Volos.

Solana, J., 2004, *The Stability Pact and Long Term Conflict Prevention in Europe*, available at:
http://www.stabilitypact.org/special

Uvalic, M., 2001, *Regional Co-operation in South East Europe*, available at: http://www.one-europe.ac.uk/pdf/wp17.pdf

UNDP Report, 1999, Human Security in South-East Europe, New York.

Salavrakos, D., 1999, *The Black Sea Co- operation (BSEC): Macro and Microeconomic Dimensions of integration with the Global Economy,* Athens Kritiki.

Valinakis, Y. and Karaganov, S., 1997-1998, The creation and evolution of the BSEC: An Assessment, *The Southeast European Yearbook,* 1, pp. 256-289.

Weidenfeld, W., 1995, *Central and Eastern Europe on the way to the European Union,* Gutersloh Bertelsmann Foundation Publishers.

World Bank, 2000, *The Road to Stability and Prosperity in South Eastern Europe: A Regional Strategy Paper*, Washington D.C.

Yusufi I., 1999, *The Stability Pact and Its Role in the Development of Regional Co-operation in South East Europe*, available at:
http://www.policy.hu/yusufi/spregcooperation.pdf.

OPTIMAL CHOICE OF AN EXCHANGE RATE ARRANGEMENT IN THE NEW EU MEMBER STATES: SOME EMPIRICAL EVIDENCE FROM BULGARIA

SILVIA TRIFONOVA

Abstract

The main objective of the paper is to make an analysis of the typology of the existing exchange rate arrangements and to describe the arguments for the optimal choice of an exchange rate system. A comparative analysis of the past and the present IMF classification systems of exchange rate systems is made. In addition, the main pros and cons of the fixed vs. the floating exchange rates are analyzed. The main focus in this paper is placed on the Bulgarian experience with a Currency Board Arrangement (CBA) as a specific hard peg system. The current performance and development of the Bulgarian CBA is analyzed and its role for maintaining the financial stability in the country during the recent global financial crisis is explored. The Bulgarian CBA was adopted in July 1997 after an unprecedented financial and economic crisis experienced in the country in 1996-1997. The recent experience of the Bulgarian economy demonstrates that the CBA is the key stabilization tool for safeguarding the soundness of the Bulgarian financial system. In fact, the global financial crisis has affected the Bulgarian financial system to a lower extent than other Central and Eastern European countries and an important factor determining this trend was the prudential framework established under the conditions of the CBA. However, problems associated with the withdrawal of foreign investors from the country, lower consumer and business confidence, and fall in employment, are still crucial for the domestic economy and are needed to be overcome.

Introduction

The structure of this paper is organized as follows: section 2 represents an analysis of the process of monetary integration of Bulgaria to the EMU (European Monetary Union) and the progress made by Bulgaria in fulfilling the Maastricht nominal convergence criteria. In section 3 the Bulgarian currency board system, its institutional framework, operational characteristics and main advantages and disadvantages are analyzed. The paper concludes with summarizing the results of the analysis.

Typology of exchange rate arrangements

The pioneering work of Robert Mundell (1961) posed the beginning of the long-lasting policy debate for the optimum currency areas (OCAs) and the discussion for the fixed versus flexible exchange rates. This debate was especially encouraged in the last decades along with the growing integration of the world economy. On its own, the growth of international trade in goods and assets has raised the transactions benefits from common currencies and led, thereby, to a decline in the number of independent currencies. Moreover, the emergence of a new fixed exchange-rate system among the European Community in 1972 and the establishment of the European Monetary Union (the Euro area) in 1999, were the most important present steps in the evolution of the fixed vs. flexible exchange rates debate. However, fixed and flexible exchange rates are only two alternatives defining the extremes of exchange-rate systems. In between of these extremes are a number of other hybrid systems of exchange rates that have been practiced in various times.

The so-called "father" of the optimum currency area theory is Robert Mundell (London School of Economics) who started to develop the concept for the OCA in 1955-56 as a doctoral student of James Meade. His initial interests were associated with the real side of the capital movements – the transfer problem, stability conditions, welfare implications, factor mobility, transport costs and so on, and not with the flexible or fixed exchange rates. During this time, the flexible exchange rates were billed as a free market alternative to fixed exchange rates. Flexible exchange-rate systems existed in the United States, United Kingdom, Canada and many other countries. In this regard, Mundell placed emphasis on the currency area concept. He argued that an optimum currency area is an area the members of which have a single currency regime or- what is almost the same thing – a fixed exchange-rate system with guaranteed convertibility of currencies. Mundell demonstrated that it is necessary to ask what economic characteristics determine the optimum size of the domain of a single currency. As McKinnon (1963, p. 717) argues, the term "optimum" is used to describe a single currency area within which monetary-fiscal policy and flexible external exchange rates can be used to give the best resolution of the following three (sometimes conflicting) objectives: i) the maintenance of full employment; ii) the maintenance of a stable internal average price level; iii) the maintenance of balanced international payments. Existing national borders are used to define the single currency area to which flexible external exchange rates would or would not be applied.

The International Monetary Fund (IMF) publishes on a regular basis classification of the countries' de facto exchange rate arrangements. As Ghosh and Ostry (2009, p. 38) argue a perennial question in international economics– whether in academia or in politics circles– concerns the optimal choice of exchange rate system. After the breakdown of the Bretton Woods system in the early of 1970s, and the subsequent adoption of the Second Amendment to the IMF Articles of Agreement, member countries have been free to adopt the exchange rate system of their choice. Since then the countries weren't obliged to peg their exchange rates in a system overseen by the IMF, they need a sound basis for selecting the regime best suited to their needs– to be fixed, floating or intermediate. There is an extensive academic literature on the relative merits of the fixed versus flexible exchange rates and on the issues concerning the optimal choice of exchange rate arrangement. Such major analytical studies are those elaborated by Ghosh et al. (1997), Ghosh et al. (2002), Levy-Yeyati and Stuzenegger (2003), Mussa et al. (2000), Rogoff et al. (2004), Reinhart and Rogoff (2004), etc. Reviews which were made also by the IMF staff, helped to inform member countries of how their choice of exchange rate regime can affect their own macroeconomic performance – inflation, growth, vulnerability to crisis – and to contribute to the stability of the international monetary system.

In practice, the preferred exchange rate regime, particularly for developing and emerging economies has considerably been evolved over the past couple of decades. Pegging the exchange rate to a strong convertible foreign (anchor) currency (often the US dollar or the deutsche mark) was very attractive in the early 1990s – especially for nations in transition from command to market economies that were seeking to stabilize their economies after their initial price liberalizations. During this period a spate of capital account crisis were also observed in the emerging economies. It has led to massive reversals of capital inflows and therefore to collapsing currencies and increasing fragility of the fixed exchange rate arrangements. On the basis of the IMF review in 1998 a broad consensus was generated for the fact that the simple pegs were too prone to crisis. This revealed the need for introducing more restrict or "hard" pegs such as monetary unions or currency board arrangements (CBAs). The other available option was the adoption of free floats in which the market determines a currency's value without government intervention.

Table 1. IMF classification of exchange rate systems (before February 1, 2009)

1. *Exchange arrangement with no separate legal tender* – the currency of another country circulates as the sole legal tender or the member belongs to a monetary or currency union in which the same legal tender is shared by the members of the union.
2. *Currency board arrangement (CBA)* – a monetary regime based on an explicit legislative commitment to exchange domestic currency for a specified foreign currency at a fixed exchange rate, combined with restrictions on the issuing authority to ensure the fulfillment of its legal obligation.
3. *Other conventional fixed peg arrangement* – the country pegs its currency (formally or de facto) at a fixed exchange rate to a major currency or a basket of currencies where the exchange rate fluctuates within a narrow margin of at most ± 1 % around a central rate.
4. *Pegged exchange rate within horizontal band* – the value of the currency is maintained within margins of fluctuation around a formal or de facto fixed exchange rate that are wider than ± 1 % around a central rate.
5. *Crawling peg* – the currency is adjusted periodically in small amounts at a fixed, pre-announced rate or in a response to changes in selective quantitative indicators (rate of inflation, GDP, interest rate, etc.)
6. *Exchange rate within crawling bands* – the currency is maintained within certain fluctuation margins around a central rate that is adjusted periodically at a fixed pre-announced rate or in a response to changes in selective quantitative indicators.
7. *Managed floating with no pre-announced path for the exchange rate* – the monetary authority influences the movements of the exchange rate through active interventions in the foreign exchange market without specifying or pre-committing to, a pre-announced level and path for the exchange rate.

8. *Independent floating* – the exchange rate is market determined, with any foreign exchange intervention aimed at moderating the rate of change and preventing undue fluctuations in the exchange rate, rather than at establishing a level for it.

Source: IMF.

In February 2009, the existing IMF classification of exchange rate arrangements was revised in order to better meet the challenges resulting from the new developments in the international monetary system such as the following: i) the overly heterogeneous residual category of managed floating; ii) the increasing complexity of the intervention practices that are used in characterizing exchange rate arrangements. As Habermeier et al. (2009, p. 3) argue the main changes to the classification system consist of the following:

- Replacing the current distinction between managed and independent floating exchange rates with two new categories – floating and free floating with clear definitions. In fact, this distinction has been often cited as too heavily on judgment before the revision of the classification system.
- Drawing a distinction between conventional fixed exchange rates and crawling pegs, and arrangements that are merely peg-like or crawl-like. First distinction is made between de facto arrangements that are floating (market-determined) and those that are not. Second distinction is made between the following two types of non-floating exchange rate systems - peg-like (or stabilized-like) and crawl-like. These categories are defined on the basis of easily verifiable quantitative and qualitative criteria.
- Increasing the transparency of the classification system by basing it on rules that can be implemented using specified information, with a more circumscribed role for judgment.

Those changes are undertaken in order to increase the consistency and objectivity of classifications across countries and improve transparency, with benefits for the IMF's bilateral and multilateral surveillance. The new system is compatible with the current trend of much more countries that actively manage their exchange rate in the recent years. As concerns the intervention practices, many countries are now able to switch between domestic and foreign currency debt on commercial terms, while others have had income flows (in particular from oil) that may or may not be channeled through the central bank, and longer-term investment funds. As a result, conventional measures of intervention may understate the degree to which floating exchange rates in some countries are managed. The problems are compounded by the lack of available information in many countries.

Table 2. IMF classification of exchange rate systems (after February 1, 2009)

Hard pegs
1. *Exchange arrangement with no separate legal tender.* Classification as an exchange arrangement with no separate legal tender involves the confirmation of the country authorities' de jure exchange rate arrangement. The currency of another country circulates as the sole legal tender (formal dollarization or euroization). Adopting such an arrangement implies the complete surrender of the monetary authorities' control over domestic monetary policy. Note: effective January 1, 2007, exchange arrangements of the countries that belong to a monetary or currency union in which the same legal tender is shared by the members of the union are classified under the arrangement governing the joint currency. The new classification is based on the behaviour of the common currency, whereas the previous classification was based on the lack of a separate legal tender. The classification thus reflects only a definitional change, and is not based on a judgment that there has been a substantive change in the exchange arrangement or other policies of the currency union or its members.
2. *Currency board arrangement (CBA).* Classification as a CBA involves the confirmation of the country authorities' de jure exchange rate arrangement. A CBA is a monetary arrangement based on an explicit legislative commitment to exchange domestic currency for a specified foreign currency at a fixed exchange rate, combined with restrictions on the issuing authority to ensure the fulfilment of its legal obligation. This implies that domestic currency will be issued only against foreign exchange and that it remains fully backed by foreign assets, eliminating traditional central bank functions such as monetary control and lender-of-last-resort, and leaving little scope for discretionary monetary policy. Some flexibility may still be afforded, depending on the strictness of the banking rules of the CBA.

Soft pegs
3. *Conventional pegged arrangement.* For classification as a conventional pegged arrangement, the country formally (de jure) pegs its currency at a fixed rate to another currency or a basket of currencies, where the basket is formed, for example, from the currencies of major trading or financial partners, and weights reflect the geographic distribution of trade, services, or capital flows. The anchor currency or basket weights are public or notified to the IMF. The country authorities stand ready to maintain the fixed parity through direct intervention (i.e., via sale or purchase of foreign exchange in the market) or indirect intervention (e.g., via exchange rate related use of interest rate policy, imposition of foreign exchange regulations, exercise of moral suasion that constrains foreign exchange activity, or intervention by other public institutions). There is no commitment to irrevocably keep the parity, but the formal arrangement must be confirmed empirically: the exchange rate may fluctuate within narrow margins of less than ±1% around a central rate – or the maximum and minimum value of the spot market exchange rate must remain within a narrow margin of 2% - for at least six months.
4. *Stabilized arrangement.* Classification as a stabilized arrangement entails a spot market exchange rate that remains within a margin of 2% for six months or more (with the exception of a specified number of outliers or step adjustments), and is not floating. The required margin of stability can be met either with respect to a single currency or a basket of currencies, where the anchor currency or the basket is ascertained or confirmed using statistical techniques. Classification as a stabilized arrangement requires that the statistical criteria are met, and that the exchange rate remains stable as a result of official action (including structural market rigidities). The classification does not imply a policy commitment on the part of the country authorities.
5. *Crawling peg.* Classification as a crawling peg involves the confirmation of the country authorities' de jure exchange rate arrangement. The currency is adjusted in small amounts at a fixed rate or in response to changes in selected quantitative indicators, such as past inflation differentials vis-à-vis major trading partners or differentials between the inflation target and expected inflation in major trading partners. The rate of crawl can be set to generate inflation-adjusted changes in the exchange rate (backward looking) or set at a predetermined fixed rate and/or below the projected inflation differentials (forward looking). The rules and parameters of the arrangement are public or notified to the IMF.

6. *Crawl-like arrangement*. For classification as a crawl-like arrangement, the exchange rate must remain within a narrow margin of 2% relative to a statistically identified trend for six months or more (with the exception of a specified number of outliers), and the exchange rate arrangement cannot be considered as floating. Normally, a minimum rate of change greater than allowed under a stabilized (peg-like) arrangement is required. However, an arrangement will be considered crawl-like with an annualized rate of change of at least 1%, provided that the exchange rate appreciates or depreciates in a sufficiently monotonic and continuous manner.
7. *Pegged exchange rate within horizontal bands*. Classification as a pegged exchange rate within horizontal bands involves the confirmation of the country authorities' de jure exchange rate arrangement. The value of the currency is maintained within certain margins of fluctuation of at least ±1% around a fixed central rate, or the margin between the maximum and minimum value of the exchange rate exceeds 2%. It includes arrangements of countries in the Exchange Rate Mechanism (ERM) of the European Monetary System (EMS), which was replaced with the ERM II on January 1, 1999, for those countries with margins of fluctuation wider than ±1%. The central rate and width of the band are public or notified to the IMF.
Floating arrangements
8. *Floating*. A floating exchange rate is largely market determined, without an ascertainable or predictable path for the rate. In particular, an exchange rate that satisfies the statistical criteria for a peg-like or a crawl-like arrangement will be classified as such unless it is clear that the stability of the exchange rate is not the result of official actions. Foreign exchange market intervention may be either direct or indirect, and serves to moderate the rate of change and prevent undue fluctuations in the exchange rate, but policies targeting a specific level of the exchange rate are incompatible with floating. Indicators for managing the rate are broadly judgmental (e.g., balance of payments position, international reserves, parallel market developments). Floating arrangements may exhibit more or less exchange rate volatility, depending on the size of the shocks affecting the economy.
9. *Free floating*. A floating exchange rate can be classified as free floating if intervention occurs only exceptionally, aims to address disorderly market conditions, and if the authorities have provided information or data confirming that intervention has been limited to at most three instances in the previous six months, each lasting no more than three business days. If the information or data required are not available to the IMF staff, the arrangement will be classified as floating.

Residual exchange rate arrangements
10. *Other managed arrangement.* This category is a residual, and is used when the exchange rate arrangement does not meet the criteria for any of the other categories. Arrangements characterized by frequent shifts in policies may fall into this category.

Source: Habermeier, et al. (2009), op.cit., pp. 11-14.

Table 3. Overall composition of exchange rate arrangements using the previous and revised classification systems

	1998 de facto system		*2009 de facto system*	
Hard pegs		23		23
	Exchange arrangement with no separate legal tender	10	Exchange arrangement with no separate legal tender	10
	Currency board arrangement	13	Currency board arrangement	13
Soft pegs		81		78
	Other conventional fixed peg arrangement	68	Conventional pegged arrangement	45
			Stabilized arrangement	22
of which:		13		11
Intermediate pegs				
	Pegged exchange rate	3	Pegged exchange rate within horizontal bands	3
	Crawling peg	8	Crawling peg	5
	Exchange rate within crawling band	2	Crawl-like arrangement	3

Floating arrangements		84		75
	Managed floating with no pre-announced path for the exchange rate	44	Floating	39
	Independently floating	40	Free floating	36
Other managed arrangements (residual)		n.a.		12
Total		188		188

Source: Habermeier et al., (2009), op.cit., p. 4.

An important argument for adopting another country's currency or maintaining a currency board is seen as more credible commitment devices than a simple fixing of the exchange rates (Alesina et al., 2002, p. 301). Moreover, the memory of the inflationary episodes encouraged inflation control, thereby generating consideration of irrevocably fixed exchange rate as a possible instrument to achieve price stability. Third, recent episodes of financial turbulence have promoted discussions about "new financial architectures". In particular, the key characteristics of the fixed and flexible exchange-rate systems could be summarized as follows.

First, key advantage of the fixed exchange rate systems is the improved inflation performance. As Mishkin (2000, p. 1) argues, the most important principle that can serve as useful guidance for the central bank's operation is the price stability – the low and stable inflation rate – since the price stability provides substantial benefits to the economy. He describes three main benefits of price stability such as the following: a) price stability prevents overinvestment in the financial sector and helps individuals and business to avoid some of the costs of inflation; b) price stability lowers the uncertainty about relative prices and the future price level, making it easier for firms and individuals to make appropriate decisions; c) price stability also lowers the distortions from the interaction of the tax system and inflation. One of the best solutions for achieving prince stability in the economy is to adopt an explicit nominal anchor or a strong commitment to a fixed exchange rate. Such nominal anchor also helps restrain fiscal policy. Many empirical studies have sought to test the anti-inflationary effects of the pegged exchange rates and the currency boards. For instance,

Ghosh et al. (1998) found that economies with fixed exchange rates and particularly with currency boards do have better inflation experiences. They also reported that average inflation under CBAs was significantly lower than under floating exchange rates. Moreover, this improved inflationary environment promotes a better economic growth.

Second, national authorities have a strong commitment to carry out restricted domestic macroeconomic policies. In particular, the monetary policy is significantly restricted, and the exchange rate policy is fully abolished. Fixed exchange rate systems are rule-based systems – they provide discipline for the macroeconomic policies. As Ghosh and Ostry (2009, p. 40) argue especially pegged exchange rate systems severely contain the use of other macroeconomic policies. The "impossible trinity" of simultaneously maintaining a pegged exchange rate, an open capital account, and an independent monetary policy is well established. Bain and Howels (2003, p. 285) use the term "inconsistent quartet", which states that national government cannot at the same time maintain all of the following: a) free trade; b) full capital mobility; c) fixed exchange rates; d) national autonomy in the conduct of monetary policy. The authors argue that this does not apply to the strong country (or the so-called "leader") of the system, which is able to determine its own monetary policy, as long as it is able to withstand the political pressure emanating from other members in cases where interests conflict. In contrast, flexible exchange rate systems provide a monetary autonomy – they enable each country to operate an independent monetary policy. Moreover, they restore the monetary autonomy enabling each country to determine its own rate of inflation.

Third, an automatic adjustment mechanism of the balance of payments (BoP) is applicable in the fixed exchange rate systems. It is called an "interest-rate adjustment mechanism" which relies on the effect of the BoP on the money supply. If the effects are not sterilized, a BoP deficit will reduce the money supply and a surplus will increase it. With a gold standard this occurs because a deficit means a gold outflow and a shrinking money supply, and a surplus means a gold inflow and an increasing money supply. In the gold-exchange and dollar standards, an in the European Monetary System, the money supply also declines after deficit and rises after surplus. In these cases the money supply changes because of intervention in the foreign exchange market. A deficit requires the national monetary authority to purchase its currency to keep the value up. Thus, money is withdrawn from circulation. Similarly, a surplus requires the central bank to sell its currency and hence increase the money supply. In this way, the interest-rate adjustment mechanism can be explained by the current account of the BoP.

The interest-rate adjustment via the capital account works in the following manner: if a deficit occurs, it will reduce the money supply and raise the interest rate. However, the interest rate will not increase as a result of a reduction in the money supply if there is a liquidity trap, which occurs if the demand for money is perfectly elastic. The deficit means surpluses elsewhere; therefore, the money supplies of other currencies will be rising, which will reduce their interest rates. For both reasons there is a rise in interest differentials in favour of the deficit countries. This will make investment (in securities, and so on) in that country appear relatively more attractive. The resultant inflows on the capital account should improve the BoP, thereby correcting the original deficit. The same automatic adjustment mechanism of the BoP is observed in a currency board system. In comparison with the gold standard, here the role of the gold is played by the foreign reserve currency. In contrast, in the flexible exchange rate systems there is not any legislative framework for a certain relationship between the foreign currency inflow in the domestic economy and the money supply.

Forth, fixed exchange rate systems leads to a higher degree of openness of the economy. The latter is both a prerequisite and a consequence from establishing a pegged exchange rate. Countries with fixed exchange rate systems or member states in a currency union usually have closer and deeper trade links as a result of the stability of exchange rates and of prices. Franker and Rose (2002) find that the effect of a currency board is a more than tripling of trade and thus the trade motive seems to be very important. It explains why currency boards may remain an attractive option for small economies. For achieving such a growth in the international trade, a free mobility of production factors (capital, labor) is needed. With this regard, a strong liberalization of foreign trade and of capital movements is particularly important.

However, a disadvantage of the fixed exchange rates is that they impose high vulnerability of the domestic economies. In contrast, the floating exchange rate systems can insulate the economies from the negative international market events (macroeconomic shocks) through changes in the exchange rate.

Currency board arrangement in Bulgaria

The CBA was introduced in Bulgaria on July 1, 1997 when the new Law on the Bulgarian National Bank (BNB) entered into force. Its introduction was a logical step after the unprecedented financial crisis experienced at the end of 1996 that pushed the country to a disastrous hyperinflation and a dramatic devaluation of the national currency – Bulgarian lev. In 1996 the GDP fell by some 8 % to 9 %, inflation soared to 310 %, and the budget deficit reached about 12 % of GDP. Cumulative inflation from 1991 to the end of 1996 was 24,000 %, and wages fell sevenfold (in dollar terms) over the same period. In early February the currency exchange rate was set at 2,608 levs against the US dollar, from 500 levs to the dollar in early January. Many retail stores were closed down. Restaurants, shops, and wholesale suppliers still in business started to accept payment in dollars only, despite an official ban of trading in hard currency. The economy was characterized by extensive adoption of the dollar and barter exchange. Bulgaria's foreign exchange reserves fell to the critical level of under USD 400 million and the service of the country's foreign debt was put into jeopardy (BNB, 1998, p. 11). The fuel shortage has paralyzed public transport and road traffic in large parts of the country. Grain supplies have been depleted; the authorities have warned that the prices of a loaf of bread may rise from 250 levs to 2,000 levs if grain must be imported at market conditions.

Ninety percent of the population was living below the World Bank poverty level of $4 a day; in fact, due to raging hyperinflation, many pensioners now receive less than $4 a month, according to a recent Washington Post editorial. The public was seized by fear about banks' prospects of survival; the commercial banks were decapitalised and systematically refinanced by the BNB in the expectation of avoiding the social and political implications of a banking system collapse. However, at the end of 1996 and beginning of 1997 a quarter of the commercial banks in Bulgaria were liquidated. Under these conditions the BNB lost control over exchange rate and the money supply. Major monetary tools ceased to have an effect on the banking and monetary systems. Moreover, the BNB was subordinated to the budget and government priorities and constantly covered fiscal losses by printing money thus pushing the country into hyperinflation.

In the light of the failed stabilization programs in 1997 there was growing awareness that a rapid restoration of normality would require a visible and credible departure from the past policies (Gulde, 1999, p. 6). The IMF mission in Bulgaria held in November 1996 initiated the first discussion with the Bulgarian authorities and major interest groups on the merits of a currency board system. Finally in April 1997 a new (5th) standby agreement with the IMF was concluded that played the role of a financial anchor for the forthcoming launch of the currency board in Bulgaria.

A currency board is a set of rules providing for a 100 % cover of reserve money with highly liquid foreign exchange assets. The exchange rate is fixed against a reserve (anchor) currency. The central bank is committed to exchange unlimited amounts of national currency against the anchor currency at an irrevocable fixed exchange rate (Ghoch et al., 1998, p. 10). Bulgaria chose initially the German mark as a reserve currency and as of January 1, 1999 - the Euro (1 Euro = 1.95583 Bulgarian levs) thus reflecting the prospects for future accession to the EU and affiliation to the EMU. As the BNB declares, this level of the fixed exchange rate was expected to be maintained until the accession of Bulgaria to the Euro area (Iskrov, 2005, p. 2). A CBA significantly differs from a central bank as far as their key features, design and policy implementations are concerned.

The CBA adopted in Bulgaria is characterized as a modern-day or quasi system. It distinguishes from the pure CBAs since it retains some features of central banking (Bennett, 1994; Williamson, 1995; Gulde, et al., 2000; Ghoch, et al., 2000). Quasi-currency boards are established in countries where the central bank continues to exist, but its structure is reorganized. Institutionally the remaining central bank is divided into two departments with separate balance sheets and different functions: a) An Issue department (ICA) which takes the function of a currency board; b) A Banking department (Monetary Agency) which takes the residual functions of a typical central bank. The quasi CBAs might hold deposits of commercial banks (that are subject to reserve requirements), also might hold domestic securities or might extend loans to commercial banks (i.e. to act as a lender of last resort). Therefore, they may conduct an active monetary policy and may use monetary policy instruments such as reserve requirements, discounting policy, interest-rate policy.

In 1997 institutionally the BNB was divided into three departments in order to function under the CBA's rules:

- Issue Department
- Banking Department
- Banking Supervision Department.

The Issue Department represents "the currency board proper", which manages the country's foreign reserves and issues domestic currency (Enoch and Gulde, 1997, p. 10). Its balance sheet includes the most liquid assets and liabilities. The main function of the Issue Department is to maintain full foreign exchange cover of the total amount of monetary liabilities of the BNB at the fixed exchange rate of Bulgarian lev against euro (BGN 1.95583 per a euro), by taking actions needed for the efficient management of the central bank's gross foreign reserves. The aggregate amount of the monetary liabilities of the BNB consists of all banknotes and coins in circulation issued by the BNB and any balances on accounts held by other parties with the BNB, with the exception of the accounts held by the IMF. The gross foreign reserves of the BNB are equal to the market value of its following assets: a) banknotes and coins held in freely convertible foreign currency; b) funds in freely convertible foreign currency held by the BNB on accounts with foreign central banks or with other foreign financial institutions; c) the Special Drawing Rights (SDRs) of the IMF held by the BNB; d) debt instruments held by the BNB and issued by foreign countries, central banks, other foreign financial institutions or international financial organizations; e) the balance on accounts receivable and accounts payable on forward or repurchase agreements of the BNB, concluded with or guaranteed by foreign central banks, public international financial organizations or other foreign financial institutions. The Issue Department and the Banking Department have separated balance sheets.

In contrast to the Issue Department, Banking Department of the BNB plays the residual functions of a typical central bank, with the exception of banking supervision (which is exercised by the Banking Supervision Department). It may hold domestic securities, to maintain gold and other precious metals, to have equity investments in domestic entities or to extend loans and advances to banks. By law, the BNB may not extend loans to banks under the conditions of the CBA, except in the case of emergence of a liquidity risk that may affect the stability of the banking system. In this case, the Banking Department may extend credits denominated in Bulgarian levs to banks under the following general conditions (BNB Ordinance 6): 1. only in case of emergence of a systemic liquidity risk; 2. only to solvent domestic banks that experience acute need of liquidity that cannot be provided from other sources; 3. only against collateral of liquid assets (monetary gold; foreign currency; paper or book-entry liquid securities issued by the Bulgarian government, or guaranteed by it; prime-rate liquid securities issued by foreign governments and central banks or guaranteed by them); 4. the loan repayment term could not exceed 3 months.

Since the currency board's introduction, the BNB has stopped to maintain domestic government securities in its assets and its government securities portfolio has been restructured. The BNB ended its direct purchases and sales of government securities and its repurchase agreements (REPOs). As concerns the base interest rate (BIR), since the CBA's introduction in Bulgaria, it has been determined as the level of the yield on 3-month discount T-bills on the primary market. This practice was remained until the introduction of LEONIA index (Lev OverNight Index Average) on February 1, 2005. LEONIA is a reference rate of the concluded and settled overnight deposit transactions in domestic currency. It is computed by the BNB as a weighted average of all overnight unsecured deposit transactions in Bulgarian levs undertaken in interbank market in Bulgaria by a specified number of data contributing banks. Since February 2005 the calculation of the BIR has been based on the simple average of the values of the LEONIA for the business days in a concluded month.

The only monetary policy instrument that the BNB can use without any legal restrictions under the conditions of the CBA is the required reserves ratio. The BNB determines the minimum reserve requirements the banks of which must keep with the central bank, the method of their calculation, and the terms and procedure for interest payments to them. According to the BNB all banks and foreign banks' branches based on Bulgaria should maintain minimum reserves with the BNB. Banks maintain minimum reserves on their settlement accounts in levs and euro with the BNB. The required reserves ratio is amounted to 10 % of banks' deposit base (bank's attracted funds in levs and in foreign currency). The deposit base is composed by banks' attracted funds in levs and foreign currency, with the exception of funds attracted: a) from other local banks; b) through the branches of a local bank abroad; c) through debt/capital (hybrid) instruments; d) as subordinated debt.

The Banking Supervision Department of the BNB exercises strict supervision over the banking system. It carries out off-site supervision in order to identify the bank risk. In this regard, the Banking Supervision Department collects, processes and examines information received by banks (accounting, supervisory and statistical data). An analysis of the financial performance of each bank and its compliance with bank supervision regulations is made. In case of violations this Department makes recommendations for sanctions to be imposed. The state of each bank and its risk profile is periodically assessed using a set of indicators. The Banking Supervision Department also undertakes on-site inspections, i.e. it analyzes the commercial bank activity in order to establish the reasons causing problems in a particular bank. Review and valuation of credit portfolio (credit risk), market risk, operational risk, foreign exchange risk, liquidity, solvency, as well as assessment of banks' management and internal controls received special attention. Finally, the Banking Supervision Department also carries out examinations of non-bank financial institutions such as financial brokerage houses and exchange bureaux.

Bulgarian economy development

In September 2004, the BNB's Governing Council adopted a Strategy for Bulgarian National Bank development (BNB, 2004). According to this strategy, the BNB takes the commitment to work for the successful integration of Bulgaria into the European Exchange Rate Mechanism II (ERM II) after the EU accession in 2007. It is committed to maintain unilaterally the CBA until the Euro area membership at the current fixed exchange rate of BGN to the euro. De Haan et al. (2005: 182) argue that a country with a currency board system has a natural "strong exit" in the form of EMU membership. As Gulde et al. (2000, p. 24) argue the CBA is compatible with the ERM II framework, entailing a discipline which is in line with that one required by the economies in the EMU.

On the basis of the adopted strategy, in November 2004 the BNB and the Government of the Republic of Bulgaria signed an Agreement on the Introduction of the Euro to the Republic of Bulgaria, outlining the policy and commitments to be pursued in the process of changing over to the euro in Bulgaria. The Government and the BNB have undertaken a unilateral commitment to adhere to zero deviation of the exchange rate from this fixed level. They have avowed Bulgaria's acceptance into the ERM II and agreed for the country's membership in this exchange-rate mechanism on the following principles of: (1) Maintaining the CBA until the Euro area entry at the existing fixed exchange rate of BGN 1.95583 per euro; (2) Renouncing any variation of the currency board conditions and exchange rates during ERM II membership; (3) Adhering to the minimum term set in EU legislation for ERM II membership and timely performance of each necessary step for Euro area membership; (4) Introducing the euro as the national currency at the time of entering the Euro area. As a result, as the earliest possible date for the euro adoption in Bulgaria (and for accession of the BNB into the Eurosystem) was determined the year 2010. However, the global financial crisis which hit the economy in 2009 made impossible the euro adoption at the scheduled phase.

A survey of 30 analysts of emerging markets by Reuters news agency established an estimate that Bulgaria would adopt the euro in 2012 and Romania, the other country joining the EU in 2007, would adopt the European currency in 2013 (The Sofia Echo, 2009). Previous forecasts indicated that Hungary, which has repeatedly surpassed its budget deficit targets, might join the ERM II in 2014. As concerns the statements of the Ministry of Finance of the Republic of Bulgaria it was stated that

> "Bulgaria is going to replace its currency, the lev (BGN), with the euro (EUR), in 2012 or 2013. We have a chance in the last year of the mandate to introduce the euro. Bulgaria will meet all criteria for the implementation of euro by the end of 2009. However, if the budget deficit exceeds 3% it will put off our Eurozone entry by two more years. Bulgaria plans to apply for ERM2 (a two-year currency stability test for euro hopefuls) by the end of 2009." (Sofia News Agency, 2009).

As many authors argue, the consistency, predictability and the clear and transparent operational mechanism of the CBA created the nominal anchor in the economy and stabilized inflationary expectations (Zaimov and Hristov, 2002, p. 8). In the post 1997 period Bulgaria achieved the lowest and most stable inflation rates since the beginning of the economic reforms and the most stable output growth.

However, this situation has been preserved until mid 2008 when Bulgarian economy was hit by the global financial crisis. The financial turmoil which emerged with the US sub-prime mortgage market grew into the deepest and fastest developing crisis in a Century. Financial difficulties at leading transnational investment banks funds completely eroded confidence among financial institutions, while the Lehman Brothers' failure practically paralyzed international financial markets.

During the period 2000-2008 Bulgaria maintained stable and consistently strong growth rates, among the highest in Central and Eastern European countries, and significantly higher than in the Euro area countries. The economic growth speeded up to 6.2% on a year-to-year basis in 2007, followed by the negative impact of the unfavourable global economic conditions. Accelerated growth in Bulgaria during the reviewed period was combined with relatively lower growth in the Euro area. Recent years' fixed capital investment trends in Bulgaria were the major factor contributing most to GDP growth. Production capacity renewal covered all sectors. Government spending under the restrictive government fiscal policy was neutral as regards economic growth.

As the world financial crisis hit real sectors worldwide in the fourth quarter of 2008, the Bulgarian economy was no exception in terms of economic activity, with annual real GDP growth slowing to 3.5%. In the context of increasing uncertainty, shrinking external demand, and falling international commodity prices since mid-2008, exports and imports started to slow down, with declines in 2007 in the fourth quarter. The adverse international environment affected mainly manufacturing whose exports had a large share of total sales. Due to the recession in the Euro area – Bulgaria's major trading partner, in the fourth quarter of 2008, the exports of goods and non-factor services decreased in real terms by 6% on an annual basis. Imports, reflecting intensive investment in Bulgaria, began to fall (mainly commodities and investment goods), though this lagged behind exports.

Despite worsened international financial markets, local economic agents retained access to foreign finance. Foreign direct investment (FDI) remained relatively high, ensuring almost 74% cover of the BoP current and capital account deficits (BNB, 2009, p. 10). The inflow of finance into the BoP exceeded the current and capital account deficits thus boosting the country's international reserves. The contraction of current account and trade balance deficit was due to the substantial drop in export of Bulgarian goods as a result to steep falls in external demand and fall in import. Due to the reduced household consumption, weaker demand and the tightening of banks' credit standards, a clear downward trend in the credit growth was observed. In particular, the lending to households was relatively weak. Fourth quarter household consumption growth slowed to 1.5% in 2008, with non-food consumption and net tourism revenue bringing negative contributions.

The global financial and economic crisis was deepened and expanded during 2009. The real GDP declined in the Euro area by 4.8% and in the

US by 3.6%. The sharp decline in external and domestic demand, combined with the weaker foreign investment inflows, and the tighter bank lending led to a decline of 2009 real GDP by 3.8% on an annual basis. The increased macroeconomic uncertainty and higher risk to the financial system was accompanying the contraction of economic activity in Bulgaria. In 2009 the domestic demand, especially for investment goods, had a negative contribution to GDP dynamics, while net exports of goods and services recorded a high positive contribution of 11.6 percentage points to the change in GDP. The physical import volume retained its decline rate above 20% in the three quarters of the year. The pace of decline in exports gradually decelerated from 17.4% in the first quarter of 2009 to 6.7% in the third quarter (on an annual basis).

Between January and October 2009 all groups, excluding animal and vegetable products, food, drinks and tobacco, contributed to the negative growth of exports, with the dynamics of base metals (-9.7 percentage points), mineral products and fuels (-6.8 percentage points), machines, transportation vehicles and appliances (-2.8 percentage points) and textile, clothing and footwear (-2.1 percentage points) contributing most to this. In the structure of imports by use, raw materials registered the highest negative contribution (-12.2 percentage points), followed by investment goods (-10.6 percentage points) and mineral products and fuels (-9.6 percentage points) due to lower production and investment activity in Bulgaria.

In addition to the industry and trade whose investments have declined since the beginning of the year of 2009, the third quarter saw a large deceleration in real estate operations and business services. In response to the decreased demand, firms reduced their stocks of materials, goods for resale and finished goods. During 2009 the final consumption fell by 4.4% in real terms compared with the same period of 2008, its contribution to GDP growth turning negative at 3.7 percentage points. Although current household income retained its positive growth, household consumer expenditure fell by 5.7% in real terms which may be ascribed to the uncertainty about future incomes and postponement of durables purchases. The increasing unemployment also affected consumption declines.

In 2009 the labor market in Bulgaria was hit by the overall economic downturn – the unemployment started to raise faster reaching 9.1% unemployment rate at the year-end. The worsened labour market conditions led to increased uncertainty among households about employment and future income. According to the consumer survey data of the National Statistical Institute (NSI) the consumer confidence remained subdued and expectations of upward unemployment dynamics increased. Against this background, households postponed purchases of durables and increased the savings rate. Similar behaviour was recorded by household budget survey data which show a clearly pronounced upward trend in savings from 7% of total income in October 2008 to 12% in November 2009. Concurrently, growth in net household claims on banks over the year confirms the increased propensity to save.

Following the introduction of the CBA, inflation rate in Bulgaria declined from extremely high levels to one-digit levels. However, despite the currency board system, the actual inflation in Bulgaria remained higher than in the Euro area member states reflecting the higher risks in the domestic economy. Since 2003 the inflation rate has risen again. These developments have mostly taken place against the background of dynamic economic conditions, but they also reflect external factors. Since December 2006, the accumulated inflation in Bulgaria reached 6.5% at the end of the year, followed by comparatively high rates in 2007. Annual rate of inflation reached 11.6% at the end of 2007 mainly due to the increased food prices (with average annual growth of 21.1%). During this period, the domestic pro-inflation factors included: changes in indirect taxes as required under the commitments to harmonize them with minimum EU levels; changes in administered prices; price convergence with Euro area levels; considerable credit growth and low real interest rates; increased domestic demand and strong private consumption spending underpinned by robust growth in disposable income.

After high rates in 2007, annual inflation moderated to 7.2% at the end of 2008 due to the decreased food and fuel prices. In the first half of 2009 inflation on an annual basis continued to go down underpinned by moderating growth in the prices of all major groups of goods and services (excluding tobacco products). The downward trend was sustained till the end of 2009 when the average annual inflation reached 2.8%. This was a result of the slowdown in domestic demand and the ongoing impact of the lower international raw material and fuel prices compared with those of 2008. The fall in some administratively controlled prices was also conducive to the fall in inflation. The Ministry of Finance of the Republic of Bulgaria expects an average inflation of 2.3% in the period of 2010-2013.

As concerns the banking system development during the first years of the new monetary system a general trend of financial stabilization was observed. There was a growing confidence in the national currency and the monetary system. In a CBA the international reserves entirely covered the BNB monetary obligations. For five consecutive years the banks in Bulgaria continued to pursue a policy of conservative market behaviour and maintained low-risk assets and high capital adequacy ratio. The higher own capital reported by the most banks was used as a prerequisite for expanding their activity. This was a clear sign that banks were extremely prudent in terms of risks related to economic processes in the country. Deposits accumulated by the banking system, earning assets, and total assets, rose significantly during the reviewed period. Moreover, an accelerated bank privatization in Bulgaria was observed. As a result the equity structure of a number of banks experienced serious changes during this period.

Since the year of 2002 the banking system was characterized by a considerable lending expansion which reflected the major part of the banks' assets growth. A sustained credit increase occurred both as a share of total assets and in absolute terms. Mostly their nominal non-government sector claims grew. This prompted the BNB to take extra measures to maintain banking stability and defend borrowers' interests. The BNB continued imposing, maintaining, and encouraging good banking practices. Banks enjoyed quality assets, net steady revenue from core operations, and a strong capital position sufficient to offset any risk in their assets. Liquidity was high, and the system was effective and competitive. The structure of the banking system balance sheet by bank group matched the policy pursued: enhancement of bank intermediacy through lending and the introduction of new banking services; an increase in the volume of securities in the investment portfolio; and maintenance of a high asset liquidity structure through a prudent level of bank deposits and securities in the trading portfolio. On 2 June 2003 the BNB launched Real-time Interbank Gross Settlement System (RINGS). As a result the systemic risk fell and settlement effectiveness, security, and speed grew significantly.

Nevertheless, the Bulgarian banking system during the period 2008-2009 was subject to two major influences. The global financial and economic crisis impacted the national economy and financial system most clearly in the second half of 2008. The other group of factors are related to the effect which the measures initiated to strengthen financial stability, including the actions of various institutions in Bulgaria, had on the banking system and business activity (BNB, 2009, p. 38). The change had effect on several aspects: (1) a significant slowdown in lending growth in the third and particularly fourth quarters of 2008; (2) a decline in general economic activity and attempts to stabilise finance sources through more aggressive deposit taking; (3) positive expectations from the cut in minimum required reserves and boosted deposit guarantees. Under the uncertain macroeconomic conditions during the period 2008-2009 a clear downward trend in the credit growth was sustained due to the weaker demand and the tightening of banks' credit standards. These factors mainly continued to curb growth in claims on non-financial corporations and households. There was also a high degree of uncertainty surrounding the developments in interest rates in the country. The reduction in interest rates in the interbank money market in the Euro area and in Bulgaria was not passed through to lending interest rates. A possible gradual decrease in deposit rates is likely to help lower the cost of borrowed funds.

During the period 2008-2009 the BNB was focused on maintaining banking stability, managing country's international reserves, ensuring smooth payments and currency circulation, and acting as official fiscal agent and state depository. The BNB priority is to maintain the banking stability and to regulate in a manner supportive of banks' own efforts to neutralize the global crisis and weaker economic activity in Bulgaria.

After the Bulgaria's membership into the EU in 2007, the BNB Governor is a member of the General Council of the European Central Bank (ECB) and participant in informal ECOFIN meetings. Therefore, he took part in deliberating the global crisis and the EU measures against it. Bulgaria joined other EU members' decision on minimum deposit guarantees by amending the Bank Deposit Guarantee Law cover from BGN 40,000 to BGN 100,000. The government adopted three packages of measures for counteracting the crisis, with relevant finance included in the 2009 State Budget Law. Amendments to Ordinance 21 on the Minimum Required Reserves Maintained with the Bulgarian National Bank by Banks also aimed to help Bulgarian banks manage their liquidity better. The Government and the BNB measures correspond to the common EU decisions while being specific to Bulgaria's particular needs.

A sharp decline in banks' deposits and international reserves was observed in 2008-2009 due to cuts in minimum required reserves (as of January 1, 2009 – the minimum required reserve ratio is of 5% for banks' funds attracted from abroad and 0% for banks' fund attracted from state and local government budgets). The released liquidity was used by banks mainly for reducing their foreign obligations. Slowed down annual growth of the money supply was observed in 2009 due to contracted economic activity and lower inflation. Due to the macroeconomic uncertainty and its negative effects on the credit demand and the lending policies, the Bulgarian banks changed significantly their behavior in direction of more prudent management, spending restrictions and staff optimization.

The maintenance of the fiscal discipline is a key pillar of the macroeconomic stability in a CBA. The solid fiscal performance in Bulgaria during the period 1997-2008 resulted from the over performance in revenues collection mainly due to higher growth of GDP and imports, improved tax and customs control and effects of ongoing tax reform. Appropriate structural reforms broadened the economy's tax base by cutting tax rates, encouraging entrepreneurship, improving the revenue function, and boosting tax collectability. State finances were additionally reinforced and the lasting maintenance of a balanced or surplus budget was attained without social tensions. In 2006-2007 the fiscal stance was tightened further (aiming to react on the deterioration of the current account of the BoP), which resulted in fairly large budget surplus - 3.5% of GDP in 2006 and 3.0% of the GDP for 2007. Over 2008 the fiscal policy remained its important role in maintaining macroeconomic stability and investor confidence in the Bulgarian economy. The consolidated fiscal program surplus came to 3.0% of the GDP for the year.

As regards the government fiscal stance in 2009, there were wide-spread warnings for deterioration of the budget position. The tax revenues were shrinked due to the economic downturn and the Bulgarian government needed to cut spending and to risk missing its budget surplus target and face a deficit for the first time in nearly a decade. Despite the expenditure-reducing contingency buffer in the budget, the general government budget balance deteriorated to a deficit of 3.8% of GDP in 2009, according to the European Commission forecasts. As a result, the discontinuation of an additional discretionary spending and the conduct of strict expenditure control were crucial for the outcome in the context of scarce revenues. Assuming that there is no government policy change, the budgetary outcome in 2010 is expected to be at a deficit of around 0.25% of GDP.

Table 4. Macroeconomic indicators in Bulgaria

Indicators	2005	2006	2007	2008	2009
Gross value added (ml BGN)	35 220	40 350	46 401	54 851	55 502
Gross value added (annual real growth rate, %)	5.3	6.6	6.3	6.1	-3.8
CPI average annual change, %	5.0	7.3	8.4	12.3	2.8
HICP average annual change, %	6.0	7.4	7.6	12.0	2.5
Unemployment, %	10.7	9.1	6.9	6.3	9.1
Broad money, % of GDP	59.0	65.0	74.4	68.6	72.1
Domestic credit, % of GDP	42.8	42.7	59.2	66.7	61.9
Base interest rate, %	2.04	2.69	3.93	5.12	2.40
Current account, % of GDP	-12.4	-18.4	-26.8	-24.0	-9.4
Trade balance,% of GDP	-20.2	-22.0	-25.1	-25.2	-12.1
Capital and financial account, % of GDP	19.3	28.8	45.3	34.2	7.8
Foreign direct investment, % of GDP	14.4	24.7	31.3	19.6	9.5
Gross external debt, % of GDP	79.0	82.0	100.2	108.7	111.3
Public sector, % of GDP	23.8	18.0	14.2	11.4	12.3
Budget deficit (-)/surplus(+), % of GDP	1.9	3.0	0.1	1.8	-3.9

Source: BNB.

Conclusions

The chosen monetary policy instrument of a currency board backed by a policy of low budget deficit and structural reform, ensured Bulgaria's macroeconomic stability, and maintained conditions for relatively high growth. Bulgaria made significant progress with economic growth and development, but important challenges have come to the fore. The global financial and economic crisis affected Bulgaria in mid-2008 mainly in terms of weaker exports and limited external capital inflows. The negative impact of this process was substantial, faded slowly and caused secondary effects on the entire domestic economy. As concerns the academic and business forecasts for the future Bulgarian economic development, a recovery of the domestic economy is expected to begin after 2011. The foreign trade balance contribution is expected to remain positive. In line with the external environment improvement and world trade revival, Bulgarian enterprises' exports are expected to begin rising and to have a major contribution to the industrial recovery. High uncertainty of the global economic environment will continue to push down investment goods demand by enterprises. Consumer demand is anticipated to contract further due to the lower employment and retention of wages at the level attained at the end of 2009.

References

Alesina, A., Barro, R.J. and Tenreyro, S., 2002, Optimal Currency Areas, *NBER Macroeconomics Annual*, 17, pp. 301-345.

Bain, K. and Howels, P., 2003, *Monetary Economics. Policy and Its Theoretical Basis*, Houndmills, Basingstoke, Hampshire, Palgrave Macmillan.

Bennett, A., 1994, Currency Boards: Issues and Experiences, *IMF Working Paper*, 97, Washington D.C., International Monetary Fund.

BNB, 1998, *Annual Report 1997*, Sofia, Bulgarian National Bank.

—, 2009, *Annual Report 2008*, Sofia, Bulgarian National Bank.

Enoch, C. and Gulde, A.M., 1997, Making Currency Board Operational, *IMF Paper on Policy Analyses and Assessment*, 10, Washington D.C., International Monetary Fund.

Frankel, J. and Rose, A., 2000, Do monetary handcuffs restrain Leviathan? Fiscal policy in extreme exchange rate regimes, *Discussion Paper CEPR*, 2692.

Ghosh, A.R. and Ostry, J.D., 2009, Choosing an Exchange Rate Regime. A new look at an old question: Should countries fix, float, or choose something in between, *Finance and Development*, December 2009.

Ghosh, A.R., Gulde, A.M. and Wolf, H., 1998, Currency boards: the ultimate fix?, *IMF Working Paper*, 98/8, January, Washington D.C., International Monetary Fund.

Ghosh, A.R., Gulde, A.M. and Wolf, H., 2002, *Exchange Rate Regimes: Choices and Consequences*, Cambridge, Massachusetts, MIT Press.

Ghosh, A.R., Gulde, A.M., Ostry, J.D. and Wolf, H., 1997, Does the nominal exchange rate regime matter?, *NBER Working Papers*, 5874, Cambridge: Massachusetts: National Bureau of Economic Research.

Gulde, A.M., 1999, The Role of the Currency Board in Bulgaria's Stabilization, *IMF Working Paper*, 3, Washington D.C., International Monetary Fund.

Habermeier, K., Kokenyne, A., Veyrune, R. and Anderson, H., 2009, Revised System for the Classification of Exchange Rate Arrangements, *IMF Working Paper,* 09/211, September, Washington D.C., International Monetary Fund.

IMF, 2010, *Global Financial Stability Report: Meeting New Challenges to Stability and Building a Safer System*, Washington D.C., International Monetary Fund.

Iskrov, I., 2005, The Economic and Monetary Union and the new member states: one year after accession, Speech of BNB Governor Iskrov, 3 - 4 October, Sofia.

Levy-Yeyati, E. and Stuzenegger, F., 2003, To float or to fix: evidence on the impact of exchange rate regimes, *American Economic Review*, 93 4, pp. 1173-1193.

McKinnon, R.I., 1963, Optimum Currency Areas, *American Economic Review*, 53, 4, September, pp. 717-725.

Mishkin, F., 2000, What should central banks do?, Federal Reserve Bank of St. Louis, November/December.

Mundell, R.A., 1961, A Theory of Optimum Currency Areas, *American Economic Review*, LI, 4, November, pp. 509-517.

Mussa, M., Masson, P., Swoboda, A., Jadresic, M.P. and Berg, A., 2000, Exchange rate regimes in an increasingly integrated world economy, *IMF Occasional Paper*, 193, Washington D.C., International Monetary Fund.

Reinhart, C. and Rogoff, K., 2004, The modern history of exchange rate arrangements; a reinterpretation, *Quarterly Journal of Economics*, 19 1, pp. 1-48.

Rogoff, K., Husain, A., Mody, A., Brooks, R. and Oomes, N., 2004, Evolution and performance of exchange rate regimes, *IMF Occasional Paper*, 239, Washington D.C., International Monetary Fund.

Williamson, J., 1995, *What Role for Currency Boards? Policy Analysis in International Economics*, 40, September, Institute for International Economics.

Zaimov, M. and Hristov, K., 2002, Shadowing the Euro: Bulgaria's Monetary Policy Five Years On, *BNB Discussion Papers*, 27/2002, November, Sofia, Bulgarian National Bank.

PROBLEMS OF BULGARIAN FARMS CONCERNING THE PROCESS OF ADJUSTING TO THE CONDITIONS OF THE COMMON AGRICULTURAL POLICY (CAP) OF THE EUROPEAN COMMUNITY

PETER POCHALEEV AND STELA TODOROVA

Abstract

After Bulgaria's accession to the European Community, the farms in the country were forced to work under the conditions of the Common agricultural policy which turned out to be a new ambience for them. The objective of this study is to consider the basic problems Bulgarian agricultural producers encounter in the process of adjusting to the conditions and regulations set by the common agricultural policy of the European Community, as well as giving instructions to their solving. In this relation an investigation was conducted among 40 agricultural producers with different legal and organizational status in 4 communities in the region of Plovdiv. For collecting information, as well as confirming or rejecting the investigation hypotheses, regressive, dispersive, and chi-square analysis was applied. The problems faced by agricultural producers in Bulgaria, turned out to be dependent on the organizational form and size of farms to a great extent.

Introduction

Since Bulgaria's accession to the EU in 2007, the agriculture of Bulgaria has been facing a new environment in which it has to operate. This new environment is the Common agricultural policy of EU. The article examines the major problems encountered by Bulgarian farmers in the process of their adaptation to this environment which is new for them. The article also summarizes the Common agricultural policy and the experience of some member countries in their process of adjustment to it, and the state of Bulgarian agriculture, as well. An analysis of the functioning of farms from Plovdiv region is made. The purpose is to point out their main problems and propose solutions.

The Common Agricultural Policy of the EC as a new environment for the development of Bulgarian agriculture The Experience of EU countries in their adjustment to CAP

The CAP sets only the general philosophy of development, common institutions, and common goals and measures (Ritson, Harvey, 1997). It does not preclude the formulation of national goals, initiatives and actions in the field of agriculture. In the European constitution, agriculture is defined as an area of shared competence between the EU and the member states, which means that both the EU and the member states may adopt laws and approve legally binding acts in the field of agriculture. In addition, member states are given the opportunity to exercise their competence to the extent not contrary to the terms of the EU. A restriction in this case is that all national agricultural programs and measures are required to be in accordance with the Community.

The acceptance of the CAP by the member states is identical with the acceptance of its objectives, principles and tools. Since the CAP replaces most of the tools used by different countries, it is an expression of the refusal of full sovereignty in the formulation and implementation of national agricultural policy (see, van Berkum, De Bont, 2003, p.23). Thus, it forms the requirements and restrictions on development of agriculture in Bulgaria.

The problems of Bulgarian agriculture have their analogue in some European countries in the 1950s and 1960s of the 20th century and in Greece, Spain, and Portugal which joined EU later in the 1980s of the 20th century. In contradistinction to them, in the countries of Central and Eastern Europe (CEE) these are problems which have not yet been overcome. Therefore, Bulgaria could benefit from the successful solutions of other countries by adapting them to the specific national characteristics, and take preventive actions on the basis of the adverse effects being identified in the other countries.

The Agrarian policy pursued in France in the 1960s was marked by a significant state intervention. Measures were taken in the following areas: keeping young producers by supporting the modernization of their farms, management of the land market by the government aiming at accelerating the creation of larger viable farms and expanding agricultural exports. France's negative experience consists in reducing the number of farms and people working in agriculture: during the period 1975 – 1995, the number of farms and people employed in agriculture decreased by half (Verot, 1988, p.11), due to the uneven development of different regions of the country. Unlike France, the approach used in Italy placed the emphasis on the development of institutions. The experience of Italy is defined rather as negative since it did not led to increased efficiency and competitiveness of the agricultural industry but to further problems due to deformations occurring under strong influence of private interests using public resources to their advantage.

The situation in Bulgarian agriculture is largely similar to that in the Netherlands but with a time separation of 30 years. The experience of the Netherlands in this field shows that the only effective means are training and advising farmers so that they can develop and manage their farm adequately. The positive experience of this country is based on the realization that in this case the changes on the micro-level are of much greater importance.

Experts from the World Bank derived the following common features in the field of agriculture in the CEE countries:

- The activity of a significant part of farms is oriented to meet their own needs rather than the needs and the requirements of the market. The production structures in the agrarian sector are relatively stable;
- The opportunity for modernization of agriculture during the period of structural reforms was missed.
- The market of land does not function successfully.
- Low prices of farm products, underdeveloped economic exchanges, difficulties in lending.

Agriculture is essential for the development of the rural areas, rural communities and individual households as a source of principal or additional income (Popov, 2000). In other words, agriculture can be seen as a sector reducing social problems and regional disparities.

There are several general trends in the agricultural sector that are characteristic of the countries of CEE:

- Relatively less agricultural production per hectare of utilized agricultural area and lower yields compared to the old member states of the EU;
- Mixture of products that is less intensive;
- Smaller use in quantitative and qualitative aspects of materials and equipment which are the main limiting factors for increasing yields in crop and livestock production;
- Low investment activity in the sector and low living standard of the people dealing in agriculture.
- The relatively low labour productivity is characteristic for all the countries as a result of the large number of employees in the agricultural sector.

Two paradoxes are to be observed in the CEE countries: (1) regardless of low labour productivity in the semi-commercial farms, these farms are essential for agricultural production and are a source of employment, (2) in the more modern farms having the form of legal persons and sole traders, the reduction of production is to be observed despite the better supply with resources and production factors

The agriculture in Bulgaria

The economic role of agriculture in Bulgaria is still significant (Mishev, Ivanova, 2004), unlike most European countries where the share of agriculture in the created GDP is negligible. Besides this fact, the changes in the CAP impose on European agriculture both social and ecological functions. The role of agriculture in Bulgaria in the creation of GDP is presented in Figure 1.

Figure 1 shows that the share of Bulgarian agriculture in the created GDP decreases continuously, and for 2008 its share was 6%. This is relatively higher than the share of agriculture in the EU as a whole - about 2%, and its share in the U.S. is only 1.5 percent of GDP. This greater contribution of agriculture in developing Bulgaria's GDP, is within the global trend worldwide, that consists in decreasing the share of the agriculture in creating GDP.

Figure 1. The share of the agriculture in the GDP of Bulgaria

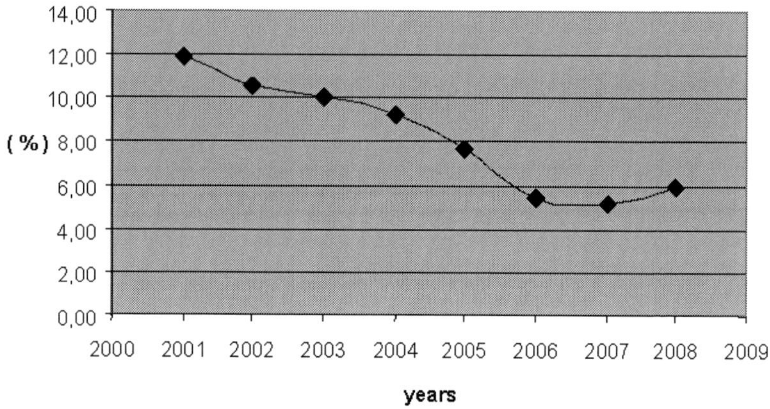

Source: NSI, statistical yearbooks 2001 - 2008

Since Bulgaria's accession to the European Union, the domestic market has become a part of the internal market of the Community, and Bulgarian producers and merchants have faced many challenges related to size and structure of exports of agricultural products.

Bulgaria's membership in the European Union played a very positive role in the growth of trade in agricultural goods to other countries in the Community. In recent years, the member countries of the EU have been the preferred trade partners for the Bulgarian business, and since January 1, 2007 the trade in agricultural goods has increased significantly. In 2007 the share of exports to other member countries of the EU-26 in value was 59.92% of the total agricultural exports, while that of imports was 75.33%.

Characteristic of Bulgarian agriculture in the last 20 years is the ineffective land use, one of the underlying factors of competitive advantage. Abandonment of fertile land and its further passage in the category of unusable land is a hindrance to the development of efficient land market. In addition, the ineffective land use and the abandonment of land lead to the deterioration of one of the most important inputs for this sector and was contrary to the European requirement for direct payments under CAP - the compliance with the so-called good agricultural practices.

During the years of transition to market economy, and even up today the agriculture has been a sector with important social functions.

Employment levels in agriculture in Bulgaria are considerably higher than those in EU countries. For example, during the period 1990 - 2007 the share of people employed in the agricultural sector in Bulgaria was between 18% and 25%, while in Germany this parameter is below 3 percent, and in France - less than 2%. In the Czech Republic, Poland and Hungary the share of the employment in agriculture do not also exceed 10% of all employees. However, the trend in reducing the number of employed in agriculture is to be observed for the period 2003 -2007, but this reduction has very slow rates.

The large number of people employed in agriculture in Bulgaria makes the Bulgarian model of agricultural production significantly different from the European model, the model of developed countries.

Another unfavourable trend of the native agriculture in the last 20 years is the age structure of employees in the sector. In 2007 only 8.08% of the employed in the agriculture are under the age of 35 years, and 33.59% are over 64 years old.

Another problem of Bulgarian agriculture is the relatively low educational level. More than half of the employees have primary and secondary education according to the National Institute of Statistics, and only 3% of farm managers have agricultural education. The CAP and its implementation in Bulgaria requires specific qualifications: knowledge in the fields of information technology, management, environmental practices, etc.

Another characteristic of agriculture in Bulgaria is that the majority of the farms are marked by low mechanization. The low level of mechanization and its absence in some of the farms and the use of mostly old equipment (over 85% of the used equipment is older than 10 years) involves the development of primitive, low-productive and inefficient production, which poses serious constraints to competitiveness.

From the analysis on the status of agriculture in Bulgaria, it is clear that the future development and transformation of the agricultural sector into a competitive one, into a sector that can withstand the competitive pressures of both the European and world markets appears to be an infinitely complex and responsible task.

The structure of the agricultural sector that has been established in respect to the amount of utilized agricultural area (UAA) is abnormal and does not contribute to the development of the agrarian sector in Bulgaria. In 2007, 54.1% of Bulgarian farms in size are smaller than 0,5 ha, and only 0.8% of the farms are over 100 ha in size, i.e. more than half the farms in the country cultivated only 1.5% of the total UAA. This reveals a structure of agriculture in which small farms predominate. The main reason for the existence of such a structure is the method of land restitution in its real boundaries which was adopted. The dimensional structure of farms in Bulgaria is the factor which most greatly restricts the creation of viable farms. The small farms that are prevailing are characterized by low profitability, which cannot attract young people to be involved in agriculture. The permanent establishment of semi-commercial farms is an inhibitory factor for the formation of market-oriented farms.

The above constraints can create the following problems: establishing a lasting trend of low-income and decreasing competitiveness due to low efficiency of the production factors. It is therefore necessary the dimensional structure of the farms should be transformed in the direction of medium and large family farms and cooperatives, as the output produced in small farms can hardly withstand the competitive pressures of both the EU and international markets (Tracy, 1993).

Characteristic of Bulgarian agriculture is the presence of the following legal forms of farms:

1. Sole (individual) forms of organisation
2. Cooperative forms of organisation
3. Corporation (company) forms of organisation
4. Physical persons

Some differences in the objectives and the way of functioning are observed between the farms of natural and legal persons. The first exist mainly to meet their own needs. They participate in the market with products only when their amount exceeds their own needs. They are known as semi-commercial farms. The farms of the legal persons fully sell their production to the market.

Table 1. Structure of agricultural farms by legal status

Legal status	2003				2004				2005			
	farms		UAA		farms		UAA		farms		UAA	
	number	%	daa	%	number	%	daa	%	number	%	daa	%
Physical persons	648274	99.00	8796778.2	30.29	515300	99.00	9147394.6	33.51	476956	98.97	10334681.7	33.88
Sole proprietors	2870	0.44	3408613.8	11.74	2158	0.41	3545969.4	12.99	1828	0.38	4087862.1	13.40
Cooperatives	1973	0.30	11693094.7	40.26	1525	0.29	8908700.4	32.64	1156	0.24	7263054.5	23.81
Companies	1331	0.20	4691970.9	16.15	1312	0.25	5225591.5	19.15	1763	0.37	7818844.7	25.63
Associations and other	360	0.05	454338.9	1.56	234	0.04	466245.4	1.71	217	0.05	1003006.6	3.29
Total	654808	100.0	29044796.5	100.00	520529	100.00	27293901.3	100.00	481920	100.00	30507449.6	100.00

Source: MAF, "Agrostatistics"

Unlike the European agricultural structures, the transformation of which lasted for many years, and their adaptation to the challenges of external environment was conducted continuously, the CEE countries and Bulgaria in particular are faced with the task the process of restructuring to take place in much shorter time. The peculiarity in the case of the new member states is that they cannot literally follow the steps and stages through which the European agriculture passed because of the differences in the types of factors of external environment, their strength and direction of action, as well as because of the specific national features.

The basic methodology of the study

The main methodological approach applied to the analysis and evaluation of the problems of the farms is the system approach. It is a methodology which views the objects of study as systems that are in steady touch with other systems. On their part, the systems are influenced both by their internal structure and the external environment. In conducting the study, the main principles of the system approach were taken into account: purposefulness, integrity, organisation, complexity.

To achieve the objectives of the study and to collect data on individual farms, the method of study based on questionnaires was chosen. Through the study, information was collected on typical farmers, on their production and economic indicators. To implement the survey, a questionnaire was developed comprising 44 open and closed questions.

The open questions were prevailing. They were aimed at revealing the characteristics of the farm, its quantitative indicators and parameters. Another group of open questions required the expression of the owner's opinion and / or intention. The purpose of the inclusion of the closed questions was the differences in assessments of the respondents to be revealed.

Chi-square analysis, analysis of variance, and correlation analysis were chosen for processing the empirical data. These types of analysis have proved to be the most appropriate statistical methods to confirm or deny the research hypotheses and to achieve the objectives of the study. The need for the use of the three statistical methods of research of the relationships was caused by the presence of both quantitative and qualitative variables in search of the correlations.

In applying the methods of verification of statistical hypotheses, we have to specify what is meant by null hypothesis and alternative hypothesis. In this study, they are defined as follows:

1. Null hypothesis Ho: It states that there is no statistically significant relationship between the studied factors
2. Alternative hypothesis H1: There is a statistically significant relationship between the two variables.

Taking into account the difficulties in collecting data at national and regional level and the lack of information in some farms (data on the results of their activity), the research hypotheses subject to verification are the following:

Hypothesis A: The ability of farms to obtain credit funds depends on their organizational form.

The variable – the organizational form is chosen to demonstrate that the relatively smaller farms such as having the organizational status of farmers have less opportunity to benefit from external resources of funding.

Hypothesis B: The degree of adjustment of farms and their production to the requirements imposed by EU depends on their organizational form

To confirm or reject this hypothesis, the question arises whether there is a substantial difference in the degree of fulfillment of the requirements in different forms of organisations.

The variable - organizational form is chosen to demonstrate that relatively smaller farms such as these having the organizational status of farmers have less opportunity to meet these requirements.

Hypothesis C: The choice of a measure under The Rural Region Development Program 2007 - 2013 that the farms want to apply to, depends on one hand on the degree of their awareness and availability of funds and on the other of their organizational form.

Hypothesis D: The direction of change in income received by the farms after the accession of Bulgaria to the EU largely depends on their production specialization.

One of the main methodological issues of this paper is the determination of the scope of the research. In this context, the object of study, are the farms in the district of Plovdiv. The choice of the region subject to this research is based besides the subjective reasons on a sufficient number of objective reasons which make this decision not only applicable but also-expedient. Plovdiv is located in the central part of South Bulgaria and covers a western part of the Upper Thracian Valley, Karlovo valley, and the north slopes of the Rhodopes. The following agricultural sectors are highly developed in this region: vegetable growing, grain production, fruit growing, vine growing, growing of oil-bearing crops, production of paddy rice, and livestock breeding.

In the selection of municipalities for study, the purpose was to capture the diversity in the Plovdiv region in terms of:

- structure of the economy in the municipalities
- level of municipal development
- level of infrastructure development,
- natural climatic diversity
- economic activity of the population.

The four selected municipalities in Plovdiv District are: the Municipality of Saedinenie, the Municipality of Maritsa, the Municipality of Stamboliyski, and the Municipality of Rodopi.

The sample selected under the study is nested, with formation of four constituent units representing all farms in the four municipalities in the first level of selection. On the second level, each of the four nests is divided into four sets, which represent four organizational structures in each municipality - registered farmers, sole traders, companies, and agricultural cooperatives. The farms subject to the survey were selected among these 16 constituent units by simple random selection.

Analysis of the functioning of farms from Plovdiv region in the conditions of the CAP

Opportunities for obtaining loans in dependence of the organizational form of the farm

Characteristic of Bulgarian agriculture during the transition period is the relatively low rate of loans granted. The main reason is the specificity of this sector, resulting in banks' overstating the credit risk due to their inability to assess the effectiveness of investment. Table 2 presents the results of the survey about the level of the taken loans conducted among farms in the Plovdiv region.

Table 2. Loans used by the farms in dependence of their form

Loans utilized/ form of organization	Sole trader	Registered farmer	Cooperatives	Companies	Loans utilized %
They have used loans	1	2	3	6	34.28
They have not used loans	3	17	1	2	65.72

Table shows that only 34.28% of the surveyed farms have used loans. The highest such percentage is with companies – 75%, and the lowest is with registered farmers - 10.5%. In this context, the aim of the study was to determine whether there is a statistically significant relationship between the organizational form of the farms and the possibility of obtaining loans, and to point out the main problems about taking loans.

For the purposes of the analysis the following hypotheses were composed:

H0: There is no significant relationship between the organizational form of the farm and the availability of loans.

H1: There is an essential correlation between the organizational form of the farm and the availability of loans.

The statistical values that show the power of the relationship between the organizational form of farms and the availability of loans were calculated by using the statistical program SPSS and the chi-square analysis. The estimated empirical characteristic is 13.742. For determining the theoretical value, the admissible error used in economic research was selected as to $\alpha = 0.05$, and the number of the degrees of freedom - as to v = (r-1). (C-1) = 3. The null hypothesis should not be confirmed on the hand of these values because t theor.. <t emp., 7.82 <13 742. But as one of the conditions of the chi-squared analysis was not satisfied (in some cells the expected values are less than 5), we should be skeptical of the result obtained. The coefficient of Chuprov was calculated in order to confirm or reject the result obtained. The relationship between organizational form and the used loans is determined as average, because the coefficient value is 0.36. As a result, the alternative hypothesis is accepted to be true. This average relationship is due to the different opportunities the organisational forms have regarding taking loans. Some of them because of their small size have financial limits and are unable to provide collateral security or cannot meet the necessary requirements.

The problems that farmers have had regarding taking loans indicate that a major drawback for farmers is the big bureaucracy and the difficulties in the process of taking loans, followed by their inability to provide collateral security. Another drawback is the insufficient information on lending and the high interest rates. Finally corruption is another problem. This proves that the procedure and the great documentary report, which is part of it, hamper farmers, and extend the time for preparation and allocation of funds requested. The specificity of the industry creates a seasonal cyclic in both the revenue received and the need for loans in certain moments. This hinders the owners of agricultural enterprises in payment of loans in equal monthly installments. Another serious problem is the inability to provide the necessary collateral for loans. Farmers have difficulty in securing them, as banks require collateral as prime real estate in cities, and other deposits, whereas the land and equipment are not accepted as such.

Degree of adjustment of farms and their production to the requirements imposed by EU

With the accession of Bulgaria to European Union the farms in the country are facing a number of requirements imposed by the Common Agricultural Policy. At present, most of these farms have difficulties in meeting these requirements. The goal is to outline the main factors that determine the adjustment to these requirements and the problems faced by the farmers in their implementation. In this context, the attention will be directed towards two factors: the organizational form of the farm and the level of farmers' awareness of the requirements imposed on their farms.

a. the relationship: organizational form - degree of compliance with the requirements

The data from the survey conducted for estimating the degree of adjustment of the farms in dependence of their organisational form are presented in Table 3.

Table 3. Degree of compliance with the requirements in dependence of organisational form

Degree of compliance with the requirements/ organizational form	Sole trader	Registered farmer	Coopera-tives	Compa-nies	Degree of adjustment of the farms to the requirements in %
Comply with any requirement	2	1	1	2	17.14
Comply with a great number of the requirements	0	7	3	5	42.86
Comply with a small number of the requirements	1	7	0	1	25.71
Do not comply	1	4	0	0	14.29

Table 3 shows that 42.86% of the surveyed farms meet a great number of the requirements imposed on them by EU, and only 14.29% of the farms have not fulfilled them. For the purposes of the analysis the following hypotheses were composed:

H0: There is no significant relationship between the organizational form of the farm and the degree of its adjustment to the requirements imposed by the CAP.

H1: There is a significant relationship between the organizational form of the farm and the degree of its adjustment to the requirements imposed by the CAP.

Again, using the chi-squared analysis, statistical values are calculated to show the power of the relationship between the organizational form of the farms and the degree of their adaptation to the requirements of CAP. The estimated empirical characteristic is 13.207. For determining the theoretical value, the admissible error used in economic research was selected as to $\alpha = 0{,}05$, and the number of the degrees of freedom - as to v = (r-1). (C-1) = 9. The null hypothesis should not be confirmed on the hand of these values because t theor.. >t emp., 16.92> 13 207. But as one of the conditions of the chi-squared analysis was not satisfied (in some cells the expected values are less than 5), we should be skeptical of the result obtained. The coefficient of Chuprov was calculated again in order to confirm or reject the result obtained. The relationship between the organisational form and the degree of compliance with the requirements is determined as weak, because the coefficient value is 0.20. As a result, the null hypothesis is accepted to be true, i.e. the organisational form of farms does not affect the degree of compliance with the requirements of the EU in the field of agriculture.

b. relationship between the levels of awareness - the extent of fulfillment of the requirements

Another factor which influences the degree of fulfillment of the requirements is the level of awareness of farmers. It turns out that the farms that are familiar with the requirements of the CAP have responded to these requirements to a much greater extent than the farms that are lacking this information.

To determine the strength of the relationship between the level of awareness and the degree of fulfillment of the requirements of the CAP the following hypotheses were composed:

H0: There is no significant relationship between the level of awareness and the degree of fulfillment of the requirements.

H1: There is a significant relationship between the level of awareness and the degree of fulfillment of the requirements.

The results of the survey concerning the level of awareness of the farmers and the degree of fulfillment of the requirements are listed in Table 4.

Table 4. Level of fulfillment of EU requirements in dependence of the awareness of farms

Level of fulfillment of EU requirements/ Awareness of farms	I am aware of all requirements	I am aware of a part of the requirements	I am not aware
Fulfillment all the requirements	6	0	0
Fulfillment of a great number of the requirement	7	7	1
Fulfillment of a small number of the requirements	0	7	2
No fulfillment of any requirements	0	1	4

In this case, using the chi-squared analysis, the alternative hypothesis was assumed to be true. It states that there is a significant relationship between the level of awareness and the level of fulfillment of the requirements (t theory. <t emp., 12.59 <29.29).

One of the main problems faced by farmers in the fulfillment of these requirements is the lack of sufficient funds. 45.71% of the farms surveyed indicated that because of lack of funds they cannot adjust their farms to the requirements imposed by the EU, since the preservation of the farms is much more important to them now. Another significant obstacle which hinders them in fulfilling the requirements is the bureaucracy. According to 14.28% of the farms, because of the high level of bureaucracy they failed to adjust their farms to European norms.

The choice of a measure under The Rural Region Development Program 2007 - 2013

Characteristic of Bulgarian agriculture is the relatively weak activity of farms in applying for support under a measure of the The Rural Region Development Program. One of the main reasons for this low activity is the poor awareness of the owners of these farms, with the result that they are not aware of the opportunities presented by these program. Another major problem that farmers encounter is the complex procedure of the application for support under the regulations of these measures. Taking into consideration the relatively low level of education of the people employed in agriculture in the country, it should be pointed out that the application for support under the terms of one of the measures of the program and its approval become almost impossible without the help of a specialist.

The results of the survey show that 63% of the farms have not applied up to now under some of the measures of The Rural Region Development Program. This percentage is even higher for registered farmers: 79% of the respondents have not applied for support. This percentage is the lowest for the sole traders - only 36.7 percent of them have not applied. In this case it is alarming that about 66% of the farms that have not applied up to now do not intend to do so in the future, pointing out the already mentioned problems they encounter as reasons for their intention.

It is interesting that the choice of a measure of The Rural Region Development Program largely depends on the organisational form of the farm. For example, farms that operate as registered farmers apply primarily in terms of the measures "Creating Young Farmers" and "Support for semi-subsistence farms undergoing restructuring“. Farms operating in the form of agricultural cooperatives or companies mainly apply in the terms of the measures "Modernisation of farms" and "Adding value to agricultural and forestry products". The observation shows that the farms apply primarily to purchase equipment. This was expected, since the machinery used by the farms in the country is quite old.

Changes in farm income after the accession of Bulgaria to the EU

Bulgaria's accession to the EU has affected differently the incomes of the farms. The results of the survey show a negative trend in farm incomes. 48.57% of the farm owners say that their income has been reduced significantly since 2007. The main reason for this trend is the high competition in the common EU market, for which Bulgarian farms are not prepared. About 31.43% of farm incomes have remained unchanged, and only 20 percent of the incomes have increased.

We want to find out the relationship between the specialization of the farm and the direction of the change in its income after the accession of Bulgaria to the EU. Thus, if there is a relationship between farm specialization and farm incomes, it will be possible to identify the sectors in which the farms can be competitive on the European market. In this context, the following hypotheses were composed:

H0: There is no significant relationship between the specialization of farm production and the changes in farm income.

H1: There is a significant relationship between the specialization of farm production and the changes in farm income.

The results of the distribution of respondents' answers are listed in Table 5.

Table 5. Change in farm income in dependence of production specialization

Income changes/ Production specialization	Grain production	Vegetable growing	Vine and fruit growing
Incomes decrease	4	10	3
Incomes do not change	3	6	2
Incomes increase	6	1	0

The following trend is to be seen based on Table 5: after Bulgaria's accession to EU the income of farms dealing in grain production increased and those involved in vegetable growing, vine and fruit growing has decreased.

Using the chi-squared analysis, statistical values are calculated to show the power of the relationship between the specialization of farm production and the changes in farm income. The estimated empirical characteristic is 9.86. For determining the theoretical value, the admissible error used in economic research was selected as to α = 0,05, and the number of the degrees of freedom - as to v = (r-1). (C-1) = 4. The alternative hypothesis should be confirmed on the hand of these values because t theor. < t emp., 9.49 < 9.86. But as one of the conditions of the chi-squared analysis was not satisfied (in some cells the expected values are less than 5), we should be skeptical of the result obtained. We assume there is a relationship between the specialization of farm production and the changes in the income of the farm. Thus, the farms should aim their efforts at the production specializations that affect their incomes positively.

Conclusion

The analysis shows that Bulgarian agriculture is facing a very difficult task - its adaptation to a new environment called the Common Agricultural Policy of EU. The survey results show that the farms encounter a lot of problems connected with their normal functioning in the conditions of the CAP. Some of the main problems relate to the lack of sufficient resources for the modernization of the farms; difficulties in obtaining loans, high competition in the European market, difficulties and sometimes inability to acquire funding from EU programs. In this regard, urgent measures are to be taken, in order these and many other problems to be resolved, and the process of adapting to the new environment to be accelerated, and Bulgarian agriculture to become agriculture at a European level.

References

Berkum S., De Bont, K., 2003, Policies for agriculture in Poland and the Netherlands, *Contributions to a policy dialogue*, Agricultural Economics Research Institute (LEI), pp. 23.

Marinov, B., Savov, M., Marinov, M., Slavova, M., Hadjinikolov, D., Krustev, S., 2004, European economic integration, *Publishing House "Farm"*, Sofia, Bulgaria.

Mishev, P., Ivanova, N., 2004, The impact of CAP on production of agricultural products in Bulgaria after EU accession, *Yearbook of the University of National and World Economy*, pp. 221-258.

Popov, R., 2000, Adaptation of the regulation of incomes in Bulgarian agriculture to the Common Agricultural Policy of the European Union, *Economic Thought*, pp. 49-59.

Ritson, C., Harvey, D., 1997, The Common Agricultural Policy, CAB, International, Wallingford, USA.

Tracy, M., 1993, Food and Agriculture in a Market Economy: An Introduction to Theory, Practice and Policy, APS, pp. 286.

Verot, D., 1998, Agriculture Biologique, Evaliation D'un Gisement D'emplois, p. 11.

PART TWO:

REGIONAL DEVELOPMENT

PROBLEMS ON THE IMPLEMENTATION OF REGIONAL DEVELOPMENT STRATEGIES IN ALBANIA

ALKETA BEJKO, KRISTAQ ÇOMBI AND DANIELA QIQI

Abstract

Regional Development Strategies provide economic and social analysis of a region according to the objectives, identify the regional challenges, goals and provide a full and comprehensive strategy for development. At the time when our country is looking further to integrate its economy and markets within the global context and in particular to join the EU market, it is necessary that all regions of the country should be able to compete in this market. In this paper, there is an analysis of the concrete problems that local authorities in Albania have encountered in implementing their regional development strategies, documents that contribute to a sustainable socio-economic development of each region. The paper is divided into 3 parts. In the first part, a general overview about the development strategies in Albania is given. In the second part an overview about regional development strategies in Albania is presented and in the third part some important problems that have hampered the implementation of the regional development strategies are identified. Finally, some conclusions and recommendations that will hopefully contribute to improve this situation are given.

Introduction

All the districts in Albania have devised their strategies for regional development since 2005. These strategies aimed at achieving a sustainable economic and social development in the respective regions (Kume, 2005). The aim of this study is to identify the specific problems faced by the local authorities in Albania in their efforts to implement these regional development strategies. A large amount of detailed information based on development strategies on a national, regional and sectoral level, was collected and analysed in order to carry out this research work. The paper reflects the current Albanian legislature as well as the direct consultation with local council and district members, who are directly responsible for the developmental process. Despite the careful study of all the elements concerned, this paper has the following limitation: The lack of statistical data on a regional level, which does not allow us to give a full overall picture of the impact of these strategies on the regional development leading to social and economic improvements in the respective regions. Despite the limitations of the survey, it did suggest some general trends and must be taken into careful consideration by regional and national policy makers when formulating and following their developmental strategies. In this way, they will stop being hollow documents, but they will be workable and effective strategies that will contribute to the improvement of the quality of life of the Albanian population in all the Albanian regions.

A general overview about the regional development strategies in Albania

During the last two decades of democracy, Albania has experienced major political and social changes, as well as an ambitious economic growth. It is transformed from a centralized into a free initiative economy, where 80% of the gross domestic product is provided by the private sector and where the per capita income is 20 times higher than 1992 (National Strategy for Development and Integration 2007–2013). In spite of this economic growth, the problems of the steady development are evident. Serious problems are present in the inequality that exists between the different regions of the country, in some of which the level of poverty is rather high. For instance, poverty in the rural areas is 66% higher than in Tirana and 50% higher than in other main urban centers. Tirana possesses a GDP index of 0.772 versus the GDP index of 0.252 for a number of mountainous areas and the index for the human development is 0.830 versus 0.632 for the mountainous areas. The level of unemployment in Kukës is three times higher than in Tirana, the level of poverty in Kukës is double higher than in Vlora, the population in Vlora has a double access to the water supply than the population in Dibra, the citizens of Tirana have an access of 2,5 more than the population of Kukësi concerning the medical visits (Intersectional strategy for the regional development - final draft) etc.

During this period of transition, the term strategy has been the focus of debates on the economic and social development of Albanian and is also present in the government programs and policies or either included in the recommendations made by the foreign donators. There have been made continuous attempts to draw the strategies of economic development, but these initiatives have been coupled with the dilemma: Which is the best strategy of the economic and social development versus the challenges of integration and effects of globalization? (Civici, 2005).

In this framework, the first years of transition demonstrated continuous attempts to compose sectional strategies that resulted as ineffective due to the lack of experience among the individuals who participated in its compilation. The first strategic national document drawn was: the National Strategy for the Economic and Social Development (NSESD), which is being applied since November 2001. In order to support the application of this strategy, there were drawn policies of national development such as a package of objectives, priorities and measures oriented towards attainment of a sustainable social and economic development in the Republic of Albania. Under the new development circumstances that the country was experiencing, like the request to become a NATO member or the Agreement of Stabilization and Association with the European Union; this development strategy was not coherent and did not fulfill the new requirements to achieve a socio-economic development.

Due to the political changes occurring in 2005, and the necessity to harmonize in a single document the agenda of social and economic stable development and the agenda of integration in NATO structures, the European Union, the National Strategy for the economic and social development, as the main document of the government until 2006, was replaced by the National Strategy for Development and Integration, (NSDI) from 2007 to 2013. Besides the considerable improvements concerning the transparency of the compilation process, this strategy fulfilled the aspirations of Albania for the NATO membership and EU integration. At the same time the compilation process of National Strategy for Development and Integration is closely related to the problems of short-term budgeting. During the process of drawing this budget, the Sectional Strategies of Development will serve as the reference documents. It is useful to provide these strategies with the appropriate budget sustainability so as they can be successfully realized.

Meanwhile, Albania intends to fully integrate its economy and markets within the global context, particularly in the EU market. Thus, it is necessary that all the areas of Albania should be able to compete in this market. After the '90s Albania has been confronted with serious problems of regional inequality (Civici, 2008). The social and economic performance between the different areas of our country has engendered the necessity to have an integrated and coherent regional policy.

In line with this, the regional development occupies an important part in the National Strategy for Development and Integration. The regional development aims at achieving a sustainable economic and social development of these regions through identification, stimulation and management of the potentials in certain regions. Also this target is achieved by the Intersectional Strategy for the regional development compiled by the Ministry of Economy, Trade and Energetic. This strategy intends to coordinate the socio-economic development of all regions of the country on the whole and particularly mountainous and peripheral zones, in order to achieve a more balanced development, reduce the present social economic inequalities between the regions and accelerate the integration process of Albania in the European Union.

Within the frame of a steady development, it is of primary importance not only to compile effective national strategies, but to effectively implement these strategies. Although Albania possesses a national development strategy, its progress is related to the success of its dissolving into regional development strategies.

Regional development strategies in Albania

Albania has serious problems of regional inequality. The Albanian government has identified the need for a more integrated and coherent regional policy, based on the concern about the deepening gap existing in the social-economic performance between different parts of the country. This is clearly demonstrated by the following Table.

Table 1. Regional inequality in Albania

Nr	District	Population according to INSTAT	The level of poverty/ national average %	The level of unemployment / national average %	Local income/ national average %	Access to water supply/ national average %	Number of medical visits/ national average%	The compulsory education/ national average %
1.	Berati	181.901	96	99	74.6	114	107	368
2	Dibra	166.367	59	85	61.4	54	70	55
3.	Durrësi	280.996	102	117	106	131	68	53
4.	Elbasani	380.593	80	110	70	83	62	147
5.	Fieri	380.737	85	133	77	91	83	76
6.	Gjirokastra	80.646	131	118	112	97	132	385
7.	Korca	263.586	94	126	78	97	127	202
8.	Kukësi	102.036	63	42	74	91	56	54
9.	Lezha	159.882	69	61	78	58	89	162
10.	Shkodra	250.351	77	52	67	74	120	75
11.	Tirana	677.871	108	168	160	123	140	
12.	Vlora	202.295	139	89	139	132	92	506
	Total	3.127.261						

Source: Intersectional strategy for the regional development (final draft)

Apart from the compilation of nationwide strategies, regional development strategies play a significant role in the development of the country (Kume, 2005). These strategies are important documents that provide analysis about the economic and social indexes of a region; they identify the regional challenges, set the objectives and goals, while they make comprehensive and radical suggestions for the development. The compilation of these strategies should theoretically take into consideration an entirety of factors, which are related to the economic, cultural and demographic specifics. This is achieved through a better combination of the equilibrium between the economic and social development, with the environment protection, as well as the protection from the effects and inevitable pressures of globalization.

The strategies of regional development are drawn by the district councils, which are the local government authorities of the second level

(Local government in Albania is organized in two levels. The first level comprises municipalities and communes and the second level the councils of districts). The district council holds the legal responsibilities for the compilation and implementation of the regional policies that should conform with the state policies (Law Nr.8652, dt 31.7.2000 "About the organization and functioning of the local government"). In this framework, since 2005, with the assistance of PNUD, World Bank, SIDA, and SNV, the regional development strategies are compiled and approved in all districts of the country. These development strategies were conceived as a combination of regional interests on the one hand and on the other, as political engagements on a national and international scale. To give a better explanation, we should say that the Objectives of the Development of the Millennium (Objectives of the development of the Millennium are measurable objectives, endorsed by Albania and other countries in the Declaration of the Millennium, and these objectives should be achieved by 2015) are at the basis of these strategies and all other local oriented policies should intend to reach these objectives. The main set objectives that these strategies aim at are: setting up a steady development framework and improvement in the communities' lifestyle, such as diminishing the poverty, education and health service improvement, stimulating the development of small and medium business, stable environment and also a better governing.

In the last years, the regional developments are seen within the scope of a new dimension. The regional development is declared as one of the government priorities and holds a very important part in NSDI (National Strategy for Development and Integration). Concerning the regional progress, there were two objectives included in this strategy:

- Districts should be given the possibility to make their own contribution in their sustainable development. This is thought to be achieved through strengthening the districts capacities in order to be able to manage their development potentials. Relevant to this achievement, new elements are involved in NSDI as:
    - National Program for the development of districts, which intends to facilitate the establishment of a unique management and planning system and is expected to bring forth new changes and development in the regional policy. In order to produce the desired function, it should be set up:

    - A unique frame of policies for the district social and economic development, taking into consideration their specific needs for the development;
    - A partnership between the interested sides on a national, regional and local level;
    - The Agency for the district development will function as a local agency that coordinates the actions towards implementation of district development strategies.
    - The agreement for the district development, a financial and strategic operational plan, which defines the central government support in relation to the development of the priorities for each district.
    - An effective system of monitoring, evaluating and reporting.
  - The program of development in unfavorable zones, which intends to reduce the inequality existing between these areas and the average in Albania, through encouraging cooperation between the national, regional and local actors to intensify the possibilities for the development of these areas. In line with this, the government plans to develop these zones and allocate a special budget line to operate with particular backing schemes for the districts and municipalities, as well. In this context, a special importance should be given to define the unfavorable zones for at least a 5- year time period.

- Establishment of an efficient management framework for the regional development, creation of a unified legal frame and also an efficient and coordinated institutional infrastructure for the regional policy.

In order to fulfill these objectives, new elements have been included in NSD as:

- Establishment of consulting structures.
- The council of national partnership will monitor the efficiency and implementation of regional development policies, as well as towards reaching a consensus;
- Councils of districts consortium that will plan the strategy of district development. They will also monitor the efficiency, the application of this strategy and the procedures towards consensus.
- The setting up of implementation structures on a national and regional level.

Although, there have been serious attempts and good strategies operating on a national and regional level, their implementation leaves much to be desired. The implementation of regional development strategies is closely related to collaboration, transparency, financial support by the local government and main institutions of the state administration.

Implementation problems of regional development strategies

Regional development strategies are important instruments that should assist the local authorities to manage optimally their potentials with the intention of achieving the improvement of the welfare quality for its citizens. Until the end of 2005, all the districts in Albania had drawn their development strategies, while the fact that these development strategies have had a little impact on the economic and social life of these regions seems to be astonishing. Some of the most specific problems which have been identified on the way to implementation of the regional strategies are:

- By the time the strategies of regional development were compiled (2004 – 2005), they were coordinated and linked with the National Strategy for Economic and Social Development, whereas the endorsement of the National Strategy for Development and Integration should of course be associated with the appropriate adaptations in the regional development strategies. Although there have passed almost three years from the endorsement, none of the districts in Albania has attempted to reach any suitability relevant to this process. It may be stated that these development strategies have been transformed into formal documents, which do not make any contribution for a stable development in the regions and the country in general.

- Based on the study we have carried out, about 76% of the municipalities and communes of Albania have not dissolved the regional development strategies into local strategies in order to stimulate the development of cities and rural areas on the basis of their competitive advantages. It is worth emphasizing that the local governing bodies included here, are those facing considerable and noticeable economic and social development problems. Even the municipalities and communes that have compiled strategies of local development have not associated them with working and financial plans in order to implement the strategies. Hence, within this frame, the structure of planning document on a national level, their compulsory content, the methodology of compilation and other issues related to them should be unified.

- The local authority bodies like District councils, municipalities and communes in order to reach the necessary investment for the strategies implementation might find recourse to the following financing sources:
  - The income deriving from the local taxes. A part of these incomes goes to the financing of institution expenditure; the rest is used for investments. Denationalization of the local government can't be an effective process in case it does not secure high rates of regional development. Due to the fiscal denationalization, the local authority bodies gain more profits from the local taxes every year. We think that this additional income should be used in a way that priority is given to public investments.
  - Unconditioned grants given by the government. These grants should be used to meet the local needs. In most of the cases they are used to cover the expenses. We think that the local authority bodies should improve the expense structure aiming at growing the capital expense capacity within the expense total in general.
  - Competitive grants given by the government to reduce the problems related to the implementation of regional development strategies and combine the national budget policies with the local budget policies. Consequently, in the 2010 budget the government has planned a special fund called the Fund of Regional development (Ligji Nr. 1010 datë 26.11.2009 "Për buxhetin e vitit 2010"). This fund comprises the competitive grants for the local infrastructure, water supply and drainage systems, educational, health service, cultural and sport buildings, irrigational and draining systems, setting up the grocery markets etc. To gain these grants the local authorities enter a competition through different projects they present to the line ministry and those considered the most appropriate are to be financed by this grant. Through perfection and completion, in the long run, it is thought to meet in an integrated way, the demands of the local governing bodies with the public investment for the above mentioned sections. Allocation of this fund avoids the fragmentation of the state budget, rises the degree of cooperation between the local and central government and stimulates the domestic and foreign factors to invest in the regions they are interested in. Thus, the role of district councils seems to be very important, because they are to propose the funds

distribution for the investments in their region based on the development strategies for these regions. This fund is gained by the local authority bodies not only as an economic possibility for the regional development stimulation, but it is also a process which helps them to preliminary exercise themselves in absorbing funds not only from the State Budget, but also from the financial institutions of the European Union.

- Apart from the regional development, all the districts in Albania have also compiled the document: "A monitoring system for the regional strategy of development", which defines the most significant indexes which should be monitored in order to achieve the objectives of the strategy successfully. Theoretically, this document should facilitate the work of the District councils with the evaluation about the progress of the achieved objectives for all years. Obviously, there are not concrete initiatives from the districts in Albania to compile a progress rating for each year, so as to identify the degree of the achieved objectives from the strategy. This occurs mainly due to the fact that these district councils are well aware that the objectives they have set are somewhat beyond their possibilities. The principals of these districts refer that there exist low levels of collaboration between the institutions that grant the public investments funds. They are not satisfied with the way the local authorities and the ministries operate with the distribution of public investments with the regions. The state administration institutions, municipalities and communes have direct relations with the relevant ministries that provide the funds for public investments and consequently submit their requests for investments without taking into consideration whether this investment is part of the regional development strategy. Thus, although there is a strategy for regional development, this document is never used as a reference document during the process of distribution of these funds meant for public investments. This is a consequence of the legal framework which should regulate the relationships between the state administration bodies with the local government bodies and apparently has been deficient.

- Based on these emerging problems, it is seen as a necessity that the compilation and implementation process should be supported by a legal platform. This will be useful in order to prevent the distortions and preferential policies about the issues concerning the social and economic development of these regions. To resolve this matter and to be provided with the district council's support about the implementation of development strategies, it is compiled a legal draft on the regional development in the Republic of Albania. This draft defines the objectives, principles, instruments and the institutional framework about the management of the regional development and the impetus of an equilibrated regional development in the Republic of Albania (Project-low for regional development in Republic of Albania). We think that under these circumstances, it is an urgent need to pass this law and the articles which support its application.

- Partnership and cooperation between the public sector, private sector, NGO and the society is of particular importance and should have a closer relationship. It is essential that the private business should be given the necessary institutional and legal space, which is considered as the engine of the economic development. In this aspect, applying the concessionary agreements: designing- financing- construction-implementation – is a significant means through which the direct investment of private sectors are encouraged concerning certain regions' development and their urgent needs for investment, but possesses limited sources to exploit.

The regional development is indisputably the most efficient means towards stimulation of economic development, vitalization of the periphery and reduction of poverty. The above mentioned problems were identified in order to provide grounds about the fact that besides the importance of compiling the regional development strategies, their implementation seems to gain more importance. Therefore, the whole work of all decision taking authorities on a municipality, commune, district and central governing level should be focused on this framework. It is unacceptable if the following saying found in the majority of books on development strategies would be coherent: "the bad thing about each development strategy is the limited government mandate". The continuous political antagonism, denying attitude towards the reciprocal economic achievement is a bad consequence for the country and its social and economic development.

Conclusions

- The social and economic development on the whole and the reduction of the differentiations in the regional development are important problems which should be the main focus in the political and social debate. The development strategies on a national, regional and local level should be considered as the main instrument for the stable economic and social development. They should be long-term strategies almost extended to 15-20 years and should enjoy a broad political consensus. The cooperation between the central and local government, donators, NGO and the civil society raises the efficiency of each strategy.

- The legal frame is crucial in relation to the implementation efficiency of the regional strategies. Consequently, the law approval about the regional development in the Republic of Albania is a necessity.
- A better management of the region capacities increases the strategy effectiveness, especially during the implementation process serving to the stable development of the regions.
- The utilization of the Regional Development Fund, which is initially included in the 2010 budget, appears to be of a great importance to the regional development. Thus, it is helpful that all structures involved in the law like the National Council of partnership, the District council of Partnership etc. should be functional. The improvement of these structures operation will bring forth improvement in the process of counseling, consulting, compilation, implementation and monitoring of the regional development strategies.

References

Civici, A., 2005, Modelet bashkëkohore të zhvillimit ekonomik e social, Konferenca V e Bankës së Shqipërisë, Durrës 24-25 Mars, faqe 68. (Contemporary models of the social and economic development, 5th Conference of the Bank of Albania, Durres 24-25, March 2005, p. 68)

—. 2008, Roli dhe kontributi i ekonomistëve në shoqëritë moderne, ECONOMICUS 1, faqe 12, (Role and contribution of the economists in the modern society, ECONOMICUS 1, 2008, p.12).

Kume, V., 2005, Planifikimi Strategjik në organizatat publike dhe jofitimprurëse, faqe 241, 245 (Strategic Planning in public and nonprofit organizations, pp. 241, 245).

Ligji Nr. 1010 datë 26.11.2009 "Për buxhetin e vitit 2010". (Low Nr. 1010 dt. 26.11.2009 "For bugdet 2010")

Ligji Nr. 8652, datë 31.7.2000 "Për organizimin dhe funksionimin e qeverisjes vendore", neni 13. (Low Nr. 8652 dt. 31.07.2000 "For organization and functioning of the local government, Article 13).

Projekt – Ligj për Zhvillimin Rajonal në Republikën e Shqipërisë, Ministria e Ekonomisë Tregëtisë dhe Energjetikës, (Project-low for regional development in Republic of Albania, Ministry of Economy, Trade and Energetic)

Strategjia Kombëtare për Zhvillim dhe Integrim 2007 – 2013, Këshilli i Ministrave, Republika e Shqipërisë, faqe 9. (National Strategy for Development and Integration 2007–2013, Council of Ministers, Republic of Albania, p. 9)

Strategjia Ndërsektoriale për Zhvillimin Rajonal-drafti final, Shtator 2007, Ministria e Ekonomisë Tregëtisë dhe Energjetikës, faqe 7. (Intersectional strategy for the regional development-final draft , September 2007, Ministry of Economy, Trade and Energetic, p.7).

EVOLUTION OF REGIONAL DISPARITIES IN NUTS III LEVEL IN GREECE

ANESTIS D. MANTATZIS

Abstract

The paper attempts to investigate the long-term development progress of Greek region in NUTS III level for the last 16-year period as it is demonstrated by annual Gross Domestic Product and Per Capita GDP. The focus of our analysis is on the evolutionary performance in the dispersion in the development level of Greek NUTS III geographical units. In other words, we audit the assumption of the reduction in the overall deviation of the NUTS III development level according to the mean, following the σ-convergence method, as well as the assumption of economic and geographic dualism in the Greek region. Despite the fact that data reveal the existence of important peripheral inequalities, both the level and the progress of such inequalities vary according to the statistic and economic index used. However, this study confirms that regional disparities in Greece constitute a permanent status during the last decades. The following inferences are reported in combination with a brief review of the Greek literature related to the issue as well as a substantial inspection of the primary causal factors that form the regional problem in Greece.

Introduction

The matter of regional disparities has become a focal issue of controversy in both theoretical and policy decision making level. In the past 30 years there have been many research efforts to identify the causal factors which lead to different development levels among regions as well as the consequences that may result from such an unbalanced distribution of development level.

Towards this direction, in the next section, a critical approach of the existing situation in Greece is attempted, through the deliberate examination of those special features that characterize Greek region. In addition, a short review of the bibliography relevant to the issue is presented.

This work also contains a study that aims at the interpretation of the official regional accounts and hopefully at the discovery of useful conclusions concerning regional development.

Critical Assessment of the Issue and Previous Approaches

Speaking generally about inequalities, there is reference to the difference in the development level among a sum of territorial units. Considering a NUTS III region as a single territorial unit, the term regional disparities refers to the modification that the distribution of an economic variable is able to subject in these NUTS III regions.

Most studies that are focused on the long-term evolution of regional inequalities in Greece have used data ranging from 1970 to 1994. Because of the fact that since 1995 the estimation method of GDP has been changed, many methodological problems emerge whereas commonly research outcome results were contradictory. The above problems were not possible to be tackled - even with the introduction of contemporary and sophisticated analytical and statistical tools - due to the fundamental weaknesses of any estimation methods based on the GDP indicator.

It has now become obvious that GDP and per capita GDP are not capable to provide sufficient clues of the real differentiation of development level and welfare among the regions of our country, without considering additional factors. In addition, the introduction of further macroeconomic indicators, such as labour productivity, employment rate, population, as well as information about the structure of production activities, tend to provide a more reliable perspective of Greek regional development. However, for simplification reasons, the present study is limited upon GDP and per capita GDP data acknowledging any disadvantages or advantages of such method.

Considering the above, GDP data are subject to many warps concerning the estimation of the actual development progress of NUTS III regions. In particular, the most developed NUTS III regions, Attiki and Thessaloniki, are quite low in the classification based on per capita GDP data whereas above are classified Voiotia, Kozani, Korinthia and island regions as well. This paradox is often caused by the "special" location of some particular economic activities. With further details, electricity plant in Kozani as well as industrial accumulation in areas located in the borderlines of Attiki are examples of monitoring registration according to their allocation boosting per capita GDP in these regions. In fact, these economic activities do not have any significant interaction with the local economies as can be extracted by the declared income examination for these NUTS III regions.

Taking into account the above specialities, Petrakos and Psicharis created a complex indicator of development including indicators about the structure of production activities, the geographic position and the social structures. They finally reached the conclusion that there is an undoubted domination of Attiki despite the overestimated data of the cases aforementioned.

In another study Syriopoulos, Labrianidis and Asteriou (1997) conducted econometric tests of β-convergence and conditional β-convergence for the decade 1981-1991 and concluded that not any particular convergence in the NUTS III development progress or economic dualism was evident. Instead, standard deviation in per capita GDP increases implying an exacerbation rather than a decrease of regional inequalities.

Opposing the previous study, Tsionas (2001) claims that indeed exist strong indications of intense economic and geographic dualism among NUTS III regions as far as per capita GDP are concerned.

The study conducted by Giannias, Liargovas and Manolias expanded its analysis in demographic, land-planning, social, educational, consumptive and quality of life indicators adopting similar methodology with that used by Petrakos and Psycharis via the complex development indicator. Through this method they were able to describe better the complex notion of "welfare" and reached the conclusion that regional inequalities were decreased during the period 1961-1991 and especially between 1961-1971, a result which is rather opposite to those of previous studies.

Venos and Karagiannis also reached a similar conclusion having used annual census data for a time period between 1971-2003. In fact, they detected indications of β-convergence with a convergence rate estimated about 2%-3%. Contrary to this, σ-convergence method did not show any converging behaviour or any possibility of economic and geographic dualism.

A very interesting view was presented by Petrakos and Saratsis (2000) who claimed that regional disparities follow the frequency of economic cycles. With further details, inequalities are increased when economic activity is accelerated and similarly decreased when economy reaches depression periods.

Another important survey conducted by the Observatory of Egnatia Street concerning mainly NUTS III regions of northern Greece revealed a diffusing trend in a territorial model different from that of centre-periphery. In other words, it became evident that in case of Thessaloniki, the second largest pole of development, there was not any significant diffusion of development in the near NUTS III regions (Kilkis, Chalkidiki) compared to the impact on regions with transportation connection like Ioanninina or NUTS III regions of Thrace as a result of the construction of Egnatia Street.

Finally, closing this short review of the existent bibliography related to the issue, it is important to mention that it is common for β-convergence and σ-convergence methods to disagree in their estimations.

For example, results of Petrakos, Saratsis (2000) for the existence of β-convergence are not confirmed by σ-convergence method, which detects a slight decline between the NUTS III regions. This fact, as well as the overall disagreement among researchers can be attributed to the time gap examined and the presumptions of the regression type used in cases of β-convergence.

Methodology Analysis

In this section of our study we examine the long run development progress of Greek region in the last 16-year period. Greece is the geographical unit where convergence hypothesis was tested and NUTS III level is the territorial unit that the present research was focused on.

The annual data that were used for any process and extraction of results were based on GDP time series of the country's 51 NUTS III regions between 1991-2006 and on per capita GDP time series between

1995-2006 as the Greek National Statistics Office provided these. However, it is important to state that for the years 1991-1994 and 1996 GDP value was calculated in million Drachmas while for the rest of the years the value was calculated in million Euros. Equally, for per capita GDP, the value was calculated in Euros with the exception of 1996 when it was calculated in Drachmas. The conversion from Drachmas to Euros was made according to the official currency rate (1€ =340.75 drachmas) in nominal values. In addition, any data from 2003 onwards were provincial according to Greek National Statistics Office.

Considering the above, we have followed σ-convergence method, examining whether the dispersion of NUTS III regions' growth level tends to get decreased in the long run. In other words, we examined whether any reduction in the overall deviation on their growth level occurred compared to the mean. The statistical indicators used for this purpose are linear correlation coefficient r(x,y), weighted variation coefficient (CVw) and Gini coefficient. Finally, the long-term evolution of such indicators was examined in comparison with the long-term evolution of national GDP and per capita GDP average, the growth rate of Greek economy as well as the max/min ratio calculated for both national GDP and per capita GDP.

Linear Correlation Coefficient

In order to test the hypothesis of economic and geographic dualism in the NUTS III regions we have used the linear correlation coefficient, which is defined as below:

$$r(x,y) = \frac{\operatorname{cov}(x,y)}{\sqrt{\operatorname{var}(x)}\sqrt{\operatorname{var}(y)}}$$

Cov(x, y): co-variance of variables x, y
Var(x), Var(y): variance of variables x, y

The numerical inputs vary from zero (0) for full independence of variables x and y to one (1) for full correlation between variables x and y. Considering the formula above, estimated linear correlation coefficients for both GDP and per capita GDP are given in the Tables below. The results of the Tables and the estimated linear regressions are also depicted in the Graphs below.

Table 1. GDP linear correlation coefficients

Year	1991	1992	1993	1994	1995	1996	1997	1998
Correlation coefficient (GDP-population)	0,9977	0,9983	0,9971	0,9991	0,9977	0,9959	0,9968	0,9971
Year	1999	2000	2001	2002	2003*	2004*	2005*	2006*
Correlation coefficient (GDP-population)	0,9974	0,9961	0,9958	0,9952	0,9951	0,9946	0,9948	0,9945

Table 2. Per capita GDP linear correlation coefficients

Year	1995	1996	1997	1998	1999	2000
Correlation Coefficient (per capita GDP-population)	0,1063	0,1899	0,0541	0,0611	0,0721	0,2650
Year	2001	2002	2003*	2004*	2005*	2006*
Correlation Coefficient (per capita GDP-population)	0,2972	0,3768	0,4138	0,4327	0,4112	0,4195

Graph 1. Linear correlation between GDP and population

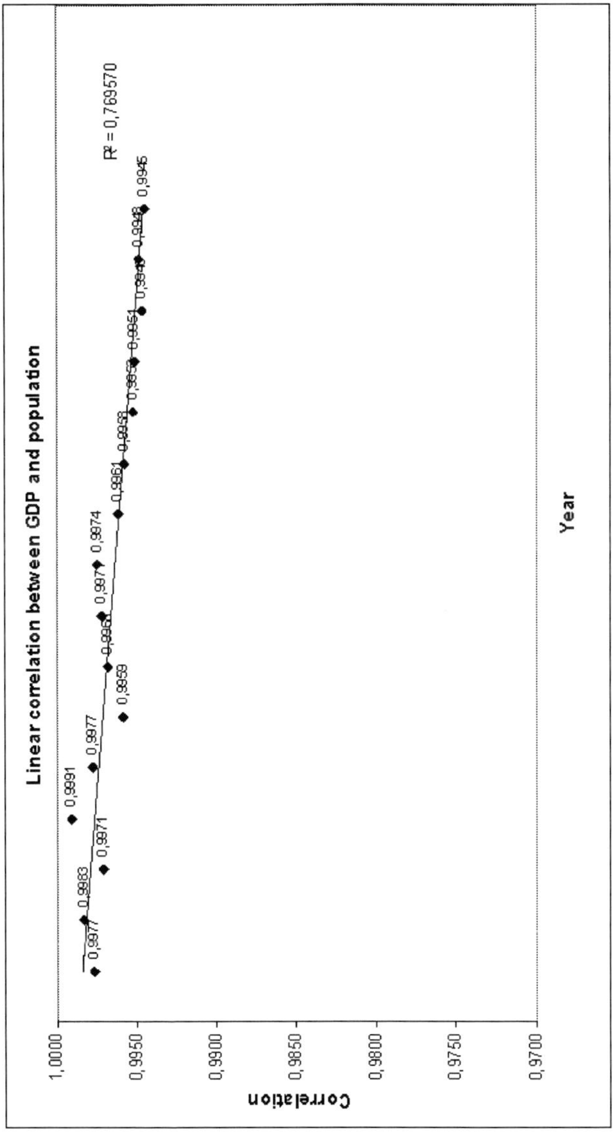

Graph 2. Linear correlation between per capita GDP and population

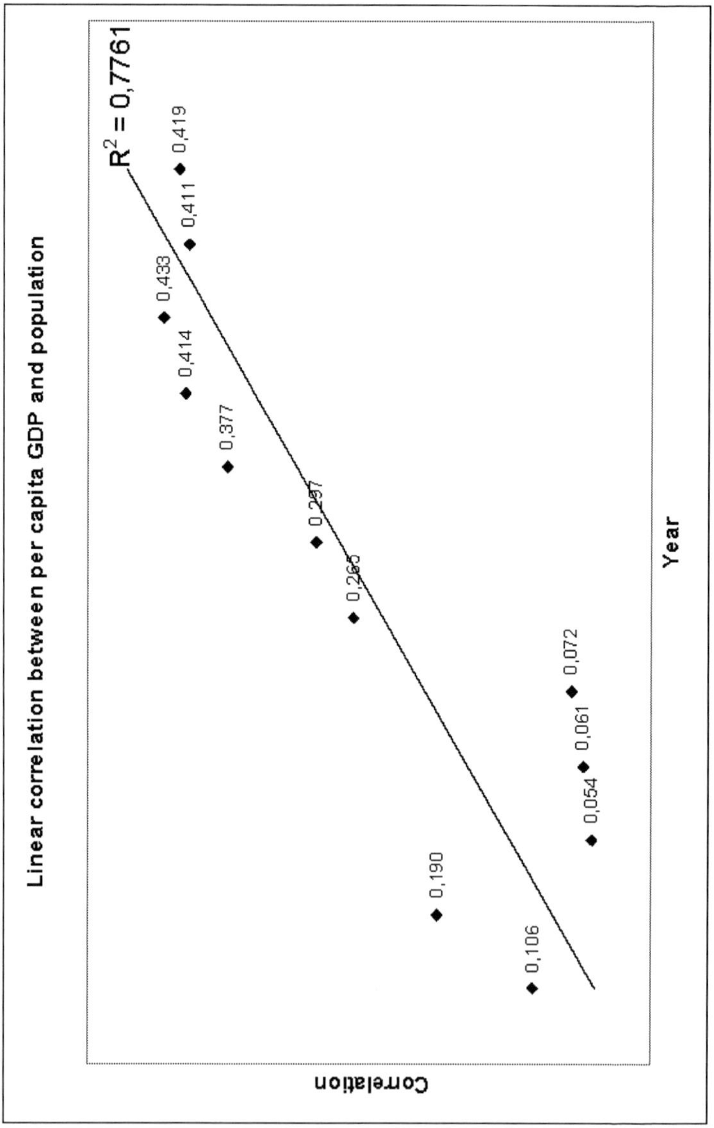

Taking into account the above results, as far as GDP is concerned, the correlation with the population remains stationary in very high levels in the long run and the total sum square (R2) of the estimated linear regression is satisfying (0.769570). These definitely confirm the hypothesis of regional polarity in the economic results activity, as indeed the GDP distribution is strengthened in NUTS III regions with higher population accumulation such as NUTS III regions including big urban formations and especially in Attiki. However, it is still unclear whether such unequal distribution of economic activities attracts big parts of the population or the opposite occurs. In other words, it is not possible to know the actual direction of the causal relation between GDP distribution and population allocation.

As far as per capita GDP is concerned, there is wider dispersion of our results (0.054-0.433), while the correlation between per capita GDP and population becomes stronger in the long run. Compared with the respective correlation between GDP and population, in this case any correlation is weaker because correlation coefficients are in lower levels, whereas the total sum square of the estimated regression is satisfying as well (0.7761). From these results it is obvious that the per capita GDP distribution between the NUTS III regions is not affected by the population as much as in the case of GDP or the opposite. However, considering the evolution of the coefficients in the long run, this situation is rather changing.

Concluding the above results, any data behaviour related to the correlation between population with either GDP or per capita GDP is rather differentiated depending to the case. Considering per capita GDP as a representative prosperity indicator*, it becomes evident that it does not show any particular trend of accumulation in big urban formations (which consists a rather encouraging fact), however this situation cannot be characterized as status quo while there is a long term change as was previously shown by Graph 2.

---

* Such an assumption includes many weaknesses while human welfare is often characterized by many other qualitative factors. However, at this particular level of analysis in the present study it becomes a very convenient assumption.

Gini Coefficient

Gini coefficient was firstly introduced by Gini in 1912 and since then it has consisted a very useful analytical tool for many researches. It estimates the variations of a single observation from all the other observations relevant to a specific variable and is defined from the formula below:

$$G=\left(\frac{1}{2n^2\mu}\right)\sum_{\iota=1}^{n}\sum_{j=1}^{n}\left|y_i-y_j\right|$$

However, for simplification reasons this formula is transformed as below:

$$G=1-\left(\frac{1}{n^2\mu}\right)\sum_{\iota=1}^{n}\sum_{j=1}^{n}Min\left(y_{i,}y_j\right)$$

where from finally results the simplest mathematic expression (Amartya, 1972):

$$G=1+\frac{1}{n}-\frac{2}{n^2\mu}\left[y_1+2y_2+\ldots+ny_n\right]$$

$$y_1\geq y_2\geq\ldots\geq y_n$$

n: number of NUTS III regions
μ: average of variable y

The following analysis will be based on the above mathematical expression whose numerical inputs vary from zero (0) for full equality between NUTS III regions to one (1) for full inequality in regard with a particular structural factor. It is also important to point out that the main advantage of Gini coefficient compared with other dispersion indicators is that it is not subject to high sensitivity from the existence of any radical data.

Although in regions like Attiki or Thessaloniki the existence of such radical data is almost ensured, however it is really important to focus on the evolution of disparities in the rest of the NUTS III regions.

Considering the above we implemented Gini coefficient for NUTS III regions' GDP for the time period between 1991-2006 in order to detect both stationary inequalities between NUTS III regions and their long run change. Our relevant processed results are provided in the table 3 below. Moreover, the evolution of Gini coefficient is also depicted in the graphs followed for the same time period in comparison with the national GDP average, the national GDP growth rate and the max/min ratio.

Table 3. Gini Coefficients

Year	1991	1992	1993	1994	1995	1996	1997	1998
Coefficients	0,60782	0,60202	0,61201	0,61085	0,62194	0,61358	0,60727	0,60946
Year	1999	2000	2001	2002	2003*	2004*	2005*	2006*
Coefficients	0,61073	0,65092	0,65381	0,66542	0,66696	0,67650	0,67406	0,67986

Graph 3. Gini coefficient and NUTS III GDP average

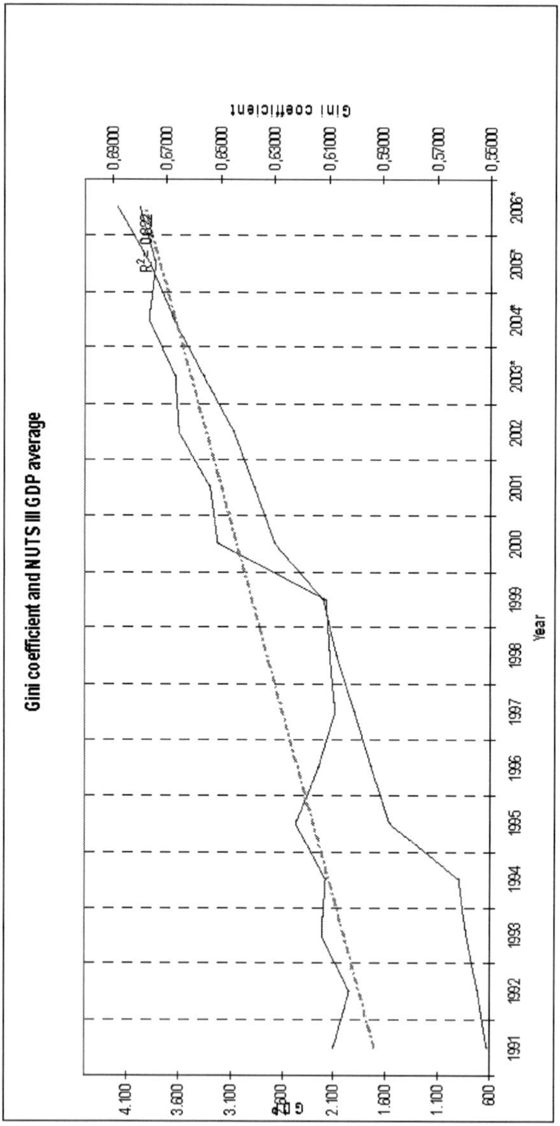

Graph 4. Gini coefficient and GDP growth rate

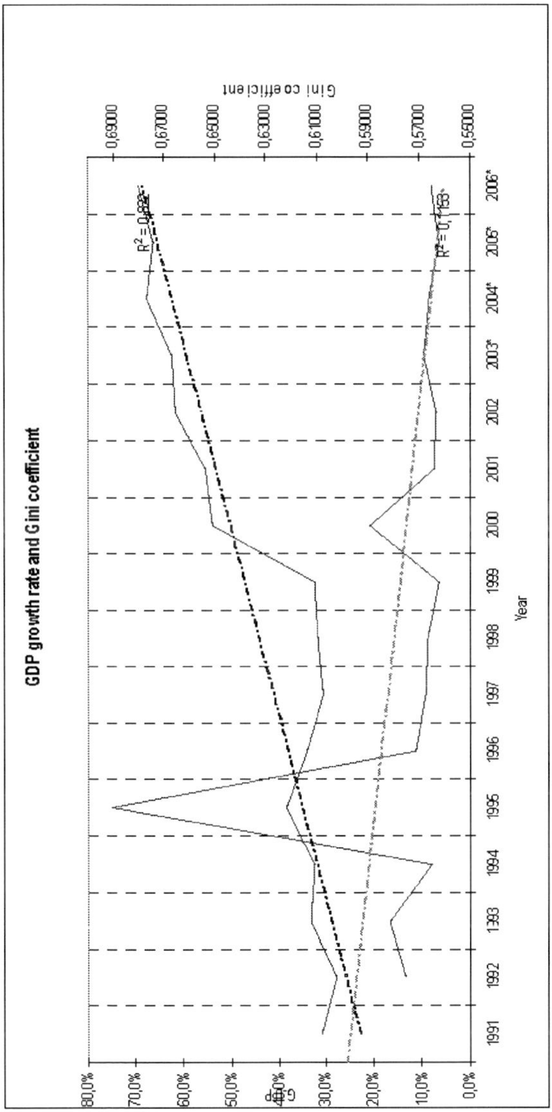

Graph 5. Gini coefficient and max/min ratio

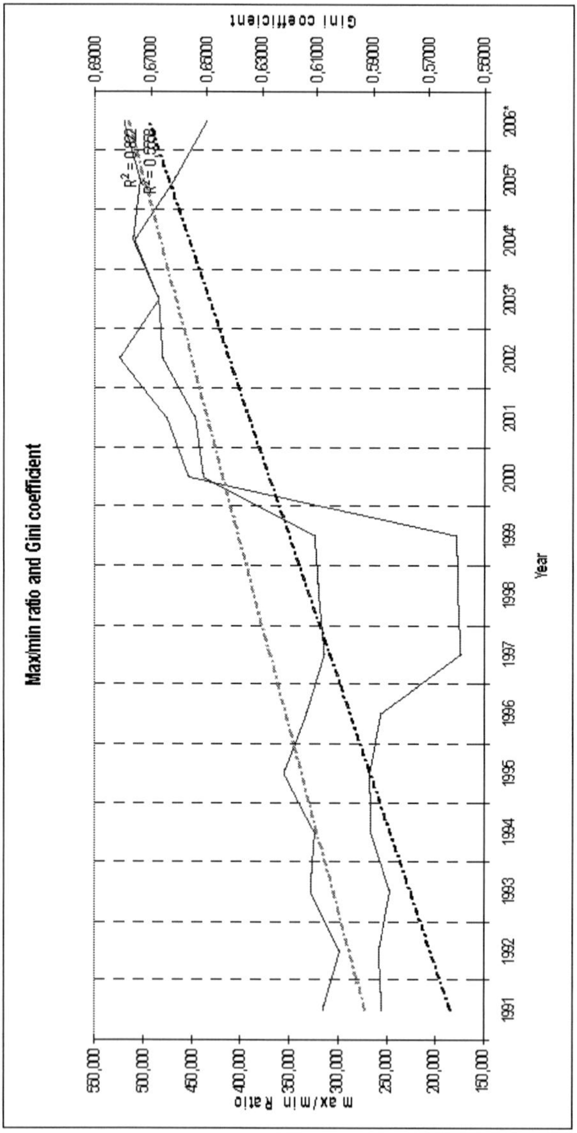

Having studied the above graphs, it can be seen that the long-term growth of average GDP is accompanied by a slight increase on the regional disparities (from 0.60782 to 0.67986). The disparity level, as described by Gini coefficient, is comparatively high whereas the total sum square is satisfying (0.822). However, it is obvious that this indicator is ultimately affected by radical data (this view is also confirmed by the comparison of Gini coefficient with the max/min ratio). More specifically, between the years 1993-1995 and 1999-2000 we can see a rapid growth in the GDP of Attiki (in particular between 1993-1995 GDP of Attiki is almost doubled whereas GDP of other NUTS III regions is increased as well) which is also seen on the increase of the average national product, however with not any similar impact in the proceeding. These changes also have an effect on the disparity level among NUTS III regions as there is a strong diverting behaviour for the same time periods (from 0.61201 to 0.62196 and from 0.61073 to 0.65092 respectively).

The evolution of disparity level in comparison with the growth rate of Greek economy as it was calculated by National Statistics Office's data seems indeed to be very interesting. With further details, for the time periods between 1992-1993, 1994-1995 and 1999-2000 the GDP growth rate was increased, nonetheless soon it has been reverted to its initial level (the change during the period 1994-1995 was approximately 73.8 %!). It is also important that the acceleration of the Greek economy is also revealed by Gini coefficient as since the periods 1993-1996 and 1999-2000 are detected many important deviations between the NUTS III regions' product. As a result in the short run, views of Petrakos and Saratsis are confirmed as the growth rate becomes increased when disparity level between NUTS III regions become higher. However, in the long run, estimated trends show rather inconsistent results revealing an odd long term trend which cannot be taken under serious consideration mainly because of the very low total sum square of the regression estimated for the growth rate (0.1171).

Finally, the depiction of Gini coefficient in comparison with max/min ratio confirms the fact that Gini coefficient is ultimately affected by any existence of radical data (a fact which consists a serious weakness), as there are similarities between the evolutions of two indicators. This outcome becomes clear for the time period between 1999-2000 when the exacerbation of regional disparities is followed by a rapid increase of max/min ratio at about 273 million Euros, whereas the total sum square of the estimated regression is relatively satisfactory (0.5558) despite the many deviations detected.

Weighted Variation Coefficient (CVw Williamson)

The last indicator which was used is weighted variation coefficient (CVw) also known as Williamson coefficient (Williamson, 1968, p. 122). This indicator is defined as below:

$$CV_w = \frac{\sqrt{\sum_i (x_i - \overline{x})^2 \frac{P_i}{P}}}{\overline{x}}$$

x_i: annual product of i NUTS III region
x: annual national average product
P_i: annual population of i NUTS III region
P: national population

The indicator above was used upon time series for GDP and par capita GDP for the time periods between 1991-2006 and 1995-2006 respectively. Its more interesting characteristic is the ratio $\frac{Pi}{P}$, which consists the weight of country's NUTS III regions according to their population. Consequently, regions including large urban formations are expected to have a stronger impact on the long-term evolution of the above indicator. By theoretical perspective, such an effect is quite objective and fair; however, it brings into surface many doubts for any possible distortion of the outcome results caused by radical data. The higher numerical value the coefficient has, the larger regional disparities exist, whereas the more the indicator tends to zero (o) numerical valid the more disparities are limited.

Weighted variation coefficients for the whole country are quoted in the following table for the time period between 1991-2006. The analysis presented for the long run evolution of regional inequalities in Greece is based on the outcome results of table 4 regarding GDP. In the tables included in the appendix at the end of the present paper, there is a presentation of Williamson coefficients for any NUTS III region separately for the time period between 1991-2006.

Based on those results, any comparison between NUTS III regions is possible regarding to their annual product for each year. In addition, the long term evolution of weighted variation coefficient for GDP is also depicted in the graphs that follow regarding the time period between 1991-2006 in comparison with the long term evolution of national product, national GDP growth rate and max/min ratio for the same time periods.

Table 4. GDP Williamson coefficients (country's total)

Year	1991	1992	1993	1994	1995	1996	1997	1998
CVw Country's Total	0,86808	0,86621	0,86570	0,86416	0,86216	0,86582	0,86543	0,86450
Year	1999	2000	2001	2002	2003*	2004*	2005*	2006*
CVw Country's Total	0,86284	0,84658	0,84461	0,84152	0,84068	0,83797	0,83762	0,83546

Graph 6. Williamson coefficient and NUTS III GDP average

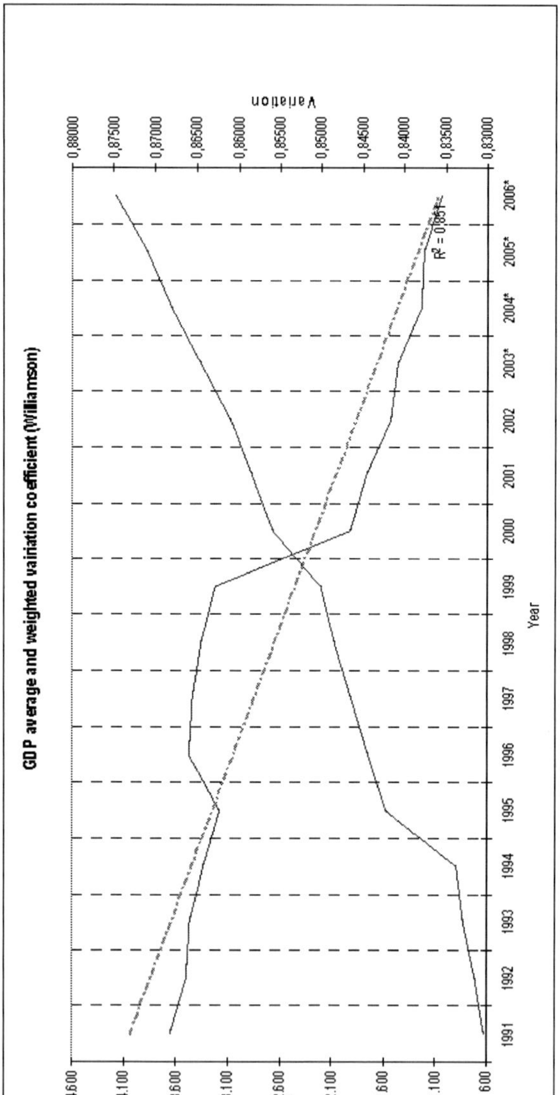

Graph 7. Williamson coefficient and GDP growth rate

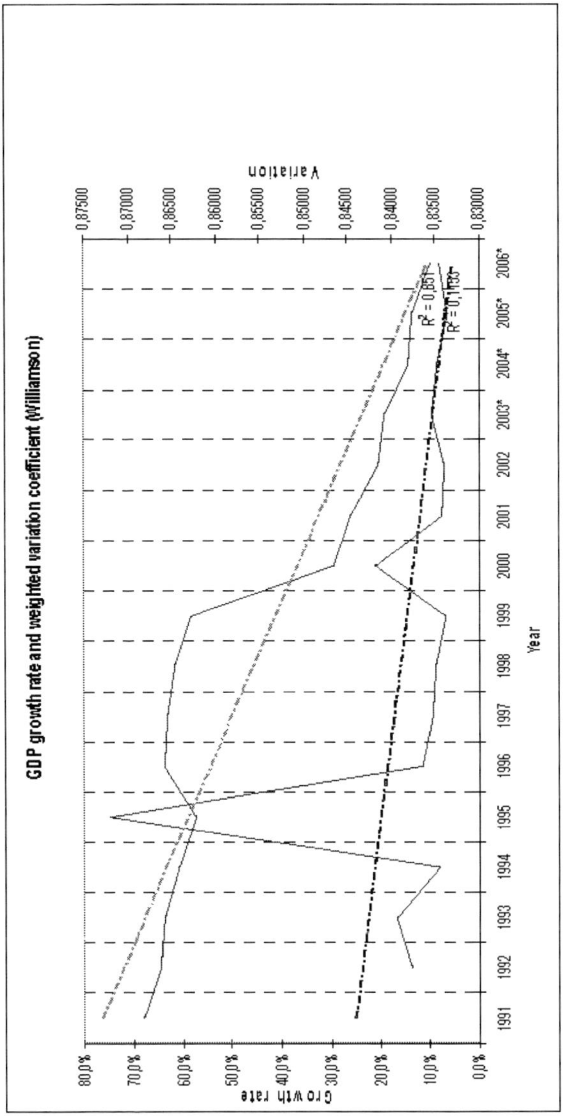

Graph 8. Williamson coefficient and GDP max/min ratio

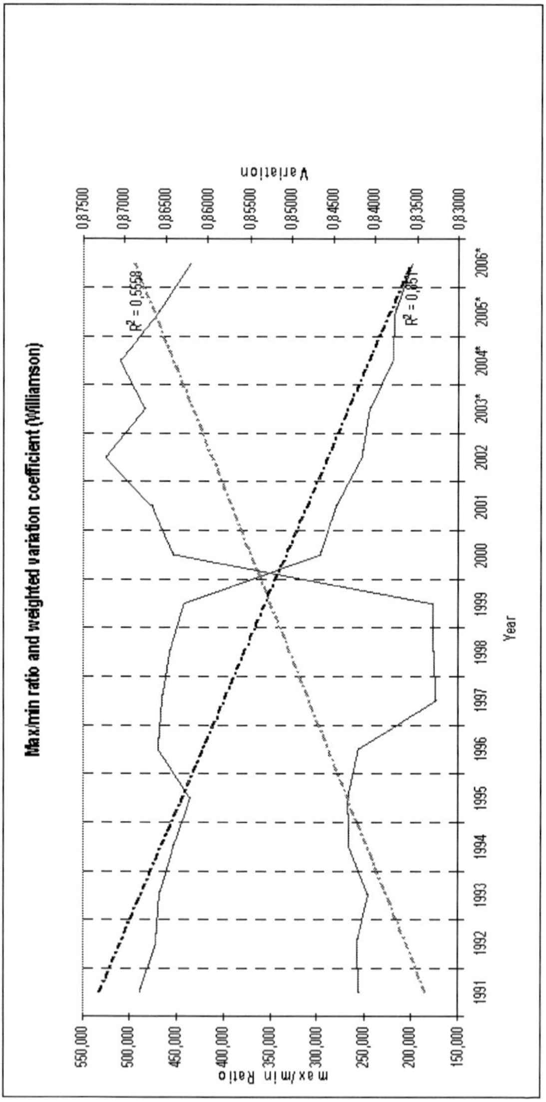

According to the weighted variation coefficient (CVw-Williamson), regional disparities are estimated in considerably high levels varying from 0.86808 to 0.83546. In general, it is possible to see that the long-term evolution of average GDP is smoothly increasing with a considerable rating, while the evolution of regional inequalities is rather steady in the long run with weak converging trends (only 0.0363 for a 16-year time period). The long-term evolution of the indicator does not have any significant fluctuations with the exception of the period 1999-2000 when a rapid fall is detected. Given that fall implies that, despite the growth of Attiki's product, the overall GDP growth in the other NUTS III regions led to the overall decrease of disparity level even that such a fall is rather small in absolute terms. However, it is rather absurd that such a general increase in the GDP of all the NUTS III regions does not affect the evolution of the GDP average for the same time period. Last but not least, the total sum square of the estimated regression is very satisfying (0.851).

It is also interesting to examine the Williamson coefficient in comparison with the evolution of GDP growth rate. It can be seen that these indicators change with a rather reverse way while whenever an acceleration of economy's activity is detected, regional disparities show a weak converging behaviour and the opposite. These outcomes are very clear especially during the periods between 1994-1996 and 1999-2001 a fact that does not confirm the claims of Petrakos and Saratsis.

As noted in the previous similar case, long run trends show a weak convergence behaviour which is probably caused by the low numerical value of total sum square of the estimated regression for the GDP growth rate (0.1171).

Finally, any comparison between Williamson coefficient and the max/min ratio is indicative of the fact that this particular indicator is not severely affected by the existence of any radical data as we had initially assumed because any fluctuations in the max/min ratio are not followed by similar changes of the Williamson coefficient for any time period examined.

Expanding the analysis on per capita GDP time series, all Williamson coefficients for any NUTS III level region are quoted in the appendix below separately for the time period from 1995 to 2006.

According to these outcome results, any comparison between NUTS III regions in regard with per capita GDP is possible for any time period.

In addition, weighted variation coefficients for the national per capita GDP are quoted in the table below as they have been calculated for the time period between 1995-2006. Moreover, the long term evolution of weighted variation coefficient for per capita GDP is also depicted in the graphs that follow regarding the time period between 1995-2006 in comparison with the long term evolution of national per capita product, national per capita GDP growth rate and max/min ratio for the same time periods.

Table 5. Per capita GDP Williamson coefficients (country's total)

Year	1995	1996	1997	1998	1999	2000
CVw Country's Total	0,97622	0,97506	0,97713	0,97706	0,97696	0,97428
Year	2001	2002	2003*	2004*	2005*	2006*
CVw Country's Total	0,97403	0,97326	0,97316	0,97263	0,97291	0,97264

Graph 9. Williamson coefficient and NUTS III per capita GDP average

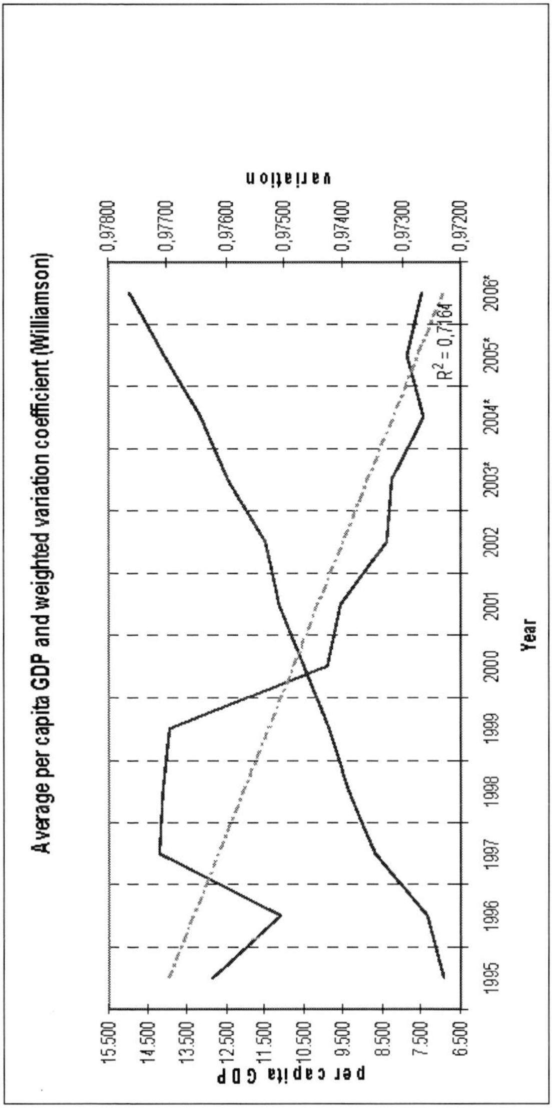

Graph 10. Williamson coefficient and per capita GDP growth rate

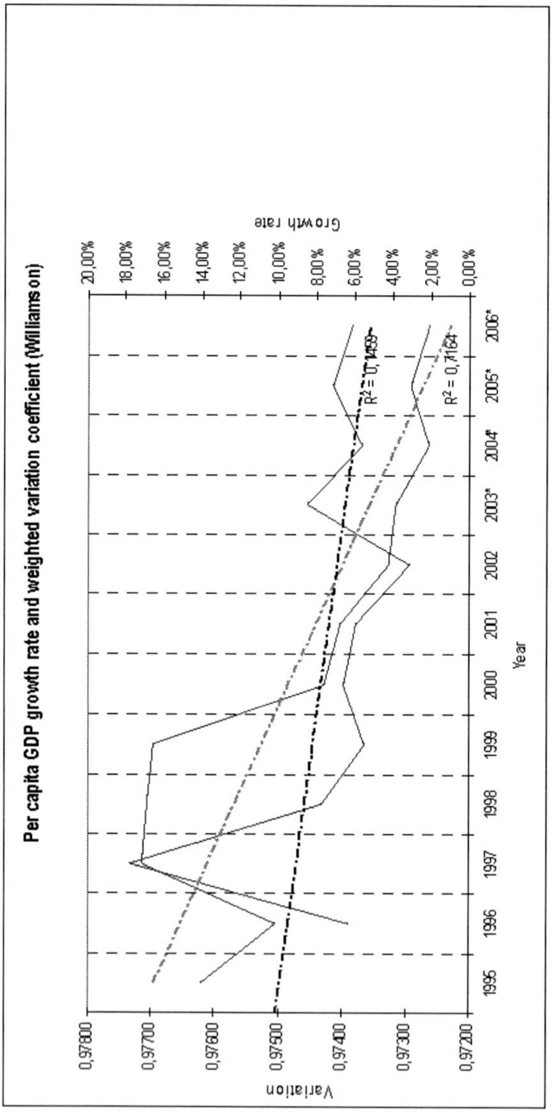

Graph 11. Williamson coefficient and per capita GDP max/min ratio

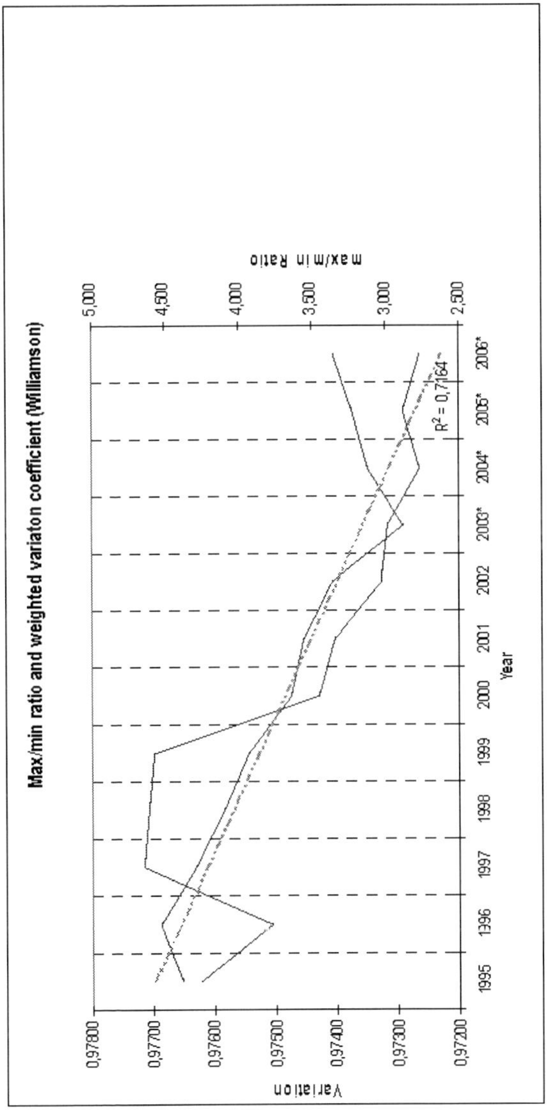

From the diagrammatic analysis for per capita GDP it can be concluded that regional inequalities are in considerably high levels and vary narrowly from 0.97713 to 0.97263. In the long run, there is not any significant convergence between NUTS III regions (only 0.00358), which is described sufficiently from the total sum square of the estimated regression (0.7164). Average per capita GDP is significantly raised from 6,914 to 14,943 Euros for the time period between 1995-2006 with only minimum changes on its long-term evolution. The most considerable fall of Williamson indicator within this period is also detected between 1999-2000 when a simultaneous increase of per capita product occurs in most NUTS III regions including Attiki. An also considerable change is detected within the period 1996-1997 when in spite of the fact that per capita GDP is increased in most NUTS III regions, there is a small decrease on Attiki. The emphasis put on per capita GDP of Attiki can easily be explained by our presumption that the higher population ratio of Attiki could more easily affect any progress in per capita GDP rather than the overall GDP from the other regions. However, the initial view held has not been confirmed by the data.

There is also great interest in the long-term progress of per capita GDP in comparison with per capita growth rate for the time period between 1995-2006. More specifically, the growth rate shows a slight falling trend from 6.4% to 6.2%; however, the total sum square for the estimated regression is significantly low (only 0.1459). In general, the evolution of Williamson indicator for per capita GDP follows any changes on the relevant growth rate a fact that confirms once again the views of Petrakos and Saratsis. In other words, it becomes evident that any acceleration on the per capita GDP growth increases regional disparities and the opposite, even that these changes are particularly small.

Finally, closing the diagrammatic analysis for per capita GDP, there is a presentation of the long-term progress of Williamson indicator in comparison with max/min ratio for the same time period. It is evident that max/min ratio shows a long term fall from 4.5 to 2.5 points without having any significant fluctuations on its progress. As a result, it is possible to reach the conclusion that the long-term progress of Williamson coefficient is not affected by any radical data in the per capita GDP of NUTS III regions.

Conclusions

Summarizing the results of this work, it becomes evident that the issue of regional disparities consisted and still consists a dynamic field of research and controversy for both theoretical and implemented policy level. After the short review in a substantial part of the bibliography related to the issue, it has been emphatically revealed that Greek bibliography is far from the adoption of a compound view about whether any inequalities exist, as it is obvious that any approach is differentiated according to the method adopted, the available data and the time period referred.

Focusing on the findings of the present study, the conclusion that the Greek region is characterized by intense indications of economic and geographic dualism which ultimately affect any distribution of GDP and per capita GDP among NUTS III regions was reached. However, after the implementation of Gini coefficient and Williamson Coefficient upon the time series, relatively differentiated results were produced. More specifically, as far as GDP is concerned, regional inequalities are underestimated by Gini coefficient compared with the Williamson coefficient, which results to a sufficiently higher disparity level. In the long run, any converging behaviour of the estimated regression trends is regarded insignificant and in many cases could have been considered steady. In addition, the implementation of these indicators upon per capita GDP time series proved that inequalities among NUTS III regions are rated higher if expressed in welfare terms rather than in overall product amount, whereas in this case any long run converging trends can be regarded steady as well (it was aforementioned in previous section that per capita GDP can be considered as interposed variable for all the other aspects of human development).

References

Amartya, S., 1972, *On Economic Inequality*, Oxford University Press.

—. 1973, *On Economic Inequality*, Clarendon Press, Oxford.

Giannias, D., Liargovas, P., Manolias, G., 1997, Regional Inequalities in Greece 1961-1991, *Review of Urban and Regional Studies*, 13, pp. 47-61.

Glytsos, N., 1988, *Peripheral Inequalities in Greece: Demographic and Economic features*, Centre of Planning and Economic Research, Athens.

Kalogirou, N., Karagianni, S., Labrianidis, L., 1989, Impacts of Motivation towards Regional Development of Greek Industry, *The Greek review of Social Research*, pp. 39-77 .

Labrianidis Lois. «Entrepreneurship in European Continent: The Case of Greece». Pataki Press. Athens 2005.

Labrianidis, L. and Papamichos, N., 1990, Regional Distribution of Industry and the Role of State in Greece, *Journal of Environment and Planning C: Government and Policy*, 8, pp. 455-476.

Petrakos, G. and Psicharis, G., 2003, Regional inequalities in Greece: An Alternative Method of Estimation, *Research Papers Series*, 9, 28. pp. 621-644.

Petrakos, G. and Psicharis, G., 2004, *Regional Development in Greece*, Kritiki Press, Athens.

Petrakos, G. and Saratsis, Y., 2000, Regional Inequality in Greece, *Papers in Regional Science*, 776, pp. 57-74.

Prodromidis, P.I., 2006, *A Regional Analysis of Declared Income in Greece*, Centre of Planning and Economic Research, Athens.

Seitanidis, S., 2008, *Transport policy and territorial cohesion – the case of the Egnatia motorway in northern Greece*, Observatory of Egnatia Street.

Syriopoulos, K., Labrianidis, L., Asteriou, D., 1997, Convergence of per capita GDP in Regions of Greece, *Review of Urban and Regional Studies*, 13, pp. 63-76.

Tsionas, E.G., 2001, Another look at regional convergence in Greece, *Regional Studies*, 36, 6, pp. 603-609.

Venos, N. and Karagiannis, S., 2008, *Convergence and Economic Performance in Greece: New Evidence at Regional and Prefecture Level*, Centre of Planning and Economic Research. Athens.

Williamson, J.G., 1968, *Regional Inequality and the process of National Development: a description of the patterns*, Penguin Books.

Appendix

Table A1. GDP Williamson Coefficients

CVw	1991	1992	1993	1994	1995	1996	1997	1998	1999	2000	2001	2002	2003*	2004*	2005*	2006*
Aitoloakarnania	0,14554	0,14464	0,14426	0,14311	0,14281	0,14218	0,14159	0,14098	0,14051	0,14026	0,13986	0,13984	0,13985	0,13957	0,13882	0,13851
Argolida	0,09547	0,09536	0,09539	0,09550	0,09564	0,09576	0,09589	0,09595	0,09599	0,09608	0,09605	0,09604	0,09603	0,09588	0,09556	0,09536
Arkadia	0,09621	0,09543	0,09473	0,09420	0,09365	0,09311	0,09255	0,09199	0,09158	0,09121	0,09078	0,09053	0,09033	0,08989	0,08917	0,08879
Arta	0,08572	0,08511	0,08458	0,08418	0,08377	0,08342	0,08304	0,08269	0,08232	0,08205	0,08173	0,08135	0,08089	0,08055	0,08025	0,07988
Attiki	0,37873	0,37474	0,37403	0,37103	0,36773	0,37917	0,37960	0,37817	0,37510	0,32848	0,32344	0,31435	0,31201	0,30589	0,30758	0,30338
Achaia	0,16708	0,16626	0,16658	0,16655	0,16634	0,16630	0,16634	0,16627	0,16636	0,16673	0,16678	0,16725	0,16778	0,16863	0,16913	0,16973
Voiotia	0,10851	0,10806	0,10775	0,10730	0,10559	0,10498	0,10500	0,10474	0,10450	0,10466	0,10424	0,10466	0,10491	0,10462	0,10447	0,10427
Grevena	0,05656	0,05628	0,05602	0,05579	0,05556	0,05538	0,05509	0,05492	0,05471	0,05462	0,05448	0,05428	0,05403	0,05379	0,05352	0,05325
Drama	0,09554	0,09580	0,09599	0,09583	0,09593	0,09591	0,09600	0,09597	0,09597	0,09602	0,09609	0,09582	0,09558	0,09528	0,09496	0,09465
Dodekanisos	0,12319	0,12446	0,12527	0,12589	0,12658	0,12696	0,12720	0,12760	0,12782	0,12831	0,12872	0,12912	0,12936	0,12957	0,12969	0,12964
Evros	0,11751	0,11725	0,11709	0,11664	0,11652	0,11627	0,11587	0,11569	0,11557	0,11558	0,11564	0,11541	0,11511	0,11477	0,11498	0,11473
Evoia	0,13774	0,13725	0,13665	0,13652	0,13603	0,13604	0,13585	0,13566	0,13559	0,13588	0,13563	0,13550	0,13531	0,13498	0,13464	0,13429
Evritania	0,04463	0,04433	0,04403	0,04374	0,04345	0,04324	0,04294	0,04271	0,04248	0,04234	0,04220	0,04211	0,04196	0,04174	0,04229	0,04206
Zakynthos	0,05608	0,05689	0,05746	0,05788	0,05821	0,05848	0,05866	0,05887	0,05901	0,05913	0,05935	0,05977	0,06015	0,06005	0,05987	0,05983
Ileia	0,12883	0,12866	0,12874	0,12858	0,12893	0,12897	0,12894	0,12885	0,12876	0,12867	0,12840	0,12799	0,12751	0,12710	0,12687	0,12643
Imathia	0,11466	0,11438	0,11415	0,11392	0,11381	0,11361	0,11350	0,11329	0,11313	0,11289	0,11294	0,11303	0,11318	0,11302	0,11283	0,11272
Irakleio	0,15649	0,15697	0,15788	0,15732	0,15801	0,15814	0,15854	0,15874	0,15886	0,15904	0,15908	0,15894	0,15925	0,15939	0,15957	0,15954
Thesprotia	0,06383	0,06365	0,06351	0,06339	0,06328	0,06317	0,06308	0,06305	0,06302	0,06297	0,06296	0,06275	0,06254	0,06233	0,06205	0,06185
Thessaloniki	0,27896	0,27970	0,28136	0,28078	0,27962	0,27763	0,27707	0,27757	0,27775	0,28534	0,28616	0,28742	0,28809	0,28876	0,28858	0,28904
Ioannina	0,12101	0,12083	0,12071	0,12059	0,12047	0,12043	0,12012	0,12001	0,11992	0,11993	0,11988	0,12030	0,12065	0,12175	0,12206	0,12313
Kavala	0,11320	0,11266	0,11227	0,11229	0,11235	0,11237	0,11255	0,11260	0,11258	0,11272	0,11267	0,11236	0,11207	0,11184	0,11165	0,11138
Karditsa	0,10865	0,10794	0,10751	0,10678	0,10658	0,10608	0,10561	0,10514	0,10476	0,10462	0,10427	0,10376	0,10326	0,10286	0,10239	0,10199
Kastoria	0,07203	0,07156	0,07131	0,07112	0,07080	0,07062	0,07037	0,07019	0,07004	0,06998	0,06986	0,06970	0,06958	0,06945	0,06943	0,06928
Kerkyra	0,09955	0,09984	0,10010	0,10017	0,10032	0,10029	0,10012	0,10003	0,09992	0,09993	0,09991	0,10071	0,10138	0,10245	0,10314	0,10417
Kefallinia	0,05602	0,05658	0,05699	0,05733	0,05760	0,05783	0,05800	0,05819	0,05832	0,05851	0,05858	0,05877	0,05892	0,05872	0,05845	0,05829
Kilkis	0,08598	0,08675	0,08726	0,08737	0,08768	0,08779	0,08782	0,08792	0,08799	0,08817	0,08834	0,08844	0,08844	0,08817	0,08797	0,08763
Kozani	0,11903	0,11866	0,11828	0,11815	0,11781	0,11760	0,11734	0,11708	0,11696	0,11720	0,11716	0,11697	0,11695	0,11678	0,11654	0,11636

Korinthia	0,11170	0,11198	0,11254	0,11250	0,11311	0,11331	0,11315	0,11308	0,11308	0,11302	0,11316	0,11349	0,11375	0,11345	0,11332	0,11304
Kyklades	0,09437	0,09542	0,09603	0,09665	0,09704	0,09746	0,09782	0,09820	0,09857	0,09879	0,09904	0,09912	0,09910	0,09903	0,09873	0,09857
Lakonia	0,09369	0,09304	0,09259	0,09231	0,09216	0,09197	0,09183	0,09179	0,09171	0,09176	0,09165	0,09180	0,09186	0,09153	0,09153	0,09122
Larisa	0,15919	0,15917	0,15493	0,15888	0,15867	0,15839	0,15780	0,15747	0,15713	0,15734	0,15713	0,15703	0,15668	0,15669	0,15678	0,15695
Lasithi	0,08238	0,08202	0,08192	0,08192	0,08209	0,08222	0,08230	0,08246	0,08256	0,08276	0,08271	0,08256	0,08238	0,08217	0,08204	0,08180
Lesvos	0,10128	0,10069	0,10024	0,09988	0,09939	0,09916	0,09891	0,09875	0,09857	0,09885	0,09879	0,09862	0,09839	0,09811	0,09763	0,09732
Lefkada	0,04524	0,04511	0,04501	0,04500	0,04493	0,04494	0,04482	0,04480	0,04474	0,04475	0,04469	0,04499	0,04525	0,04504	0,04494	0,04476
Magnisia	0,13569	0,13541	0,13557	0,13507	0,13526	0,13519	0,13506	0,13493	0,13488	0,13491	0,13470	0,13440	0,13413	0,13395	0,13359	0,13326
Messinia	0,12387	0,12339	0,12302	0,12291	0,12288	0,12275	0,12273	0,12266	0,12252	0,12248	0,12227	0,12213	0,12199	0,12156	0,12111	0,12066
Xanthi	0,09405	0,09498	0,09550	0,09571	0,09580	0,09590	0,09596	0,09599	0,09607	0,09623	0,09634	0,09644	0,09649	0,09654	0,09678	0,09682
Pella	0,11416	0,11405	0,11392	0,11384	0,11386	0,11372	0,11360	0,11354	0,11351	0,11361	0,11367	0,11385	0,11413	0,11392	0,11358	0,11332
Pieria	0,10413	0,10486	0,10530	0,10549	0,10586	0,10602	0,10615	0,10630	0,10640	0,10653	0,10667	0,10675	0,10682	0,10667	0,10665	0,10653
Preveza	0,07446	0,07411	0,07383	0,07367	0,07349	0,07335	0,07313	0,07299	0,07284	0,07272	0,07262	0,07239	0,07216	0,07193	0,07183	0,07167
Rethimno	0,08144	0,08187	0,08218	0,08241	0,08273	0,08304	0,08330	0,08365	0,08395	0,08421	0,08442	0,08445	0,08444	0,08439	0,08445	0,08440
Rodopi	0,10016	0,10046	0,10044	0,10046	0,10036	0,10028	0,10015	0,10010	0,10005	0,10011	0,10011	0,10003	0,09985	0,09966	0,09965	0,09951
Samos	0,06436	0,06408	0,06389	0,06376	0,06363	0,06357	0,06340	0,06334	0,06324	0,06322	0,06313	0,06284	0,06258	0,06234	0,06213	0,06188
Serres	0,13303	0,13272	0,13265	0,13222	0,13248	0,13233	0,13211	0,13201	0,13192	0,13195	0,13197	0,13166	0,13126	0,13076	0,13007	0,12951
Trikala	0,11323	0,11455	0,11378	0,11317	0,11240	0,11176	0,11126	0,11058	0,11007	0,10985	0,10943	0,10905	0,10865	0,10826	0,10818	0,10785
Fthiotida	0,12442	0,12431	0,12397	0,12410	0,12374	0,12359	0,12330	0,12317	0,12309	0,12317	0,12291	0,12277	0,12259	0,12217	0,12137	0,12107
Florina	0,07134	0,07112	0,07091	0,07080	0,07068	0,07059	0,07039	0,07030	0,07016	0,07016	0,07011	0,07011	0,07013	0,07003	0,06982	0,06962
Fokida	0,05979	0,05957	0,05939	0,05933	0,05922	0,05916	0,05902	0,05895	0,05886	0,05884	0,05870	0,05891	0,05904	0,05872	0,05854	0,05831
Chalkidiki	0,09113	0,09058	0,09212	0,09246	0,09284	0,09314	0,09331	0,09359	0,09383	0,09417	0,09433	0,09451	0,09459	0,09446	0,09432	0,09416
Chania	0,11199	0,11255	0,11309	0,11310	0,11336	0,11199	0,11373	0,11395	0,11416	0,11462	0,11500	0,11518	0,11536	0,11521	0,11486	0,11475
Chios	0,07169	0,07126	0,07093	0,07071	0,07046	0,07027	0,07001	0,06986	0,06971	0,06960	0,06945	0,06921	0,06890	0,06861	0,06847	0,06821

Table A2. Per capita Williamson Coefficients

CVw	1995	1996	1997	1998	1999	2000	2001	2002	2003*	2004*	2005*	2006*
Aitoloakarnania	0,14278	0,14215	0,14161	0,14097	0,14047	0,13996	0,13955	0,13946	0,13946	0,13914	0,13839	0,13806
Argolida	0,09455	0,09469	0,09492	0,09497	0,09500	0,09497	0,09493	0,09487	0,09484	0,09470	0,09435	0,09417
Arkadia	0,09254	0,09229	0,09140	0,09076	0,09037	0,08984	0,08949	0,08918	0,08897	0,08850	0,08771	0,08732
Arta	0,08296	0,08269	0,08233	0,08197	0,08156	0,08122	0,08086	0,08045	0,07998	0,07964	0,07936	0,07899
Attiki	0,58012	0,57948	0,58245	0,58286	0,58314	0,57882	0,57862	0,57727	0,57690	0,57695	0,57866	0,57912
Achaia	0,16763	0,16747	0,16771	0,16761	0,16763	0,16752	0,16755	0,16795	0,16849	0,16925	0,16982	0,17039
Voiotia	0,10272	0,10296	0,10243	0,10221	0,10206	0,10208	0,10174	0,10230	0,10264	0,10215	0,10204	0,10185
Grevena	0,05485	0,05483	0,05415	0,05398	0,05376	0,05388	0,05373	0,05350	0,05327	0,05305	0,05261	0,05233
Drama	0,09494	0,09487	0,09525	0,09522	0,09522	0,09512	0,09519	0,09489	0,09465	0,09434	0,09407	0,09372
Dodekanisos	0,12592	0,12595	0,12664	0,12705	0,12724	0,12737	0,12780	0,12814	0,12838	0,12858	0,12877	0,12865
Evros	0,11585	0,11529	0,11519	0,11500	0,11487	0,11468	0,11475	0,11451	0,11418	0,11380	0,11402	0,11378
Evoia	0,13571	0,13596	0,13567	0,13546	0,13538	0,13539	0,13510	0,13490	0,13468	0,13428	0,13396	0,13356
Evritania	0,04255	0,04268	0,04200	0,04179	0,04155	0,04183	0,04170	0,04163	0,04143	0,04121	0,04173	0,04143
Zakynthos	0,05739	0,05754	0,05789	0,05812	0,05824	0,05783	0,05798	0,05842	0,05886	0,05881	0,05859	0,05856
Ileia	0,12855	0,12854	0,12865	0,12855	0,12845	0,12819	0,12790	0,12745	0,12692	0,12649	0,12630	0,12587
Imathia	0,11290	0,11268	0,11276	0,11254	0,11238	0,11182	0,11194	0,11200	0,11224	0,11200	0,11186	0,11177

Irakleio	0,15882	0,15869	0,15947	0,15966	0,15978	0,15954	0,15955	0,15930	0,15959	0,15963	0,15984	0,15977
Thesprotia	0,06252	0,06254	0,06235	0,06231	0,06224	0,06205	0,06195	0,06178	0,06155	0,06133	0,06107	0,06090
Thessaloniki	0,30484	0,30387	0,30536	0,30580	0,30618	0,30738	0,30795	0,30883	0,30977	0,31034	0,31032	0,31087
Ioannina	0,11988	0,11993	0,11954	0,11940	0,11929	0,11905	0,11899	0,11935	0,11969	0,12073	0,12110	0,12215
Kavala	0,11141	0,11134	0,11180	0,11187	0,11181	0,11181	0,11174	0,11137	0,11109	0,11084	0,11063	0,11038
Karditsa	0,10573	0,10527	0,10482	0,10432	0,10396	0,10384	0,10348	0,10290	0,10238	0,10198	0,10154	0,10119
Kastoria	0,06978	0,06948	0,06934	0,06917	0,06903	0,06907	0,06896	0,06875	0,06860	0,06853	0,06846	0,06828
Kerkyra	0,09928	0,09920	0,09912	0,09904	0,09893	0,09878	0,09875	0,09953	0,10022	0,10135	0,10205	0,10313
Kefallinia	0,05679	0,05692	0,05714	0,05733	0,05743	0,05752	0,05748	0,05767	0,05781	0,05765	0,05741	0,05719
Kilkis	0,08665	0,08670	0,08679	0,08690	0,08694	0,08702	0,08720	0,08735	0,08731	0,08698	0,08677	0,08630
Kozani	0,11680	0,11653	0,11647	0,11618	0,11607	0,11618	0,11614	0,11579	0,11584	0,11563	0,11536	0,11518
Korinthia	0,11211	0,11265	0,11213	0,11197	0,11195	0,11145	0,11173	0,11213	0,11250	0,11211	0,11192	0,11156
Kyklades	0,09587	0,09605	0,09666	0,09707	0,09744	0,09726	0,09741	0,09746	0,09739	0,09736	0,09711	0,09690
Lakonia	0,09132	0,09128	0,09096	0,09094	0,09085	0,09087	0,09075	0,09086	0,09091	0,09059	0,09060	0,09027
Larisa	0,15940	0,15887	0,15868	0,15831	0,15794	0,15768	0,15743	0,15720	0,15684	0,15677	0,15689	0,15700
Lasithi	0,08084	0,08091	0,08101	0,08118	0,08126	0,08153	0,08143	0,08126	0,08107	0,08091	0,08068	0,08039
Lesvos	0,09834	0,09780	0,09791	0,09773	0,09747	0,09795	0,09782	0,09766	0,09734	0,09709	0,09662	0,09628
Lefkada	0,04432	0,04430	0,04397	0,04395	0,04388	0,04407	0,04397	0,04427	0,04450	0,04428	0,04420	0,04404
Magnisia	0,13494	0,13474	0,13486	0,13471	0,13465	0,13437	0,13411	0,13371	0,13340	0,13317	0,13285	0,13244

Messinia	0,12229	0,12225	0,12226	0,12220	0,12205	0,12184	0,12160	0,12141	0,12123	0,12076	0,12031	0,11984
Xanthi	0,09487	0,09475	0,09511	0,09511	0,09521	0,09526	0,09533	0,09546	0,09547	0,09551	0,09576	0,09584
Pella	0,11303	0,11287	0,11287	0,11284	0,11282	0,11278	0,11283	0,11296	0,11332	0,11307	0,11274	0,11244
Pieria	0,10505	0,10518	0,10542	0,10559	0,10568	0,10563	0,10577	0,10584	0,10590	0,10574	0,10573	0,10563
Preveza	0,07260	0,07254	0,07227	0,07212	0,07196	0,07161	0,07154	0,07133	0,07112	0,07089	0,07082	0,07067
Rethimno	0,08167	0,08189	0,08217	0,08251	0,08280	0,08290	0,08314	0,08310	0,08318	0,08308	0,08316	0,08318
Rodopi	0,09965	0,09944	0,09947	0,09942	0,09933	0,09927	0,09911	0,09910	0,09893	0,09874	0,09877	0,09873
Samos	0,06279	0,06254	0,06254	0,06247	0,06236	0,06233	0,06219	0,06190	0,06163	0,06145	0,06123	0,06096
Serres	0,13216	0,13201	0,13186	0,13175	0,13166	0,13148	0,13150	0,13115	0,13072	0,13017	0,12952	0,12893
Trikala	0,11163	0,11097	0,11061	0,10984	0,10932	0,10909	0,10866	0,10822	0,10780	0,10736	0,10730	0,10698
Fthiotida	0,12299	0,12301	0,12259	0,12245	0,12240	0,12226	0,12202	0,12186	0,12173	0,12122	0,12032	0,12005
Florina	0,06982	0,06969	0,06943	0,06931	0,06916	0,06916	0,06916	0,06913	0,06913	0,06903	0,06883	0,06864
Fokida	0,05805	0,05840	0,05778	0,05774	0,05767	0,05788	0,05781	0,05800	0,05811	0,05775	0,05762	0,05741
Chalkidiki	0,09171	0,09218	0,09206	0,09237	0,09262	0,09295	0,09314	0,09334	0,09339	0,09325	0,09314	0,09295
Chania	0,11245	0,11237	0,11291	0,11313	0,11332	0,11358	0,11392	0,11403	0,11422	0,11403	0,11366	0,11356
Chios	0,06967	0,06935	0,06916	0,06900	0,06884	0,06863	0,06848	0,06818	0,06779	0,06746	0,06740	0,06708

ECONOMIC DEVELOPMENTS IN ALBANIA IN THE FRAMEWORK OF THE GREEK ECONOMIC CRISIS

LINDITA ROVA AND ILIRJANA ZYBERI

Abstract

With the end of the totalitarian era thousands of Albanian emigrants crossed the border with Greece. Nowadays more than 600.000 Albanians (according to EUROSTAT 640.000 Albanians live and work in Greece) officially live and work in the neighbour country, but the nonofficial number is much greater. Thus, both countries are organically linked to each other. Together with the whole of the Balkan region and the whole world Greece is suffering from the recent economic crisis, which started initially from the United States of America as a financial one. The aim of this paper is to analyze the consequences of the Greek economic crisis on Albanian economy such as: the decrease of the remittances from the emigrants, the decrease in the import level associated with the devaluation of the domestic currency, the reduction of Foreign Direct Investments including even the Greek ones, the prospect of the continuation or not of foreign development programs financed by Greece. After having a full image of the situation some recommendations for the Albanian Government are given.

Introduction

The last crisis spread rapidly throughout the world, including Europe, which originally remained passive waiting for further developments of the situation in America, assessing at the same time possible impacts of this crisis on the European Community. This crisis divided the once "powerful" states of the Eurozone into two big groups: the powerful countries and the weak countries (Portugal, Italy, Greece, and Spain – PIGS as they were nicknamed by the London financiers). With the starting of 2010 Greece revealed its problems with the high debt and budget imbalance. Greece and Albania are neighbour countries with a lot of connections between them. In the conditions of an increasingly globalized world economy, the success or the crisis of a country is, in all probability, certain to affect the economy of other countries. The higher the speed at which the impact spreads to other countries, the more closely linked the countries are in terms of economic interaction, which is perfectly illustrated by the relationship between Greece and Albania. The Greek economic crisis and its developments in the following months should not be simply seen as "a phenomenon occurring in the neighbouring country", but as an element which is certainly going to affect the Albanian business and economy.

The paper is divided into five parts starting with a brief description of the last economic crisis and a few words about the Greek crisis. The aim of this paper is to analyze the consequences of the Greek economic crisis to the Albanian economy using official data revealed by Albanian institutions. However, the data collected pose two problems:

Firstly: the official data were released until the third quarter of 2009 so, it was not possible to find data beyond that point of time.

Secondly: we strongly believe that Albanian attitudes have interfered with the official data in a misleading way.

In order to show the effect of the crisis on the Albanian economy a survey based on 200 questionnaires filled out by different subjects in the South of Albania (30% of them businesses and self-employed people) was conducted. As in all surveys based on questionnaires the interviewees are not totally sincere. Finally, some general recommendations are given.

A brief description of the last economic crisis

The financial crises' history goes back a long time ago. Form 1863 the author Joseph Holbrey expressed his desire to identify their cause and find the proper remedy to each crisis. Studying his conclusions, it can be said, with no hesitation, that crises are the same harmful and they do not depend on the period they happened. The recent economic crisis which started in the USA in the year 2008 rapidly spread in almost the whole world. Over the last decade many countries around the world were hit painfully by such events, but global economy was not affected by such crisis since 1929

(The Great Depression). The early examples of financial crisis are Mexico (1973-1982) and Argentina (1973-1981). A few years later several countries in Europe (1992-1993), Mexico again (1994-1995), East Asia and Russia (1998) followed by Brazil (1999). The years after Turkey suffered a financial crisis (2000-2001) and Argentina (2001-2002) too.

According to Kissinger (2008) various specific reasons have been defined as being responsible for every crisis so far, but it is certain that all of them have definitely two things in common:

- Speculations beyond control and
- Underestimation of risk.

Pol Samuelson, the 94-year-old dean expresses himself as follows: "The fault for this crisis is ours, it is America's fault. The economic disaster was born in Wall Street and there were our professors- frankly speaking, some students of mine- who developed the theories on the distribution of risks leading to this situation; theories, which were technically accurate, although they failed to take into consideration the human greed" (Gaggi 2009, p. 53).

The last crisis spread rapidly throughout the world, including Europe, which originally remained passive waiting for further developments of the situation in America, assessing at the same time possible impacts of this crisis on the European Community. Despite the "strong resistance put up by the anti-crisis alliance" for almost two years, the American financial crisis changed into an economic crisis, deeply affecting many countries in the world. The European Union claimed a real increase of its GDP of 1% in the year 2009 compared to 3% in the previous year, whereas the GDP levels in the USA seemed to fall from 2% in the 2008 to 1.3% in 2009 (EUROSTAT, European Commission 2010). The last crisis rocked the foundations of the banking system and generated what could be defined, above all, as a loss of confidence. Gaggi (2009, p. 88) says: "The last hours of the Lehman Brothers are a part of history, which will be written and rewritten, even though this bankruptcy is considered as a demarcation line in the history of modern capitalism."

Taken as a countervailing measure against the recession caused by the financial crisis, the USA decided to make a figure available which approximates to 6% of the DNP, supporting the up to then approved state interference in the banking system with the intention of helping its recovery. The European Union did not manage to provide more than 1.5% of the income generated by its member countries. Europe suffers the disadvantage of a more complicated administration brought about by the fact that each of its member countries is allowed to follow a policy which is considered to be perfectly reasonable by its authorities. Thus, France supported its enterprises; Great Britain reduced its VAT from 17.5% to 15% with the intention of increasing the consumption. Despite a slight interference in the exports, Germany does not intent to interfere by adopting a supplementary package of fiscal measures aiming boost the economy, as UK did.

Nevertheless, the prospect that the United Europe would remain unaffected by the crisis, seemed to last but a short while. The first inflictions were felt in the summer of 2009, in the French and Swiss banking system. Later the impact reached The United Kingdom with a total nationalization of some institutions and a partial nationalization of The Royal Bank of Scotland. Germany was obliged to spend 20% of GDP to avoid the phenomenon of bankruptcy in its banking system whereas Holland nationalized ABN, the Dutch branch of Fortis Group.

The financial crisis divided the once "powerful" states of the Eurozone into two big groups: the powerful countries and the weak countries (Portugal, Italy, Greece, and Spain – PIGS as they were nicknamed by the London financiers).

The Greek crisis

At a time when welcome news about the recovery of the situation from the crisis was coming from the American continent, bad news for a crisis situation, with a major impact on the South-eastern Europe was reported from the heart of the Balkans, from Greece, -the sixth member of the CEM, a member of the European Union as well as Euro zone. Among the most important bonds between the situation in Greece and South eastern Europe are:

- Greek banks have credited several banks in the region with approximately 55 billion Euro ($70bn), or 22% of GDP. Four of the major Greek banks are supossed to control 40% of banking in FYROM, 35% in Albania, 30% in Bulgaria, 20% in Romania (Stoke et al., 2010).

- One fourth of the Greek exports is conducted with Southeast European countries. In terms of importance for the Greek exports, the Bulgarian market is ranked fourth, with 6% of the total amount.

Greece occupies only 2.7% of the Eurozone. The question whether Greece is the problem of Europe or Europe itself is facing problems, is a subject of heated debate. The specific gravity of the countries that have been deeply affected by this crisis in the Eurozone, such as Greece, Spain, Portugal and Ireland, otherwise considered to be for the moment the most seriously ailing "patients" of Europe, is naturally not of considerable significance for the economy and finances of the Eurozone. However, they became "Achilles' heel" in the financial complications that Eurozone is developing and is certainly going to develop in the future.

The concern is made more real when analyzing the latest information that Greek obligations worth 230 thousand Euros were bought by European banks, which may turn out to be a "Lehman Brothers" for the Eurozone. Nevertheless, some of the European countries, especially Germany, were astringent and hesitant in their willingness to help Greece ease the burden of the crisis, for fear that other countries followed the same scenario, in order to balance their public finances, thus setting a dangerous precedent. In a few words, the reasons for the Greek crisis are:

Firstly, budgetary and financial imbalance Greece has a high budget deficit of 12,7%, of which 3.7% is a home loan and 9% is a foreign loan at a time when the Maastricht Treaty has set the budget deficit limit to 3% and the Greek Government claimed to run a budget deficit of 6%. At the end of April 2010, ratings agency Moody's downgraded Greece's credit rating by one notch to A3 (which means "state bankruptcy") from A2, citing in part the upward revision to the country's deficit and debt levels. The agency said the figures underline the challenges the Greek government faces in meeting its deficit-reduction goals (Goldstain, 2010). Eurostat, the European Union statistics agency, pushed up its estimate of Greece's 2009 deficit to 13.6% of GDP, compared to Greece's earlier projection of 12.7%. Eurostat reiterated concerns about the veracity of Greece's budget data (Whats, 2010). The total debt of the Greece is almost 125% (Manasse, 2010) of GDP, whereas there are other sources valuating it 170.5%.

Secondly, unreal statistics released by the Greek government for several years, starting with the year 2001. Greece underwent a number of assessments and was given strong negative opinions regarding the quality, transparency and the reality of the figures and indices provided by its authorities to measure macroeconomic and financial indicators (Seseri, 2009). More specifically, with regard to compilation issues, the investigation of Eurostat has revealed weaknesses in the national services principally responsible for EDP data: the National Statistical Service of Greece (NSSG), the General Accounting Office (GAO) and the Ministry of Finance (MOF) (EUROSTAT, Europian Commission 2010). It is difficult to say that the figures were deliberately manipulated, or that the statistical system could not manage to accurately reflect the country's economic and financial situation due to inefficiency. However, it is absolutely certain that the unreal figures which were on the basis of the most important decisions determining the economic and financial policies (for almost 10 years), had a major negative impact on the current crisis situation.

Thirdly, compared to the economy of the other countries of the European Union in general and that of the Eurozone member countries, in particular, Greece has a fragile and uncompetitive economy. Since 2001, the time when Greece entered the Eurozone, the Greek economic growth, although high and much appreciated for its growth rates (with an average of 4.2% annually (Civici, 2010a), is considered to be "a delicate economic growth, which is not well-grounded on long-term, sustainable basis." This growth was brought about by major public investments, by frequent and often artificial pay rises and an increase in domestic demand (factors which provided the basis for the Greek financial crisis), by the initial effect of the use of Euro as a strong currency, etc.

On the other hand, the Greek economy seems to reflect a weak exporting and competing potential, a growing trade deficit, a substandard productive and industrial sector, a tourist industry affected by the world crisis, etc. (Angjeli 2009). The above mentioned are considered to be the major factors that caused the current Greek crisis. At the same time these factors are predicted to make it more difficult for the Greek authorities to defuse the grave crisis situation and to generate positive results in the near future.

Despite the difficulties, the European Commission is going to approve an economic plan for Greece, alongside with putting it under "a special, monthly monitoring". The main aim of this plan is the reduction of the budget deficit from 8.7% in 2010 to2.8% by the end of 2012. The Greek government has announced a special, ambitious plan of action and reforms aiming at balancing the public finances and stabilising the financial situation.

In the conditions of an increasingly globalized world economy, the success or the crisis of a country is, in all probability, certain to affect the economy of other countries. The higher the speed at which the impact spreads to other countries, the more closely linked the countries are in terms of economic interaction. This is perfectly illustrated by the relationship between Greece and Albania. The Greek economic crisis and its developments in the following months should not be simply seen as "a phenomenon occurring in the neighbouring country", but as an element which is certainly going to affect the Albanian business and economy (Civici 2010b). We hope that the strict measures undertaken by the Greek government under the close and careful monitoring of IMF, as well as the significant help provided by the European Union, despite the conflicting opinions and interests of its member countries, will soon generate some elements of recovery in the Greek economy. Nevertheless, the Albanian government should take immediate action and should adopt policies with the intention of minimizing the negative impact of the Greek economic crisis on the Albanian economy, particularly on that of the Southern region (Civici 2010 b).

The impact of the Greek crisis on Albanian economy

There has been a steady increase (of 6% on average), in the Albanian economy during the last 10 years.

Graph 1. Real increase in GDP in the course of years

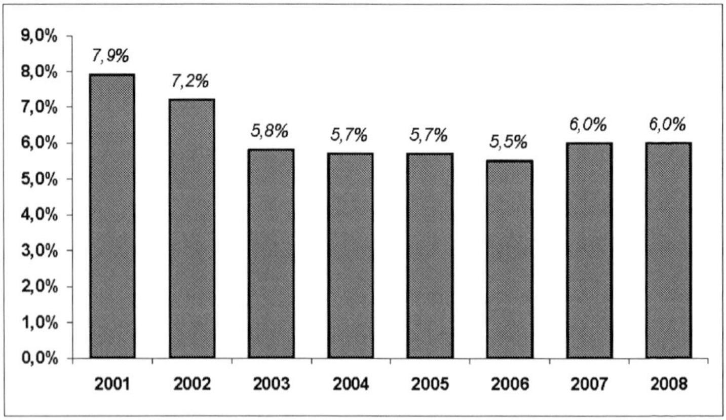

Source: INSTAT, Albania.

The economic pattern of the Albanian transition was supported by such factors as the emigrant remittances, large-scale denationalization, especially in the last two years, soft loans, etc. The Albanian economy has not yet defined its main priority pillars, which are going to support a sustainable future development of the economy. Unfortunately, we are not only closely connected to, but also dependent on all world developments, especially those of the neighbouring countries. Albania has an underdeveloped industrial sector characterized by an extremely low level of competitiveness (products "made in Albania" are not only limited in number but also unable to compete in the global market).

Even though Albania is one of the countries with the highest level of the economic freedom, it is far from being a preferable destination for foreign investors. In the last two years, the level of foreign direct investments has increased significantly, but the only factor responsible for this increase has been the denationalization process. One of the pillars of the development of the Albanian economy is considered to be the tourism industry, but with the neighbouring countries such as Greece and Turkey, whose tourism industry is much more developed and satisfies the requirements of a high quality standard, even in this sector it is difficult to have high expectations. At a time when the governments around the world were talking about a possible cut off in the pays and pensions in the framework of a crisis situation which was being transformed into a deep economic recession, Albania went on with its policy of pension and pay rise, the motto being " we are safe from the crisis". The change in IMF status in 2008 from "enforcer" to "advisor" is partly responsible for running the budget deficit out of control, almost doubling it in value. If the fact that in the years to come the foreign loans interest is expected to reach 900 million dollars is taken into account, it is not difficult to jump into the conclusion that a crisis situation similar to that in Greece may develop in Albania in the next two or three years.

A heated debate has followed since the beginning of the crisis situation in Greece, about the possible impact of this crisis on the Albanian economy. Some experts supported the idea that the Greek crisis would profoundly affect our economy. However, some other experts were optimistic and were quick to announce that we were on the safe side.

What indices might deteriorate with the Greek crisis?

A decrease in the emigrant remittances

Greece is the country with the highest number of Albanian emigrants; about 700.000 (Ministry of Labour and Social Welfare) Albanians have lived and worked there since 1992 providing income for the Albanian economy in form of remittances. These remittances have been substantial both in relative and absolute terms, culminating in the year 2007 (graph no 2). The following year (2008) presented a sharp decrease both in their level (16% less than in 2007) and in percentage of the GDP (from 14% of the GDP in 2005 to 9.2% in 2008).

As it was expected, the emigrant remittances continued to drop in the first quarter of the year 2009, resulting in a decrease of nearly 6% compared to the same period of the previous year and nearly 19% compared to the same period of 2007 and this trend continued even the second and the third quarter. The decline was, by far, a direct reflection of the impact of the world crisis. So far, there are no statistical data for the whole of the 2009, yet the level of the remittances in the first half, can be considered as a first negative sign for the future expectations.

According to IMF and IOM, emigrant remittances, have played a significant part in the poverty alleviation, especially in the mountainous region. Emigrant remittances, though considerable, have not played a major role in the investment level and have not contributed financially to a sustainable development of Albania (IOM, IASCI, 2009).

Graph 2. Emigrant remittances in several years

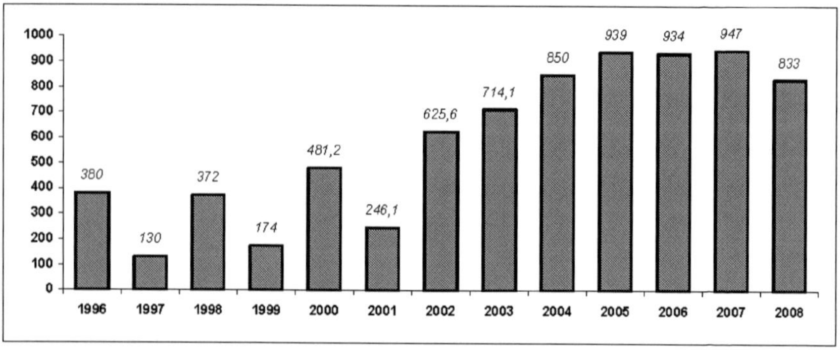

Source: INSTAT, Albania, Bank of Albania, and IOM Albania.

However, the experience of countries with a long emigration history has shown that the focus of specialist attention should not be as much on the influx of the remittances as on the development of proper financial mechanisms for the absorption of emigrant savings, which, in Albania, seem to be 4.2 (Gëdeshi, 2002) times higher than the remittances level. The Albanian government has not yet come up with any plan or mechanism to take in these savings and is not prepared yet for such a decline in the emigrant remittance level.

Deterioration in the foreign trade

The current account balance is a significant indicator, especially for countries and economies in transition, which are making great efforts to approximate to developed economies. Albania is a country with low exporting potential. Its exported products are not only limited in quantity, but also in value. The Albanian exports constitute mainly of minerals, working on materials on order demand (the row materials are imported; the manufacturing process is done in Albania and the destination for final consumptions is the country from which we imported them initially) called "fassons", which, at the same time, is a way of labour export, and recently electricity export. In the course of the last twenty years the Albanian imports have on average been 3 times higher than its exports (Bank of Albania, 2008).

Graph 3. The level of current account balance, imports, exports and trade balance in several years (in million Euros).

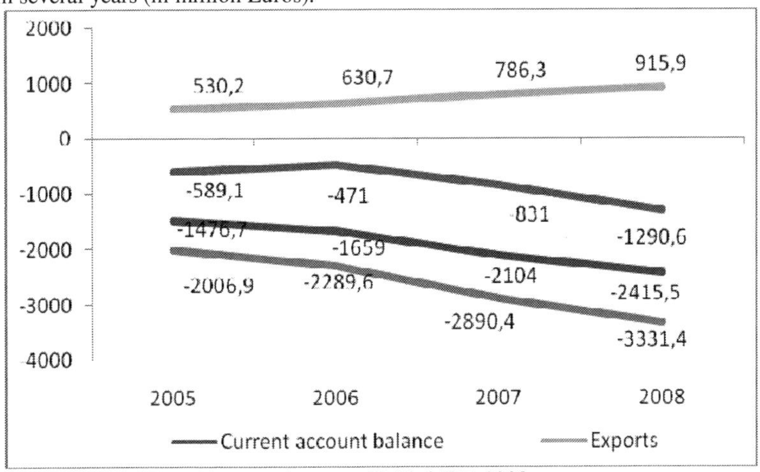

Source: Bank of Albania annual reports 2006, 2007, 2008

The official data on foreign trade for the first quarter of the year 2009 show a decrease in the import-export level. According to these data, the current transactions conducted in the period from July to September 2009 are estimated to have reached 2.68 billion Euros being 7.4% higher than the transactions in the same period of the previous year. The current account balance deficit during this period reached the figure 330.6 million Euros, thus recording an annual increase of 43%. The following table shows the results of a study of some indicators of the Balance of Payments in the third quarter of several successive years.

Table 1. Some elements of Balance of Payments in the third quarter of successive years

	In million euros				In percentage of GDP			
	T3' 06	T3' 07	T3' 08	T3' 09	T3' 06	T3' 07	T3' 08	T3' 09
Current account	-106.9	-170.1	-230.7	-330.6	-8.2	-8.4	-13.9	-17.3
Trade balance	-415.3	-527.4	-601.9	-590.8	-22.7	-25.1	-27.9	-28.4
Exports	153.2	197.3	242.0	201.8	8.3	9.7	10.9	9.2
Imports	-568.5	-724.7	-843.9	-792.6	-31.0	-34.9	-38.7	-37.6
Net current transfers	276.4	271.7	229.2	205.7	13.4	13.6	11.7	10.5

Source: Bank of Albania, Statement of monetary policies for 2009 first and second semi year.

As it can be clearly seen in the table no 1, if the figures are compared to those of the same period of the year 2008, all the indicators of the Payment Balance deteriorated in the third quarter of the 2009. This deterioration was a consequence of the interaction between two factors:

- The Albanian impossibility to decently compete in the global market and
- The impact of the world crisis.

Only 8% of Albanian foreign trade is conducted with Greece (Bank of Albania, 2008) and this is the reason why some analysts believe that the Greek crisis will not have a profound impact on the Albanian economy. Due to lack of data, this article cannot analyze in detail the impact of the Greek crisis on the Albanian foreign trade. However, it can certainly be said that it will deeply affect the economic developments in the Southern region.

The reduction in Greek investments in Albania and a decrease in the aiding programs

A possible impact of the Greek crisis is assessed to be the possible reduction of the Greek Investments in Albania and a decrease in the Greek aiding programs. We came to this conclusion analysing the fact that the financial problems in Greece will serve as a stumbling block to the projects of the Greek investors interested to invest in the Balkans, Albania included.

The impact on the small business developments, especially in the south of Albania

The south of Albania is the region which, due to direct bordering with Greece, is likely to experience more seriously the effects of the Greek crisis. The increase of raw material prices as well as the price increase in every element of production such as the increase in the price of electricity & combustible materials, the problematic process of supplying for the businesses that operate on material demanded from the consumer (fassons), particularly the various anomalies in their liquidation system, will be some of the problems that the small business in the South of Albania is going to face. These problems may bring about an increase in the unemployment level, a decline in the Tax income, a decrease in the consuming level, a general economic contraction and may result in economic stagnancy for the region. The building sector will be particularly affected by the impact of the Greek crisis, for the reason that the building sector has been mostly operating on emigrants' demand to buy Real Estates.

The prospect of emigrant return

The possible emigrant return, which may be permanent or temporary (until the recovery of the situation) might be one of the consequences of the crisis and the policies adopted by the Greek government in close cooperation with the European Community. This scenario will be accompanied by both negative and positive effects for the Albanian economy. One of the most important negative effects would be the increase in the unemployment level which is already high. If we think that most of the returned emigrants decide to live permanently in their country, then we could speak about positive economic effects for the Albanian economy. The investment of their savings in the Albanian economy combined with the knowledge and the experience gained in the country of emigration would be a factor with positive impact in the sustainable development of the country.

In order to achieve this, the Albanian Government and the decision-making authorities should adopt encouraging policies related to these investments, such as their orientation towards spheres of priority of the Albanian economy, fiscal facilities etc.

The sensitivity of the southern region inhabitants towards the crisis

In order to make this study more complete, a survey was carried out in the South of Albania, namely in Gjirokastra, Saranda and Tepelena. It was believed that the South of Albania would serve as the best survey environment if we were to study the inhabitants' perceptions related to the Greek crisis. For this reason, 200 questionnaires were filled out in the above mentioned towns in proportion to their population. 30% of the questionnaires were answered by business and self-employed people. The following graph represents the findings.

Graph 4. Answers of the question: Are you aware of the Greek economic crisis?

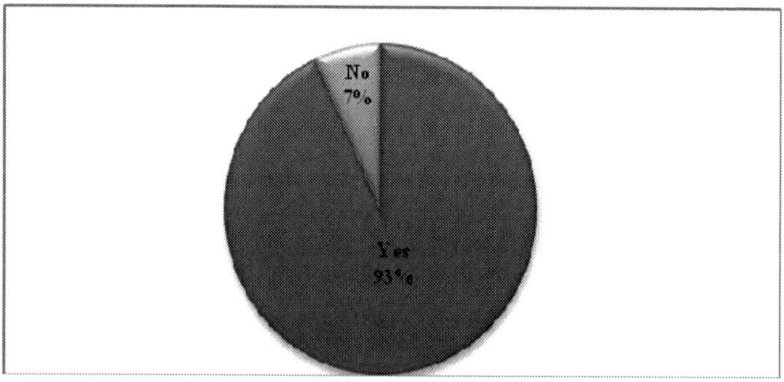

As it can clearly be seen in the graph above, 93% of the surveyed subjects confess that they are well-informed about the crisis situation in Greece.

Graph 5. Answers of the question: Do you think that the Greek crisis will affect the Albania economy?

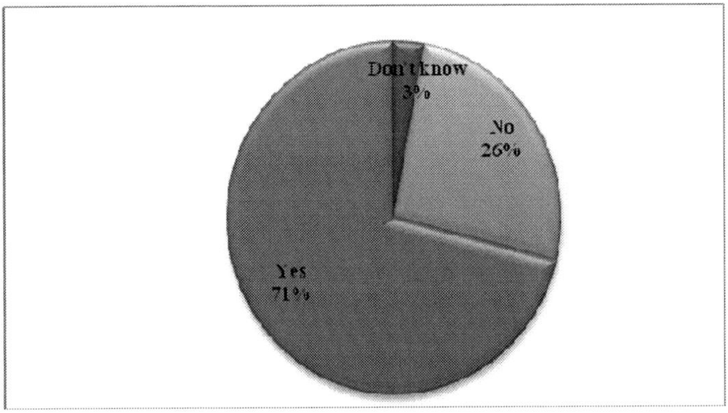

71% of the subjects have expressed the opinion that the economic crisis in Greece will have its impact on the Albanian economy. Further answers express their selection of the four out of eight economic elements most likely to be affected by the crisis. They appear to be as follows:

1. Price increase in the goods imported from Greece.
2. Decrease in the emigrant remittances
3. Devaluation of the domestic currency towards Euro
4. Reduction or cessation of the old-age pensions given to the Greek minority population in Albania

Graph 6. Answers to the question: Do you think that due to the crisis a part of Albanian emigrants will turn back in their country?

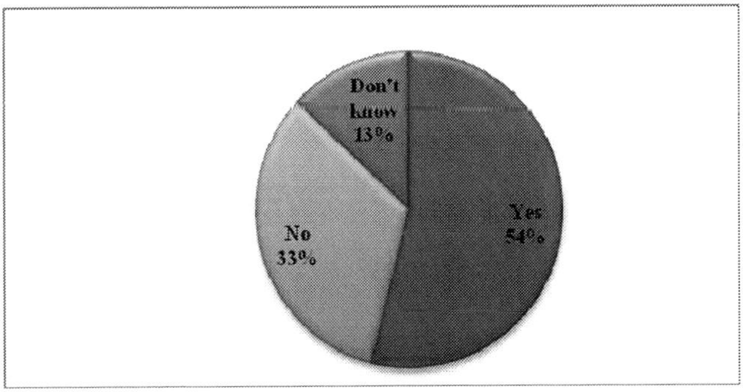

The graph makes it clear that most of the subjects in the survey express the opinion that, due to the crisis, a considerable part of the emigrants in Greece will be obliged to come back to their country of origin.

The answers to the questionnaire compiled for the business and self-employed people provide us with the following findings.

Graph 7. Answers to the question: Is your business related to the Greek economy?

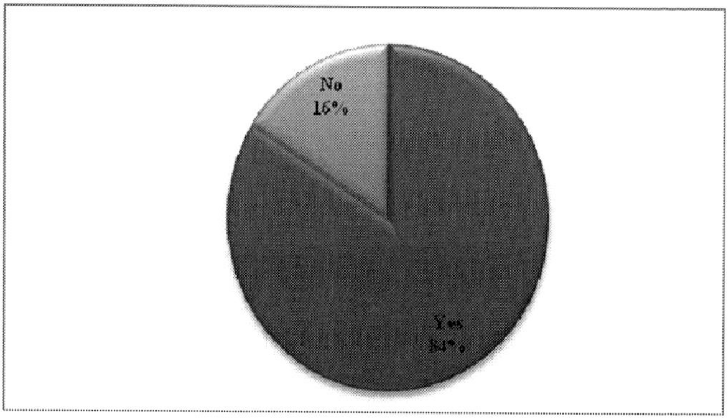

If yes, in which of the following aspects are you related to the Greek economy?

Graph 8. The nature of the relations between Greece and South Albania businesses

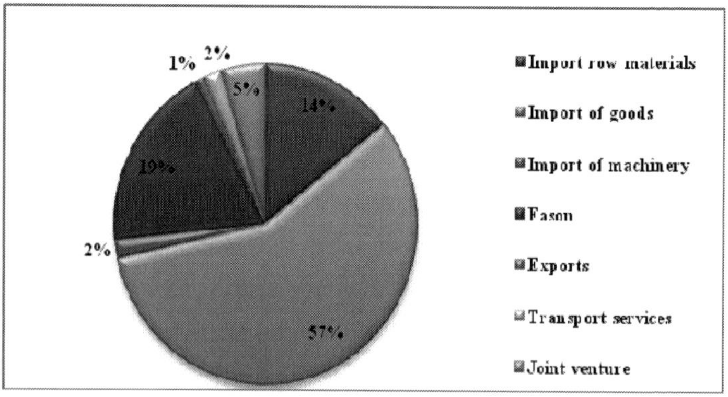

The businesses whose relation to Greece is of the raw material import-export nature or transport services gave the following answers to the question "Has the price of raw material, combustible materials and other goods imported by Greece gone up?"

Graph 9. Answers to the question: Is increased the price of goods, row materials and combustible materials?

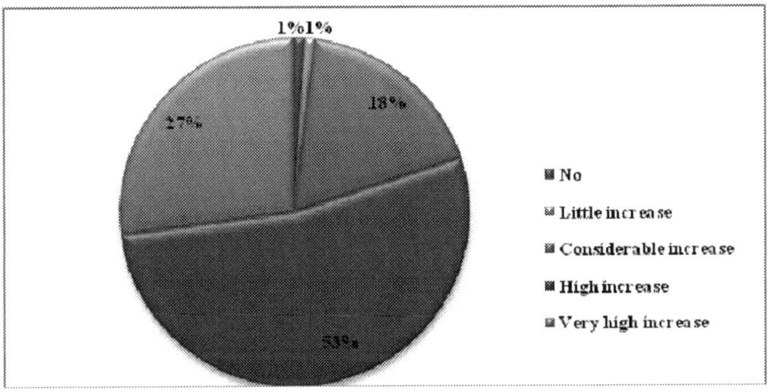

The following two questions were asked to the representatives of those business companies which offered servicing and processing of materials whose final destination was the Greek market. This was done for two reasons: first, to see how much the crisis had affected the supplying rate of these businesses and second, the order liquidation process.

Graph 10. Answers to the question: Did the supplying rate deteriorate the last four months?

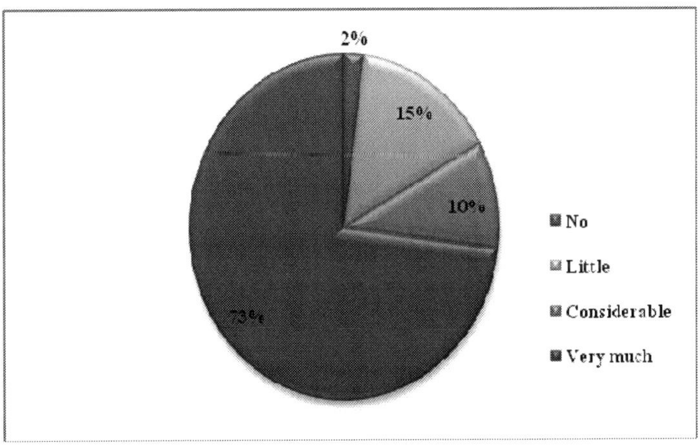

Graph 11. Answers to the question: Did you have problems with the order liquidation in the last four months?

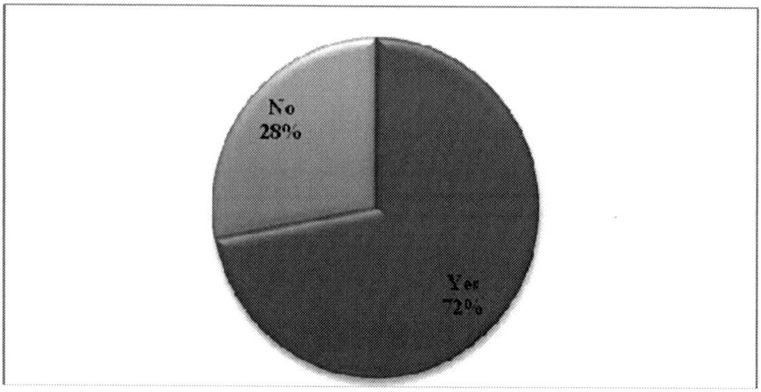

The last questions in the questionnaire have to do with the sensitivity towards the Greek banks, which play a significant role in the banking market in the Southern region of Albania.

Graph 12. Answers to the question: Do you have a bank account or a deposit in the Greek banks in Albania?

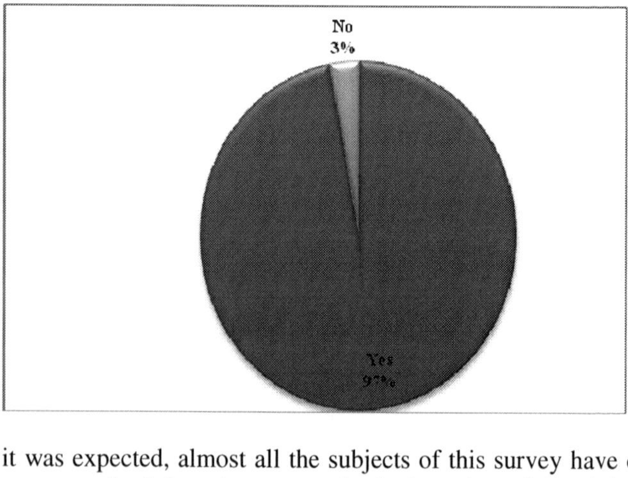

As it was expected, almost all the subjects of this survey have current bank accounts or/and deposit accounts in the branches of Greek banks in Albania. The two following questions assess the interviewees' sensitivity or fear of this Greek crisis being passed on from Mother-banks in Greece to their branches in Albania.

Graph 13. Answers to the question: have you ever thought to transfer your accounts in a non-Greek bank?

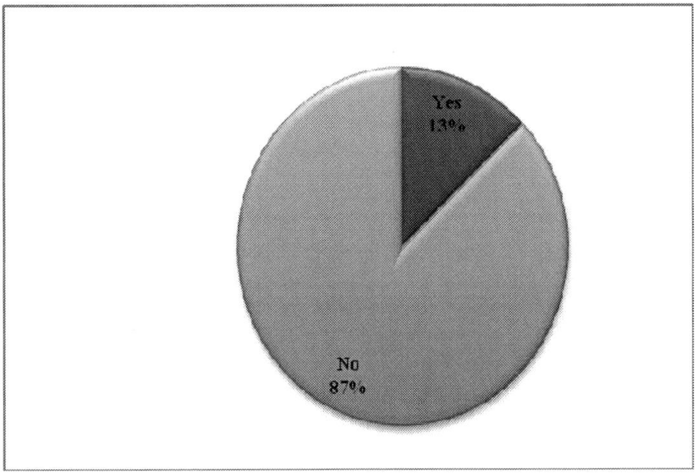

The last question was asked to those subjects, who have given the answer "yes" to the question: "Have you ever thought to transfer your accounts in a non- Greek bank?" In answer to the question if they had really carried out the transfer, it resulted that only 5% had done so, whereas the others continued to work normally with the same banks as before. This indicator makes us believe that the business in Albania is not feeling threatened by the transferring of the Greek crisis from the Greek banks into their Greek branches in Albania. The Bank of Albania has played a major role in this respect by continuously declaring that these branches are Albanian entities and the monitoring system utilized by the Bank of Albania minimizes the risks mentioned above almost to elimination.

Conclusions and recommendations

The analysis of the indicators mentioned above combined with the results of the questionnaire allows us to fully accept that the Greek crisis has undoubted impact on the Albanian economy. The degree to which this phenomenon will be expressed depends on manifold factors of which the most important are:

- The ability of the Greek state to renew its economy and to defuse the crisis.
- The policy going to be followed by the Albanian government to minimize the effects of the crisis on the Albanian economy. It is a must that institutions responsible for it follow closely the dynamics of this crisis in the neighbouring country and every possible negative impact it might have on the Albanian economy and react quickly with protective measures. The ministry of Finance and the Bank of Albania should be the two leading actors, playing the most important role in this respect.
- This crisis should serve as an example for the Albanian Government, which should learn a lesson and benefit from the experience, in order to avoid such a crisis situation in Albania by an estimation of the real risks of the public loan and the budget deficit, taking into consideration the low rates of the development of the Albanian economy, which, although not accepted as such by the Albanian Government, are declared to be problematic by international institutions such as IMF and World Bank.

References

Angjeli, A., 2009, Dy vjet pas krizës globale, *Panorama Journal*, 276, issue, p. 13. (Two years after the global crisis).

Annual Report, Bank of Albania, 2006, 2007, 2008, available at: www.bankofalbania.org

Bank of Albania, 2009, Monetary policies settlement for the first semi year 2009, *Bank of Albania publications*, available at: www.bankofalbani.org

—. 2009, Monetary policies settlement for the second semi year 2009, *Bank of Albania publications*, available at: www.bankofalbani.org

Civici, A., 2010a, Leksionet e krizës greke për Shqipërinë, *Gazeta Panorama*, 225, p. 14. (The lessons of Greek crisis for Albania).

—. 2010b, Kriza financiare greke dhe Shqiperia, *Panorama*, 187, p. 12 . (The greek financial crisis and Albania).

—. 2010c, Leksionet e krizës greke për Shqipërinë, *Gazeta Shqiptare*, 219, issue, p. 11. (The lessons of the Greek crisis for Albania.).

European Commission, 2010, *Report on Greek government deficit and debt statistics*, Brussels, 8.1.2010, COM final, available at: http://epp.eurostat.ec.europa.eu/cache/ITY_PUBLIC/COM_2010_REPORT_GREEK/EN/COM_2010_REPORT_GREEK-EN.PDF

Gaggi, M.,. 2009, *La valagna, Dalla crisi Americana alla recessione globale*, Gius, Laretza & Figli. (The avalanche from American crisis to the global recession).

Gedeshi, I., 2002, Role of Remittances from Albanian Emigrants and Their Influence in the Country's Economy, *Eastern European Economics*, 40, p. 5.

Goldstain, S., 2010, Eurostat chides Greek data as bonds slammed, LONDON (MarketWatch), available at: www.marketwatch.com/story/eurostat-greek-data-as-bonds-slammed-again-2010-04-22

IASCI and IOM Vienna, *Maximizing the development impact of migration related Financial Flows and Investment from Austria to BiH* ", IOM (International Organization for Migration), IASCI (International Agency for Source Country Information) available at: http://www.iom.int/jahia/Jahia/activities/europe/south-eastern-europe/bosnia-and-herzegovina#md

Kissinger, H., 2008, Paradoksi i dyfishtë i globalizimit, The International Herald Tribune, (Globalizations and its discontents). Available at: www.henryakissinger.com/articles/iht052908.html

Manasse, P., 2010, *Help Greece save herself*, Roubini Global Economy.

Seseri, R., 2009, Kriza greke, kriza shqiptare dhe te dyja sebashku, *Shekulli*, 227, p 12.(Greek crisis, Albanian crisis and the both).

Stokes, M., Vucotic, J., 2010, What Greece's fiscal crisis could mean for Eastern Europe, *Roubini Global Economy*, available at: http://www.roubini.com/euro-monitor/258437/what_greece___s_fiscal _ risis_could_mean_for_eastern_europe

Whats, W.L., 2010, *Moody's cuts Greek credit rating*, London (MarketWatch).

QUALITATIVE ANALYSIS OF IN-HOUSE SUSTAINABILITY INDICATORS: THE CASE OF MANUFACTURING SECTOR IN EAST MACEDONIA AND TRACE REGION, GREECE

MICHAEL NIKOLAIDIS, CHRISTOS BATZIOS, ATHANASIOS MANDILAS, ATHANASIOS NIKOLAIDIS AND PERSEFONI POLYCHRONIDOU

Abstract

The role of the manufacturing sector in the economic activity of a region and in general of a country is discussed widely nowadays, and in contradiction to the increasing role of tertiary sector. Today, even though, manufacturing constitutes an important sector of the economy, the growth and more specifically the sustainability of the manufacturing enterprises presents significant problems and particularly at the less developed regions. Under this frame, we considered that, the estimation and the qualitative analysis of in-house sustainability indicators/ratios of the sector will lead to useful ascertainments that can constitute a base for the elongation of the enterprises' life duration, as well as for the recognition of priorities in research, aiming at the configuration of a more effective manufacturing policy for the particular sector. For identifying precisely the in-house sustainability indicators of the manufacturing enterprises, we considered that the statistical research and analysis of these, based on various qualitative characteristics, will offer useful information.

Introduction

Nowadays, sustainability has become an operational issue for management (Reinhardt, 2000). Although, the concept of sustainability is understood intuitively; it remains difficult to express it in concrete operational terms but certainly entails the incorporation of the objectives of sustainable development, social equity, economic efficiency and environmental performance, into a company's operational practices (Labuschagne et al., 2003). However, the sustainability of a national economy, a total region or a firm must be considered in the context of the entity's overall economic activity (Reinhardt, 2000).

The manufacturing sector in Greece, despite its declining tendency, still constitutes one of the most core sectors (Chassid, 1980; KEPE, 1984b; Marinos, 1990). The continuously increasing importance of manufacturing for the Greek economy growth is attributed mainly to the fact that it is the one that mainly contains the best potentials for self-reliant growth against the rest of the sectors and generally is the key for the exploitation of new economy knowledge (Chassid and Katsos, 1992; Chassid et al., 2003; SEV, 2006). Moreover, manufacturing industry can attribute the regional growth in various ways (Xanthakis, 1989).

It has internationally been appreciated that many governments tried occasionally, via industrial policy, to divert the territorial distribution of growth towards confrontation of unemployment and income improvement of the least developed regions (Kottis, 1980; KEPE, 1984a; Walker and Chapman, 1992).

As long as it concerns the course of manufacturing sector of East-Macedonia and Thrace (EMT) Region, it has been done through various phases. Since the 70's, the sector began to present considerable remarks of dynamic growth which was intensified during the next decade. This growth resulted in an increase in employment in the industrial sector within the period 1978-1988 by 47.2% (Programme RITTS - EMT). The enterprises that were established, exploited primarily the low cost of labour and moreover the motives of the Development Law and other Operational Programmes.

Despite the fact that high developmental motives are provided in the manufacturing units of the Region, since the second half of the 90's onwards, the sector presented indications of weakening. Thus, many enterprises were unable to continue their operations, while others shrank or transplanted their activities into other countries of the Balkans and some others simply maintained their existence. So, the manufacturing sector of EMT Region devolved to recession and in particular without any obvious ways of recovering to exist (Labrianidis and Kalantaridis, 1997). Given the competition between 'peripheral' regions to supply firms and industries, the role of local physical and socio-economic factors which may induce investment is thought to be of considerable importance. However, the EMT Region appears to be relatively disadvantaged in comparison to other parts of the mainland (Labrianidis and Kalantaridis, 1997).

An interesting element of the manufacturing sector course in the particular Region is the ascertainment that many enterprises suspended their operations, or even stopped functioning completely. Indicatively, from the statistical data of the EMT Region's Chambers, can be identified that the enterprises that were deleted/erased over the last two decades from the Chambers' records, due to their termination, approaching e.g. for the prefectures of Kavala and Xanthi, 40% of the total registered enterprises (Chamber of Kavala, 2005; Chamber of Xanthi, 2008). Nowadays, the participation of the Region's manufacturing sector to GNP is 4.4%.

This implies the weakness of enterprises to cope with the requirements and challenges that are formed and also signifies the importance of a more general query about enterprises' survival and simultaneously the importance of an investigation about the reasons that cause such operational terminations. In other words, it is vital to investigate the factors that determine the enterprises' life duration of the Region and their inclusion in the wider frame of policies that are engraved and materialised in a national and/or regional level aiming to support entrepreneurship.

In this frame, the estimation and the qualitative analysis of enterprises' in-house sustainability factors/indicators present exceptional interest as much for the intermediary management agencies, as for the enterprises of the sector. The main objective of the present research is the imprinting and analysis of in-house indicators/ratios that influence the sustainability of manufacturing units in the EMT Region.

The research is structured as follows. In the next section the sustainability factors are determined. Section 3 describes the research methodology used, the sample selection and its structure, while in section 4 the Exploratory Factor Analysis process is presented. Moreover, section 5 notes the in-house sustainability indicators/factors and the variables/themes that they incorporate, and in section 6 the analysis of subjects'/themes' reliability of each in-house sustainability indicator is presented. Afterwards, section 7 determines the in-house sustainability indicators and section 8 provides a statistical analysis and investigation of the results of the in-house sustainability indicators based on every qualitative classification. At last, section 9 summarizes and concludes the research ascertainments.

Determination of the sustainability factors

From the existing relevant literature only few studies focus on basic factors that affect the sustainability of new established enterprises, too small or perennial, too big - multinational enterprises (Royal Dutch/Shell, 1983). Especially in Greece, at least to our knowledge, there are no studies focusing on the subject; there are only a few about the advantages and disadvantages of such enterprises operation and their general development problems (Papadopoulos, 1986; Katsou, 1988; Kiriazopoulos and Terzidis, 2000; Kanellopoulos, 1994; Karvounis, 2000). The first goal of the paper is to construct the questionnaire of the empirical research conducted on the manufacturing enterprises' sustainability of the EMT Region. Towards that direction, several factors which according to the relevant bibliography are important, are examined.

According to (Esenwein, 1961; Holt, 1972; Georgi and Giersch, 1977; Collins and Porras, 1994; Richard et al., 2000) most of the empirical research different samples concerning the enterprises' size, type, and branch are studied. Thus, their results cannot be compared. Most of the studies focus on specific matters of the enterprises' activities, like profitability, reasons of success or failure, reasons of suspension or shrinkage, problematic SME (Small and Medium-sized Enterprises), characteristics of successful enterprises (Peters and Waterm, 1990, Goddard and Willson, 1996; Hunt and Puetz, 2003). Likewise, in Greece, there are theoretical approaches which aim at the description and the interpretation of general causes for failure or interruption of the SME (Papadopoulos, 1986; Kiriazopoulos and Terzidis, 2000; Kanellopoulos, 1994; Karvounis, 2000). What is more, there are efforts at developing theoretical survival prediction models or practical manuals/guides for establishing successful enterprises (Feeser and Willard, 1990; Shepherd and Shanley, 1998; Shepherd at al., 2000).

In this paper, the determination and the systematization of the factors that affect the enterprises' sustainability is based on the internal and external environment of the enterprise, assuming the overall acceptance that the factors of that kind are explicitly relevant with the enterprises' survival (Wernerfelt, 1984; Collis and Montgomery, 1995; Theodoropoulos, 2003; Theriou, 2002). Furthermore, the factors' list is enriched by additional factors resulted by the experience of successful businessmen who are discriminated because of the long life duration and success of their business activities, by executives in charge of promoting and by our experience and estimation based on the specific business/economic environment in Greece.

Based on the above, the sustainability factors of the manufacturing sector in our Region (Nikolaidis, 2007) are grouped as follows:

- Function of production
- Function of sales and marketing,
- Function of research and development,
- Function of suppliers,
- Financial function,
- Organizational and managerial function,
- Entrepreneurship of the enterprise's founders,
- Enterprise's size,
- Enterprise's legal form,
- Enterprise's type and
- Enterprise's sector of activity.

Research Methodology

As it was mentioned above, the main objective of this research is to estimate and qualitatively analyse the in-house indicators that influence the longevity of EMT Region's manufacturing units. Therefore, in order to accomplish this objective the type of structured questionnaire with "closed answers" in a five-level Likert scale, which is considered as the most efficient tool for such type of measurements, was used. This scale is proposed from researchers as it allows the creation of a uniform structure, which is easy to be followed from the researcher, but also from the responder due to its similar potential answers. Also, in contrary to the satisfaction scale which tends, according to the decriers, to produce an excessively large number of positive answers, the Likert scale avoids this type of partiality as it allows the existence of negatively formulated questions (Dimitriadis, 2002).

Sample Selection

For the selection of the sample manufacturing enterprises the records of the existing manufacturing enterprises with legal form of a Public Limited Company (S.A.) or a Limited Company from the corresponding departments (handicraft and industrial department) of each prefecture's Chambers of EMT Region were used. The other categories of enterprises

(General Partnership, Limited Partnership, Sole Proprietorship, etc.) that are not obligated by the current law to publish their financial statements (Balance Sheet, Income Statement, etc.) were excluded.

Moreover, the enterprises that were presented in the records of Chambers but did not function anymore were excluded, as well as those that did not have at least five years life duration since their foundation. This was done in order to ensure a satisfactory level of long-lasting operational experience and activity, an essential element for the quality of research's results. Also, the methodology of stratified random sampling was followed in terms of the legal form, the prefecture and the basic activity subsector of the manufacturing enterprises (Petridis, 2000; ICAP, 2005).

The questionnaire was answered by a total sample of 148 manufacturing units in EMT Region by an on-the-spot survey at enterprises' premises. Furthermore, for gaining additional information, executives of the sample's enterprises and of the intermediary management agencies (Regional Development of EMT Service, Banks, Consultant companies) that were involved in the concretisation of relative actions/projects at the EMT Region were interviewed.

Geographical – Sector-based structure of the sample

For the needs of the research, the total 37 manufacturing subsectors were unified into the next five subsectors:

1) "Food & Beverages",
2) "Clothing & Accessories",
3) "Construction & Materials - Industrial Goods & Services",
4) "Lumber & Wood Production" and
5) "Remainder Manufacturing Subsectors".

The unification of subsectors was realised in order to achieve more effective data handling as many subsectors had small and even no representation.

In regard to the geographical structure of the sample, 21% of enterprises were functioning at the prefecture of Drama, 20% at the prefecture of Kavala, 27% at the prefecture of Xanthi, 21% at the prefecture of Rodopi and 11% at the prefecture of Evros (Figure 1).

Figure 1. Geographical structure of the sample

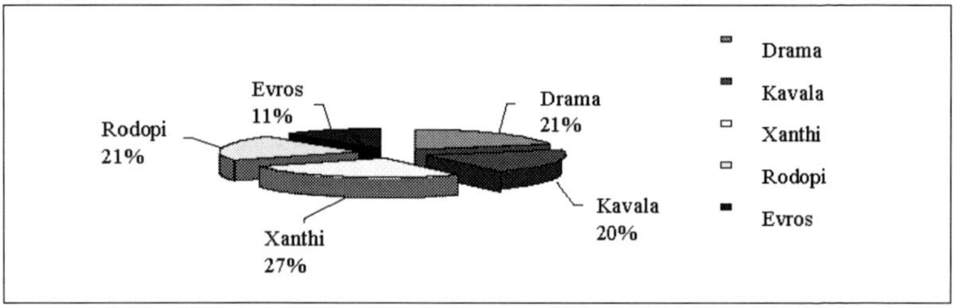

Moreover, in regard to the sector-based structure, as well as the legal form structure of the sample, 24.3% belong to the "Food & Beverages" subsector, 22.9% to the "Construction & Materials - Industrial Goods & Services", 9.5% to the "Clothing & Accessories", 12.9% to the "Lumber & Wood Production" and 30.4% to the "Remainder Manufacturing Subsectors" (Figure 2). Finally, most of sample enterprises were functioning as Public Limited Companies (S.A.) (97.3%), while only 2.7% as Limited Companies.

Figure 2. Sector-based structure of the sample

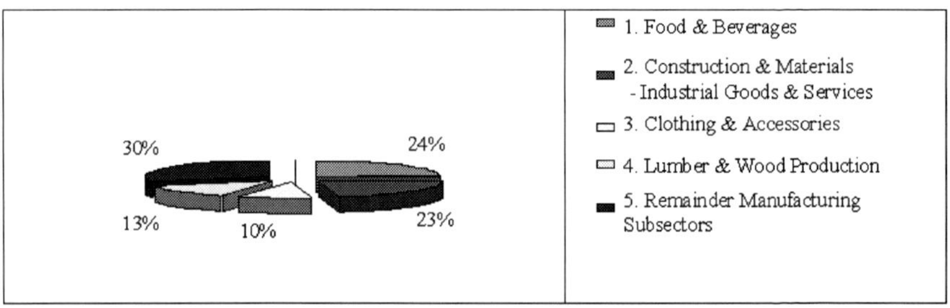

The primary data collection from the 148 sample enterprises was submitted in a prime treatment-evaluation based on which were grouped and coded. Then, there is identification and determination of the factors/indicators that influence sustainability of the manufacturing enterprises in EMT Region were identified by the Exploratory Factor Analysis (EFA) method (Chu and Murrmann, 2006; Dimitriadis, 2002; Samanda-Roundi, 2007).

Factor Analysis produced useful results when the variables are overall or partially correlated. In order to test the first type of correlation, the Barltlett's test of sphericity was used while to test the second type of correlation the Kaiser - Meyer - Olkin Measure (KMO) of Sampling Adequacy test (MSAs) was used to test the second type of correlation. Finally, K-Means clustering analysis was implemented aiming at factors' cluster/thematic grouping.

Factor analysis of questionnaire's themes/subjects

In order to export the factors and estimate the sustainability indicators that influence manufacturing enterprises' life duration the principal component method was selected while they were only certified as significant/important factors only those the eigenvalue of which was higher than 1.

After repetitive EFA processes by the use of the orthogonal rotation method (Varimax) (Dimitriadis, 2002; Hair et al., 1995), finally come up at eight (8) in-house indicators, which interpret 65.6% of the total variation (variability), while KMO indicator was appreciated at 0.849, and was evaluated as sufficient enough (Sharma, 1996). Moreover, the Barltlett's test of sphericity was found statistically significant ($p \leq 0.05$) and all the variables of the corresponding factors were also found statistically significant ($p \leq 0.05$).

It is noted that all variables having the same factor loadings on more than one factor were removed (Hair et al., 1995; Dimitriadis, 2002). In total, 27 variables were removed from the EFA process.

The following ascertainments were concluded (see, Table 1, in Appendix) from the results of EFA analysis and the factors that were finally shaped:

- Based on the estimations, the most important factor of manufacturing enterprises' sustainability appears to be the one that incorporates the variables-themes that concern the areas of "sales & marketing" and "research & development" as it interprets 15.474% of the total variance.

- The next, more important, factor includes the variables-themes that concern the areas of “financial management” and “special characteristics” of an enterprise and it interprets 13.401% of the total variance.

- The third factor contains the variables-themes that concern the areas of “administration –management” and “entrepreneurship”, interpreting 8.262% of the total variance.

- The fourth, more important, factor contains the variables-themes that concern the areas of “infrastructure - supply”, interpreting 6.35% of the total variance, while the fifth factor concerns “characteristics of entrepreneurs”, interpreting 6.11% of the total variance.

- The sixth important factor contains the variables-themes that concern the areas of “fame of products-enterprise” interpreting 5.88% of the total variance, while the seventh factor includes the variables that concern “technology and production systems” interpreting 5.67% of the total variance.

- Finally, as eighth, more important in-house factor was proved the “size of enterprise” interpreting 4.46% of the total variance and more specifically, the excellent size, that is interrelation of experience and abilities of entrepreneur as well as of the market size.

Identification of in-house sustainability indicators

The identity of each in-house factor of sustainability is characterized by each variable-theme that encompasses, which will constitute the base for the creation of particular **“in-house sustainability indicators”** of manufacturing units. The quantification of these themes and their statistical expression will constitute the estimated material of the sustainability indicators. So, based on the above there are the following in-house sustainability indicators:

The first sustainability indicator ($\Delta\Delta 1_{\text{in-house}}$) reflects the enterprise’s capacity in the areas of **“sales & marketing and research & development”** and incorporates the following variables-themes:

- Specialisation - products’ differentiation,
- Width of offered products,
- Planning and production of new products,

- Briefing and service of customers,
- Level-continuation of investments for research and development,
- Adoption and development of new products,
- Laboratory equipment of research and development,
- Level of education-experience of research and development executives and
- Adoption of innovative processes

The second sustainability indicator ($\Delta\Delta2_{in\text{-}house}$) reflects the enterprise's capacity in the areas of **"enterprise's financial management and special characteristics"** and is characterized by the following variables-themes:

- Availability of reliable economic elements,
- Availability of equity and total capital,
- Availability of working capital,
- Level of education-experience of financial executives,
- Guarantee of financial liquidity,
- Administrative – organizational – managerial skills,
- Appropriateness of legal form,
- Type of enterprise and
- Reliability of entrepreneur-enterprise

The third sustainability indicator ($\Delta\Delta3_{in\text{-}house}$) reflects the enterprise's capasity in the areas of **"administration -management and entrepreneurship"** and incorporates the following variables-subject:

- Existence of vision and concrete objectives,
- Initiative and tendency for action,
- Perspicacity of enterprising opportunities/threats and
- Entrepreneur's actions plenitude before the foundation of unit

The fourth sustainability indicator ($\Delta\Delta4_{in\text{-}house}$) reflects the enterprise's capasity in the areas of **"infrastructure - equip"** and incorporates the following variables-subject:

- Place of enterprise's infrastructure,
- Availability of raw and supplementary materials and
- Relationships-collaborations with the suppliers

The fifth sustainability indicator ($\Delta\Delta5_{in\text{-}house}$) reflects the enterprise's capasity in the areas of **"characteristics of entrepreneurs"** and incorporates the following variables-subject:

- Previous experience with such occupation,
- Academic - technological education and
- Financial capasity - assets

The sixth sustainability indicator ($\Delta\Delta6_{in\text{-}house}$) reflects the enterprise's capasity in the areas of **"fame of products -enterprise"** and incorporates the following variables-subject:

- Fame of enterprise in the market and
- Fame of products in the market

The seventh sustainability indicator ($\Delta\Delta7_{in\text{-}house}$) reflects the enterprise's capasity in the areas of **"premises technology & production systems"** and incorporates the following variables-subject:

- Development of infrastructure technology and
- Adoption of flexible production systems

Finally, the eighth sustainability indicator ($\Delta\Delta8_{in\text{-}house}$) reflects the enterprise's capasity in the areas of **"size of enterprise"** and is one-theme factor:

- Excellent size of enterprise in relation to the experience and the skills of entrepreneurs as well as with the size of the market.

Themes' reliability analysis of each indicator

The analysis of reliability, as it is known, is reported in the internal cohesion of each theme of a multi-theme variable (Chu and Murrmann, 2006). The application of EFA methodology had as result the identification of eight in-house sustainability indicators that were presented above. After the identification, it followed a reliability test of all sustainability indicators' themes based on the criterion/factor Cronbach's alpha, as it is proposed by Churchill (1979). The value of Cronbach's alpha is recommended to be at least 0.70 (Nunnally, 1978; Spector, 1992). In this particular case, the price of alpha varied from 0.641 to 0.900.

Determination of in-house sustainability indicators

It was stated above that the sustainability indicator, e.g. $\Delta\Delta 1_{\text{in-house}}$ reflects the enterprise's ability in the areas of **"sales & marketing and research & development"** and incorporates nine (9) variables-themes, which are: 1) Specialisation - products' differentiation, 2) Width of offered products, 3) Planning and production of new products, 4) Briefing and service of customers, 5) Level-continuation of investments for research and development, 6) Adoption and development of new products, 7) Laboratory equipment of research and development, 8) Level of education-experience of research and development executives and 9) Adoption of innovative processes.

Thus, in the effort to quantify this indicator, they have to be taken into consideration the themes that it incorporates (θ_i, where i = 1,.2,3,.., n) and the "value-grade" that receives each theme, based on the answers that noted the responded entrepreneurs in the five-scaled questionnaire of the research ("Very much" = 5, "Much"= 4, "Somewhat"= 3, "A little" = 2 and "Not at all" = 1). So, the quantitative expression of a sustainability indicator ($\Delta\Delta i_{\text{in-house}}$) arises from the following:

ΔΔi = [Sum of all themes' scores of θ_i indicator **x** Maximum score of five-scaled answers]/[Sum of maximum score of all themes]

Based on the five-scaled answers used, if the result of an indicator's quantification is more than three (> 3) that means that the enterprise accomplishes the sustainability criterion for the particular factor/indicator. Moreover, the enterprises can be characterized as "very much" sustainable, or "very" sustainable. Respectively, if the value, that the indicator receives, is less than three (< 3), then the enterprise does not accomplish the sustainability criterion for the particular factor/indicator (not sustainable). Finally, if the price, that the indicator receives, is three (= 3), then the enterprise can be characterized as marginally sustainable for the particular indicator.

Statistical analysis and investigation results of the in-house sustainability indicators of the manufacturing sector in EMT Region

The results of the estimation and statistical description of the in-house sustainability indicators that express the longevity identity of manufacturing units in EMT Region had their main statistical measures are described in this section.

This description concerns estimations of in-house sustainability indicators in the manufacturing sector in total as well as in its structure based on various qualitative criteria of enterprises' classification, such as the "sector of activity", the "size of enterprise", the "type of enterprise", the "former profession of entrepreneur" and the "education level of entrepreneur".

Results of statistical analysis and investigation of the in-house sustainability indicators in the total of manufacturing sector

From the examination of the descriptive statistics of the estimated in-house sustainability indicators of the manufacturing units in EMT Region resulted the following ascertainments (see, Table 2, in Appendix).

In general, most of the manufacturing enterprises in EMT Region present relatively high mean in-house sustainability indicators (> 3). This means that the responded entrepreneurs focus on all the in-house sustainability indicators of their enterprises. The above ascertainment is strengthened by the relatively small dispersion that characterizes the individual prices of indicators around their means, as it is impressed by the low standard deviation (from 0.03354 to 0.05372), a fact which implies that, in general, there is significant homogeneity among the opinions of entrepreneurs.

- Significance of the longevity of the enterprises appear to attribute to the respondent entrepreneurs, at first, the degree of enterprise's capacity in the area of "administration - management and entrepreneurship" (4.3193 ± 0.03354), which, as it was aforementioned, incorporates the variables: existence of vision and concrete objectives, initiative and tendency for action, perspicacity of enterprising opportunities/threats and entrepreneur's actions plenitude before the foundation of unit.

- As second, more important, in-house sustainability indicator the responded entrepreneurs considered the degree of enterprise's capacity in the areas of **"fame of products - enterprise"** (4.1622 ± 0.04102), the capacity of which is incorporated in the variables: fame of enterprise in the market and fame of products in the market.

Results of statistical analysis and investigation of the in-house sustainability indicators based on various qualitative criteria

Subsector of activity

From the examination of the descriptive statistics of the estimated in-house sustainability indicators based on the subsectors of the manufacturing enterprises in EMT Region (see, Table 3, in Appendix) the following ascertainments resulted:

- The estimations of in-house sustainability indicators by subsector of enterprises' activity are not differentiated from the general picture of the total manufacturing sector in the EMT Region. The above report of in-house sustainability indicators $\Delta\Delta 3_{\text{in-house}}$ [Administration - Management and Entrepreneurship] and $\Delta\Delta 6_{\text{in-house}}$ [Fame of Products-Enterprise] appeared to be statistically significant in the aspect of survival in all the manufacturing subsectors against the other in-house sustainability indicators, presenting the highest mean prices/values.

- In the rest of in-house sustainability indicators differentiations appeared among the subsectors with regard to the significance that the respondent entrepreneurs attribute. The enterprises that function in the subsectors "Lumber & Wood Production" (4.0532) and "Construction & Materials - Industrial Goods & Services" considered as equally important as the sustainability indicator $\Delta\Delta 4_{\text{in-house}}$ [Infrastructure - Equip]. The other subsectors appeared not to be particularly influenced by the above indicator as the price of indicator is appreciated in lower levels than the mean (3.9522 ± 0.03509) of the total manufacturing sector in EMT Region, except from the subsector "Food & Beverages" where it was appreciated marginally above the mean indicator.

- Corresponding picture is also observed in the mean of the sustainability indicator $\Delta\Delta 5_{\text{in-house}}$ [Characteristics of Entrepreneurs] where the subsectors "Construction & Materials - Industrial Goods & Services" and "Food & Beverages" are differentiated against the rest of the subsectors, presenting higher values than the mean of the total manufacturing enterprises. Small differentiation presented also the subsector “Lumber & Wood Production” as it was appreciated marginally above the total mean.

Type of Enterprise

From the examination of the descriptive statistics of the estimamted in-house sustainability indicators based on the type of the manufacturing enterprises in EMT Region (see, Table 4, in Appendix) the following ascertainments arose:

- The estimations of in-house sustainability indicators by the type of the enterprises are not differentiated from the general picture of total sector. More specific, indicators $\Delta\Delta3_{\text{in-house}}$ [Administration - Management and Entrepreneurship] and $\Delta\Delta6_{\text{in-house}}$ [Fame of Products-Enterprise] are significantly affecting the aspect of manufacturing enterprises’ survival.

- In the rest of in-house sustainability indicators differentiations appeared due to the type of enterprise, with regard to the significance that the responded entrepreneurs attribute. In the types “Relocation or other” and “Parental” the indicator $\Delta\Delta4_{\text{in-house}}$ [Infrastructure - Equip] is considered equally important. The other types appeared not to be particularly influenced by the above indicator as the price of indicator is appreciated in lower levels than the total mean (3.9522 ± 0.03509) in EMT Region.

- Corresponding picture is also observed in the mean of the sustainability indicator $\Delta\Delta5_{\text{in-house}}$ [Characteristics of Entrepreneurs] where the type of enterprise “Parental” and “Affiliated” are differentiated against the rests of the types, presenting a higher indicator than the total mean.

Size of Enterprise

From the examination of the descriptive statistics of the estimated in-house sustainability indicators based on the size of the manufacturing enterprises in EMT Region (see, Table 5, in Appendix) the following ascertainments were concluded:

- The estimations of in-house sustainability indicators by the size of enterprise are not differentiated by the general picture of the total sector. More specifically, indicators $\Delta\Delta 3_{\text{in-house}}$ [Administration - Management and Entrepreneurship] and $\Delta\Delta 6_{\text{in-house}}$ [Fame of Products-Enterprise] are significantly affecting the aspect of manufacturing enterprises' survival.

- In the rest of in-house sustainability indicators differentiations appeared due to the size of the enterprise, with regard to the significance that the respondent entrepreneurs attribute. The entrepreneurs that represented large or intermediate enterprises considered as equally important the indicators $\Delta\Delta 1_{\text{in-house}}$ [Sales & Marketing and Research & Development], $\Delta\Delta 2_{\text{in-house}}$ [Financial Management and Special Characteristics] and $\Delta\Delta 8_{\text{in-house}}$ [Size of Enterprise]. In the other categories of enterprises' size, the above sustainability indicators appreciated in lower levels than the total mean of manufacturing sector in EMT Region.

- Miscellaneous picture is observed in indicators $\Delta\Delta 4_{\text{in-house}}$ [Infrastructure - Supply], $\Delta\Delta 5_{\text{in-house}}$ [Characteristics of Entrepreneurs] and $\Delta\Delta 7_{\text{in-house}}$ [Technology and Production Systems] where the "small" and "large" enterprises had identical opinions and considered as more important the above indicators, comparatively with the mean estimation of the corresponding indicators for the total of the enterprises.

Former profession of the entrepreneur

From the examination of the descriptive statistics of the estimated in-house sustainability indicators based on the former profession of the entrepreneurs of the manufacturing enterprises in EMT Region (see, Table 6, in Appendix) the following ascertainments arose:

- The estimations of in-house sustainability indicators by former profession of the entrepreneurs are not differentiated from the general picture of the total sector. More specifically, indicators $\Delta\Delta 3_{\text{in-house}}$ [Administration - Management and Entrepreneurship] and $\Delta\Delta 6_{\text{in-house}}$ [Fame of Products-Enterprise] are significantly affecting the aspect of manufacturing enterprises' survival.

- In the rest of in-house sustainability indicators differentiations appeared due to former profession of the entrepreneurs, with regard to the significance that the respondent entrepreneurs attribute. More specifically, the entrepreneurs with former experience in such enterprises considered as equally important all the other in-house sustainability indicators. The other categories of entrepreneurs presented insignificant differences, as the estimated prices of the indicators are marginally equal to the mean price of the indicator of the total manufacturing sector in EMT Region.

Education level of entrepreneur

From the examination of the descriptive statistics of the estimated of in-house sustainability indicators of the manufacturing enterprises in EMT Region based on the education level of entrepreneur (see, Table 7, in Appendix) the following ascertainments resulted:

- The estimations of in-house sustainability indicators by former profession of the entrepreneurs are not differentiated from the general picture of the total sector. More specifically, indicators ΔΔ3in-house [Administration - Management and Entrepreneurship] and ΔΔ6in-house [Fame of Products-Enterprise] are significantly affecting the aspect of manufacturing enterprises' survival.

- In the rest of in-house sustainability indicators differentiations appeared due to former profession of the entrepreneurs, based on the education level of entrepreneur, with regard to the significance that the responded entrepreneurs attribute. Entrepreneurs with level of education "Undergraduate Studies" and "Postgraduate studies" considered the indicator $\Delta\Delta4_{\text{in-house}}$ [Infrastructure - Equip] equally important. The other categories of entrepreneurs' level of education appreciated that their enterprises' sustainability is not significantly influenced by the above indicator as the price of indicator is appreciated in lower levels than the total mean (3.9480 ± 0.0383) in EMT Region.

- Corresponding picture is observed in the sustainability indicators $\Delta\Delta5_{\text{in-house}}$ [Characteristics of Entrepreneurs] and $\Delta\Delta7_{\text{in-house}}$ [Premises' technology & Production systems] where entrepreneurs with level of education "Undergraduate Studies" appreciated that their enterprises' sustainability is significantly influenced by the above indicator as the price of indicator is appreciated in higher levels than the mean of the total enterprises in EMT Region.

Conclusions

Based on the exploratory factor analysis (EFA) the factors that influence the manufacturing enterprises' sustainability in EMT Region were determined. More specifically, there are, by the level of importance, the following in-house sustainability indicators:

1. Sales & Marketing and Research & Development
2. Enterprise's Financial Management and Special Characteristics
3. Administration – Management and Entrepreneurship
4. Infrastructure – Equip
5. Characteristics of Entrepreneurs
6. Fame of Products – Enterprise
7. Premises' technology & Production Systems
8. Size of Enterprise

From the statistical analysis of the total of the estimations, it has been proved that, in general, all the indicators, based on the entrepreneurs' opinion, influence considerably the longevity of manufacturing enterprises in EMT Region. However, differentiations are presented concerning the importance of certain in-house sustainability indicators, as well as relative differences depending on the qualitative classification of enterprises (sector of activity, type of enterprise, size of enterprise, education level of entrepreneur and former profession of entrepreneur).

Specifically, the following observations arose from the appreciated in-house sustainability indicators' analysis:

Manufacturing Sector:

- Entrepreneurs consider as the most important in-house sustainability indicators the enterprise's ability in the areas of "administration – management and entrepreneurship" and "fame of products-enterprise".

Activity Subsector

- The in-house sustainability indicators' estimations by enterprises' subsector of activity are not differentiated from the general picture of the total sector, where in-house sustainability indicators $\Delta\Delta3_{\text{in-house}}$ [Administration - Management and Entrepreneurship] and $\Delta\Delta6_{\text{in-house}}$ [Fame of Products-Enterprise] are significantly affecting the aspect of manufacturing enterprises' survival.

- In the rest of in-house sustainability indicators differentiations appeared among the subsectors with regard to the significance that the respondent entrepreneurs attributed. Thus, e.g. enterprises that function in the subsectors “Lumber & Wood Production” and “Construction & Materials - Industrial Goods & Services” considered as equally important the sustainability indicator $\Delta\Delta4_{\text{in-house}}$ [Infrastructure - Equip]. The other subsectors, based on the entrepreneurs’ opinion, appeared not to be considerably influenced by the above indicator as the price of indicator is appreciated in lower levels than the mean of the total manufacturing sector in EMT Region. The subsector “Food & Beverages” where the estimated prices of the indicator appreciated marginally above the mean constitutes an exception.

Type of Enterprise

- With regard to the general picture of in-house sustainability indicators based on the entrepreneurs’ type, the ascertainments are the same as the ascertainments produced by the reported estimations based on the enterprise’s activity sector.

- In the rest of in-house sustainability indicators, depending on the type of enterprise, different estimates are presented with regard to the importance that the entrepreneurs attributed to them. Thus, e.g. in the types “Relocation or other” and “Parental”, the indicator $\Delta\Delta4_{\text{in-house}}$ [Infrastructure - Equip] is considered equally important while the other types appeared not to be particularly influenced by the above indicator as the price of indicator is appreciated in lower levels than the mean of the total manufacturing sector in EMT Region.

Size of Enterprise

- As long as it concerns the general picture of in-house sustainability indicators, based on the enterprise’s size, the ascertainments are not significantly different from the ascertainments produced by the reported estimations based on the enterprise’s activity sector, enterprise’s type or entrepreneurs’ level of education.

- However, there are certain differences with regard to the importance or not of certain in-house sustainability indicators based on the enterprise’s size. Thus, e.g. large or intermediate enterprises consider as equally important the indicators $\Delta\Delta1_{\text{in-house}}$ [Sales & Marketing and Research & Development], $\Delta\Delta2_{\text{in-house}}$ [Enterprise’s Financial Management & Special Characteristics] and $\Delta\Delta8_{\text{in-house}}$ [Size of

Enterprise] while in the other categories of enterprises' size, enterprises considered that sustainability is not significantly influenced by the above indicators as they were appreciated in lower levels than the total mean of the total manufacturing sector in EMT Region.

Former profession of the entrepreneur

- As long as it concerns the general picture of in-house sustainability indicators, based on the entrepreneur's former profession, the ascertainments are the same as the ascertainments produced by the reported estimations based on the enterprise's activity sector, enterprise's type or entrepreneurs' level of education.

- However, there are certain differences with regard to the importance or not of certain in-house sustainability indicators based on the entrepreneur's former profession. Thus, e.g. entrepreneurs with former experience in such enterprises considered as equally important all the rest of in-house sustainability indicators, while the other categories of entrepreneurs presented insignificant differences, as the estimated prices of the indicators are marginally equal to the mean price of the indicator of the total manufacturing sector in EMT Region.

Education Level of the entrepreneur

- With regard to the general picture of in-house sustainability indicators based on the entrepreneurs' level of education, the ascertainments are the same as the ascertainments produced by the reported estimations based on the enterprise's activity sector or type.

- However, there are certain differences with regard to the importance or not of certain in-house sustainability indicators based on the entrepreneurs' level of education. Thus, e.g. entrepreneurs with level of education "Undergraduate Studies" and "Postgraduate studies" considered equally important the indicator $\Delta\Delta4_{\text{in-house}}$ [Infrastructure - Equip] while other categories of entrepreneurs' level of education appreciated that their enterprises' sustainability is not significantly influenced by the above indicator.

References

Chamber of Kavala, 2005, Registration list of enterprises, Lists of registration and deletion of enterprises at the time interval 1980 – 2001, Kavala (in Greek).

Chamber of Xanthi, 2008, Registration list of enterprises, Lists of registration and deletion of enterprises at the time interval 1980 – 2008, Xanthi (in Greek).

Chassid, I., 1980, The Greek industry and EEC: Study on the repercussions by the integration, Special Studies, *Foundation for Economic & Industrial Research*, 6, 1, Athens (in Greek).

Chassid, I., Katsos, G., 1992, European unification and Greek industry: Structure - records - prospects, *Foundation for Economic & Industrial Research*, 17, Athens (in Greek).

Chassid, I., Papagiannakis, E., Konstantelou, A., 2003, *Technological Prospect Investigation in Greece*, Theme: Industrial production and transformation, Drawing of thematic report, Athens (in Greek).

Chu, K. H., Murrmann, S.K., 2006, Development and validation of the hospitality emotional labor scale, *Tourism Management*, 27, pp. 1181-1191.

Churchill, G. A., 1979, A paradigm for developing better measures of marketing constructs, *Journal of Marketing Research*, 16, pp.64-73.

Collis, D., Montogomery, C. A., 1995, Competing on Resources: Strategy in the 1990s, *Harvard Business Review*, pp. 118-128.

Collins, J., Porras J., 1994, *Built to Last: Successful Habits of Visionary Companies*, Harper Business, New York.

Dimitriadis, E., 2002, *Statistical Applications with the use of SPSS*, Kritiki, Athens (in Greek).

Esenwein, E. R., 1961, Die Persistenz von Industriebetrieben in strukturschwachen Wirtschaftsgebieten, *Industrialisierung ländlicher Räume, Forschungs- und Sitzungsberichte der Akademie für Raumforschung und Landesplanung*, Veröffentlichungen der Akademie für Raumforschung und Landesplanung, Bd. 17, Hannover, S. 60-82.

Feeser, H. R., Willard, G.E., 1990, Founding strategy and performance: A comparison of high and low growth high tech firms, *Strategic Management Journal*, 11 2, pp. 87–98.

Georgi, H., Giersch, V., 1977, Neue Betriebe an der Saar, Bestandsaufnahme, Analysen, Perspektiven, Saarbruken.

Goddard, J.A., Willson, J. O. S., 1996, Persistence of Profits for UK Manufacturing and Service Sector Firms, *The Service Industries Journal*, 16, 2, pp. 105-117. Published by Frank Cass, London.

Hair, F., Anderson, R., Tatham, R., Black, W., 1995, *Multivariate Data Analysis with Readings*, 4th Ed, London, Prentice-Hall International.

Holdt, W., 1972, Industrieansiedlungen und Ihre Auswirkungen auf das Arbeitsplatzangebot- dargestellt am Beispiel ausgewählter Städte und Kreise des Landes Nordrhein-Westfalen, Düsseldorf.

Hunt, R. E., Puetz, J. E., 2003, *Predicting small business mortality using high risk marketing: an exploratory consideration, Rockhurst College* (available online at: www.usasbe.org/knowleadge/proceedings/1998/36-hunt.pdf.).

ICAP, 2005, The Greek Manufacturing Sector, Estimates for 2004 and expectations for 2005: Results of the fourth annual sampling research, *ICAP HELLAS SA*, Athens (in Greek).

Kanellopoulos, C., 1994, *SME Management and Entrepreneurship*, 2nd Edition, Athens (in Greek).

Karvounis, S., 2000, *Entrepreneurship and new business activities*, Stamouli, A., Athens (in Greek).

Katsou, C. G., 1988, Problematic enterprises in Greece: Reasons, Predictions, Prevention and Cleansing, Scientific Studies, *Center of Economic Planning and Researching*, 28, Athens (in Greek).

KEPE, 1984a, Licensing and Industrial Development, Scientific Studies, 4, *Planning and Economic Researches Centre*, Athens (in Greek).

—. 1984b, Sector-based & territorial analysis of Greek Manufacturing Sector, *Scientific Studies*, 12, Athens (in Greek).

Kottis, G. Ch., 1980, Industrial decentralisation and Regional Development, *Foundation for Economic & Industrial Research, Special Studies*, 7, Athens (in Greek).

Kiriazopoulos, P. G, Terzidis, K. P., 2000, *SME Management*, Athens (in Greek).

Labrianidis, L., Kalantaridis, C., 1997, Globalization and local industrial development in the European periphery: Enterprise strategies in Eastern Macedonia and Thrace, *European Planning Studies*, 5, 4, pp. 477-494.

Labuschagne, C, Brent, A., Erck, R., 2003, Assessing the sustainability performances of industries, *Journal of Cleaner Production*, 13, pp. 373-385.

Marinos, I. 1990, Greek Industry: The peak of the spear for the survival and modernisation of Greek economy, *Economic Postman*, 14 June, 1990 (in Greek).

Nikolaidis, M., 2007, *The sustainability (duration of life) of the manufacturing units' function-development and its contribution in the regional development. An empirical application for the Prefecture of East Macedonia and Thrace*, PhD thesis (in Greek).

Nunnally, J. C., 1978, *Psychometric Theory*, New York, NY: McGraw-Hill.

Papadopoulos, D., 1986, *Introduction of enterprises' economy and management*, Thessaloniki (in Greek).

Peters, T. J., Waterman, R. H., 1990, *In Search of Excellence: Lessons from America's Best – run Companies*, New York: Harper.

Petridis, D., 2000, *Applied Statistics: Science of Foods*, Omiros, Thessaloniki (in Greek).

Programme RITTS - EMT, *Regional Innovation Technology Transfer Strategy*, Operational Programme, Athens (in Greek).

Reinhardt, F., 2000, Sustainability and the Firm, *Interfaces*, 30, 3, pp. 26-41.

Richard, J., Boden, J. R, Nucci, A. R., 2000, On the survival prospects of men's and women's new business ventures, The University of Toledo, Toledo, OH USA b U.S. Bureau of the Census, Washington, DC USA, *Journal Business Venturing*, 15, 4, pp. 347-362.

Royal Dutch/Shell Group Planning PL/I., 1983, Corporate Change: A Look at How Long-Established Companies Change.

Samanda-Roundi, E., 2007, The aid of competitiveness of intermediate size enterprises, *File of Economic History*, 2, pp. 141-168 (in Greek).

SEV, 2006, *The Greek industry in 2005*, Association of Greek Industrialists, Athens (in Greek).

Sharma, S., 1996, *Applied Multivariate Techniques*, Willey, New York

Shepherd, D. A., Shanley, M. T., 1998, *New Venture Strategy: Timing, Environmental Uncertainty and Performance*, Sage Publications, Thousand Oaks, CA.

Shepherd, D. A, Douglas, E.J., Shanley, M., 2000, New venture survival Ignorance, external shocks, and risk reduction strategies, *Journal of Business Venturing*, 15, 5-6, pp. 393-410.

Spector, P. E., 1992, Summated rating scale construction: An Introduction, *Quantitative Applications in the Social Sciences*, p. 34, Sage, Beverly Hills C.A.

Theodoropoulos, A., 2003, *Strategic Operational Planning: How you achieve development in your enterprise*, Series: Labour market and Management, Athens (in Greek).

Theriou, N., 2002, *Strategic management of enterprises*, Athens (in Greek).

Walker, D., Chapman, K., 1992, *The arrangement of industry, translated in Greek*, Papazisi, Athens (in Greek).

Wernerfelt, B., 1984, A Recourse-Based View of the Firm, *Strategic Management Journal*, July-August.

Xanthakis, M., 1989, *The crisis of Greek Manufacturing Sector and the intervention of state*, Papazisi, Athens (in Greek).

Appendix

Table 1. Results of Exploratory Factor Analysis

		In-house sustainability factors							
a/a	Variables	F1	F2	F3	F4	F5	F6	F7	F8
f1.1	Specialisation - Products' differentiation	0.656	**F1=9 Sales & Marketing and Research & Development**						
f1.2	Width of offered products	0.575	15.474[a]						
f1.3	Planning and production of new products	0.660	9.676[b]						
f1.4	Briefing and service of customers	0.651	0.900[c]						
f1.5	Level-continuation of investments for R&D	0.707							
f1.6	Adoption and development of new products	0.810							
f1.7	Laboratory equipment of R&D	0.786							
f1.8	Level of education-experience of R&D executives	0.743							
f1.9	Adoption of innovative processes	0.653							
f2.1	Availability of reliable economic elements		0.584	**F2=9 Financial Management & Special Characteristics**					
f2.2	Availability of equity and total capital		0.828	13.401[a]					
f2.3	Availability of working capital		0.848	3.107[b]					
f2.4	Education-experience level financial executives		0.600	0.872[c]					
f2.5	Guarantee of financial liquidity		0.575						
f2.6	Administrative - organisational abilities		0.505						
f2.7	Appropriateness of legal form		0.614						
f2.8	Type of enterprise		0.661						
f2.9	Reliability of entrepreneur-enterprise		0.529						
f3.1	Existence of vision and concrete objectives			0.740	**F3=4 Administration - Management & Entrepreneurship**				
f3.2	Initiative and tendency for action			0.672	8.262[a]				
f3.3	Perspicacity of enterprising opportunities/threats			0.689	1.941[b]				
f3.4	Entrepreneur's actions plenitude before unit's foundation			0.614	0.735[c]				

(continued)

f4.1	Place of enterprise's infrastructure	0.700	**F4=3 Infrastructure - Equip**
f4.2	Availability of raw and supplementary materials	0.772	6.357[a]
f4.3	Relationships-collaborations with the suppliers	0.578	1.684[b]
			0.609[c]
f5.1	Previous experience with such occupation	0.835	**F5=3 Characteristics of Entrepreneurs**
f5.2	Academic - technological education	0.651	6.116[a]
f5.3	Economic "surface" - assets	0.666	1.511[b]
			0.681[c]
f6.1	Fame of enterprise in the market	0.827	**F6=2 Fame of Products - Enterprise**
f6.2	Fame of products in the market	0.812	5.888[a]
			1.440[b]
			0.823[c]
f7.1	Development of infrastructure technology	0.706	**F7=2 Premises Technology & Production Systems**
f7.2	Adoption of flexible production system	0.765	5.673[a]
			1.170[b]
			0.641[c]
f8.1	Excellent size of enterprise in interrelation with the experience and the abilities of entrepreneurs as well as with the size of market	0.807	**F8=1 Size of Enterprise**
			4.462[a]
			1.130[b]
			0.652[c]

[a] Variance Explained
[b] Eigen values
[c] Crobach's α
K.M.O=0.849 Barltlett's test of Sphericity=2569.19
Significance Level=0.000 Total Variance Explained=65.633

Table 2. Estimation of the manufacturing sector in-house sustainability indicators of EMT Region

In-house sustainability indicators	Sample	Mean	Standard Deviation	Skewness	Kurtosis
$\Delta\Delta1_{in\text{-}house}$ sales & marketing and research & development	148	3.7441	0.04574	-0.511	1.431
$\Delta\Delta2_{in\text{-}house}$ enterprise's financial management and special characteristics	148	3.7385	0.03995	0.782	-0.135
$\Delta\Delta3_{in\text{-}house}$ administration -management and entrepreneurship	148	4.3193	0.03354	-0.561	1.827
$\Delta\Delta4_{in\text{-}house}$ infrastructure - equip	148	3.9522	0.03509	0.048	0.423
$\Delta\Delta5_{in\text{-}house}$ characteristics of entrepreneurs	148	3.8696	0.04681	-0.326	1.043
$\Delta\Delta6_{in\text{-}house}$ fame of products -enterprise	148	4.1622	0.04102	0.142	0.147
$\Delta\Delta7_{in\text{-}house}$ premises technology & production systems	148	3.9122	0.05090	-0.837	2.585
$\Delta\Delta8_{in\text{-}house}$ size of enterprise	148	3.8311	0.05372	0.038	-0.375

Table 3. Estimation of the in-house sustainability indicators based on the Subsector of Activity

Subsector of Activity	ΔΔ1	ΔΔ2	ΔΔ3	ΔΔ4	ΔΔ5	ΔΔ6	ΔΔ7	ΔΔ8
Food & Beverages	3.9129±0.1822	3.9529±0.1607	4.5357±0.0902	3.9921±0.1193	4.0243±0.1797	4.2143±0.1252	3.8929±0.2577	4.0714±0.1645
Clothing & Accessories	3.4341±0.1167	3.6768±0.0696	4.1765±0.0735	3.9494±0.0697	3.7753±0.0654	4.0441±0.0800	3.7206±0.1120	3.5882±0.1202
Construction & Materials - Industrial Goods & Services	3.8126±0.1284	3.8005±0.1411	4.2632±0.1138	4.0532±0.1306	4.0705±0.1384	4.3684±0.1070	4.1579±0.1433	3.8421±0.1578
Lumber & Wood Production	3.7433±0.0839	3.8142±0.0864	4.4167±0.0660	4.0006±0.0822	3.8892±0.0910	4.2222±0.0900	3.9444±0.0739	3.8056±0.1040
Remainder Manufacturing Subsectors	3.8973±0.0494	3.6318±0.0585	4.3056±0.0514	3.8604±0.0432	3.7922±0.0961	4.1000±0.0738	3.9333±0.0834	3.9556±0.0896
Total Sample	3.7441±0.0457	3.7385±0.0399	4.3193±0.0335	3.9522±0.0350	3.8696±0.0468	4.1622±0.0410	3.9122±0.0509	3.8311±0.0537

Table 4. Estimation of the in-house sustainability indicators based on the Type of Enterprise

Subsector of Activity	ΔΔ1	ΔΔ2	ΔΔ3	ΔΔ4	ΔΔ5	ΔΔ6	ΔΔ7	ΔΔ8
Parental	3.8040±0.1354	3.8484±0.1051	4.4000±0.0816	4.0812±0.0874	4.0276±0.1399	4.2200±0.1044	3.8000±0.1633	3.9600±0.1222
Affiliated	3.8291±0.0827	3.6759±0.0902	4.3295±0.0724	3.8564±0.0619	3.9086±0.1354	4.3182±0.0961	3.9318±0.1243	4.2273±0.1126
New	3.7241±0.0546	3.7097±0.0511	4.2849±0.0435	3.9239±0.0443	3.8354±0.0526	4.1129±0.0524	3.9839±0.0553	3.7312±0.0651
Relocated or Other	3.5550±0.3050	3.9025±0.1497	4.4375±0.1619	4.1413±0.2165	3.6663±0.2176	4.1250±0.1567	3.3750±0.2630	3.5000±0.3273
Total Sample	3.7441±0.0457	3.7385±0.0399	4.3193±0.0335	3.9522±0.0350	3.8696±0.0468	4.1622±0.0410	3.9122±0.0509	3.8311±0.0537

Table 5. Estimation of the in-house sustainability indicators based on the Size of Enterprise

Subsector of Activity	ΔΔ1	ΔΔ2	ΔΔ3	ΔΔ4	ΔΔ5	ΔΔ6	ΔΔ7	ΔΔ8
Very Small	3.5853±0.1001	3.6437±0.0800	4.3000±0.1019	3.8507±0.0855	3.7557±0.0887	4.0167±0.0943	3.6833±0.1085	3.6667±0.1298
Small	3.7483±0.0748	3.7395±0.0650	4.3633±0.0468	4.0328±0.0518	3.9069±0.0631	4.1797±0.0633	3.9688±0.0824	3.8125±0.0829
Medium	3.8030±0.0719	3.7450±0.0687	4.2386±0.0513	3.8900±0.0589	3.8864±0.0969	4.2273±0.0679	3.9886±0.0882	3.9091±0.0849
Large	3.9340±0.1861	3.9880±0.1575	4.4500±0.1040	4.0140±0.1515	3.8990±0.2679	4.2000±0.1855	3.9000±0.1453	4.1000±0.2333
Total Sample	3.7441±0.0457	3.7385±0.0399	4.3193±0.0335	3.9522±0.0350	3.8696±0.0468	4.1622±0.0410	3.9122±0.0509	3.8311±0.0537

Table 6. Estimation of the in-house sustainability indicators based on the Entrepreneur's Former Profession

Subsector of Activity	ΔΔ1	ΔΔ2	ΔΔ3	ΔΔ4	ΔΔ5	ΔΔ6	ΔΔ7	ΔΔ8
Independent Agent	3.7180±0.0827	3.8184±0.0721	4.3550±0.0589	3.9248±0.0702	3.7472±0.1001	4.1300±0.0780	3.8500±0.1022	3.7000±0.0869
Employee in Public/Private Sector	3.7770±0.1646	3.8940±0.1055	4.3500±0.1000	3.9385±0.1179	4.0170±0.0852	4.2000±0.0917	3.9500±0.1400	3.9000±0.1000
Businessman in other activity	3.8142±0.1338	3.6950±0.1612	4.4583±0.0965	4.0117±0.1082	4.1383±0.1447	4.3750±0.1393	3.8750±0.1642	3.9167±0.1930
Businessman in the same activity	3.6746±0.0784	3.4796±0.0650	4.2054±0.0364	3.8364±0.0559	3.8689±0.0791	4.0357±0.0440	3.9107±0.0892	3.7500±0.1219
Other	3.7900±0.0888	3.7561±0.0773	4.2961±0.0810	4.0618±0.0570	3.8687±0.0875	4.2105±0.0973	3.9868±0.0970	4.0000±0.1250
Total Sample	3.7441±0.0457	3.7385±0.0399	4.3193±0.0335	3.9522±0.0350	3.8696±0.0468	4.1622±0.0410	3.9122±0.0509	3.8311±0.0537

Table 7. Estimation of the in-house sustainability indicators based on the education level of entrepreneur

Education level	ΔΔ1	ΔΔ2	ΔΔ3	ΔΔ4	ΔΔ5	ΔΔ6	ΔΔ7	ΔΔ8
Elementary school	3,7440±0,1800	3,6460±0,1464	4,3000±0,1572	3,9260±0,1312	3,8680±0,1737	4,1500±0,1675	3,9000±0,2081	3,7000±0,1527
Secondary school	3,8338±0,0918	3,8100±0,0850	4,3382±0,0699	3,9524±0,0898	3,6765±0,1206	4,1324±0,0974	3,9265±0,1037	3,8824±0,1098
Technical education	3,5384±0,1086	3,6444±0,0964	4,2400±0,0859	3,7804±0,0832	3,7344±0,1262	4,2800±0,0960	3,7800±0,1609	3,4800±0,1306
University	3,7289±0,0741	3,7333±0,0659	4,3727±0,0471	4,0213±0,0530	4,0302±0,0594	4,1455±0,0617	4,0000±0,0756	3,9636±0,0819
Master studies	3,7156±0,2756	3,8400±0,1222	4,0000±0,2124	3,9733±0,1507	3,7411±0,1731	4,0000±0,1443	3,5556±0,2421	3,4444±0,2421
Total Sample	3,7202±0,0492	3,7368±0,0414	4,3083±0,0363	3,9480±0,0383	3,8524±0,0503	4,1579±0,0428	3,9023±0,0558	3,7970±0,0562

PART THREE:

FDI, ENTERPRISE FINANCE AND BANKING

FOREIGN DIRECT INVESTMENT (FDI) IN THE BALKANS: THE ROLE OF GREECE

DIMITRIOS MADITINOS,
DIMITRIOS KOUSENIDIS
AND DIMITRIOS CHATZOUDES

Abstract

The fall of communism in the early 1990's and the subsequent social and economical developments, placed the spotlight on the potential of the Balkan economies (Albania, Bulgaria, FYROM, Montenegro, Romania and Serbia). Nowadays, 20 years after the dramatic change in the economical status quo, the markets of the Balkan countries seem to be successfully integrated into the free market economy. Foreign Direct Investment (FDI) has a significant role in encouraging and supporting such a transition, making it a matter of growing importance to the countries of the whole Balkan region. Greece, an E.U. member country that has always been integrated into the free market economy, plays a significant regional economic role, especially when it comes to FDI. The present study aims to clarify Greece's economic regional role in the Balkans, provide both qualitative and quantitative data concerning Greek FDI in the Balkans, analyze the current and future investment climate and make predictions about future FDI trends in the region. Results offer interesting observations that can be used by policy makers and companies.

Introduction

During the process of the industrialisation of the Greek economy (1960-1980), Greek outward investment to western and developing countries had been marginal and government policy had only emphasised on attracting inward investment. The scenery was drastically changed by the opportunities that arose from the collapse of the centrally planned regimes and the consequent process of transition to the market economy of the Central and Eastern European Countries. Greece shifted from being a receiver of Foreign Direct Investment (FDI) into an exporter of capital, with the Balkans being the main destination of direct investment abroad (Labrianidis et al., 2004).

Greek organisations started investing in foreign countries as a result of two, almost simultaneous events: (a) the Greek economy reached a point in it's development cycle that allowed outward FDI to be commenced, (b) in a proximal geographic area high opportunities were created overnight (shift in the economic system of the Central and Eastern European Countries: from protected economy to the free market system).

Given the aforementioned circumstances, Greece has emerged during the last two decades (1990-2010) as a key regional player and one of the largest investors in the Balkans (Bastian, 2004; Demos et al., 2004; Kekic, 2005; Stoian and Filippaios, 2008a). With the opening of neighbouring markets in the early 1990s, Greek organisations and entrepreneurs took the opportunity to exploit their ownership advantages and expand in abroad economies (Dunning, 2001; Stoian and Filippaios, 2008a). Greece has, thus, transformed from a peripheral European country to a regional centre, especially to its neighbouring South-Eastern European countries (Stoian and Filippaios, 2008a).

The whole investment process was enhanced by: (a) the political support of the Greek Government and it's desire to acquire a regional economic role, (b) Greek policies that were specifically designed and implemented in order to transform the country into a key player in the region (policies such as the 'Hellenic Plan for the Economic Reconstruction of the Balkans -HiPERB), (c) the upgrading of the Athens Stock Exchange (ASE) from a developing to a developed financial market (reliable source for raising funds for investment purposes) (Bastian 2004; Labrianidis et al., 2004; Stoian and Filippaios, 2008a; Stoian and Filippaios, 2008b; Totev, 2005).

Within the context described above, the aim of this study is to describe the regional role of Greece in the Balkan investment reality, provide qualitative information about the Greek expansion to the north, present contemporary quantitative data concerning Greek FDI in the Balkans, analyze the current and future investment climate and make predictions about future FDI trends in the region. The present study, describing the methods that a small-medium peripheral economy used in order to upgrade it's regional role through outward FDI, may offer the ground for understanding the emerging patterns of outward FDI from small peripheral economies, particularly in the context of the expanded European Union.

The following two sections include a reference to the importance of FDI on developing countries and an analysis of the investment climate in the Balkan countries. The phases and the determinants of the Greek investment in the Balkans are included in the following two sections, while the paper is concluded with the presentation of the Greek investment in the Balkans (quantitative and qualitative data), the analysis of the current economic crisis and the future prospects and, of course, the general conclusions.

The importance of FDI on developing countries

One of the most important developments of the 1990's has been observed in the number of emerging opportunities and challenges for cross-border direct investments and co-operative ventures (Dunning, 1993). FDI has been, in the last twenty years, a matter of growing importance to the economies of both developed and developing countries (Lankes and Venables, 1996; Liu and Zou, 2008; Tatoglu and Glaister, 1996, 1998).

FDI can be defined as a category of cross-border investment made by a resident entity in one economy (the "direct investor") with the objective of establishing a "lasting interest" in an enterprise resident in an economy other than that of the investor (the "direct investment enterprise") (Dunning, 1993; Hosseini, 2005). The role of FDI in generating technology transfers and positive spillovers to domestic firms, creating job opportunities, improving the balance of payments, increasing foreign currency stocks etc., has motivated policy makers in recipient countries to implement specific policies for attracting FDI (Deichmann et al., 2003).

FDI's role on developing countries is considered to be significant, since FDI is responsible for GDP development, welfare increase in the host country due to technology spillovers and innovation introduction, new managerial techniques, development of additional management and production skills (Perez, 1997), increased capital flows, job creation and improvement of the job environment, and the development of the industrial sector in the host country (Haddad and Harrison, 1993;

Markusen and Venables, 1999). The positive FDI effects have, thus, led the majority of the developing countries to seek new ways to increase FDI inflows. The competition for attracting FDI aims at strengthening the advantages of each country and eliminating its disadvantages, so as to motivate investors to choose one FDI location over another (Botric and Skuflic, 2006).

Although FDI represent an important source of financial support for developing and transition economies, most of the FDI transactions are concentrated within the developed countries. The economic literature has identified a significant gap between the FDI inflows to the developed countries and those to developing countries (Markusen and Venables, 1999). Surprisingly enough, the global economic crisis seems to have limited that effect. According to the United Nations (2009), investments to developing and transition economies increased to 43% in 2008. More specifically, Africa FDI inflows rose to a record level, with the fastest increase in West Africa (a 63% rise over 2007); inflows to South, East and South-East Asia witnessed a 17% expansion to hit a new high; FDI to West Asia continued to rise for the sixth consecutive year and inflows to Latin America and the Caribbean rose by 13%. Finally, it should be underlined that the expansion of FDI inflows to South-East Europe witnessed an eighth year consequent raise, but are still in an embryonic state, compared to other regions with same characteristics.

The investment climate in the Balkan countries

According to various scholars (Botric and Skuflic, 2006; Kekic, 2005; Zagkos et al., 2007), the South-Eastern European countries are considered to be generally less developed, receive less FDI flows, have weaker relationships with the European Union, and are generally lagging in the transition speed of the Central European countries (Botric and Skuflic, 2006; Kekic, 2005; Zagkos et al., 2007). Specifically, the private sector of the South Eastern European countries is not as developed as the one in the Central European countries, while, at the same time, the public sector has not yet been fully reformed. Furthermore, the informal economy (gray economy) plays, as a rule, a significant role (Hunya, 2004), while week government structures, political instability, corruption and unemployment are further deteriorating the economic condition. Additionally, the worriers of the Balkan transition point to the possible future upsurge of violence in the region (having the 2004 Kosovo incident in mind) and raise concerns about the threat of a return of old regime forces in Serbia and elsewhere (Kekic, 2005).

Therefore, one might conclude that despite the liberation process, the Balkans still represent a region with barriers and restrictions, a region that is trade averse and may not be considered as a region of free and full growing trade development (Zagkos et al., 2007).

Despite the above, it is considered that the Balkan region shows great potential. The emergence of a global system of open trade (unrestricted transferability of capital, goods and services), the anticipated completion of the reforms in the economic structures of the Balkan states and the increased flow of foreign capital, combined with the integration of Balkan states to international organisations (EU, NATO), have highlighted a unique and historically significant opportunity for all Balkan states to align themselves permanently to the Western economy and, therefore, become more influential participants in the world community (Bastian, 2004; Botric and Skuflic, 2006; Carstensen and Toubal, 2004; Demos et al., 2004; Nimetz, 2005). The democratization, economy liberation and fulfilment of the EU requirements will improve the reputation of the Balkan countries and will enable their full integration in the European family (Kekic, 2005).

The accession of ten new member states to the EU on 1st May 2004, and the accession of Bulgaria and Romania in 1st January 2007 (first Balkan states to enter EU since the accession of Greece in 1981), made the Balkan countries close neighbours to an enlarged European Union. As a result, the attractiveness of the region for Foreign Direct Investment is expected to improve due to diminished perceived geographic distance to the core of Europe (Hunya, 2004). These positive regional effects can be enhanced by the progress in economic transformation and democratic consolidation that has been already made, thus reducing the risk to invest in the area.

The problems occurred in the ongoing free market integration process of the Balkan states that are described above, had an impact on the quantity of the FDI attracted in the whole region. This can be better observed by comparing South-Eastern European countries with Central European countries, concluding that the latter have received more FDI per capita than their Southern-Eastern counterparts (Pournarakis and Varsakelis, 2002; Slaveski and Nedanovski, 2002). The uneven political and economic progress of the countries of the region have made them less attractive for FDI, while for the time being, most of these countries receive less FDI than their size and location would normally suggest (Hunya, 2004).

Hence, it is not surprising that, overall, most Balkan countries were unable to fully seize the momentum of transition, lagging significantly behind Central European countries, especially in the early 1990s (Fischer et al., 1996). Their poor performance is clearly demonstrated when compared to the FDI flows directed to the Czech Republic, Hungary or Poland. Investment interest for Romania and Bulgaria scaled up only recently, driven by the progress in the negotiation process and their accession to EU, that led to a substantial improvement in the political and economic environment. By contrast, FDI flows to Albania, Serbia and FYROM remain relatively low, as a result of the serious ethnic and political problems these countries have faced in the recent past (Kitonakis and Kontis, 2008).

During 2003 to 2008, FDI in the Central and Easter European countries experienced a five-fold increase, rising from $30 billion to $155 billion. The credit crunch and consequent recession coincided with a collapse of FDI inflows to the region. In the region as a whole, FDI inflows were 50% lower in 2009 when compared to 2008. This negative distribution is uneven between the countries of the region, with weaker countries having the most severe problems. Looking ahead, FDI is projected to recover only modestly from 2010 onwards and could reach around $172 billion by 2014 (Price Waterhouse Coopers, 2010; Roberts, 2010).

The phases of the Greek investment in the Balkans

Foreign Direct Investment (FDI) has been encouraged in Greece since the early 1950s, in an effort to revive and expand the industrial base of the country (Louri et al., 2000). Historically, the number of Greek companies producing abroad was relatively insignificant, the two main exceptions being shipping (a strong point of the Greek Economy) and the trading of oriental tobacco leaves (a traditional Greek product). Another exception was the productive activity of some construction companies in the Middle East during the 1960s and 1970s (Labrianidis, et al., 2004).

Until the opening of the Balkan economies in the early 1990s, there were fewer than 10 Greek companies that had invested abroad. The expansion of Greek organisations abroad is a phenomenon of the last two decades, with a large number of diverse investment projects being implemented abroad in a very short space of time (Kamaras 2001). Most of these investments have been realised in the Balkans.

The evolution of the Greek investment activity can be defined in four phases/ stages (Demos et al., 2004; ELKE, 2006; Kitonakis and Kontis, 2008; Labrianidis, 2001; Labrianidis et al., 2004; Louri et al., 2000):

- A' Phase (1989-1993 / 'The El Dorado' period): The Balkan countries were seen as areas where one could gain high and easy profits. Most of the Greek companies entering the Balkan markets during that period were small and medium-sized. The underlying idea was that one could enjoy quick profits with no long-term strategic commitment ('stack and run' strategy). This phase was characterized by low capital transfer and lack of long-term strategy, mainly due to political risk and inexperience in foreign investment. These initial attempts were not always successful in terms of profitability and strategic positioning, but Greek companies acquired valuable information, knowledge about the markets and evaluated potentials for further investment. Nevertheless, they were examples of entrepreneurs who enjoyed extremely high profit rates (not exactly playing inside the legal framework). However, in most of the cases it was soon realised that the investment procedure was tougher than expected and numerous entrepreneurs quit and returned home.

- B' Phase (1994-1997 / 'The Mafia' period): After the fortune-hunter investors of the first period completed their run and fled, the companies that remained in the Balkans during the following years started to understand that the investment environment was not an ideal one. The countries of destination were characterised by the predominance of illegal practices, the lack of proper market institutions, the lack of intra-state agreements for the protection of investments, and so on. The newly-born Greek investment community became conscious of the hardships of investing in a country with social, political and economic instability (high rates of inflation, wide use of semi-illegal practises), in many cases through the bankruptcy of many businesses.

- C' Phase (1997-2000 / The 'Wake of the Big Greek Players' period): The gradual stabilization of the social, political and economic environment intensified the investment interest, attracting, mostly, larger Greek organisations. Banks, metal industries, food industries, telecommunications and retail trade companies entered the Balkan markets, either by greenfield investments (establishment of new companies) or by acquiring local companies. Big Greek State companies, such as the Hellenic Telecommunications Organization (OTE), Hellenic Petroleum (ELPE) and the National Bank of Greece became increasingly involved in large expansion projects in the area. This is a period of rationalisation for the Greek internationalisation process, since most investments were made with long-term prospects.

- D' Phase (2001-today / The 'Normalisation' period): The further stabilization of the social, political and economic environment, the significant funds that Greek companies have accumulated from the Athens Stock Exchange (ASE) and the experience that has been gathered from the 'Balkan endeavour', led the Greek investment in the Balkans into the period of normalisation. This period triggered an even larger and wider stream of investment projects: FDI outflows from Greece in 2004 totalled 1,8 billion Euros (more than double than the FDI inflows in the country), from 1,6 billion Euros in 2003 and 1,2 billion Euros in 2002, confirming the increasing internationalization of the Greek economy.

When taking under consideration the revised version of the 'Investment Development Path (IDP) theory' (Dunning and Narula, 1996), in which five main stages of development are recognised, one could argue that Greece can be considered as a stage three country. Countries in that stage experience a deterioration of the comparative advantage in the domestic labour intensive industries (increase in the domestic wages that exceed the level of productivity) and the consequent investment flow into one and two stage countries, so as to take advantage of the cheap labour and/or the natural resources. According to Dunning (1993), outward investment for countries on stage three could be either market seeking or resource seeking. Experience has shown that the Greek outward FDI is mostly market seeking. Overall, it can be said that the investment path of Greece is compatible with the theory of internationalisation (Johanson and Vahlne, 1977).

The determinants of the Greek investment in the Balkans

The analysis of the key determinants of the Greek FDI in the Balkan region can be better achieved by making the following categorisation: (a) General factors, (b) Push factors, (c) Pull factors (Labrianidis et al., 2004; Pournarakis and Varsakelis, 2002; Totev, 2005).

Firstly, the development of the Greek investment in the Balkan economies can be understood in the context of various factors of general applicability (Brada et al., 2004; Kitonakis and Kontis, 2008; Labrianidis et al., 2004):

- The increasing importance of FDI at a global level.
- The increasing trend towards the internationalisation of SMEs during the 1990s.
- The radical social and economic developments of the late 1980s (fall of communism).
- The development pattern of Greece (the country has been gradually transformed into a fully industrialised country).
- The spillover effects of the foreign investments that improved the Balkan economies (motivating even more companies to invest in the area).
- The ongoing progress in economic transition towards capitalism.
- The economic policies toward FDI (both in an EU and a regional level).

The most important factors pushing Greek companies away from the Greek (domestic) market, and leading them to invest in other countries (mostly Balkan) are (Kitonakis and Kontis, 2008; Labrianidis et al., 2004):

- The saturation of the Greek market and the intensification of imported competition in many sectors (gigantic multinationals with wide-known and extremely successful products had put the Greek companies on a hard competitive spot).
- The high labour costs in labour-intensive sectors.
- The favourable economic conditions in Greece (introduction of Euro, raising of significant capital from the Athens Stock Exchange, the GDP development and accumulated experience deriving from the Olympic Games of 2004).
- The need to pursue a 'follow the leader strategy' (the decision of many companies to invest in the Balkans motivated others to do so,

transforming the whole process of Greek FDI into a self-reinforcing loop).

- The difficulty in finding local trade partners in the Balkan region, the segmented and unreliable trade networks of merchants-distributors (the choice of internalization was a one way road).
- The opportunity to establish first mover's advantages.
- The opportunity to gain strategic positions.
- The opportunity to produce substantial revenues, thus empowering the mother company and gaining an advantage over domestic competitors.
- The opportunity to take advantage of the rare, valuable and difficult to imitate (Barney, 1991) resources that Greek companies possessed over their Balkan competitors. For example, in developed industries such as banking and mobile telecommunications, the long experience gained in Greece was a valuable asset for cultivating advance marketing skills and transferring integrated services abroad. The development lag between Greek and Balkan companies made these skills the penetrating force for successfully entering local markets.

Finally, there are various possible motives for Greek companies to make and investment in the Balkan region. These can be regarded as 'pull factors' (Botric and Skuflic, 2006; Kitonakis and Kontis, 2008; Labrianidis et al., 2004; Pournarakis and Varsakelis, 2002; Totev, 2005):

- The geographic proximity between Greece and Balkan countries.
- The low cost of raw material and workforce (companies exploited the opportunity to reduce labour costs -especially in labour intensive industries- and acquire a proximity to cheap raw materials that are significant in their production procedure).
- The large size of the Balkan markets as compared to Greece. The FDI literature in Central and East European countries has recognized market size as the most significant factor affecting the decision to invest in these economies. There is a widespread argument that most Balkan FDI has been market seeking rather than production seeking.
- The favourable conditions concerning rivalry, because of the absence of Western firms (companies from advanced industrialized countries hesitated to undertake the risk of operating in the Balkan region). Delays in investment programmes, currency deprecations, political instability and various cultural barriers have provided Greek investors with an initial breathing space, since the international capital was hesitant (at first) to invest in the area (the western competitors would have been extremely dangerous, because of their experience in

internalisation, their financial capabilities and their globally recognised brand name, among others).

- The fact that the Balkan markets are at an early stage of development and, therefore, competition is still based on prices and not on quality / differentiation of the product.
- The low density of local competition (relatively easier to build competitive advantages).
- The avoidance of tariff or non-tariff obstacles.
- The exploitation of existing relations within Balkan States. An investment in one Balkan country can be used for intra-regional trade, taking advantage of reduced tariffs, existing traditional trade channels, etc.
- The integration of Bulgaria and Romania into the EU.
- The prior existence of Greek companies and Greek communities encouraged the establishment of more Greek companies.
- The cultural proximity between Greece and Balkan states. Greek companies have a relatively good knowledge of the specific cultural characteristics of the Balkan countries, thus enhancing their product placement and acceptance.

On the other hand, the disadvantages of investing in the Balkans can be summarised as follows (Kitonakis and Kontis, 2008; Totev, 2005):

- Weak infrastructures.
- Hazy legal framework. There are continuing changes to regulations and laws.
- Lack of political and administrative continuum.
- Bureaucracy. There is an unwillingness of some state authorities to do their job and, therefore, the decisions of the administration are implemented slowly. There is, moreover, lack of information and failure to provide sufficient information on how to run a business.
- Weak tertiary sector.
- Delay in reforms. The reforms in the region lag behind similar processes in other transition countries (e.g. Slovenia, Czech Republic, Poland, the Baltic countries).
- The instability in the region as a whole.
- Corruption.
- Domestic firms are illegally avoiding taxes and there is a differential attitude to firms by the administration (both creating unfavourable competition).
- Week assistance from both National and International organisations.

The Greek investment in the Balkans

Since the political shift in the regimes of the former communist countries in the early 1990s, both trade and investment relations between Greece and the neighbouring Balkan states have followed an upward trend. A large number of Greek companies have undertaken numerous investment projects, thus reviving the traditional production and trade networks of the region or creating new ones (Kitonakis and Kontis, 2008). For the majority of the countries of the Balkan region, Greece represents the most important market in the area, a commercial crossroad, so to say. As such, it can contribute to the efforts of the transition economies in the restructuring and the stabilisation of their economies.

Generally, it can be said that the Greek economic performance in South-Eastern Europe has been positive, but not overwhelming (Demos et al., 2004; Stoian and Filippaios, 2008b). Greek organisations, being inexperienced in investing abroad, achieved satisfactory, but not optimal, results. There is no doubt that a county with significant experience in foreign direct investment would have achieved better results.

When it comes to trade, South-East European countries are among the first market destinations for Greek products. The volume of trade presented constant increase during the last 3 years with available official data (2006-2008), exceeding 8 billion Euros in 2008, showing a 7,1% raise compared to 2007 (7,4 billion Euros). The most significant trade partners of Greece are Bulgaria and Romania, having a share reaching 60% of the total trade volume of Greece with the countries of the Balkan region (Katseli, 2010).

As far as investments are concerned, Greece holds an important position in Balkan markets. The total invested Greek capital (1996-2008) exceeds 20 billion Euros (Katseli, 2010; FDI Magazine, 2010). Taking also into consideration the investments made by companies of Greek interests through their affiliates in third countries, such as the Netherlands, Luxembourg, Germany etc, the actual size of total Greek investments is significantly bigger. Greece is estimated to be first among foreign investors in Albania, FYROM and Serbia, third in Romania and forth in Bulgaria (Katseli, 2010; FDI Magazine, 2010; To Vima, 2009). In total, Greek investment capital is responsible for the creation and the retention of 200.000 jobs in the countries of the Balkan region (Mathiopoulou, 2008).

In Albania, Greece is responsible for the 40% of the invested foreign capital, reaching almost 550 million Euros, while it is estimated that approximately 270 companies of Greek interest are located in the country. In FYROM, Greece has always been the first investor, with total invested capital over 1 billion Euros. Greece, moreover, is the first investor in Serbia for the time being (2009), since Greek companies have invested approximately 2,5 billion Euros through 120 companies of exclusive Greek interests and 150 joint-ventures. Greece is, also, the third larger investor in Romania, with 4.500 Greek companies and a total of 3,1 billion Euros in invested capital. In Bulgaria, Greece holds the fourth place, with the capital invested being approximately 2,2 billion Euros. Additionally, Greek banks hold 26% of the total assets of the Bulgarian banking sector. Finally, coherent official data for Montenegro could not be retrieved (Katseli, 2010; FDI Magazine, 2010; To Vima, 2009).

Besides the above quantitative characteristics of the Greek investment in the Balkans, certain qualitative aspects should also be underlined (Bastian 2004; Demos et al., 2004; Iammarino and Pitelis, 2000; Labrianidis et al., 2004; Louri et al., 2000; Stoian and Filippaios, 2008a; Stoian and Filippaios, 2008b, Totev, 2005):

- In order to better understand the progressive growth of Greek FDI flows, one should first consider the economic geography of the target markets (Balkan countries). The position of the Balkan states provides an advantage to Greece, which has an ideal geographic proximity, since the large distance of the Balkan states from leading European markets and traditional locations of business concentration obstructs their integration into regional and international production networks. Thus, the decreased competition from market leaders allows Greece to develop competitive advantages.

- Certain circumstances that occurred in the second half of the 1990s and the beginning of the 2000s enhanced Greece's capability to invest abroad: (a) Greece succeeded in meeting the convergence criteria of the Maastricht Treaty, thus becoming a Euro-zone member and achieving fiscal stability (strong players emerged in banking, retail trade and telecommunication sectors, as well as in food industry and construction), (b) the undertaking of the 2004 Olympic Games and the subsequent heavy infrastructure spending allowed Greek companies to participate in complex projects and acquire experience that was significant for competing in the Balkan market, (c) the significant growth of the Athens Stock Exchange (ASE) provided investors with a key source of funds in order to finance their expansion strategies (it is not a coincidence that most leading Greek firms that successfully participating in the ASE started investing abroad: '3E', a Coca-Cola soft drinks subsidiary; 'Delta', dairy products, partner of Danone; 'Intracom', telecommunications, a partner of Siemens; 'Cosmote', telecommunications; 'Chipita' a PepsiCo food subsidiary). As already stated, the whole investment process was further enhanced by (a) the political support offered by the Greek Government and the desire to play a regional economic role and (b) the implementation of Greek policies that were specifically designed to transform the country into a key player in the region.

- The Greek investment flow derives from (a) purely domestic firms or (b) Greek subsidiaries of large multinational organisations. This fact is indicative of the transformation of Greece from a peripheral European country to a regional centre.

- In certain industries, a strategic move of a pioneer company was being followed by similar moves by its competitors, mainly as a reaction to actual opportunities but also out of fear of staying behind. As a result, local competition became regional.

- The majority of the Greek investment initiatives are concentrated in the fields of services, finance, construction, food industry and banking (the Greek banking sector has a predominant presence in the Balkans). Greek public corporations are also involved in the reconstruction of infrastructure networks and private companies participate in the construction of large infrastructure projects.

- Large Greek companies usually invest in more than one Balkan country, thus conducting strategic investments. For many of them, the entry was seen as an investment (Greek companies entered these markets knowing that they would operate at a loss for a period, but hoping that these losses would be compensated by the strong positions they would achieve once the markets started improving).

- Compared with other foreign companies, Greek businesses have certain socio-cultural advantages: they better understand consumers' behaviour and taste; they have better knowledge of the local markets and of the mentality of the Balkan people. These intimate socio-cultural relations play a significant role as an enhancing factor of the Greek GDI.

- Acquisitions and joint ventures are the most commonly used entry modes. Greek firms involved in FDI are larger than those engaged in domestic investment in terms of assets and turnover.

The current crisis and future prospects

The financial crisis and its impact on the Greek economy became a daily subject in the news, worldwide (BBC News, 2010). At the beginning of May 2010, a solution to help the country out of the debt crisis seemed to have been found by the means of the EU and the International Monetary Fund (IMF). The crisis has forced new levels of economic stringency, the imposition of new taxes and a public sector salary freeze. The Greek crisis has been a major test of the EU economic resilience. Moreover, it constitutes a development that may have significant impact on the Balkan countries (EU or not) which border the Greek economy (BBC News, 2010; FDI Magazine, 2010).

According to numerous economists (Bieber, 2010; FDI Magazine, 2010; Fotiadis, 2010; Jewell, 2010) the main fear in the Balkans has to do with the possible spillover of the recession from Greece to its neighbouring economies. Greece is, after all, not only a major investor in the Balkans, but also a donor and host to several hundred thousand economic migrants from the region.

A reverse Greek FDI trend is likely to follow in the next few years, while at the same time the Greek capital will struggle with recession effects back home. The Greek Central Bank has since last year advised Greek banks to adopt a restricted lending policy in the Balkans, since the region is expected to be hit hard by the ongoing recession (Fotiadis, 2010).

As a consequence of the crisis, Greek investors are also reconsidering their plans. For instance, only in the first nine months of 2009 over 70 million Euros of Greek capital left FYROM with the Greek owners of communication companies selling out and leaving the country (disinvestment strategy) (BBC News, 2010; FDI Magazine, 2010; Fotiadis, 2010).

Moreover, the role of Greece as a promoter of Balkans' integration into the EU will also be limited. The 'Hellenic Plan for the Economic Reconstruction of the Balkans' which has allocated so far 163,4 million Euros for improving public infrastructure and organising community projects in seven Balkan states is unlikely to complete its future projects under the current economic conditions (Bieber, 2010; Fotiadis, 2010).

On the other hand, various Balkan officials make positive predictions about the impact of the Greek crisis to their economies. The inward investment agencies of the Balkan states are optimistic that the Greek crisis will have a limited impact, or even a positive effect on Greek foreign investment. Official Balkan sources assume that that Greek companies may turn to investing in more competitively priced countries, since the increase in taxes in Greece have been made into a significant push factor. Moreover, it is expected that Greek companies might also export more due to the decreased demand at home, as a result of the public sector wage freeze (FDI Magazine, 2010; Jewell, 2010).

According to most predictions that have been made, the most possible scenario is that the Greek financial crisis will discourage Greek investors from over-extending themselves, both domestically and abroad. Access to capital and, likewise, general investor confidence will take a knock, at least until stability returns to the Greek economy (Bieber, 2010; FDI Magazine, 2010; Fotiadis, 2010; Jewell, 2010).

With regard to the mode of investment behaviour during the crisis, it seems that the divestment strategy is a road followed by many companies, while the stabilisation and non over-investment strategy are being the predominant ones.

Conclusions

FDI is an international phenomenon that attracts the attention of all economic entities of the globe. FDI has innumerable effects on the economy of a host country: It influences, among others, the production, employment, income, prices, exports, imports, economic growth, balance of payments, general welfare and the internalisation degree of the recipient country (Erdal and Tatoglu, 2002). The significant positive influence of FDI to the economy of the host country has created severe competition between various recipient countries. The present study focuses on FDI that have been made in the Balkan region by Greek companies.

During the last two decades, Greek companies have exploited the geographical proximity to South-East European countries as a significant advantage for the systematic international expansion of their commercial activities. At the forefront of this expansion were banks and telecommunications companies. These two sectors served as catalysts for numerous other firms of all sizes and sectors to take the courage and invest in the Balkan region. As a result, Greek companies have successfully managed to penetrate the economies of the Balkan countries, and, nowadays, Greece is estimated to be first among foreign investors in Albania, FYROM and Serbia, third in Romania and forth in Bulgaria.

Today, Greek companies are firmly anchored in the Balkan economies. The horizon of their investment is long term. They mostly count on the assumption that they will be among the first to benefit from a continuous improvement in the economic conditions of the neighbouring countries (first mover advantage). Romania and Bulgaria stand out as the favoured destinations for Greek FDI in the region, especially since their integration to the EU. New investment opportunities in the Balkans are the regional energy sectors, the modernization of electricity grids, water, oil and natural gas utilities, regional transport infrastructures (highway and bridge construction), border crossings, airport modernization and revamping railway networks.

The present concludes by attempting to bridge the gap between theory and real-life practice and suggest possible courses of action for Greek, or other companies that intend to invest in the Balkans, or elsewhere. The extended literature review of recent publications indicates that when a company decides to invest in a foreign economy it needs to be mindful of the valuable lessons learned by their predecessors:

- The most successful tactic is to make relatively small, incremental investments and use them as a stepping-stone for the next. Large ad hoc investments, made without a coherent, long-term strategy, tend to create difficulties.
- Association with international financial institutions such as the European Bank for Reconstruction and Development (EBRD) and the International Finance Corporation (IFC) can provide valuable resources and management aid.
- Strong, but flexible, corporate structure is necessary, so that the results of the company abroad in the start-up stage do not impact negatively the domestic profit and loss statement.

- Willingness to export know-how and management skills is essential. The continuous development of the human capital will help the company to achieve its targets.
- "Putting the locals in charge" is the best way of having total control over the company: local managers know the special cultural, demographic characteristics of the country, they understand better the legal issues and the verbal laws of the market and they can help with the relationships of the company with the State.
- A strong back office capable of coping with the variances of foreign currency markets is a must. Hedging is often best achieved by borrowing in the local currency but, when long term funding is not available, an ability to swap rapidly currency against debt obligations is essential.

Finally, it should be noted that with the accumulated experience from investing in the Balkan Region, sufficient critical mass and modern management skills, there is no reason that Greek companies cannot invest in places as far away as China in the same manner as their EU counterparts (Kamaras, 2008; Koutsikos, 2006). We sincerely hope that the present study points to that direction.

References

Barney, J.B., 1991, Firm Resources and Sustained Competitive Advantage, *Journal of Management*, 17, 1, pp. 99-120.

Bastian, J., 2004, Knowing your way in the Balkans: Greek foreign direct investment in Southeast Europe, *Southeast European and Black Sea Studies*, 4, 3, pp. 458-490.

BBC News, 2010, Q&A: Greece's economic woes, retrieved May 3, 2010 from http://news.bbc.co.uk/2/hi/business/8508136.stm.

Bieber, F., 2010, The Economic Crisis, Greece and The Balkans, *Eurasia Review*, retrieved May 3, 2010 from http://www.eurasiareview.com/2010/05/economic-crisis-greece-and-balkans.html.

Botric, V. and Skuflic, L., 2006, Main Determinants of Foreign Direct Investment in the Southeast European Countries, *Transition Studies Review*, 13, 2, pp. 359-377.

Brada, J., Kutan, A. and Yigit, T., 2004, The Effects of Transition and Political Instability On Foreign Direct Investment Inflows: Central Europe and the Balkans, Zentrum für Europäische Integrationsforschung Center for European Integration Studies, Rheinische Friedrich-Wilhelms-Universität Bonn.

Carstensen, K. and Toubal, F., 2004, Foreign direct investment in Central and Eastern European countries: a dynamic panel analysis, *Journal of Comparative Economics*, 32, pp. 3-22.

Deichmann, J., Karidis, S. and Sayek, S., 2003, Foreign direct investment in Turkey: regional determinants, *Applied Economics*, 35, pp. 1767-1778.

Demos, A., Filippaios, F. And Papanastassiou, M., 2004, An event study analysis of outward foreign direct investment: The case of Greece, *International Journal of the Economics of Business*, 11, 3, pp. 329-348.

Dunning, J., 1993, *The globalization of business*, Routledge, London and New York.

Dunning, J. and Narula, R., 1996, The investment development path revisited: Some emerging issues, Dunning, J. and Narula, R. (eds.), *Foreign direct investment and governments: Catalysts for economic restructuring*, London, Routledge.

Dunning, J.H., 2001, The eclectic (OLI) paradigm of international production: Past, present and future, *International Journal of the Economics of Business*, 8, 2, pp. 173-190.

ELKE, 2006, *Report on Greek investments in the Balkans and the Black Sea region*, Athens: Hellenic Centre for Investment.

Erdal, F. and Tatoglu, E., 2002, Locational determinants of foreign direct investment in an emerging market economy: evidence from Turkey, *Multinational Business Review*, 10, 1, pp. 21-28.

FDI Magazine, 2010, Greece's economy: impact on the Balkan backyard?, retrieved April 25, 2010 from http://mepra.net/index.php?view=article&catid=15:staff&id=15:tomblass&format=pdf&option=com_content&Itemid=7.

Fischer, S., Sahay, R. and Végh, C., 1996, Stabilization and growth in transition economies: The early experience, *Journal of Economic Perspectives*, 10, pp. 45–66.

Fotiadis, A., 2010, Greek Crisis Impacts the Balkans, *Inter Press Service*, retrieved April 25, 2010 from http://ipsnews.net/news.asp?idnews=50734.

Haddad, M. and Harrison, A., 1993, Are there positive spillovers from direct foreign investment?, *Journal of Developing Economics*, 42, pp. 51-74.

Hosseini, H., 2005, An economic theory of FDI: A behavioural economics and historical approach, *The Journal of Socio-Economics*, 34, pp. 528-541.

Hunya, G., 2004, *Foreign Direct Investment in South East Europe in 2003-2004*, The Vienna Institute for International Economic Studies, Vienna.

Iammarino, S. and Pitelis, C., 2000, Foreign direct investment and 'less favoured regions': Greek FDI in Bulgaria and Romania, *Global Business Review*, 1, 2, pp. 155-170.

Jewell, M., 2010, Investors should care about Greece, MSNBC, retrieved May 3, 2010 from http://www.msnbc.msn.com/id/36972794/ns/business-personal_finance.

Johanson, J. and Vahlne, J.E., 1977, The internationalisation process of the firm: a model of knowledge development and increasing foreign market commitment, *Journal of International Business Studies*, 8, pp. 23-32.

Kamaras, A., 2001, A Capitalist Diaspora: the Greeks in the Balkans, *London School of Economics and Political Science,* Discussion Paper no. 4.

—. 2008, Complementary bilateral relations, *The Bridge: A bimonthly review on European integration*, retrieved June 11, 2008, from http://www.bridge-mag.com/magazine/index.php?option=com_content&task=view&id=191&Itemid=31.

Katseli, L., 2010, Priorities of Greece, *The Bridge - A quarterly review on European integration*, retrieved April 5, 2010 from http://www.bridge-mag.com/magazine/index.php?option=com_content &task=view&id=662.

Kekic, L., 2005, Foreign direct investment in the Balkans: Recent trends and prospects, *Southeast European and Black Sea Studies*, 5, 2, pp. 171-190.

Kitonakis, N. and Kontis, A., 2008, The determinants of Greek foreign direct investments in southeast European countries, *Southeast European and Black Sea Studies*, 8, 3, pp. 269-281.

Koutsikos, P., 2006, Greece and Investment in the Balkans - Turkey and the Black Sea Region, *Trade with Greece*, 36, pp. 10-15.

Labrianidis, L., 2001, Geographical proximity matters in the orientation of FDI: Greek FDI in the CEECs, in Petrakos, G. and Totev, S. (eds), *Economic Cooperation in the Balkans: A Regional Approach to European Integration*, Aldershot, Ashgate, pp. 463–489.

Labrianidis, L., Lyberaki, A., Tinios, P. and Hatziprokopiou, P., 2004, "Inflow of Migrants and Outflow of Investment: Aspects of Interdependence between Greece and the Balkans, *Journal of Ethnic and Migration Studies*, 30, 6, pp. 1-26.

Lankes, P. and Venables, J., 1996, Foreign direct investment in economic transition: the changing pattern of investment, *Economics of Transition*, 4, 2, pp. 331–347.
Liu, X. and Zou, H., 2008, The impact of greenfield FDI and mergers and acquisitions on innovation in Chinese high-tech industries, *Journal of World Business*, 43, pp. 352-364.
Louri, H., Papanastasiou, M., and Lantouris, J., 2000, FDI in the EU Periphery: A Multinomial Logit Analysis of Greek Firm Strategies, *Regional Studies*, 34, 5, pp. 419-427.
Markusen, J.R. and Venables, A.J., 1999, Foreign direct investment as a catalyst for industrial development, *European Economic Review*, 43, pp. 335-356.
Mathiopoulou, M., 2008, Balkans: In alert the investors of the Northern Greece, Newspaper Macedonia, 30/10/2008, retrieved April 5, 2010 from http://www.makthes.gr/news/economy/27207, in Greek language.
Nimetz, M. (2005), "Southeastern Europe in the Age of Globalism", *Mediterranean Quarterly*, 16, 1, pp. 16-32.
Perez, T., 1997, Multinational enterprises and technological spillovers: an evolutionary model, *Evolutionary Economics*, 7, pp. 169-192.
Pournarakis, M. and Varsakelis, N., 2002, Foreign Direct Investment in Central and Eastern Euriopean Countries: Do Institutions matter?, *EIBA Annual Conference*, Athens, Greece.
Price Waterhouse Coopers, 2010, Foreign Direct Investment in Central and Eastern Europe: A case of boom and bust?, *Economic Views*, retrieved April 5, 2010 from http://www.pwc.com/en_CZ/cz/tiskove-zpravy-2010/fdi-in-cee-final-report-march10.pdf.
Roberts, M., 2010, Foreign investment in central and eastern Europe takes a major knock?, retrieved March 25, 2010 from http://www.balkans.com/open-news.php?uniquenumber=51707.
Slaveski, T. and Nedanovski, P., 2002, Foreign Direct Investment in the Balkans, *Eastern European Economics*, 40, 4, pp. 83-99.
Stoian, C. and Filippaios, G., 2008a, Dunning's eclectic paradigm: A holistic, yet context specific framework for analysing the determinants of outward FDI: Evidence from international Greek investments, *International Business Review*, 17, pp. 349-367.
Stoian, C. and Filippaios, G., 2008b, Foreign direct investment in Central, Eastern and South Eastern Europe: an 'eclectic' approach to Greek investments, *International Journal of Entrepreneurship and Innovation Management*, 8, 5, pp. 542- 564.
Tatoglu, E. and Glaister, K., 1998, An analysis of motives for western FDI in Turkey, *International Business Review*, 7, pp. 203-230.

To Vima, 2009, 74th International Exhibition of Thessaloniki - The crisis strikes the Greek investments in the South-Eastern Europe, retrieved April 5, 2010 from http://www.tovima.gr/default.asp?pid=2&ct=32&artid=286947&dt=06/09/2009, in Greek language.

Totev, S., 2005, Foreign direct investment in Bulgaria: advantages and disadvantages to investment, *South-East Europe Review*, 4, pp. 91-104.

United Nations, 2009, *World Investment Report*, United Nations, New York.

Zagkos, C., Kyridis, A., Golia, P. and Vamvakidou, I., 2007, Greek University Students Describe the Role of Greece in the Balkans: From Equality to Superiority, *Nationalities Papers*, 35, 2, pp. 341-367.

The Investment Attractiveness Increasing of Black Sea Post-socialists Countries: Synergetic Approach

Yuriy Makogon, Tatyana Orekhova and Oleksiy Ryabchyn

Abstract

The modern situation which has developed in global economy as a whole and economy of the Black Sea countries in particular, demands definition of the accurate purposes and clear priorities of social and economic development of cities of this region, their self-determination among objects of the internal and external environment, on regional and international markets, which will allow to build relations with investors and financial organisations, and to react adequately to strategic calls of the global economic system.

This article is devoted to the directions of investment attractiveness increasing of Black Sea post socialist countries which are formed on the base of Donetsk Investment Development Program with the usage of synergetic forming approaches.

Synergetics has arisen in response to the crisis over a stereotypical, linear thinking. Its main features are the following (Yankovskiy et al., 2010):

- representation of chaos as an exclusively destructive beginning of the world;
- review of contingency as a secondary factor;
- world is independent of micro fluctuations (oscillations) of lower life levels and cosmic influences;

- review of the disequilibrium and instability as a nuisance that must be overcome, because of negative and destructive role;
- processes occurring in the world are reversible in the time and predictable for long periods of time;
- development is a linear, progressive, non-alternative process (and if there are alternatives, they can be only casual deviations from the main flow. They are subordinated to it, and finally are absorbed by it);
- past stage is only of historical interest, and return to the old is a dialectic removal of the previous level and has a new basis; world has cause-effect relations;
- causal chains are linear, and consequence, if is not identical to reason, is proportional to it, i.e. the more energy, the greater result.

According to Synergetics, two models describe the society development as a nonlinear system: evolutionary and bifurcation. Distinctive feature of the evolutionary development is the constancy of the system quality. This is a period with well-predicted linear changes. However, it is here the growth of internal disequilibrium occurs, a growing crisis. The destruction, destabilization of each system has its own way. The system structure has its weak points, which can have the greatest impact. Therefore, destabilization depends primarily not on the specifics of external influence, but on the system structure.

Economic development, as well as economic crises, has the objective cyclical nature. The economic development is a cyclical movement from gradually developing equilibrium to its gradual disturbance, and formation of a new equilibrium at a higher level, the equilibrium of a new quality. We must not only recognize the objective character and the inevitability of the cyclical transformation of dynamic economic development, but also develop a system of measures for the application of counter-cyclical policy of States and interstate unions. In many countries the cyclical nature of economic development was ignored and countercyclical regulatory mechanisms were not included. This has extremely weakened the economic policy and led to the non competitiveness of economic systems because of incorrect forecasts of crises and catastrophes.

The approach offers an estimation of investment potential of cities and specifies directions to increase their investment appeal, which has a universal character for the majority of the post socialist countries of Black Sea Coast, considering that they share rather similar characteristics or conditions, internal and external to their environments, which have affected their development.

Introduction

Nowadays, because of the global economy, in the economies of the Black sea post socialist countries there are particular accurate and clear priorities in the socioeconomic development at the cities of this region; their self-determination among the objects of internal and external environment on regional and international markets which will enable to effectively build up relations with investors and financial organisations and to react adequately on strategic challenges of global economic system.

The methodological research of global and regional integration of economic systems was initially done by Amin, 2003; Wallerstein, 1984; Levitt, 1983; Meadows, 2004; Modelski, 2008; Myrdal, 1957; Randers, 2004; Stieglitz, 2000; Frank, 1981; Huntington, 1996; Schumpeter, 1954 and others.

The most significant works concerning this problem belong to such Ukrainian and Russian scientists as Bilous, 2001; Blank, 1995; Budkin, 2002; Kozak, 2004; Lukianenko, 2004; Novitskiy, 2003; Pakhomov, 2001; Smitienko, 2010; Shnirkov, 2000 etc.

Despite the considerable number of works of foreign and domestic scientists concerning investment attractiveness of the countries, regions and certain branches of economy, there should be a systematic approach to investigate the investment development process of cities of the Black sea countries, in the context of integration processes intensification within the boundaries of The Black Sea Economic Cooperation Organization.

The aim of this article is to define approaches of investment attractiveness growth for the cities of the Black Sea Region, based on the examples of the methods used for the creation of Donetsk Investment Development Program.

Research results

The invention of computers and the development of computer technology have had a significant impact on the methodologies used by scientists, researchers and economists. Until recently, actually, a 'life' experience served to economists as the analogue of experiment, which they have scooped from publications in scientific journals, monographs, etc. The further improvement of methods for the study of socio-economic systems may be the development of a toolkit, which makes it possible to carry out experiments with the model, but not with the system itself. Methodological basis for modelling and studying the economy as a complex nonlinear system can be Synergetics or Selforganization theory. At present, the study of socioeconomic systems from the standpoint of the new scientific directions of Synergetics – Catastrophe theory, Chaos theory, bifurcation, attractors, entropy, extra capacity and so on – is actively developing.

In spite of the increased interest in Synergetics in recent years (Yankovskiy et al., 2010), a lack of works in the field of mathematical modelling of socio-economic systems and insufficient number of teams working at a modern level are observed.

Synergetic ideas began to penetrate to the socio-economic sciences from the late 80s. Basically, with few exceptions, the authors of the first works in the field of economic synergetics were physicists and mathematicians. Results have been obtained by means of synergetics specific toolkit - identification of order parameters, design of nonlinear mathematical models, carrying out of computer experiments, which should be comprehended by economists, and they, in some sense, can change the methodology of economic researches.

'Why do economists deal with Synergetics?'. Synergetics, first of all, is of great importance as a view on events that take place in the world, differing from the traditional deterministic aspect, which has been dominating science since Newton's times. In other words, Synergetics is useful as means of scientific data interpretation in a new way. It allows you to observe and assess what, probably, would remain outside the traditional review. Thus, the initial terms of orthodox economics are the following:

- people attain to the goal: consumers – to get the maximum benefit, producers - the maximum profit;
- movement to the goal is a predefined process, clearly predicted and universal (i.e. identical in all countries). The result of the process equilibrium market – is also unambiguous;
- movement to the equilibrium market occurs spontaneously and state control for this purpose is not needed and is also not desirable.

Synergetic approach, on the contrary, bases its conclusions on the following:

- economy is a developing system and should take into account the theory of developing systems;
- when moving to the goal, due to nonlinear feedback there can be unstable and chaotic stages. This, in its turn, may lead to the different final states of market equilibrium. Modern science can estimate the probability of different options, but cannot give a definite answer which of them will take place. Therefore, modern science does not accept the unambiguous prediction of the future and, thus, it differs from the orthodox economics;
- when there are several equilibrium states, the problem of choice is aggravated. This problem should be resolved by State taking into account the peculiarities and national interests of the country.

Synergetics let us see the world from 'another system of coordinates'. Synergetic scientists' conclusions are often unexpected and contrary to accepted truths. However, it is such a view that allows us to find out what is lost in the traditional perspective, and to warn of the serious dangers that may arise during the development of society, if the critical, evolutionarily proved decisions will not be taken at the bifurcation moment of choice. Possibility of scientific study of crises and catastrophes has long been questioned because of the originality and uniqueness of these phenomena. Later, however, many common elements have been identified in development of crises and catastrophes of various natures.

According to Synergetics (Yankovskiy et al., 2010), two models describe the society development as a nonlinear system: evolutionary and bifurcation. A distinctive feature of the evolutionary development is the stability of the system quality. This is a period with well-predicted linear changes. However, it is here the growth of internal disequilibrium occurs, a growing crisis. The destruction, destabilization of each system has its own way. The system structure has its weak points, which can have the greatest impact. Therefore, destabilization depends primarily, not on the specifics of external influence, but on system structure.

The essence of the investment climate should be considered at macro- and microeconomic levels. At the macro level it includes factors that characterize political and economic situation in a host country, and the socio-psychological condition of the population. In the first case, the main focus in placed on such parameters as state policy concerning foreign investments, the tradition of observance of international agreements, the propensity to nationalization of foreign property, the solidity of state institutions, the level of state interference in the economy etc. According to conditions the political factor is dominating when evaluating the investment climate in our country by a potential investor.

In terms of the economic parameters of the investment climate, the prior ones are indexes that characterise the overall macroeconomic dynamics, the currency status, financial and credit system of the country, customs regime and the regime of the work force employment.

At the micro level the investment climate reveals itself through bilateral relations between an investor and the certain government bodies, economic entities - suppliers, buyers, banks, trade unions and working teams of a host company, while both levels are closely interrelated. The investment climate is formed under the influence of the management activity of the public authorities. The latter can be consciously directed to the establishment of the particular investment environment in the country and it can be built without taking into account the possible consequences for the foreign enterprise, but with the influence on it. Thus, every country open to the import of capital has at its disposal a specific system of capital adopting that represents a set of the elements of the regulatory and legal base and institutions which carry out state policy with regard to foreign capital investments. Generally, capital acceptance system reflects the intention of the host country to find the optimal variant to include foreign investments into the solution of foreground tasks of national development.

To implement these objectives defined in Donetsk socioeconomic development Strategy until 2020, it was provided the elaboration of Donetsk Investment Development Program, the main aim of which was to attract maximum investments from all the sources and an increase in the efficiency of their usage by concentrating on the prior directions of the socioeconomic and social development of the city. The result of this program realisation should be:

- the improvement of living standards and the population welfare, in accordance with strategy defined natural and monetary indexes of the socioeconomic growth of the city and the standard of living in Donetsk;
- the guaranteeing of constant socioeconomic development of the city on the basis of the prior activities determination and economic policy directions;
- Donetsk integration into the system of national and international flow of financial resources;
- the formation of partnership between city's executive authorities, representatives of business and general public;
- the creation of an effective control system of the city in order to solve the problems connected to the socioeconomic development.

In order to achieve this goal in the process of the work done by the executive team, the leader of the work team, who is the author of this article, has set and solved the following:

- an assessment of investment attractiveness and Donetsk potential has been made;
- the directions of investment attractiveness increase and realization of Donetsk investment potential have been elaborated in order to solve socioeconomic development tasks;
- the long-term and short-term program of measures and actions has been elaborated to mobilize investment resources from budget and off-budget funds, private domestic and foreign sources and also to use them effectively for the constant innovative development of the city;
- the system of encouraging companies, which are busy with the construction of buildings of paramount importance for the city, has been formed;
- the methodical security of the assessment of economic and social effect has been developed taking into account investment projects, which can be implemented with use of state measures of stimulation;
- the information support system of the city's investment development has been formed;
- the directions of constant monitoring system of the Donetsk investment climate have been determined.

Figure 1. System of analytical indexes, which characterize the level of economic development in Donetsk, Dnepropetrovsk, Kiev

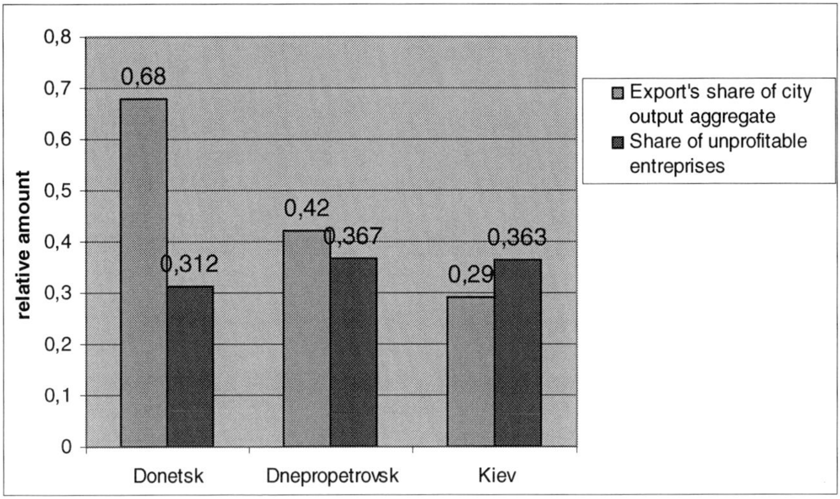

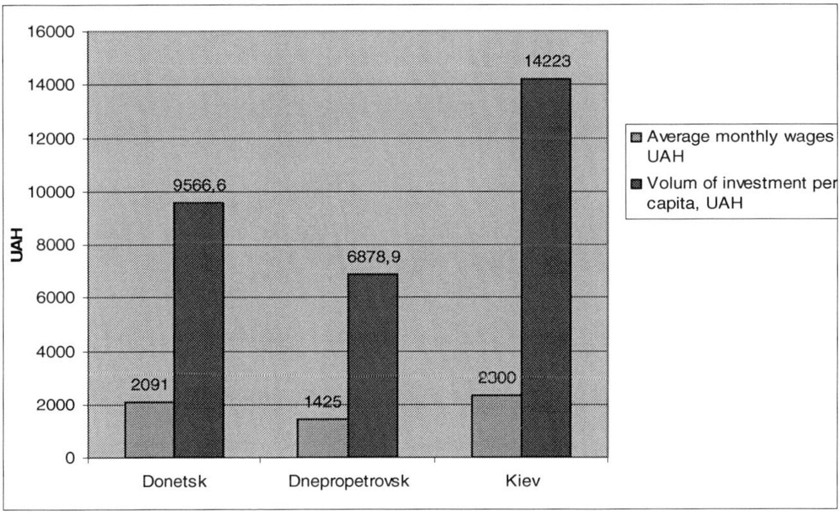

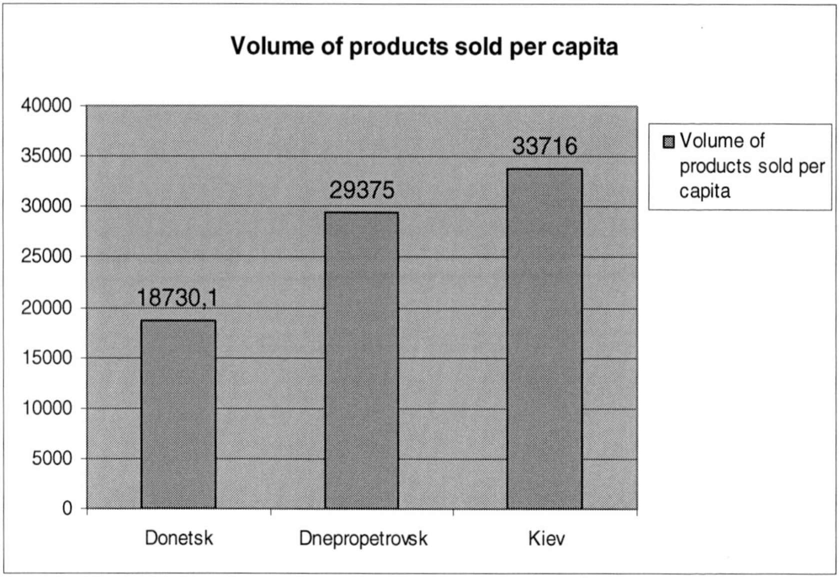

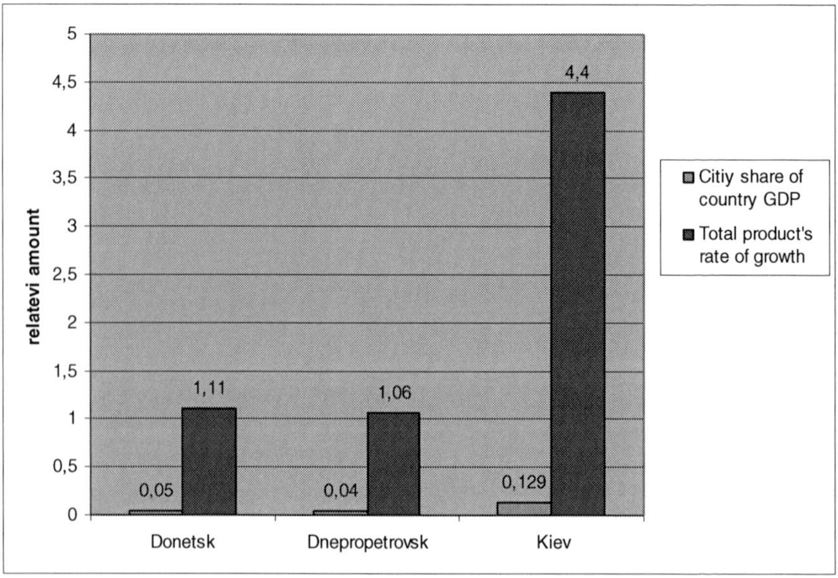

Source: Statistic department of Kiev, Donetsk and Dnepropetrovsk

The integrated index of cities' investment attractiveness, based on the author's methods (Orekhova, 2009) was used to calculate an average quantity of five synthetic indexes, which are the average quantity of the system of standard analytical indexes:

$$G = 0{,}25ED + 0{,}2II + 0{,}2SDCh + 0.15MRD + 0{,}20IP,$$

Where:

ED –the level of city's economic development;
II –the development of commercial and investment infrastructure;
SDCh –socio-demographic characteristic of the city;
MRD –the development of market relations;
IP –innovation potential of the city.

The assessment of Donetsk investment attractiveness potential was made firstly on the principals of SWOT analysis, followed by a comparative analysis of the similar indexes in Kiev and Dnipropetrovsk cities, whose leaders used to attract the direct foreign investments to Ukraine.

The comparative analysis of the indexes that indicate the level of economic growth in Kiev, Dnepropetrovsk and Donetsk allowed us to draw the conclusion that in Donetsk a number of the unprofitable businesses are lower by 15% than a similar index in Dnepropetrovsk, and by 14.01 % in Kiev. The share of export in an output aggregate of the city exceeds the similar index by 2.1 in Kiev and by 1.46 times in Dnipropetrovsk.

At the same, time the volume of the sold products per capita in Donetsk is lower than similar indexes in Dnepropetrovsk and Kiev (more than by 1.57 and 1.8 times respectively). Besides Donetsk is behind the above mentioned cities in terms of the output aggregate increase (in comparison with Kiev – almost by 4 times), and, in terms of the city's specific gravity index in the gross product of Ukraine, Donetsk 2.58 times behind Kiev. Although the Donetsk average wage rate is 1.5 higher than the index in Dnepropetrovsk, it is 1.1 times lower than the wage rate in Kiev. The level of capital investments per capita in Donetsk is higher than the similar index in Dnepropetrovsk, but 4656,4 UAH (by 1.5 times) lower than in Kiev.

The comparative analysis of the commercial and investment infrastructure development that has been carried out, has shown that the number of stock and commodity exchanges in Donetsk are the same as in Dnepropetrovsk and 1.1 times higher than in Kiev (Figure 2).

At the same time Donetsk is 2.8 times lower than in Kiev regarding the number of construction companies involved in hotel business development is by 1.5 times lower than in Kiev and by 1.53 times than in Dnepropetrovsk and as for number of telephone lines per thousand inhabitants – Donetsk is lower than Kiev by 1.24, Dnepropetrovsk by 1.11 times.

Figure 2. Indexes, which characterize the level of development commercial and investment infrastructure

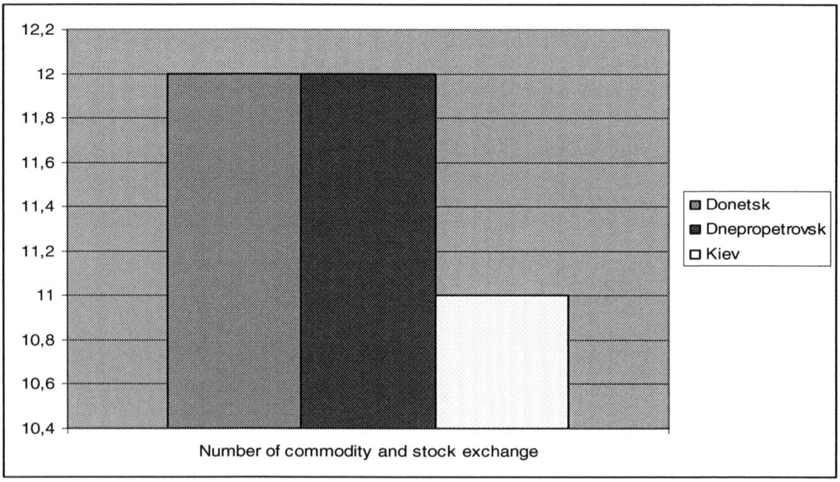

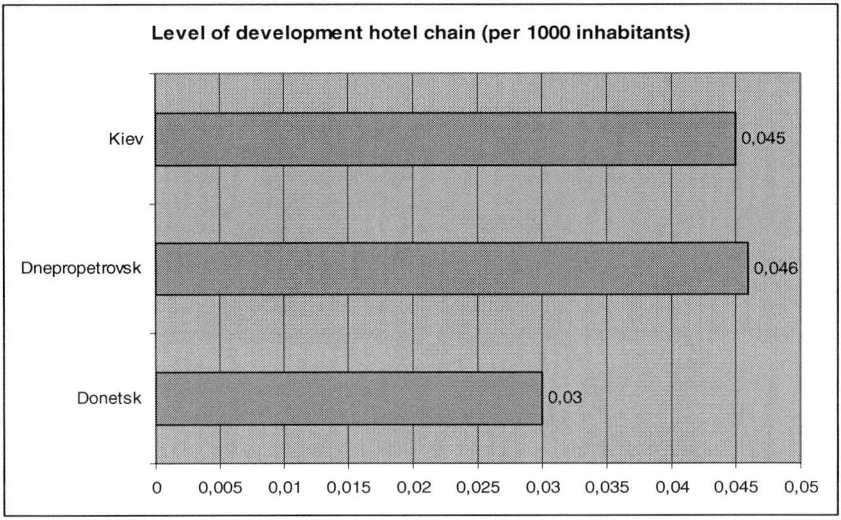

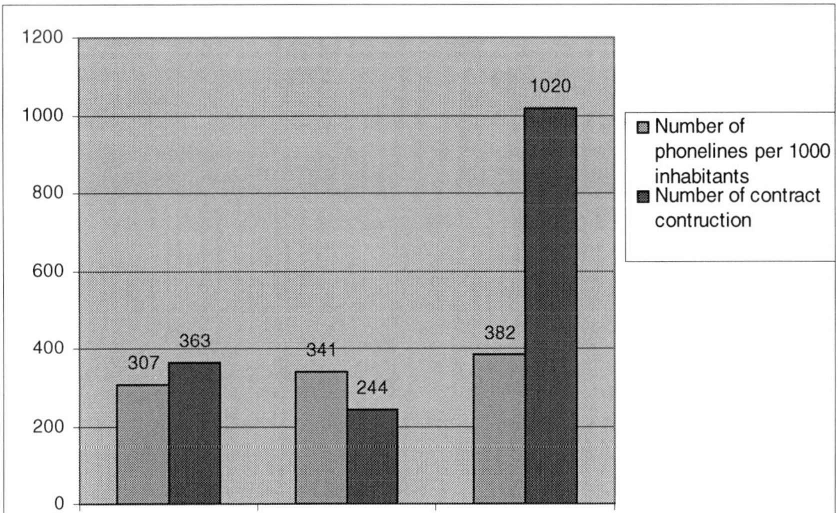

Source: Statistic department of Kiev, Donetsk and Dnepropetrovsk

According to comparative analysis of the main demographic characteristics, Donetsk has a lower ratio of University students to total population than, which is 2 times lower than Kiev.

In terms of the average monthly wage Donetsk is ahead of Dnepropetrovsk and behind Kiev (Figure 3).

Figure 3. City's social-demographic indexes

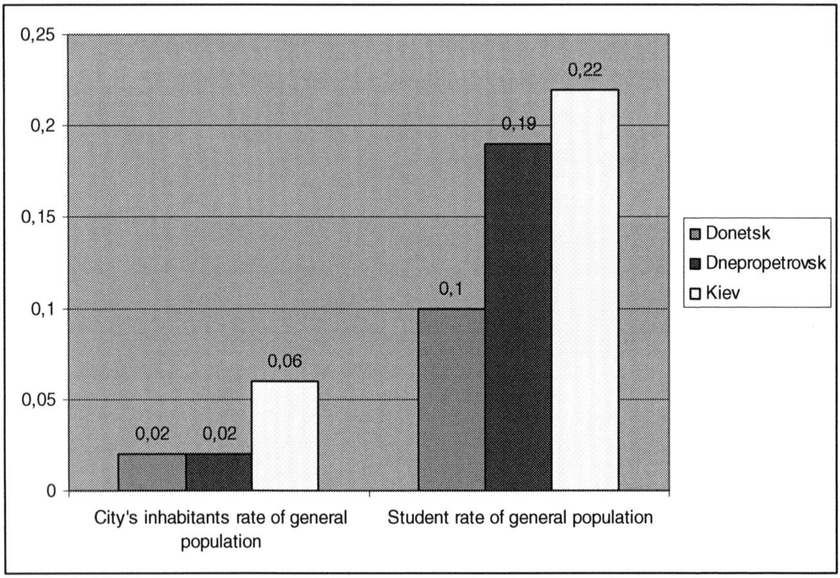

Source: Statistic department of Kiev, Donetsk and Dnepropetrovsk

The comparative analysis of the level of market relations development in the above cities has shown that Donetsk is a leader in terms of the index of a joint stock companies share in the total number of economic entities (by 6.3 times higher than in Dnepropetrovsk and by 1.73 times – than in Kiev (Figure 4).

At the same time we can see the Donetsk's weak position in terms of the number of enterprises with foreign investments (by 3.7 and 6.5 times respectively) (Figure 4).

The comparative analysis of indexes that characterise the level of innovation potential development reveals that Donetsk is behind in terms of the number of "SRACD" executives compared with Dnepropetrovsk by 1.98 times, with Kiev – by 7.28 times; in terms of share of the enterprises that introduce innovations it is 3.6 lower than Kiev; in terms of the volume of the 'SRACD" implemented – by 1.6 times than in Dnepropetrovsk and by 6.7 times than Kiev (Figure 5).

Figure 4. Status of development market relations indexes

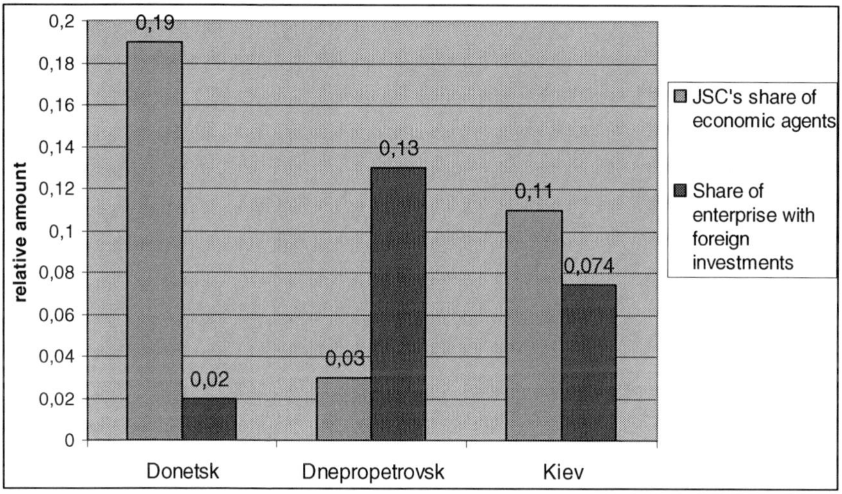

Source: Statistic department of Kiev, Donetsk and Dnepropetrovsk

Figure 5. The level of development of innovative potential in cities

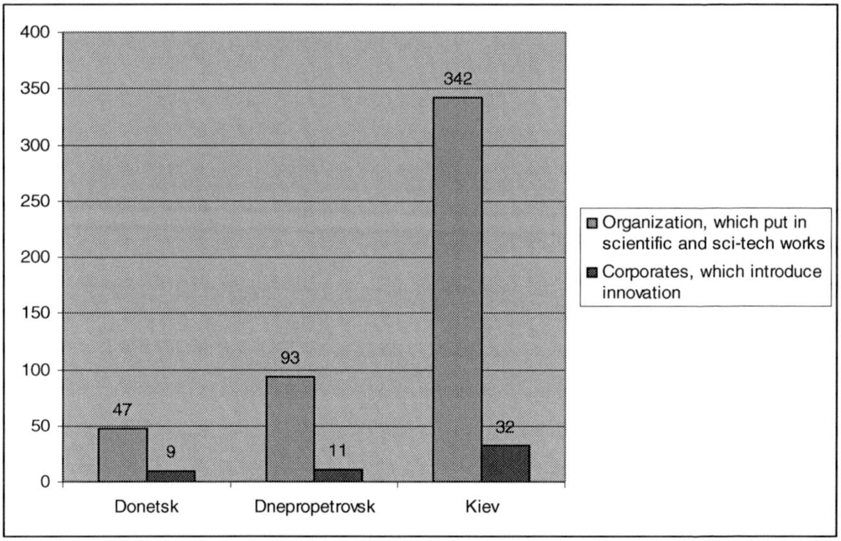

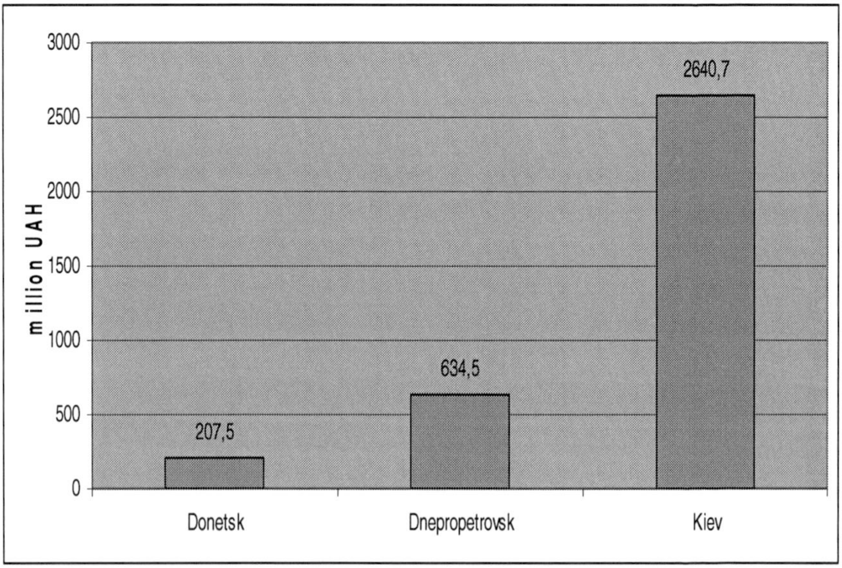

Source: Statistic department of Kiev, Donetsk and Dnepropetrovsk

So, the comparative analysis conducted on the basis of author's program of the investment attractiveness potential of Donetsk, Kiev and Dnepropetrovsk has shown that Donetsk is 1.5 lower than Kiev in terms of the integrated index of investment attractiveness potential, but it is ahead of Dnepropetrovsk by 1.2 times; this is also confirmed by data about actual attracted foreign investments in the economies of these cities (Figure 6).

Thus, strengths of investment potential of Donetsk are its economic and geographic location, high industrial potential and good raw materials, presence of large internal investors, developed system of inter-industrial links, presence of vertically-integrated businesses, high personal income, in comparison with average income in Ukraine, presence of high scientific and skilled potential, high level of education.

Figure 6. The accounting result of integrated indexes of investment potential in Donetsk, Dnepropetrovsk and Kiev.

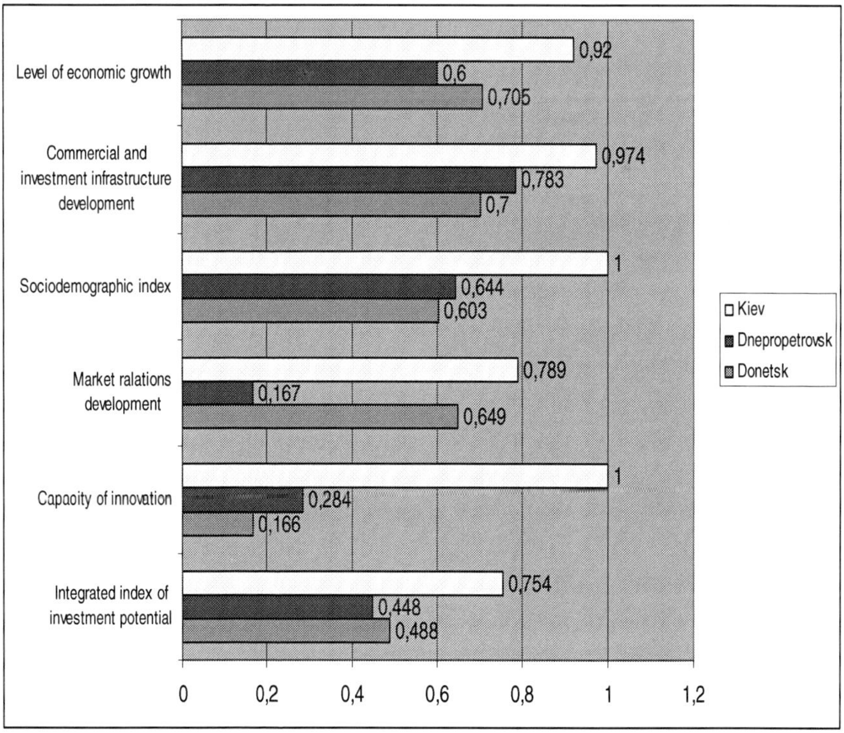

Source: Statistic department of Kiev, Donetsk and Dnepropetrovsk

Business infrastructure is a resource which makes Donetsk attractive for investors (transport, road and rail network, hotel chain, telecommunication service, housing and community amenities, informative services). Dynamic of investments from all sources of financing, development of market relations, part of low-technology branches of industrial production, enterprises innovative activity also play their role in this city's attractiveness.

The long-term and short-term programs of the city's investment development programmes need to mobilise investments within a short-term period (before 2012) for the real sector of economy – 6645682.2 thousands UAH, in the services and infrastructure sector – 12014656.1 thousands UAH, in the social sector – 572950 thousands UAH, in the innovation and energy conservation sector – 586120,015 thousands UAH, in the ecology and environment protection sector – 989134 thousands UAH; in a long-term period (before 2020): in the real economy sector – 3232189 thousands UAH, in the services and infrastructure sector – 194191117.6 thousands UAH, in the social sector – 255805 thousands UAH, in the innovation and energy-saving sector – 4944369.55 thousands UAH, in the ecology and environment protection sector – 60126 thousands UAH .

The total sum invested in perspective projects which were undertaken as a part of the Donetsk Investment Development Program before 2020 was 7652964.9 thousands UAH, the total demand for investments for these projects is 241811379.6 thousands UAH. The general systematization of financial sources of Donetsk Investment Program realization before 2020 is presented in Figure 7.

The traditional financial sources of investment in industrial projects and in services are private capital, both from private investors' funds and credit funds, not including the state owned objects.

From the above said the directions taken to increase investment attractiveness and realise Donetsk's investment potential should be:

Figure 7. Financing sources of investment development program in Donetsk to 2020

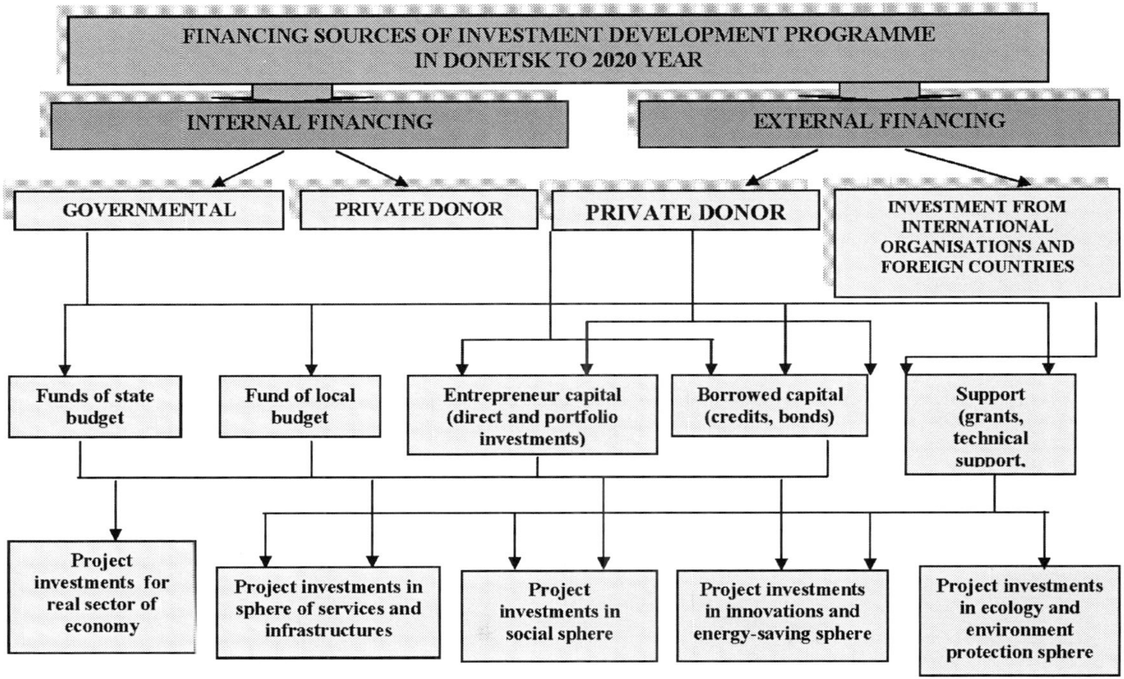

the intensification of investment attractiveness aimed at infrastructure development and, more specifically, transport infrastructure development with regard to socioeconomic needs of city's development; high speed rates of communication infrastructure development, increase of investment attractiveness of IT spheres; a substantial improvement of national telecommunication network; construction of shopping malls, offices, cultural and sport centres; development of the hotel business, reconstruction of old and construction of the new accommodation, reconstruction of engineering networks and equipping of house and municipal services, in order to provide citizens with living conditions that meet up-to-date quality standards; relocation of industrial sites way from the centre of the city;

the improvement of the normative legal regulation of the entrepreneurship: improvement of the procedure of passing and obtaining permissive documents; development of the new redaction of Donetsk building Rules in accordance with the General plan of the city; the confirmation of the normative estimated money value of Donetsk non-agricultural lands;

the investment potential development with the aim of successive transition to international standards of industrial goods production; economic stimulation of resource- and energy saving, implementation of environmentally friendly equipment and technology, extension of the technologies in which innovative resources are used; the formation of ecological works and services, market the supply of environment protection devices, the means of automation and equipment;

the development of social sphere of the city in particular: development and implementation of special programs of municipal housing construction, the formation of social housing funds; stimulation of entrepreneurship development, the creation of conditions for stable performance and increase of operating efficiency of small businesses and entrepreneurs; modernization of existing workplaces, the upgrading of their technology level, improvement of working conditions in workplaces; extra workplaces; increase high-technology and innovative workplaces share; increase in the number of working places for non-competitive workforce (disabled, women with small children); increase of capital investments in nonproduction and humanitarian sphere at the expense of local budget; increase of investments in the fixed capital for environment protection and rational use of natural resources;

the development of transport system which should include updating of the park all kinds of transport in the park, optimization of its structure and network; research of sources for covering expenses and for modernization of city's public transport; reconstruction and extension of streets; improvement of transport network planning, organization of highway exits from the city; continuation of the construction of underground passages; adjusting control systems on the major cross-roads based on the real intensity of transport and guarantee its realization using technical methods of regulation; substantiation of directions for the development of networks for trams and trolley busses and usage of methods for upgrading its work;

the informational support of the city Investment Development Program realization in particular: preparation and distribution of presentation materials about Donetsk and its Investment Development Program; creation of "Investment activity" section at the municipality and the council of the city; participation of municipality in exhibition activities (investment forums, international summits ,exhibitions etc); assistance in the development of the international exhibition activity in the city by informing and inviting businesses and organizations from other, neighbouring or not, countries to the exhibition campaigns of Donetsk; presentation of enterprises' investment projects important for the city during international business meetings, exhibitions, forums; arrangement of the contest of investment projects "Invest in Donbass – invest in future"; arrangement of the International economic Forum "Open Donbass"; development of cooperation with the main investment funds, companies and banks (EBRD, the World Bank and others) in order to submit an application for obtaining credits, grants for the development of communal system and transport infrastructure of the city; assistance in setting up the representation offices, Honourable and General consulates of foreign countries in Donetsk; cooperation with near- and far-abroad countries concerning the establishment of partnership and twin-city relations; organization of cooperation with international organizations that encourage the development of local self-administration in Ukraine; provision of informational support of investment projects;

scientific and consulting activity: the provision of consulting services to the participants of projects and programs (communal and commercial enterprises, representatives of small and medium-sized business; the participation in seminars, conferences, forums and other activities concerning the attraction of foreign investments and development of international relations; the improvement of the foreign language skills of city council specialists through offering language courses;

environmental improvement in cities by means of mining and using coalmine methane as energy vector; planting sanitary-protection zone around industrial enterprises and creation of special areas for utilization of waste to avoid air-spraying gassy toxins for a considerable distance; utilization of mine waters; increasing facilities for recycling and cascade round of water utilization in the industry; concentration of beneficial rocks and extraction of components of technologic minefields; conversion of metallurgical production wastes, with graphite; using attle for concreting exhausted mines; coffin and mining sites restoration; forestry-based, sanitary and hygienic, recreational, building, hydroeconomic; liquidation of manufacturing, domestic and building dumps; creation of so-called "waste yard"; organization of separate domestic rubbish collecting and providing of differentiate payment for heaped and sorted waste collecting and removal, charging extra for unsorted waste; setting up new factories based on current disposal plants.

Conclusions

In order to raise funds for local budget as means of financial security of investment project implementation in social sphere, land market should be created.

In addition, real property taxes, corporate profit taxes, environmental payments are substantial stakes in the reserves for increasing both private and fixed Donetsk budget source of financing.

Provided private investments for implementing certain projects will be paid back, mutual funds may be used as a method of financing. The use of mutual funds is widespread in Europe not by central authorities, interested in project implementation, but also by local authorities, when wanting to solve a problem. One possible source of funds for ecology investment is grants from International ecology organizations, as well as, government investments.

It is useful also to develop new ways for the city to accumulate extra-budgetary funds, that is, to accelerate the development of borrowed financing investments hierarchy to city projects by internal municipal bonds, such as governmentally guaranteed loans and setting up borrowed banking public institute.

The primary element of system approach to creating prosperous investment climate in city is setting up an institute for its regular monitoring, which should included: organising the work of municipal investment and innovative commission; setting up the independent investment monitoring agency in Donetsk and attract officials from local government bodies, academies and businesses to the agency. The goal of establishing this Agency should be the formation of social partnership between all aforementioned bodies, in order to settle issues of social-economy city development, to determine the investment priorities through monitoring clime indexes in Donetsk, previously mentioned in “Financing sources of investment development program in Donetsk by 2020 year” tasks, the solution of which should be directed to increase its investment attractiveness and investment potential implementation; an analysis of integrative index dynamics of city investment attractiveness by proposed methods; periodical informing of public and local government bodies about results of investment clime in Donetsk, adjustment of long-term tasks in the project “Financing sources of investment development program in Donetsk by 2020 year’, based on its results.

Providing methods for appraisal of investment potentials of city and mentioning ways of increasing their investment attractiveness are common within the majority post-socialist countries of Black Sea region, taking into account the relatively similar conditions of external and internal environment influencing their development.

Synergetics and such its direction, as catastrophe theory, chaos theory, bifurcations, attractors, entropy, extra capacity and so on combined with the now classic and long-known theories of cyclical development of the economy are able to more accurately predict the development processes of complex economic systems. Knowledge and ability to use the laws of Synergetics provide a more proper decision-making basis and efficient detection of global trends.

References

Amin, S., 2003, *Obsolescent Capitalism*, Zed Books Ldt, USA.

Blank, I., 1995, *Investment management*, Kiev: MP "INTEM" LTD, United London Trade Limited (Бланк И., 1995, Инвестиционный менеджмент. Киев: МП "ИНТЕМ" ЛТД, "Юнайтед Лондон Трейд Лимитед")

Bilorus, O., Luk`janenko, D., 2001, *Globalization and security of development,* Kiïv: KNEU (Білорус О., Лук`яненко Д., 2001, Глобалізація і безпека розвитку, Монографія. Київ: КНЕУ)

Frank, A., 1981, *Reflections on the World Economic Crisis*, Softcover, New York Univ. Pr.

Filipenko, A., Budkin, V., Gal'chins'kijj, A. ect., 2002, *Ukraine and the world economy: the interaction of turn of the millennium*, Kyiv, Libid (Філіпенко А., Будкін В., Гальчинський А. та ін., 2002, Україна і світове господарство: взаємодія на межі тисячоліть.К., Либідь)

Filipenko, A., Rogach, O., Shnirkov, O., 2000, *World economy*, Kyiv, Libid (Філіпенко А., Рогач О., Шнирков О., 2000, Світова економіка. К., Либідь)

Huntington, S., 1996, *The Clash of Civilizations and the Remaking of World Order*, Touchstone Book, NY.

Kozak, Y., Luk'janenko, D., Makogon, Y. ect., 2004, *International economy*, Kyiv, Educational books centre (Козак Ю., Лук'яненко Д., Макогон Ю. та ін., 2004, Міжнародна економіка. Київ: Центр навчальної літератури.)

Levitt, T., 1983, *The Globalization of Markets*, Harvard Business Review.

Marshall, A., 1920, *Principles of Economics*, London, Macmillan and Co., Ltd.

Meadows, D., Meadows D., Randers J., 2004, *Limits to growth : the 30-year update*, Chelsea Green Publishing Company, White River Junction, Vermon.t

Modelski, G., 2008, *Globalization as Evolutionary Process*, Modeling Global Change, Routledge, NY

Myrdal, G., 1957. *Economic Theory and Underdeveloped Regions*, Gerald Duckworth.

Novickiy, V., 2003, *International economic activity of Ukraine*, Kyiv, KNEU (Новицький В., 2003, Міжнародна економічна діяльність України. Мін-во освіти і науки України, КНЕУ.)

Orekhova, T., 2009, *Forming and Development Investment Attractiveness of the Black Sea Area Cities. Problems and Prospects of Cooperation Between the Countries of Southeastern Europe within the Context of Black Sea Economic Cooperation*, Collection of Scientific papers, Sevastopol – Donetsk, pp.47-54.

Pakhomov, Y., 2001, The market transformations in Ukraine in the context of international experience, *The bulletin of NAS of Ukraine*, 3, pp.11-

14. (Пахомов Ю., 2001. Ринкові трансформації в Україні у контексті світового досвіду. Вісник НАН України, № 3, С. 11-14)

Schumpeter, J., 1954, *History of Economic Analysis*.

Smitienko, B., 2010, *World economy*, Jurayt, Moscow (Смитиенко Б., 2010, Мировая экономика. Юрайт, Москва).

State statistic committee of Ukraine, 2010, *Social-economical development of Ukraine*, available at: www.ukrstat.gov.ua (accessed 20/05/2010).

Statistic department of Dnepropetrovsk, 2010, *Social-economical development of Dnepropetrovsk*, available at: http://www.dneprstat.gov.ua/ statinfo/ (accessed 20/05/2010).

Statistic department of Donetsk, 2010, Social-economical development of Donetsk, available at: http://www.donetskstat.gov.ua/statinform/index .php (accessed 20/05/2010).

Statistic department of Kiev, 2010, Social-economical development of Kiev, available at: http://www.gorstat.kiev.ua/p.php3?c=242&lang=1, (accessed 20/05/2010).

Stiglitz, J., 2000, *Frontiers of Development Economics: The Future in Perspective*, edited with Gerald M. Meier, World Bank.

Wallerstein I., 1984, *The Politics of the World-Economy. The States, the Movements and the Civilizations*, Cambridge, Cambridge University Press.

Yankovskiy, M., Makogon, Y., Ryabchyn, O., 2010, I*nnovative and classical theories of catastrophes and economic crises*, International Economics Department, Donetsk National University.

Assessment and Evaluation of the Results Obtained by Finance Policies of International Financial Institutions (IFIs) in the Transition Process of the Southeast European Countries

Maria-Eleni Voutsa

Abstract

The priority given to certain areas, the rate and sequencing of reforms and the orientation of financing are some of the factors that shaped the transition process in the Southeast European countries [Albania, FYROM, the former Federal Republic of Serbia-Montenegro (including Kosovo), Bulgaria, Romania, Croatia and Bosnia-Herzegovina].

The International Financial Institutions, through their financial policies, have decisively contributed to the attempted transformation of former socialist states.

The involvement of Institutions in the transition process was almost direct but after the cessation of hostilities in Kosovo in 1999, there has been a dramatic increase in financing throughout the area. The level of financing, in conjunction with the immediate and increasing needs of countries, were the main factors that configured the balance of powers among recipient countries and international financial institutions.

This paper will examine to what extent the financial assistance of the transition by the International Financing Institutions has defined the parameters of the model implemented, that is, to what extent and direction the transition process was affected. At the same time, an attempt will be made to assess the results of the financial policies implemented in the last two decades.

In order to make this assessment feasible, an examination is going to be conducted with regard to the characteristics of the financial assistance provided to the states by the major creditors of the region, the International Monetary Fund, the World Bank Group, the European Bank for Reconstruction and Development and the European Union. These institutions manage the vast majority of finances; however, their significance is not exclusively related to the amount of assistance which is provided but also to the associated conditionality accompanying financial policies, which cover a wide range of economic, social and political components. The conditionality regarding the economic and social aspects of the attempted transformation put into operation a mechanism that acts as a catalyst in shaping the model of transition, the way it will be applied by the countries and its impacts.

Introduction

The Systemic Transformation which was attempted by South East European countries after the fall of the Berlin Wall was named transition. The economic transition aimed at transforming the nature of economic relations, since their coordination would be passed from the state to market mechanisms.

In order to achieve this goal, the key areas that the effort should focus on were the following:

- Macroeconomic stabilization by controlling the monetary and fiscal policy,
- The privatisation of state enterprises,
- The liberalisation of production, trade and prices and
- Structural transformation so as to create institutions which would support the operation of market economy (Van-Brabant 1998, pp. 1-16).

In order to enable the conversion of the financial operations it was necessary to finance the attempted changes. These countries did not have the required capital adequacy as they did not possess sufficient domestic savings to support this project and, as a consequence, foreign borrowing was the only solution.

International finance has so far been the main source of capital and mainly comes from three directions: a) bilateral donors, b) international organizations and c) the European Union.

The present analysis, however, will focus on the major donors in the area, i.e.:

- the International Monetary Fund,
- the World Bank Group,
- the European Bank for Reconstruction and Development, and
- the European Union.

The above International Financial Institutions (IFIs), through their financial policies, have been instrumental in the transition process, since during the last fifteen years the per capita assistance to countries in the area has been seven times higher than the one given to Africa (Tzifakis and Xouliaras 2007, p. 18). Their importance, though, is not exclusively related to the amount of the assistance provided and to the associated conditionalities which are attached to every finance agreement.

The present paper will attempt to assess to what extent the financial assistance of the transition determined the parameters of the model which was implemented; and to evaluate the impacts of international finance on the transformation of South East Europe countries.

The financial instruments of International Financial Institutions (IFIs) for the south east European countries

Until 1999 the data available with regard to SE Europe financing are fragmented. As a result, it is not possible to achieve a comprehensive and clear picture of financial flow. The period 1999-2005 shows a steadily increasing influx of funds into the area, which in 1999 exceeded € 5.5 billion and in 2005 it is estimated to have reached 7.3 billion € (Table 1) (European Commission 2008). These figures correspond to more than 100 € per capita annually, on average, which places SEE on top of the list of areas with the highest per capita financing.

Table 1. International financing for South East Europe (Billion €)

Donors	South East Europe*						
	1999	2000	2001	2002	2003	2004	2005***
Bilateral & European Committee	3,5 (64%)	2,2 (38%)	3,9 (60%)	3,7 (55%)	3,3 (50%)	3,3 (55%)	3,0 (41%)
IFI**	2 (36%)	3,6 (62%)	2,6 (40%)	3,0 (45%)	3,3 (50%)	2,7 (45%)	4,3 (59%)
Total	5,6 (100%)	5,9 (100%)	6,5 (100%)	6,7 (100%)	6,6 (100%)	6,0 (100%)	7,3 (100%)

* Including Moldavia
** Not including the IMF
*** Estimations
Source: Economic Reconstruction and Development in South East Europe, International Assistance to South East Europe, How Much Money is Being Given, http://ec.europa.eu/enlargement/archives/seerecon/gen/howmuch.htm

The International Monetary Fund

As a rule, IMF loans to Southeast European countries are drawn from the "Stand-By Arrangement" and the "Extended Fund Facility" financial policies.

In terms of implementing the "Stand-by Agreement", the interested state contracts agreements with the IMF, which grant it the right to draw a certain amount from the General Resources Account (GRA) if it meets the conditionalities set by the supporting arrangement program.

The "Expanded Fund Facility" finances three-year projects with a view to confronting difficulties in balance of payments which result from the macroeconomic and structural problems that the country is facing.

The World Bank Group

In 2000, the World Bank Group (the World Bank Group consists of five autonomous international organisations: i) International Bank for Reconstruction and Development, ii) International Finance Corporation, iii) International Development Association, iv) Multilateral Investment Guarantee Agency and v) International Centre for Settlement of Investment) defined its activity areas and objectives for SE Europe through the "Regional Strategy Paper". For the implementation of the reform programs in each country, it created the Country Assistance Strategy (CAS). The "Country Assistance Strategy" sets the priorities and determines the level and composition of financial and technical assistance which the Bank will provide on the basis of the priority assessment within each country, its past performance and its creditworthiness. The "Poverty Reduction Strategy Papers" (PRSPs) are the main pillars supporting the "Country Assistance Strategy".

In order to achieve the objectives of the Regional Strategy Paper, in 2002 the World Bank and the European Commission decided to coordinate and inform each other on compiling and evaluating the "Poverty Reduction Strategy Papers" on the part of the Bank, as well as the "Country Strategy Papers" on the part of the European Commission (Gropa 2007). Governments in cooperation with the World Bank and IMF compile the "Poverty Reduction Strategy Papers" (Joint Office of the European Commission and the World Bank 2008).

The European countries

The EU, although it is not an IFI, through the European Investment Bank Group (European Investment Bank and European Investment Fund), its close cooperation with the World Bank Group and the development of relations with the SE Europe countries, constitutes one of the largest donors in the region, playing a significant role in their transitional state.

The EU action into the former socialist countries started with the PHARE program, which was created in 1989 and was designed to support the transition process in Poland and Hungary. Following the European Council in Essen (1994), it was converted into a financial instrument of the pre-accession strategy and it was later expanded to the Western Balkans. In line with the Agenda 2000 provisions, it became a structural type of fund with the aim of encouraging economic development. After the Zagreb summit (2000), a key policy instrument in Southeast Europe is the Stabilisation and Association Process (SAP) which introduced a new regulatory framework for financing through the CARDS program, which also replaced all previous financing programs. The actions of the European Union and the World Bank have to date been determined by the Stabilisation and Association Process and the conclusions of the Thessaloniki European Council (2003) (European Commission 2010).

The "Instrument for Pre-Accession Assistance" (IPA) which was established for the period 2007-2013, constitutes the novel financial support program of the enlargement.

The European Bank for Reconstruction and Development

The EBRD has not formally adopted a particular policy for loaning countries under transition. However, in 2007 it founded, in cooperation with 15 countries, the Western Balkans Fund in order to enhance investments and support the economic development and stability throughout the region. The decision to create this Fund was based on the assumption that the current situation in Western Balkans is very different from other former socialist European countries.

The role of International Financing Institutions (IFIs) in the configuration of the theoretical model for transition

The involvement of international financial institutions into the transformation of former socialist states was almost direct, but not simultaneous. It was from the beginning that the IMF and the EBRD took part in the transformation, whereas the World Bank and the EU did so later. However, the IMF and the WB primarily defined the core principles through which they guided the transition towards a market economy and their cultivation had begun at least a decade before, whereas in 1990 Williamson codified them under the term "Washington Consensus" (Williamson, 1990).

Some of the key elements of the "Washington consensus" constituted a common reference to suggestions with regard to developing countries, while at the same time the plan proposed for Latin America marked the official launch of the New Political Economy into the financial procedures of the IMF and the WB.

The New Political Economy suggests that market mechanisms, if released from political interventions, can act as capable regulators for the successful operation of the financial system. As a consequence of this position, the donors faced the State as the impediment to development and presented free market as its solution, even though up to that point they had been operating in the light of tracing market imperfections and guiding governments in order to improve them.

The development approach using the "Washington consensus" model has received a number of criticisms with regard to whether it has facilitated real progress in countries under development. In many cases, criticism does not merely concern the results of its application, but it extends to the theoretical background itself. The New Political Economy is based on the neoclassical model of perfectly competitive markets, which can hardly be identified as concrete reality in some industrialised countries, and it moves to the interpretation of economic phenomena through the angle of "economic science", thereby ignoring the interdisciplinary of the socio-political economy of development which incurs the market imperfections and the existence of positive impacts of the economic policy (Makris and Voutsa, 2006, pp. 352-353).

The adequacy of this approach had already begun being reviewed since the mid 90s. This occurred because there were phenomena which operated as inhibitors to development but could not be explained by the New Political Economy. As a result, international financial institutions adopted a differentiated approach to development by placing more emphasis on the social factors influencing it (World-Bank-Group, 2001). In practice, though, on no account did this change entail the acceptance of their potential responsibility for the failure of a previous policy.

Despite the reluctance to acknowledge the wrong strategy applied, the "Post-Washington Consensus", which was proposed as a term descriptive of the new development policy, would constitute an important step if it contributed towards substantial change (Table 2). But, in fact, the theoretical framework was not different but it was merely updated and completed by modernising the neoclassical model, continuing, however, to treat development and, hence, transition, as a technical problem (Makris and Voutsa, 2006, p. 353). The new components concern the implementation of more and more stringent conditionalities as well as the increase in the influence of institutions on domestic policy making (Table 3).

Table 2. The key points of "Washington consensus" and the supplementary elements of "Post-Washington consensus"

WASHINGTON CONSENSUS	POST-WASHINGTON CONSENSUS
1. Fiscal discipline	11. Corporate governance
2. Reorientation of public expenditure	12. Anti-corruption
3. Tax reform	13. Flexible labour markets
4. Financial liberalization and reduction of interest rates	14. Adherence to WTO disciplines
5. Unified and competitive exchange	15. Non-intermediate exchange rate regimes
6. Trade liberalization	16. Independent central banks/inflation targeting
7. Openness to IFD	17."Prudent" capital-account opening
8. Privatization	18. Social safety nets
9. Deregulation	19. Targeted poverty reduction
10. Secure Property Rights	20. Adherence to international financial codes and standards

Source: Yuhiro, 2003. Dragutinovi, 2004. own processing

The difference between the rhetoric, the proposed programs and the implementation of the conditionalities often creates a false impression about the priorities of international financial institutions. Nonetheless, the "Post-Washington consensus" cannot be regarded as a new development vision. It does not offer any truly innovative solutions to the transitional process since the free market mechanisms and the private sector keep having a leading role. Consequently, this justifies the reservations about whether the new approach to international financial institutions is a fundamental shift in their theoretical position.

If the development model of "Washington consensus" and "post-Washington consensus" receives criticism with regard to its effectiveness and principles, then it strengthens the reservations about whether it was duly chosen to be the appropriate framework to manage the transition of Southeast European countries. The countries of the region, with the particularities characterising them with regard to the comparison among them as well as among other developing countries, were in need of a more special treatment through specific measures tailored to operate into the transition environment (Samson, 1994, pp. 2-3).

However, the main question is not whether the specific development model was appropriate for managing the transition process, but why they chose a development model in order to implement the project of transition. The international financial institutions, having established a series of development principles, rushed to apply them as a transitional model. That is, in fact they did not study the creation of a policy framework that would correspond to the transition process but instead they used a development model in order to manage transition.

Table 3. Key fields of action, proposed policies and conditionalities through the implementation of the "Washington consensus" and the "post-Washington consensus"

	WASHINGTON CONSENSUS		POST-WASHINGTON CONSENSUS	
FIELDS	PROPOSED POLICIES	CONDI/ TIES IMPOSED	PROPOSED POLICIES	CONDI/ TIES IMPOSED
Fiscal Policy	Fiscal discipline aiming at GDP growth	X	Maintaining fiscal discipline aiming at GDP growth &	X
			the reduction in the current account deficit	-----
Public Expenditure	Tax increase	X	Tax increase with a gradual reduction of income tax, increased indirect taxation and tax collection mechanisms	X

(continued)

Public Expenditure	Downscaling of public expenditure, reduction of salaries, pensions and social benefits	X	Downscaling of public expenditure, reduction of salaries, pensions and social benefits	X
Monetary Policy	Exertion of restrictive policy aiming primarily at controlling inflation	X	Continuation of the restrictive policy and inflation control. Free setting of interest rates and in some cases preservation of a fixed exchange rate	X
Banking System	Reconstruction of the Banking Sector	X	Strengthening the competitiveness of banks	X
Trade Policy	Liberalisation of Trade	X	Full trade liberalisation and harmonisation with the WTO and EU policies	X
Business Policy	Privatisation of state enterprises	X	Completion of the privatisation process of state enterprises, even by selling them	X

(continued)

Investment Policy	Cuts in social expenditure and privatisation of enterprises in order to strengthen public investment with a view to attracting FDIs.	X	Abrogation of the remaining restrictive policies concerning FDIs and reform of the legislative framework conditioning them	X
Poverty	There are no correlations between reform programs and the impacts that these will have on poverty	----	The potential impacts of reform programs on poverty increase are acknowledged but no comprehensive proposals or policies are put forward in order to confront it	----

(continued)

Institutional Environment	Coverage of the institutional and administrative gap by providing technical assistance for the implementatio n of programs and hardly any support for bridging the gap (there are remarks which only regard the legislative framework for the protection of property rights)	----	It is acknowledged that the lack of an appropriate institutional environment may affect the course of transition and development, but no policies are recommended so as to bridge the gap and in some cases where piecemeal measures are proposed, no funds are credited.	----
Social Goods (education, health, etc.)	Their importance is recognised, but they are neither financially supported nor is it discussed to what extent they will be influenced by the transition process	----	Their importance as well as the adverse effects they may incur by the reform programs are recognised but no care is actually taken in order to protect them.	----

Source: IMF, World Bank, EBRD, own processing.

The characteristics of financing to the Southeast Europe states under transition

Financing to SE European states presents the following core features:

1. Imposition of conditionalities

The imposition of conditionalities is the world's most important feature of international finance. However, a research conducted on behalf of the United Nations shows that the SE Europe and Central Asia are the areas which are subject to the most conditionalities of quantitative performance criteria (Kapur, 2000).

In the review conducted jointly by the IMF and the World Bank (2001-2002) they raised the question of alignment of all financial benefits and financial strategies, wherever these come from, with specific conditionalities, which are included in the "Poverty Reduction Strategy Papers". Indicatively, what should be included among development programs and financial instruments, which are proposed to be aligned under specific conditionalities, are the following:

i. The IMF program "Poverty Reduction and Economic Growth",
ii. The World Bank programs "Country Assistance Strategy" and "Poverty Reduction Support Credits" (PRSCs), and
iii. The United Nations Development Assistance Framework (UNDAF), (IMF 2002).

The connection between financing and the adherence to strict political and economic conditionalities has caused loss of funds. The gradual proliferation and complexity of the conditionalities have led to the implementation of controversial policies in several cases. What is most important, though, is that the conditionalities are not related to the expected outcomes of the implemented policies but rather to the technical implementation of specific parameters which seem to be unchanged from the beginning of the transition up to now (Xatzimixail and Voutsa, 2009, pp. 328 - 329).

2. Inefficiency in the management of financing

In order for financing to reach the recipient country, what must exist is an effective internal mechanism for successful fund absorption. The sophisticated technical parameters of programs are often ineffectively manageable by the cumbersome administration mechanisms of countries (Xatzimixail and Voutsa, 2009, pp. 328-329). The incomplete and problematic legislation in conjunction with the "bureaucratic rigidity" of the public sector, in many cases rendered financing and, by extension, the absorptive capacity of the countries ineffective (UNECE, 1999). Poor design and planning have contributed to squandering the assistance on projects of dubious quality and utility. The EU Court of Auditors in a relevant report characterised half of the pre-accession assistance to Romania and Bulgaria (1.9 billion €) as problematic (Tzifakis and Xouliaras, 2007, p. 33). Market failures and phenomena of corruption and shadow economy act as catalysts in the effective utilisation of funds.

3. The Nirvana fallacy

The international financial institutions suggest that the design and implementation of financial plans can be made more effective without the participation of local institutions. This perception has been described as the "Nirvana fallacy" (Coyne, 2006). The institutions, ignoring the characteristics that should be taken into account, make policies and instruments that are not designed properly enough to operate and be implemented into the environments of the countries. This practice hinders the implementation of financial policies since a country's commitment is not enough for their successful implementation but what is needed is a wider framework of cooperation, which cannot be achieved without constructive dialogue.

The lack of significant cooperation does not promote the creation of capital gain through financing. Furthermore, the absence of a strong social contract, which would act as a breakwater against the turbulences of transformation by facilitating the smooth operation of the countries, caused irreparable damage to the social capital of the countries (Xatzimixail and Voutsa, 2009, pp. 328 - 329).

4. Technocratic & teleological approach of the transition

The International Financial Institutions treated countries in the region as a tabula rasa, ignoring completely the 'initial conditions' on which the proposed measures should be applied and placing unilateral emphasis on the economic aspects of transition. This treatment essentially led to a double distortion in the transition process. On the one hand, they completely ignored the structural transformation that was necessary in order to support the operation of market economy and, on the other hand, the serious structural weaknesses along with the considerable institutional insufficiencies impeded the transition process.

The fundamental principle which the promoted model was based on entailed that every economic action can be explained by the rational, individualist and materialistic behaviour of persons. But this approach ignores the fact that individuals and, by extension, societies do not act as perfect maximisers as they do not aim at maximising but at satisficing instead (Zoumboulakis and Kyriazis, 2009, p. 65).

What was ignored was the fact that countries are directly dependent on the path of the past (path-dependence), whereby 'significant effects on the final outcome are exerted by events distant in time, which are characterised by random data instead of systemic forces (Zoumboulakis and Kyriazis, 2009, p. 63). Once a set of rules, institutions and customs of a society have been established, it is difficult and it requires great effort to change it.

In countries where maximisation of efforts was necessary so as to restore public confidence regarding institutions and the reinforcement of their culture towards participatory processes, what was chosen was a model which removed any socio-political aspect of transition, resulting in the creation of weak or failed states and problematic societies. The non-existent or weakened regulatory mechanisms did not allow for effective state intervention in cases of dysfunction (e.g. corruption, monopolistic policies, etc.)

The neoliberal model which was implemented created a teleological conception of transition. The methods used and the policies implemented have been criticised even by executives of the international financial institutions themselves, who were called to implement them to countries under transition (Hertz, 2006, pp. 124-26). Through shock therapy, all states in the region were forced to implement a specific procedure, as a sine qua non Treaty, which in theory would lead to the establishment of democracies and to the smooth operation of market economy.

It is worth noting that the EU policy is the only one which reflected a basic effort to approach the socio-political parameters of the transition. At a theoretical level, it was through the Maastricht Treaty which in Article

49 states that "any European State which respects the principles of liberty, democracy, human rights and fundamental freedoms as well as the rule of law may apply to become a member of the Union" (European Union, 2008).

Nevertheless, in practical terms it is the only institution which finances, mostly through grants and not loans, socio-political fields, associating them with the tightening of its relations to countries in the region. It connects them with conditionalities and checks the expected results. Although it has been accused that these fields are not its top priorities and that a firm policy on the implementation of measures does not exist, what is indubitably remarkable is its effort to specify proposals and the policy measures it applies, which is a very positive first step.

The results of the international financial policies on the transition process

Financing has been the instrument used for imposing the dominant theoretical model of transition on the South-East Europe. Intertwining interests and their magnitude as well as the absence of an alternative approach constituted the key factors in shaping the balance of power between the recipient countries and the international financial institutions, leading the states under transition to granting to the international financial institutions the jurisdiction to shape the transition model.

The core characteristics of this model called for:

1. Speed of reforms

At the beginning of the transition process, the fundamental concern regarded the speed of reforms; in other words, whether the proposed policies should be either directly implemented though shock therapy or gradually. From the beginning, all international financing institutions opted for the direct implementation of reforms (Xatzimixail and Voutsa, 2009, pp. 329 - 331). Their decision, though, was not based on scientific and theoretical approaches which would indicate that this was the appropriate approach to transition, but on the political decision to approach transformation as a form of counter-revolution to communism revolution or otherwise, as a "market revolution" (Stiglitz, 2003, pp. 276, 80-81).

The institutions who defend the position that the economy should operate unaffected and away from political interference, not only enabled the policy to determine their attitude to the issue of transition, but rather rendered themselves instruments for the exercise of this policy (Stiglitz, 2003, pp. 280-81, 324-326; Hertz, 2006, pp. 56-63, 124-126). Their choices were guided by the political fears of IFIs' major shareholders (primarily the IMF and World Bank group).

There was concern that communism in some states could be recreating itself, organising its comeback. The selection of shock therapy would result in the creation of a strong group that would have an interest in capitalism, strengthening the ideological foundation of society for political change. On the other hand, the direct and complete privatisation of state enterprises would deprive the communist parties of the mechanism and the financial resources that could be used to rehabilitate them to power. The treatment, however, of the transition as a political issue placed the approach of the whole project on false and unsound foundations.

The conditionalities eventually undermined the effectiveness of the financing itself, which initially functioned as a formative mechanism of the transitional framework and subsequently was used to cover the cost of the reforms introduced by the financial institutions (Xatzimixail and Voutsa, 2009, pp. 329-331). Although in SEE the choices of transformation were not implemented throughout the period of transition with the same intensity as in other former socialist countries like Russia and Ukraine, the result obtained due to the corruption of local elites was to create disorganized and chaotic state structures. The "weak states" that emerged with strong signs of institutional weakness, in conjunction with the disorganisation of the economic system, led to the complete dependence of the transition process upon the financing of institutions and, as a consequence, to its full submission to their choices.

2. The framework for reforms

In addition to speed, the international financial institutions also determined the framework for reform which was based on the three aspects of liberalisation, macroeconomic stabilisation and privatisation (Xatzimixail and Voutsa, 2009, pp. 331-333).

In the first transition period, the implementation of the direct liberalisation and stabilisation prevented the smooth privatisation of enterprises. The prices of most products were instantaneously liberalised, fuelling strong inflationary pressures, which in some cases turned into hyperinflation, dissipating savings and bringing to the fore the issue of macroeconomic stability. The effort to reduce inflation led to the implementation of a contractionary monetary policy, which caused a rise in interest rates. Without savings and with high interest rates, privatisations could not be forwarded and investment activities could not be strengthened.

Privatisations strengthened poverty and inequality instead of relaunching growth. Since privatisations were regarded of secondary significance along with the absence of an appropriate institutional framework, public enterprises usually ended up in the hands of their old directors or under the control of a very specific group, who ripped off the assets of enterprises. Many cases of corruption and the organised informal networks that exist in the countries of the region are directly linked to the intensified privatisations during which the state monopoly was converted into a monopoly or oligopoly of private interests (Xatzimixail and Voutsa, 2009, p. 332). Arthur Kruinderink, Director of the Regional Office of the United Nations Development Programme (PNUD), believes that accelerated privatisations will prove to be one of the greatest crimes of the 20th century and lead the country into unprecedented poverty level (Negreponti-Delivani, 2001, pp. 299-300).

In the programs which were implemented, it was not deemed necessary to develop a suitable mechanism that would promote the creation of a specific economic system since the systemic transformation would be promoted by the operation of market mechanisms. As a result, recession characterised at least the entire first decade of transition and many countries became confronted with the risk of systemic collapse (Andreff, 2003, pp. 109-13).

Almost all governments of the countries throughout the region, under the pressure of the increasing social and political cost as well as the numerous practical difficulties in implementing reforms, followed the so-called 'stop and go policy'. They reduced the speed of the proposed changes in a short term but they promoted reform again as they came up against the potential suspension of credits. It goes without saying that the adoption of this policy cannot possibly be considered to be a success because neither did it manage to maintain any benefits of the rapid reform nor did it avert crises.

Conclusions

The former socialist countries resorted to international financial institutions, as they needed both guidance in their effort to select the most appropriate transformation policies and financing for their materialisation. It is very difficult, even today approximately 20 years since the beginning of transition, to say with certainty which the appropriate path to follow was.

The fact of the matter is that transition could not be achieved without cost, so the involvement of international financial institutions was expected to act towards its minimisation by reducing the negative impacts. However, expectations were falsified. Although there is no society without inequality, its magnitude in the SEE countries is surprising. If the mechanisms worked just as the institutions had promised, the expected inequality that would be created would be moderate and would move at reasonable levels. In communism, the income distribution did not exhibit large differentiations. As a consequence, the factor of inherited wealth is not included in the transition process and the resulting differentiations should be attributed to differences in productivity and employment. But the transition model, through its choices, fuelled inequality and impeded the creation of a robust and remarkable middle class.

By focusing on the idea which claims that the middle class serves as the cornerstone of democracy, the financing of economic transformation encumbered another aspect of transition, that of pluralist democracy (Economics Centre for Liberal Strategies Institute for Market, 2003). Especially if the effects of financial policies are judged according to Amartya Sen's opinion, "that economic development is meaningless if it does not offer poor people the right to access things that ensure a better material life" (Strange, 2004, p. 327), then the produced effect of transformation, which was shaped by international financing, can by no means be considered to be successful and developmental.

References

Andreff, W., 2003, *La Mutation des Economies Postsocialistes Une analyse economique alternative*, Paris: L' Harmattan.

Blue, B., 2003, *In Search of Responsive Government. State Building and Economic Growth in the Balkans*. Budapest, Center for Policy Studies Central European University.

Bonker, F., Muller, K., Pickel, A., 2002, *Post communist Transformation and the Social Science Cross-Disciplinary*, Lanham, Rowman & Littlefield.

Coyne, C. J., 2006, Reconstructing Weak and Failed States: Foreign Intervention and the Nirvana Fallacy, *Foreign Policy Analysis*, 2, pp. 343–360, accessed February 18, 2010 http://www.ccoyne.com/FPA_-_Final.PDF.

Dragutinovic, D., 2004, The IMF Supported Program in Serbia & Montenegro, *Economic Annals*, 161, accessed April 12, 2010, http://www.doiserbia.nb.rs/img/doi/0013-3264/2004/0013-32640461007D.pdf

Economics Centre for Liberal Strategies Institute for Market, 2003, *The Inflexibility Trap Frustrated Societies, Weak States and Democracy the State of Democracy in the Balkans*, Sofia, Centre for Liberal Strategies Institute for Market Economics.

European Union, 2008, *Europe in 12 Lessons*, accessed April 08 2010, http://europa.eu/abc/12lessons/lesson_1/index_en.htm

European-Commission, 2008, *International Assistance to South East Europe*, sccessed April 20 2008, http://ec.europa.eu/enlargement /archives/seerecon/gen/whoisinvolved.htm.

—. 2010, *The Western Balkan countries on the road to the European Union*, accessed January 23 2010, http://ec.europa.eu/enlargement/enlargement_process/accession_process/how_does_a_country_join_the_eu/sap/history_en.htm#sap_agreement

Geormas, K., 2006, *Globalization and Poverty. The Ideological Frameworks and the Politics of International Organizations to Fight Poverty*, Athens, Metexmio (in Greek).

Gropa, R., 2007, *Multilateral Donors: The World Bank in the Western Balkans. In The International Development Assistance in the Balkans the Contradictions of Generosity*, edited by Tzifakis, N., Xouliaras, A., pp. 113-146, Athens, Papazisi (in Greek).

Gros, D., Steinherr, A., 2004, *Economic Transition in Central and Easter Europe Planting the Seeds*, Cambridge, Cambridge University Press.

Hertz, N., 2004, *The Debt Threat. How Debt is Destroying the Developing World*, Translated in Greek by Saltapidas G., 2006, Kritiki ed.

IMF, 2002, *IMF/World Bank Comprehensive Review of the Poverty Reduction Strategy Papers (PRSP) Approach*, IMF, accessed February 03 2010 http://www.imf.org/external/np/prspgen/review/2001/index.htm.

Joint Office of the European Commission and the World Bank, 2008, *What is the Role of the World Bank*, Joint Office of the European Commission and the World Bank.

Kapur, D., Webb, R., 2000, *Governance-related Conditionalities of the International Financial Institutions*, Research papers for the Intergovernmental Group of Twenty-Four on International Monetary Affairs, In United Nations Conference on Trade and Development, United Nations Publication.

Kjaer, A. M., 2004, *Governance. UK – USA*, Polity Press.

Lavigne, M., 1999, *The Economics of Transition from Socialist Economy to Market Economy*, Second ed., Great Britain, Palgrave.

Makris, G., Voutsa M.E., 2006, The Theoretical Position of the International Financial Institutions in Relation to the Transition: The Case of the Balkan Countries, presented at *The Dimensions of Transition and European perspective of the Balkans Countries*, Greece, Florina, 10-12 November, Conference Proceeding, pp. 349-371, Thessaloniki, *Publication Mechanism University of Macedonia* (in Greek).

Negreponti-Delivani, M., 2001, *Conspiratorial "Globalization"*, Athens, Papazisi (in Greek).

Samson, I., 1994, *La stabilisation de la transition dans les sociétés post-socialistes*, accessed February 17 2010, http://web.upmf-grenoble.fr/pepse/IMG/pdf/La_stabilisation.pdf.

Stiglitz, J., 2003, *Globalization and its Discontents*, Translated by Theodoropoulos G., Athems, Livani (in Greek).

Strange, S., 2004, *The Retreat of the State. The Diffusion of the Power in the World Economy*. Translated by Kapernakou K. and Papadopoulos, I., Athens, Papazisi (in Greek).

Tzifakis, N., Houliaras, A., 2007, *Introduction: The Contradictions of International Generously to the Balkans. In The International Development Assistance in the Balkans the Contradictions of Generosity*, edited by Tzifakis, N. Xouliaras, A., pp. 15-42, Athens, Papazisi (in Greek).

UNECE, 1999, *Economic Survey of Europe, Post-war Reconstruction and Development in South-East Europe*, UNECE, accessed January 17 2010, http://www.unece.org/ead/pub/992/992_1.pdf.

Van-Brabant, J., 1998, *The Political Economy of Transition Coming to Grips with History and Methodology*, London - New York, Routledge.

Williamson, J., 1990, *Latin American Adjustment: How Much Has Happened? What Washington Means by Policy Reform*, accessed January 20, 2010,

www.iie.com/publications/papers/paper.cfm?researchid=486.
World-Bank-Group, 2001, *Report of the Task Force on the World Bank Group and the Middle-Income Countries*, World Bank.
Xatzimihail, D., Voutsa, M.E., 2009, *Contribution of Policy of the International Financial Institutions (IFIs) and the European Union in the process of Transition of the Central and Southeastern Europe: Expectations and Reality. In The Political Economy of Transition From Central Planning to Market Economy*, edited by Pelagidis, T., Xazakis, K., pp. 311-341, Athens, Papazisi (in Greek).
Yuhiro, H., 2003, *From the Washington Consensus to the Post-Washington Consensus, Retrospect and Prospect. Asian Development Review*, 20, 3, accessed February 18, 2010, http://www.adb.org/documents/periodicals/adr/adr_vol20_2.pdf.
Zoumpoulakis, M., Kyriazis, N., 2009, *Inertia and Institutional Change in Transition Economies. In The Political Economy of Transition From Central Planning to Market Economy*, edited by Pelagidis, T., Xazakis, K., Athens, Papazisi (in Greek).

E-BANKING EVALUATION OF GREEK BANKS IN GREECE AND BULGARIA

PERSEFONI POLYCHRONIDOU,
IOANNIS KAZANIDIS, GESTHIMANI ELEFTHERIADOU
AND STAVROS VALSAMIDIS

Abstract

The evolution of electronic trade and the possibility of establishing virtual companies have led banks to broaden their rendering of services and to include this new sector. The revolution of bank transactions was realized with e-banking (bringing banks into personal computers via Internet). E-banking provides direct access to bank accounts, the ability of performing transactions, observing portfolios, conduct prompt payment of bills and credit cards and many other services. At the same time, there have been rapid changes in the area of Balkans, creating new markets with a lot of opportunities for companies. As a result, many Greek companies expanded their businesses in the Balkan countries, with the Greek banks being forerunners, especially in Bulgaria. Greek banks claim that they offer the same quality of services to all their customers around Balkans. Furthermore, their web pages are also available in Bulgarian so as to ease the accessibility of Bulgarian customers. The customers' satisfaction is important for every company; therefore, the evaluation of the services that these banks provide is an important process, contributing in improving the rendering of services. In this study, we examine and compare the satisfaction level of e-banking users in both countries (Greece and Bulgaria). The results are quite similar for both, since the webpage of each bank is similar in both languages. The Bulgarian customers seem to be more enthusiastic than the Greek customers regarding the design and graphics of each webpage. This can be justified by the fact that the Bulgarians have possibly less experience in using the Internet. Finally, customers from both countries are very satisfied with the quality and quantity of the provided information, the amount and the sufficiency of information, the ease of use and the usefulness of the provided information.

Introduction

The transition in the economies of the former communist countries of the Balkan area set in motion significant changes, not only in the countries concerned but also in the economic and geo-political environment of Greece. The process of political and economic transition in these countries altered dramatically the political economy and international relations of Europe, in general, while the opening of the economies of these countries shifted the centre of gravity of the European economy to the East and altered noticeably the economic geography of the continent (Monastiriotis and Tsamis, 2007).

Moreover, for Greece, these changes signalled the end of the physical-geographic and, subsequently, economic isolation of the country, a factor that had been constraining its economic development and its firmer integration to the EU (Monastiriotis and Tsamis, 2007). On the other hand, Bulgaria went through political and economic reform, which caused socio-political turmoil about ten years ago (Xanthidis and Nicholas, 2004), but managed to achieve significant levels of internet penetration in a relatively short time. The events in both countries indicate that once a proper telecommunications infrastructure is in place and political stability is established, it is only a short time before the digital economy emerges, regardless of the rest of the problems a community maybe facing.

The development of the banking sector can play an integral and pivotal role in the successful completion of the transition process. The number of financial institutions in the Balkans quickly multiplied through the privatization of state banks and the establishment of new private institutions. In some countries the sector was immediately opened to foreign interests, as well (Glaveli et al., 2006; Hackethal et al., 2003). It can be argued that the changes in the ownership status of the banks and the closure of insolvent institutions, the entry of foreign banks, the adoption of regulations according to international standards and practices, and the implementation of tighter and more effective supervision by the central banks and currency boards have substantially transformed the banking sectors in the transitional economies of the Balkans (Hackethal et al., 2003). This has in turn affected the emphasis placed on and the level of quality of the services provided.

Based on the above, it is quite obvious that a comparison between the Balkan countries would be of interest to academics, researchers and practitioners for at least two reasons. First, the Balkan area may offer an opportunity for developing a standardized versus a customized approach to bank service quality strategies. This is important since the banking sector in this area, especially the Bulgarian banking sector, has attracted both Greek (due to the market proximity and close economic relationships) and international investors' interest. Second, the two countries have different economic, political and socio-cultural backgrounds, while their banking sectors are in different levels of maturity, thus, giving the opportunity for cross-cultural research. Indeed cross-cultural research is not very mature, since the historical emphasis has been placed on domestic and mono-cultural issues, particularly in the area of service quality (Glaveli et al., 2006). In particular, the presence of Greek banks in Bulgaria and FYROM is estimated as the strongest, while Albania follows at Greece's heel. In FYROM and Bulgaria, Greek banks are in control of over 28 percent of the banks' assets. In Albania, Greek banks are in possession of 20 percent of the assets of the state, and in Serbia 19 percent of the banking capitals are being controlled by Greek banks. The Greek banking presence in Romania is 18.5 percent, while in Turkey only 4.4 percent of the market.

The phenomenon of the information revolution has important economical and social consequences. The rules of the market are constantly changing and the banks need to come up to the demands of the new data in the market. Thus, they follow new models and methods. Nowadays, e-banking is an inseparable piece of banking, important for competitive advantages of banks and governances. The use of computer technology and telecommunications improves the relation of the banks with their customers and with other banks. E-banking provides flexible and integrated promotion solutions in the new markets, increasing the number of customers day by day. This sector of banking has lead to the creation of new chances and challenges for the markets.

Due to cultural and environmental effects in general, consumers of services in different countries have different perception of what service quality is. Indeed, several studies have identified culture as a key variable influencing service quality perceptions. Thus, managers who seek to develop international service standards may not succeed unless they are aware of the value of environmental differences between countries in terms of economic development, political ideology, cultural value system and level of sector maturity and accordingly emphasize the various dimensions of service quality differently. In addition, they can focus on similarities to introduce global or regional quality initiatives (Glaveli et al., 2006).

According to Parusheva (2005), by 2005 56 percent of the banks in Bulgaria offered Internet banking services. Several studies (Vijayan and Shanmugam, 2003; Diniz et al., 2005; Miranda et al., 2006) have tried to evaluate e-banking web sites in different countries; these studies, however, have some limitations and none of them is concerned with Balkan countries. Moreover, to the best of our knowledge, there is no research studying e-banking web sites in Greece and Bulgaria. Bojinov (2002) presents an overview of the internet services that Bulgarian banks offer to the consumers, but there is no evaluation of these services and the e-banking web sites. In the present study our aim is to evaluate and compare the e-banking sites of Greek banks in Greece and Bulgaria.

In section 2 we delineate the theoretical background and the research methodology of our study, in section 3 we present the results and, finally, in section 4 we present the study's conclusions and a discussion of the findings.

Research Methodology

Several studies attempted to measure web site quality (Huizingh, 2000; Young and Benamati, 2000; Palmer, 2002) and, more specifically, business web sites (Merwe and Bekker, 2003). However, the evaluation criteria still require theoretical justification (Miranda et al., 2006). Taking into account the above, we base our evaluation on specific theoretical models and criteria. More specifically, we use the Nielsen Heuristics (Nielsen, 1994) for the web sites' usability evaluation. These heuristics evaluate the usability of a system and can show most of the problems that may be encountered in a system.

Also, we borrow from the conceptual framework of the Technology Acceptance Model (TAM) (Davis, 1986). This model was developed in order to explain the acceptance of information systems, as well as to predict the value of related factors to the penetration of these systems (Davis et al., 1989). TAM is studying the factors that affect the intention of the user to use an information system, an environment or just information, and proposes the connection between two main factors: the perceived ease of use and the perceived usefulness. Davis (1989) defines perceived usefulness as the degree to which a person believes that a specific system will be improving his/her performance in his/her job. On the other hand, perceived ease of use is defined as the degree to which a person believes that the use of a specific system does not require effort on his/her behalf to be used. According to this model the main factors that affect the actual use of a system are perceived ease of use and perceived usefulness. Research has established the validity of the TAM model, which is widely accepted (Legris et al, 2003).

Therefore, one of the main goals is to evaluate system usefulness and ease of use. Evaluation is a process common to most of the products, including the Internet. It helps control the design and development goals of every implementation and contributes by recommending ways of improvement. It assesses whether a certain webpage is drawn near the targeted customers, if it functions efficiently and its content is full, correct and relevant to the theme. The Internet has no operation time, it is multinational and multicultural; thus, the language, images and graphics that are used must have a universal character.

The evaluation criteria, are the following: accuracy of provided information, ownership of the webpage, objectiveness, renewal and update, value and accuracy of information provided, recovery time of information, readability of the webpage, presentation with a uniform and balanced way (color, animation, etc.), so that the customers can be focused on the information provided. Additionally, according to the TAM model, ease of use and usefulness should be examined. The last two criteria are important for the actual use of the banks' web services. In our study, we examine whether users believe that the environment is simple and user-friendly and whether navigation in the system is easy and friendly. The outcome of these questions emerges the perceived ease of use of e-banking services. Additionally, the usefulness of a system is the second factor that affects the system's actual use. So, we examine the perceived usefulness of the system. In order to do that we ask users weather they feel that e-banking sites help them do their job more effectively and weather they intend to use the sites in the feature. The answers to these questions show the perceived usefulness of the e-banking services.

We develop a questionnaire with 34 questions, using a five-point Likert scale (1=very high, 2=high, 3=medium, 4=low, 5=very low) to measure the importance of the criteria. The answer to these questions will indicate whether users have positive perceptions regarding the usefulness and ease of use of a system, and by effect, on actual system usage.

Results

More than 20 banks operate both in Greece and Bulgaria. The banks that operate in both countries are quite a few, but only 4 are Greek owned. These are Eurobank, Piraeus, Alpha and National Bank of Greece. National Bank of Greece operates in Bulgaria under the name 'United Bulgarian Bank'. The questionnaire was distributed during 2008. In total, 100 Greeks and 100 Bulgarians completed the questionnaire, separately for each bank. We randomly selected these people according to the e-banking of the bank they use. 25 people from each country answered the questionnaire for each bank. In this section, we include a few representative questions with comments on the answers of Greek and Bulgarian customers and we present few graphs showing the mean percentage for both countries. For legitimate reasons we do not discriminate the 4 banks.

Regarding perceived quality of information in terms of a. credibility, b. objectiveness, c. accuracy, d. content, e. uniqueness, f. usefulness, almost all costumers believe that the credibility of information is either very high or high. It is remarkable, though, that none of the respondents rates the objectiveness of information as being high; the majority of both Greeks and Bulgarians (65% and 55%, respectively) rate it as medium. Most of the customers in both countries share similar high value on the accuracy of information, while they have different perceptions about the contents of the webpage. 67% of Greeks and 73% of Bulgarians believe that the information provided is not unique, while almost 80% of each state that the information is useful (Table 1- in appendix- and Figure 1). These results point towards an overall satisfaction with the quality of information provided.

Figure 1. How the customers evaluate the quality of information in terms of a. credibility, b. objectiveness, c. accuracy, d. content, e. uniqueness, f. usefulness.

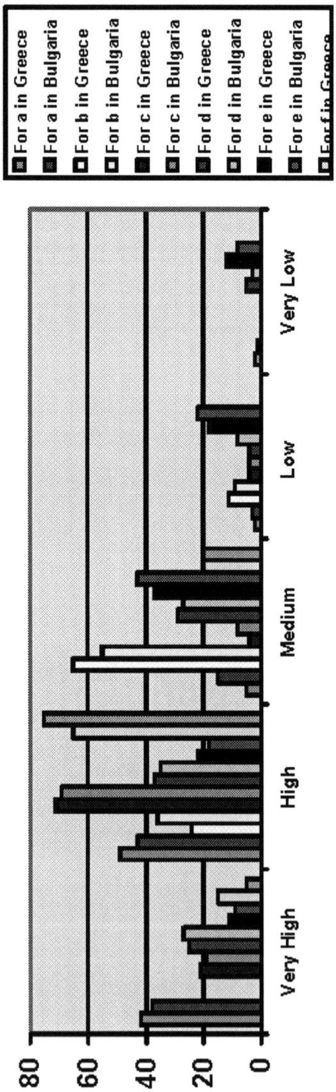

Figure 2. What is the level of satisfaction concerning a. the quantity of content, b. the quality of content, c. the ease of understanding of content, d. graphics, e. search speed, f. load speed, g. update frequency, h. total appearance, i. effectiveness.

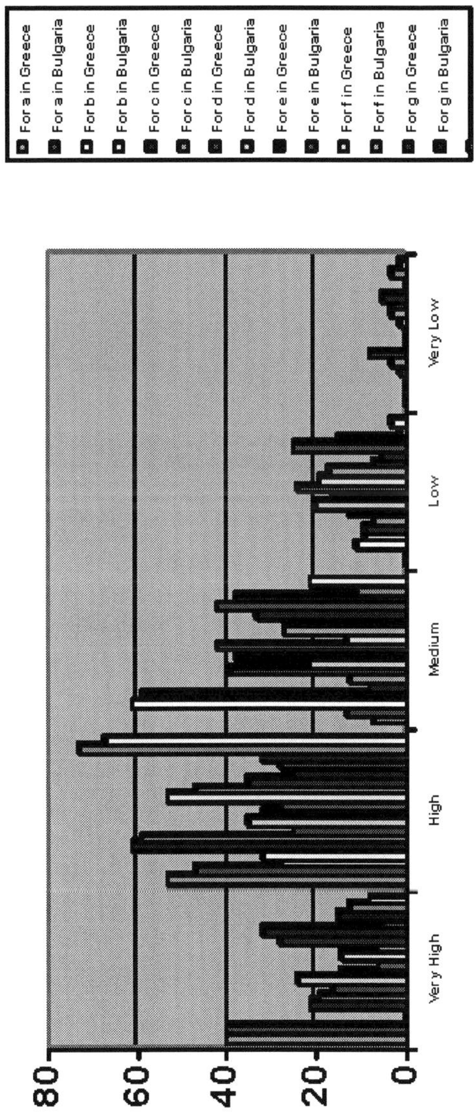

The next question assessed the level of satisfaction concerning a. the quantity of content, b. the quality of content, c. the ease of understanding of content, d. graphics, e. search speed, f. load speed, g. update frequency, h. total appearance, and i. effectiveness. More specifically, 93% of Greeks and 87% of Bulgarians say quantity of content is either high or very high. About the quality of content, 89% of Greeks and 91% of Bulgarians rate it either medium or high, while it is noteworthy that no one perceives the quality as being very high. Regarding ease of understanding of content, 61% of Greeks and 59% of Bulgarians rate it high, whilst there are a few that believe that it is very low.

Concerning the graphics, it is observed that the customers are almost equally divided between very high, high and medium in both countries. About the search speed, 16% of Greeks and 24% of Bulgarians say that they are not satisfied, while for the load speed almost 80% of each country is satisfied. Concerning the update frequency, 63% of Greeks and 57% of Bulgarians believe that it is high or very high. About the general appearance, 42% of Greeks and 38% Bulgarians rate it medium, while 25% and 15% of the Greeks and Bulgarians, respectively, rate it low. Finally, in terms of effectiveness 85% of Greeks and 75% of Bulgarians consider it high or very high (Table 2 - in appendix- and Figure 2). Customers' demand is high because their previous experiences with web applications effectiveness have been high (Table 1).

To the question of 'how you evaluate the specific webpage compared to other similar', in terms of a. design, b. use of information, c. technical characteristics, d. aesthetics, 43% of Greeks and 37% of Bulgarians believe that design is mediocre. About the use of information of content 74% of Greeks and 86% of Bulgarians say that it is high or very high. Concerning technical characteristics, 60% of the customers of both countries say that they are medium or low satisfaction level, while with respect to aesthetics, 77% of Greeks and 63% Bulgarians say that they are not satisfied (Table 3 - in appendix- and Figure 3). Overall, results suggest that the Bulgarian users are more satisfied, compared to Greeks.

Figure 3. How you evaluate the specific webpage in comparison with others in terms of a. design, b. use of information, c. technical characteristics, d. aesthetics.

Figure 4. How well designed is the webpage.

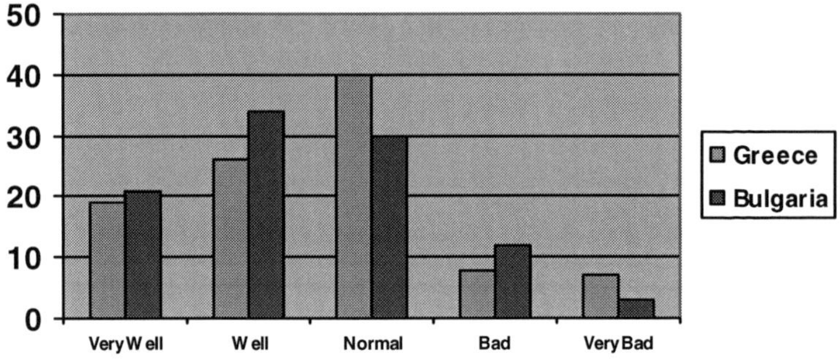

To the question of 'how well the webpage is designed', 85% of the users of each country believe that it is well designed.

Figure 5. How attractive is the webpage concerning a. the variety of colors, b. the combination of text and graphs, c. the use of multimedia

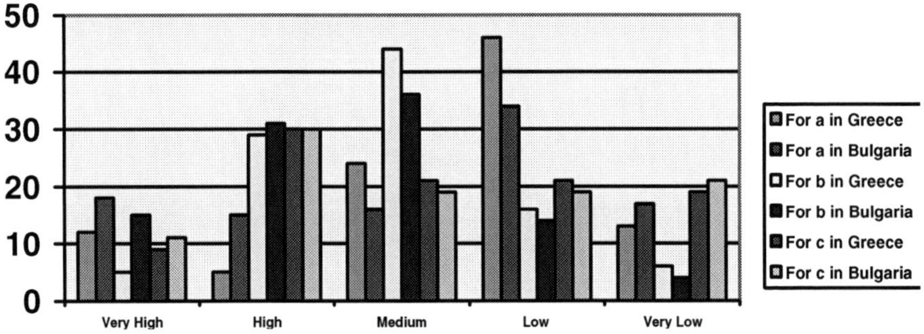

As to how attractive is the webpage in terms of a. the amount of colours, b. the combination of text and graphs, c. the use of multimedia (Figure 5), it contains, almost 25% and 40% of the respondents from Greece and Bulgaria, respective, rate each of the 3 categories of attributes very high or. Results indicate that the Bulgarian customers (Table 5- in appendix) are a little more satisfied with page attractiveness than the Greeks. Moreover, the combination of text and graphs is highly evaluated by consumers in both countries.

Figure 6. Are the links clarified in each webpage?

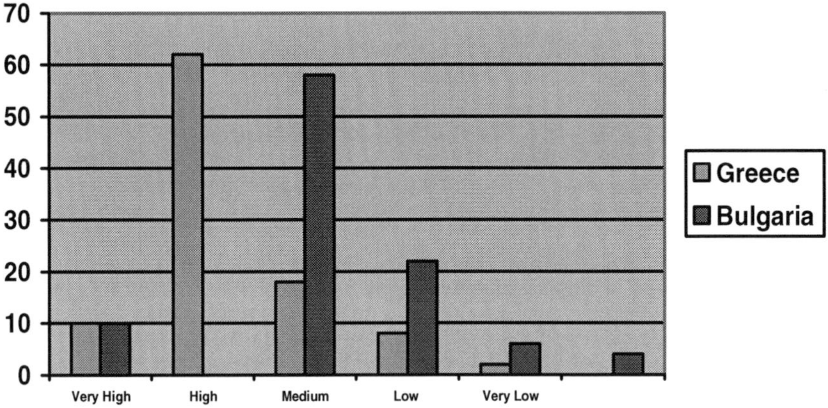

Almost 70% of the respondents from each country are satisfied with the way links are clarified in the web pages (Figure 6 and Table 6- in appendix).

Figure 7. Is there support available during the visit in the webpage?

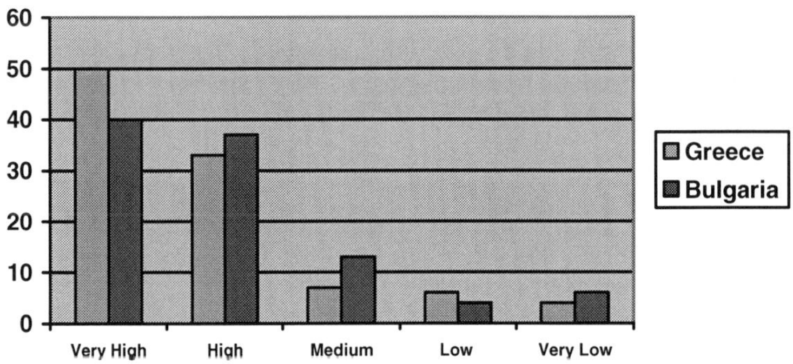

To the question of 'whether one can find adequate support during the visit to the webpage', 83% of Greeks and 77% of Bulgarians believe that such support is available (Figure 7 and Table 7- in appendix).

Figure 8. How the customers evaluate the amount and the sufficiency of information.

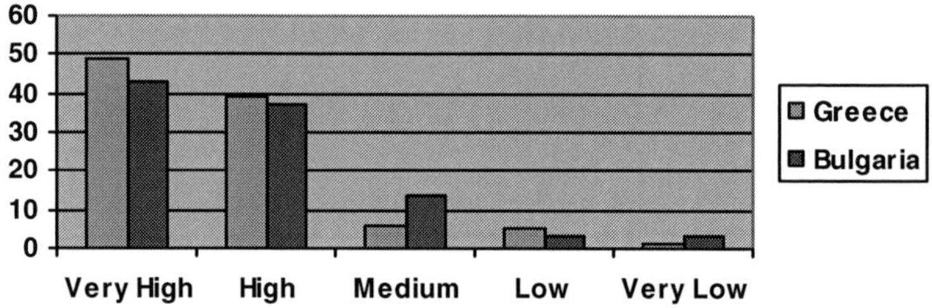

With respect to the amount and the sufficiency of information available in the web pages, 49% of Greeks and 43% of the Bulgarians find it very sufficient, while 39% of Greeks and 37% of Bulgarians sufficient (Table 8 and Figure 8- in appendix).

Discussion and Conclusions

The period after Greece's integration in EU is delicate concerning Greek banks. This is because the banking system bore the adjustment weight of the Greek economy to the standards of the Western Europe. Greek banks had to modernize in order to survive in the competitive environment of the EU. To that direction, Greek banks realized that the new technologies and communications that they were already using (Automatic Transaction Systems and on-line interface of bank branches) were not enough.

Consequentially, internet invaded the banking sector providing new effective possibilities both for banks and their customers, determining the bank transaction scheme of tomorrow. Ulterior goal is to take advantage of Internet to achieve best quality and completeness of the services provided on-line and, therefore, save time and money.

Nevertheless, e-banking services became available to Greek customers quite late, mostly because of the unsatisfactory internet networks' infrastructure and users' fear concerning safety of on-line transactions. Because of that, most banks hesitated to invest in e-banking. However, e-banking renders many benefits, such as:

- The bank approaches an additional customers' network, without the customers being physically present.
- The bank uses less personnel in sections were personal contact is unnecessary.
- Reduces operational costs, because of e-banking transactions are more cost-efficient than the transactions performed in a bank branch or through an ATM or phone banking.
- Additionally, because of reducing operational costs, the bank can offer better products, like more attractive interest rates on loans and/or deposits.
- The bank accesses customers from a broader geographical area, outside the national boarders of a country.
- Moreover, the customer's main advantage is that he can perform transaction , using a computer in the convenience of his/her home 24 hours a day.

For all the above, banks invest in e-banking in order to provide high-quality, modern, fast and useful services to their customers. Based on the results of our study we can draw the following conclusions.

- There is an overall satisfaction with the quality of information available in banks' web pages. The majority of customers from both countries value high the accuracy and usefulness of information.
- Banks' customers have high demands about the webpage's content and appearance. In comparison with other web pages, it seems that the majority of the Bulgarians and Greeks are fairly satisfied with the design and technical characteristics, while they seem to be dissatisfied with the aesthetics. Both groups of respondents are satisfied with the use of information of content.
- Both groups are satisfied with the webpage's design and attractiveness. Although Bulgarian customers seem to be a little more satisfied than the Greeks. Also, results suggest that the combination of text and graphs is rated extremely high in both countries.
- Greeks and Bulgarians value very high the links' clarification and the support available to them during the visit to the webpage.
- Customers rate very high the amount and sufficiency of information.
- Finally, customers find both useful and easy of understanding the content of e-banking pages which, according to TAM, increases the possibility of the web pages actually being used.

Consequentially, both Greeks and Bulgarians are satisfied with the quality of the provided information, the ease of use and understanding and the sufficiency of information available to the in the web pages. Both of them are restrained about the total appearance and design of the web page, with the Greeks being more restrained than the Bulgarians.

In future work we would like to expand our research to include more banks in the area and, since e-banking is constantly evolving and expanding with new possibilities like phone-banking, m-banking, tv-banking, in those services as well. Also, we would like to expand our research in others sectors of banking.

References

Bojinov, B., 2002, What Bulgarian Banks Offer via Internet: An overview. Proceedings of 50th Anniversary Financial Conference, 11-12 April, Svishtov, Bulgaria, pp. 883-989.

Davis, F. D., 1986, *A technology acceptance model for empirically testing new end-user information systems: theory and results*, PhD Thesis, MIT Sloan School of Management, Cambridge, MA.

Davis, F. D., Bagozzi, R. and Warshaw, P. R., 1989, User acceptance of computer technology: a Comparison of two theoretical models, *Management Science*, 35, pp. 982–1003.

Davis, F.D., 1989, Perceived usefulness, perceived ease of use, and user acceptance of information technology, *MIS Quarterly*, 13, pp. 319–339.

Diniz, E., Morena, R. and Adachi, T., 2005, Internet Banking in Brazil: Evaluation of Functionality, Reliability and Usability, *Electronic Journal of Information Systems Evaluations*, 8, 1, pp 41-50.

Glaveli, N., Petridou, E., Liassides, C. and Spathis, C., 2006, Bank service quality: evidence from five Balkan countries, *Managing Service Quality*, 16, 4, pp. 380-394.

Hackethal, A., Marinov, V. and Schmidt, R.H., 2003, Banking markets in central and Eastern Europe (VI): Bulgaria – emerging stronger from a crisis, Database online, In Die bank, available online at www.die-bank.de.

Huizingh, E., 2000, The content and design of web sites: an empirical study, *Information & Management*, 37, 3, pp. 123-134.

Legris, P., Ingham, J. and Collerette, P., 2003, Why do people use information technology? A critical review of the technology acceptance model, *Information and Management*, 40, 3, pp. 191-204.

Merwe, R. V. D. and Bekker, J., 2003, A framework and methodology for evaluating e-commerce Web sites, *Internet Research: Electronic Networking Applications and Policy*, 13, 5, pp. 330-341.

Miranda, F.J., Cortés, R. and Barriuso, C., 2006, Quantitative Evaluation of e-Banking Web Sites: an Empirical Study of Spanish Banks, *The Electronic Journal Information Systems Evaluation*, 9, 2, pp. 73 - 82, available online at www.ejise.com.

Monastiriotis V. and Tsamis A., 2007, *Greece's new Balkan Economic Relations: policy shifts but no structural change*, GreeSE Paper No1 Hellenic Observatory Papers on Greece and Southeast Europe, The London School of Economics and Political Science.

Nielsen, J., 1994, *Usability inspection methods*, John Willey, New York.

Palmer, J. W., 2002, Web Site Usability, Design, and Performance Metrics, *Information Systems Research*, 13, 2, pp. 151-167.

Parusheva S., 2005, Electronic Banking in Bulgaria – State and Perspectives, *Economic Studies Journal*, 3, pp. 36-64, Bulgarian Academy of Sciences - Institute of Economics.

Vijayan, P. and Shanmugam, Bala, 2003, Service Quality Evaluation of Internet Banking in Malaysia, *Journal of Internet Banking and Commerce*, 8, 1, pp.

Young, D. and Benamati, J., 2000, Difference in public web sites: The current state of large U.S. firms, *Journal of Electronic Commerce Research*, 1, 3, pp. 94-105.

Xanthidis, D., Nicholas D., 2004, Evaluating internet usage and ecommerce growth in Greece, *Aslib Proceedings: new information perspectives*, 56, 6, pp. 356-366.

Appendix

In this section we collate the tables presenting the percentages per question, presented above. First, we mention the answers of Greek customers, followed by the answers of Bulgarian customers and then mean percentage of both countries customers.

Table 1. How the customers value the quality of information in relevance with a. credibility, b. objectiveness, c. accuracy, d. content, e. uniqueness, f. usefulness.

Reply	Very High	High	Medium	Low	Very Low
For a in Greece	42	49	5	2	2
For a in Bulgaria	38	43	15	3	1
For b in Greece	0	24	65	11	0
For b in Bulgaria	0	36	55	9	0
For c in Greece	21	71	4	4	0
For c in Bulgaria	19	69	8	4	0
For d in Greece	25	37	29	4	5
For d in Bulgaria	27	35	27	8	3
For e in Greece	11	22	37	18	12
For e in Bulgaria	9	18	43	22	8
For f in Greece	15	65	20	0	0
For f in Bulgaria	5	75	20	0	0

Table 2. What is the level of satisfaction concerning a. the quantity of content, b. the quality of content, c. the ease of understanding of content, d. graphics, e. search speed, f. load speed, g. update frequency, h. total appearance, i. effectiveness

Reply	Very High	High	Medium	Low	Very Low
For a in Greece	40	53	7	0	0
For a in Bulgaria	40	47	13	0	0
For b in Greece	0	28	61	11	0
For b in Bulgaria	0	32	59	9	0
For c in Greece	21	61	8	9	1
For c in Bulgaria	19	59	12	7	3
For d in Greece	16	25	39	12	8
For d in Bulgaria	24	35	21	20	0
For e in Greece	14	32	38	16	0
For e in Bulgaria	6	28	42	24	0
For f in Greece	14	53	13	19	1
For f in Bulgaria	6	47	27	17	3
For g in Greece	28	35	27	7	3
For g in Bulgaria	32	25	33	5	5
For h in Greece	5	28	42	25	0
For h in Bulgaria	15	32	38	15	0
For i in Greece	12	73	11	1	3
For i in Bulgaria	8	67	21	3	1

Table 3. How you evaluate the specific webpage in comparison with others in terms of a. design, b. use of information, c. technical characteristics, d. aesthetics

Reply	Very High	High	Medium	Low	Very Low
For a in Greece	8	26	43	23	0
For a in Bulgaria	12	34	37	17	0
For b in Greece	27	47	26	0	0
For b in Bulgaria	33	53	14	0	0
For c in Greece	0	39	41	20	0
For c in Bulgaria	0	41	39	20	0
For d in Greece	7	16	34	32	11
For d in Bulgaria	13	24	26	28	9

Table 4. How well designed is the webpage

Reply	Very Well	Well	Normal	Bad	Very Bad
Greece	19	26	40	8	7
Bulgaria	21	34	30	12	3
Mean	20	30	35	10	5

Table 5. How attractive is the webpage concerning a. the variety of colors, b. the combination of text and graphs, c. the use of multimedia

Reply	Very High	High	Medium	Low	Very Low
For a in Greece	12	5	24	46	13
For a in Bulgaria	18	15	16	34	17
For a Mean	15	10	20	40	15
For b in Greece	5	29	44	16	6
For b in Bulgaria	15	31	36	14	4
For b Mean	10	30	40	15	5
For c in Greece	9	30	21	21	19
For c in Bulgaria	11	30	19	19	21
For c Mean	10	30	20	20	20

Table 6. Are the links clarified in each webpage?

Reply	Very High	High	Medium	Low	Very Low
Greece	10	62	18	8	2
Bulgaria	10	58	22	6	4
Mean	10%	60%	20%	7%	3%

Table 7. Is there support available during the visit in the webpage?

Reply	Very High	High	Medium	Low	Very Low
Greece	50	33	7	6	4
Bulgaria	40	37	13	4	6
Mean	45%	35%	10%	5%	5%

Table 8. How the customers evaluate the amount and the sufficiency of information.

Reply	Very High	High	Medium	Low	Very Low
Greece	49	39	6	5	1
Bulgaria	43	37	14	3	3
Mean	46%	38%	10%	4%	2%

Part Four:

Rural Developments in Specific Countries

The Perspective of Rural Development in Albania – Evidence of Microfinance in Agriculture

MATTEO BELLETTI AND ELVIRA LEKSINAJ

Abstract

Albanian farming was left totally unchanged after transition and derived from land reform. It is still characterized as being a self-sufficient agricultural model: a smallholding venture of around 1 hectare with low external inputs and labour-intensive techniques. Over the past decade Albania opened its doors to the market economy but that process does not seem to have extended and embraced the rural economy. Why? The hypothesis is that along with land reform effects enduring due to typical land market inelasticity, there is a strong pillar of this peasant household's equilibrium: farm structure consolidation during Albanian transition is a peculiar part-time smallholding venture which could be labelled "transnational part-time peasant farm household". This subject doesn't demand credits to purchase land orienting itself toward the market. It demands credit to strengthen its own self-consumption-oriented structure. The aim of this paper is to consider why the analyzed micro-credit system, and, by extent, the special smallholding, would contain elements of sustainable development dynamics in Albania.

Introduction

In Albania, even today, agricultural farm structure is almost that of agrarian reform in the early transition period. An agrarian reform that led to the division of land, which, at the moment, was dominated by state-run cooperatives, and its distribution in micro-farms, on the basis of the principle of equality (Ellis, 1992). It is easily noticeable that even though almost two decades have already passed since the transition, the regime of private ownership of land resulting from the reforms has not yet evolved towards a market-oriented structure (Swinnen and Gow, 1999). It is, rather characterized as an agricultural model labelled *self-sufficient* (Tripp, 2006) and oriented towards self-sustenance. With farms covering an average area of about 1 hectare, labor-using and low use of external inputs, the Albanian agricultural system can theoretically be classified as a case of *peasant farm household* (Ellis, 2003).

This paper constitutes a key reading on the Albanian rural development, according to the evolution and performance of the main system of rural micro-credit in Albania: the Union of Albanian Savings and Credit Associations (SCAs Union). In spite of considering the entrenched and constant effects of agrarian reform arising from the inelasticity of land market (Ellis, 1992), the dataset related to the SCAs Union points toward the presence in Albania of a process of virtuous consolidation in agricultural structure, driven and steered by self-sustenance in a long-term perspective. Peasant household farm is efficiently benefiting from the possibility of a non-subsidized credit, for almost ten years, provided by the SCAs Union with the aim of optimizing surplus production after self-sustenance to move towards the local food market. This is done through investment capable of boosting productivity with the progressive adaptation of farm to market needs, rather than in increasing size and farm specialization.

In fact, only about 1% of credits granted by SCAs Union are used for purchasing land and about 8% for rent. In Albania the peasant farm household does not require loans to buy land and to be oriented towards the market. Rather it seeks loans to strengthen its structure based on production for self-consumption. Demand for credit has led to increased productivity of land already owned and to the maximization of the part of production, by exceeding the amount necessary to guarantee an adequate level of consumption and savings in the farming household. This part of the production represents a shadow price on self-consumption less than the market prices and thereby available and price-fetching for sale (De Janvry, Sadoulet and Murgai, 2002).

However, the consolidation of the Albanian peasant farm household bases itself on another income source, except that of the possibility of loans: remittances from abroad. This way one can come into possession of a part-time farm, commonly referred to as *transnational part-time farm* (Belletti et al., 2009). Table 1 shows the structure of Albanian peasant farm households' income.

Table 1. Albanian peasant farm household income

Income	Source of provision		Income destination (in billion of Leks)					
			Consumption		Savings		Savings utilization in %	
Total	Farming activities	Out farming activities	Total	In %	Total	In %	Investment	Idle
119	80	39	83	70	36	30	19	11

Source: Skreli, Meçe, Musabelliu & Apostoli, 1997.

The presence of an internal process of wealth creation through a non-subsidized credit and in the absence of supporting policies in agricultural incomes describes an anomaly case in agriculture. This case alone can be explained on the basis of the reverse link between productivity and farm size (Ellis, 2003), which constitutes recurring phenomenon in agriculture. Thus, the Albanian peasant farms would precisely find in their small size not only a natural guide to self-sustenance but also economic and financial efficiency.

The importance of this paper lies in the attempt to identify strengths of post-transition Albanian agricultural structure in response to the opening of credit channel. Micro-credit applied in agriculture rarely achieves satisfactory results (Pillarisetti, 2007). Despite this, in 2008 the SCAs Union has ranked 19th among micro-finance institutions worldwide (Microfinance Information Exchange, 2008), being also among the first five, considering only rural micro-credit systems.

Material and methods

This paper proposes an exploratory research on the topic of rural micro-credit, based on the Albanian experience; this research started in 2006 and is still in progress, under the Scientific Cooperation Agreement between the Italian and Albanian Government. The following aspects are specified for purposes of analysis: the time lines elaborated upon are based on FAO data regarding the Albanian agricultural mix in the transition period; full interviews have been conducted with key players of SCAs Union's Board of Directors; a sample of some 15 SCAs is administered a questionnaire containing approximately 100 variables of the quantitative-qualitative type, relative to the operation and performance of the SCAs. The hypothesis formulated and the ensuing thesis is not subject to any statistical verification, due to the exploratory nature of this research.

Empirical checks will be part of a more advanced stage of elaboration on the basis of the data collected.

Result and discussions

The Union of Savings and Credit Associations is a micro-credit system, based upon the model of Grameen Bank in Bangladesh (Grameen Bank, 1988). Today, SSAs Union in Albania represents the main source of crediting, non-subsidized, in agriculture. SCAs were legally recognized as such on 3 May 2001, after a decade's development both institutional and operational. In 2001, the SCAs network were present in 175 villages, while in 2008 were present in 805 villages scattered across 14 districts, out of 36 in total existing in the nation, with an average annual rate of territory coverage of 32.6% for the period 2004-2008. In the same period (2004-2008) the number of SCAs climbed from 90 to 103, while the average number of members per SCA from 118 individuals climbed to 240, with an annual average rate of SCA size expansion equal to 27.5%.

Briefly stated, the system's expansion is verified more through the increase of "pioneer" SCAs than on the basis of the creation of new groups. The expansion of existing SCAs and the large number of members of any Association should be considered valid indicators of the presence in Albanian rural society of two main elements pointing to the success of a micro-credit program besides the need for a well-being design of rural financial intermediaries (Chavez and Gonzales-Vega, 1995): personal reliability and reputation as a form of guarantee and steering capabilities that in turn suggests the presence of a good level of social capital (Belletti at al., 2009).

During the period 2004-2008, the SCAs network average annual percentage of members' growth was 22.9%, while the ratio between active clients and members has remained almost unchanged at about 67% for the period 2004-2006. This shows that, despite the broad participation of rural society in establishing a credit cooperating system, some difficulties are present, such as the lack of profitable markets and insufficiency of financial capital, preventing the system from developing its maximum potential, in terms of the relation between effective customers and members. However, it must be noted that during the period 2007-2008 the ratio between active clients and members has increased by 72% (Figure 1). This last dataset may indicate that the ability of SCAs Union funding (active members) in relation to the majority (number of members) is starting to expand.

The evolution of SCAs Union lending performance shows a positive linear development marking an average portfolio annual growth of 32% during the period 2004-2008 (Figure 2).

Figure 1. The evolution of SCA network structure

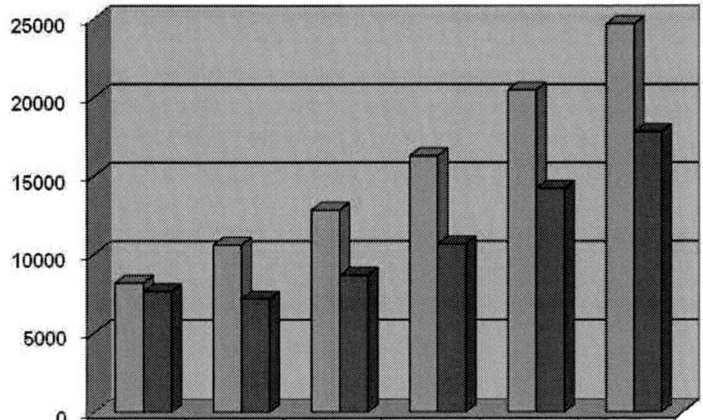

	2003	2004	2005	2006	2007	2008
Members	8161	10584	12815	16260	20457	24682
Active Clients	7621	7157	8650	10655	14209	17809

Source: elaboration on Albanian Saving & Credit Union Reports

Figure 2. The evolution of SCA Network portfolio (€)

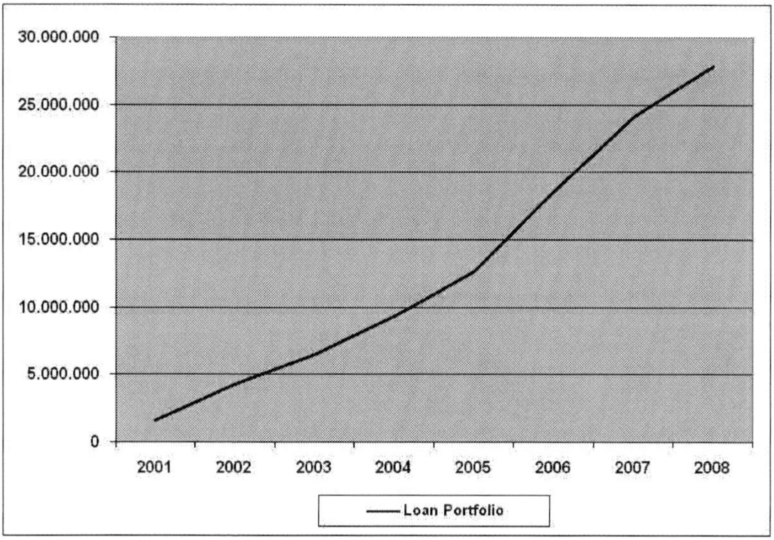

Source: elaboration on Albanian Saving & Credit Union Reports

It should be noted that the number of members of the SCAs Union in 2008, about 25 thousand, represents approximately 5% of all agricultural farms in Albania.

However, this percentage does not allow for generalizations neither regarding the behaviour nor the economic and financial potential of national agricultural sector. It is also a fact that there are not indications, based on which to suggest that the process of rapid expansion of the SCAs Union is likely to stop anytime soon.

In less than ten years the SCAs network has spread in many districts, even in those outside the periphery of the nation. So, it cannot be excluded that the evolution trend of the SCAs Union may be the result of a progressive involvement of all national rural territory, in the process of consolidating the financial and economic optimization of agricultural structure oriented towards self-sustenance.

In the period 2004-2006, the average loans (in Leks) within SCAs systems were equivalent to about 1500 Euro, a value close to the Albanian income per-capita. Portfolio at risk has decreased steadily going down from 2% to 0.5%, for the period 2001-2006. In practice, the introduction of late payment of credit is close to zero.

Most of the loans within SCAs activity go toward horticulture, livestock and fruit-trees, but also to other credits, such as extension to other commercialization activities and services, related to agriculture; the result is an overall economic growth in rural area (Figure 3).

Figure 3. The SCAs Union utilization of loans

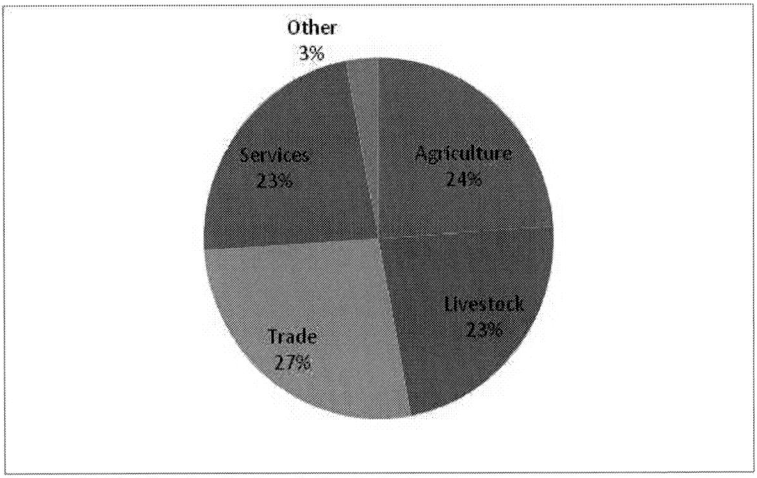

Source: 2008 Albanian Saving & Credit Union Report

Finally, Figure 4 shows the perfect balance between the loan capital and the credit capital from abroad collected by the SCAs Union in the financial markets. The conventional financial sector believes and invests in the SCAs network almost by doubling the loans cartel; this certainly is an indication of good performance and sustainability of the financial system under analysis.

The structural evolution of Albanian agriculture, orientated toward self-consumption, adapts to the evolution of the agricultural mix, represented as a time series and indexed in the base year $t_0 = 1975$ (Figure 4-5) and in the point of structural shock due to the transition (period 1990-1993).

Figure 4. The SCAs Union composition of resources

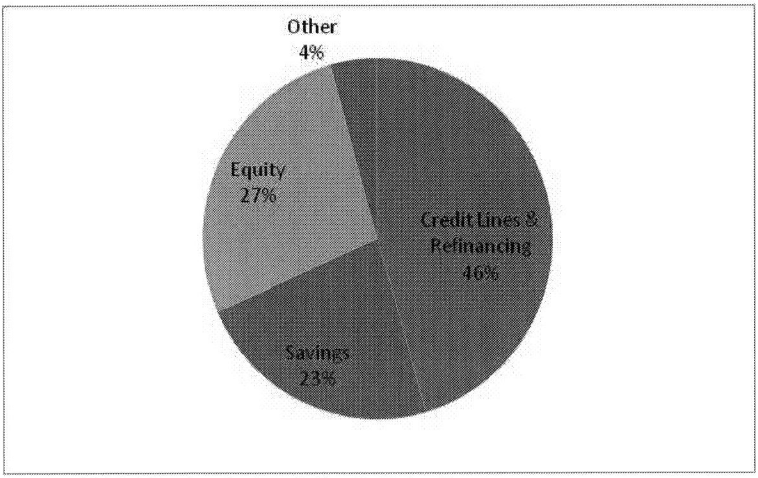

Source: 2008 Albanian Saving & Credit Union Report

Figure 5. Albanian agricultural-mix change in the transition

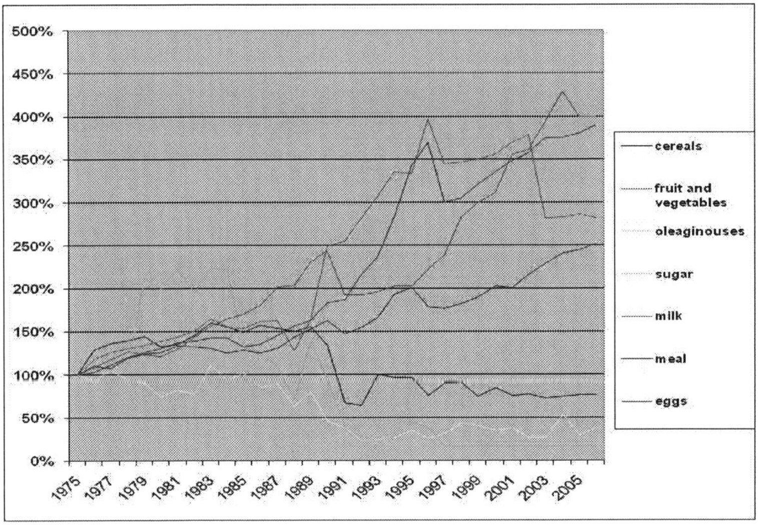

Source: elaboration on FAOSTAT dataset

In parallel, in Figure 6 one can notice that at the point of transition the national production of wheat is reduced in half, and progressively replaced by imported wheat, destined mainly for consumption by urban population, which was already currently isolated from national agricultural supply.

Figure 6. Wheat production and import in the transition

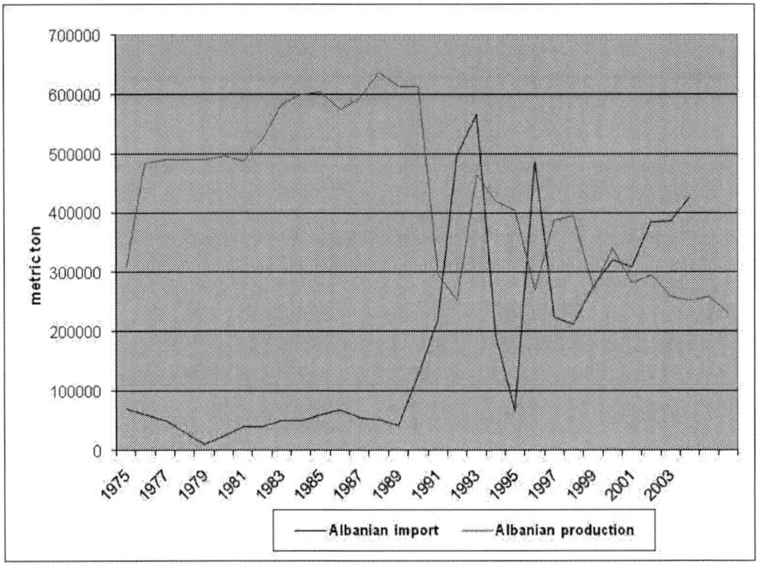

Source: elaboration on FAOSTAT dataset

Relocation of production, in the transition period, from cultivation of cereals towards livestock (Figure 5) can be explained considering that livestock provides greater food availability to the peasant farm household. This results from the transition in short cycles within an economy oriented towards production for self-consumption and further confirms the hypothesis of this paper.

In these dynamics of smallholding production cycles, farms also find an efficient way of reducing environmental risks, to which the extensive cultures are exposed. In addition, the livestock, alongside fruit and vegetable growing, exploits labour-intensive production techniques, typically adopted by Albanian farmers (Hatziprocopiou, Karagiannis and Velentzas, 1996), better than annual extensive cultures can do.

So the present work seems to confirm the numerous empirical verifications of the opposite link between productivity and farm size (Berry and Cline, 1979). Indeed, by deduction, taking the opposite link between farm size and productivity, an optimizing system of solutions, starting from the allocation of the less insufficient production source, in this case labour, will be linked to peasant farm household.

Concluding remarks

The perspective of rural development in Albania in relation to the evolution of smallholding ownership of families sets upon self-sustenance, which advances within an efficient cooperative credit system. This system is represented today by the SCAs Union (Belletti et al., 2009). Given the undeniable reverse link between productivity and farm size, the synergy between agriculture and credit could deliver a significant production capacity to be directed toward the market.

This projection also enters into the national macroeconomic framework in view of risks associated with globalization (Sadoulet, de Janvry, 1992). In this context, it is important that the Albanian agricultural sector lifts itself out of isolation through integration into the national development, which today is dangerously imbalanced by the industry connected with the international markets. Until an external development dependent on foreign capital and foreign consumer markets transforms into a sustainable and long internal development, the contribution of the agricultural sector will be a significant element, basically because of its peculiar role of a macroeconomic stabilizer, independent of its contribution to Gross Domestic Product (GDP) (Ardeni and Freebairn, 2002).

Given the recent changes in policy, economy and market implementation in Albania, the small size of self-sufficient farms might actually become a driving force of a society more egalitarian and with a more stable economy.

Reliance on a national agricultural structure based on small private property, self-sufficient and able to support a major part of national consumption demand in an open-market economy, calls for re-investing a significant part of income generated from industrial investment from abroad, particularly in rural areas which currently turn out to be excluded from development. So, representing a broad expansion and penetration of the SCAs network in the rural environment (Monteil et al., 1993) to support to this type of agricultural structure, it is possible to imagine the Albanian self-sufficient agricultural model as a model of sustainable rural development, also capable of providing stability to the national macroeconomic balance.

References

Albanian Saving and Credit Union, 2004, *Annual Report 2004,* Tirana, Albanian Saving and Credit Union.

—. 2006, *Annual Report 2006*, Tirana, Albanian Saving and Credit Union.

—. 2008, *Annual Report 2008*, Tirana, Albanian Saving and Credit Union.

Ardeni, P. G., Freebairn, J., 2002, The Macroeconomics of Agriculture, in Bruce, L., Gardner and Gordon C. Rausser, ed. *Handbook of Agricultural Economics*, Elsevier Science B.V. 2A, Chapter 28.

Belletti, M. Leksinaj, E. Petrocchi, M. Meco, M. Mussabelliu, B., 2009, *Perspectives of Rural Development and the Role of Agricultural Lending in Albania*, in: FEA (Faculty of Economy & Agribusiness), AHEED Project (Hawaii University and USAID) & GTZ (Deutsche Gesellschaft für Technische Zusammenarbeit), International Conference *"Farm efficiency and the vertical integration of actors as factors contributing to increase of competitiveness. Role of private and public actors"*, Tirana, Albania, 15 April 2009, Tirana: Faculty of Economy & Agribusiness.

Berry, R.A. and Cline, WR., 1979, *Agrarian Structure and Productivity in Developing Countries*, Baltimore, Johns Hopkins University Press.

Chavez, R.A., Gonzalez-Vega, C., 1995, The Design of Successful Rural Financial Intermediaries: Evidence from Indonesia, *World Development*, 24, 1, January, pp. 65-78.

De Janvry, A., Sadoulet, E. and Murgai, R., 2002, *Rural Development and Rural Policy*, in Bruce L. Gardner & Gordon C. Rausser, ed. *Handbook of Agricultural Economics*, Elsevier Science B.V. 2A, chapter 31.

Ellis, F., 1992, *Agricultural policies in developing countries*, Cambridge University Press.

—. 2003, *Peasant Economics,* 3rd ed. Cambridge University Press.

Grameen Bank, 1988, *16 Rules of Grameen Bank*, IRED Forum, 28.

Hatziprocopiou, M., Karagiannis, G. and Velentzas, K., 1996, Production structure, technical change, and productivity growth in Albanian agriculture, *Journal of Comparative Economics*, 22, pp.295-310.

Montiel, P. J. Agenor P. R. Haque, N. U., 1993, *Informal Financial Markets in Developing Countries: A Macroeconomic Analysis*, Oxford, Blackwell and Co.

Pillarisetti, S., 2007, Microfinance for agriculture: perspectives from India, in FARM (Foundation for World Agriculture and Rural Life), International Conference *"What microfinance for developing countries agriculture?"*, Paris, France 4-6 December 2007, available at: <http://www.fondation-farm.org/spip.php?article299, (accessed 6 September 2010).

Saudolet, E., De Janvry, A., 1992, Agricultural Trade Liberalization and Low Income Countries: A General Equilibrium-Multimarket Approach, *American Journal of Agricultural Economics*, 74, 2, pp. 268-280.

Skreli, E., Meço, M., Musabelliu, B. and Apostoli, S., 1997, *Income of rural households in Albania,* Survey study, Agricultural University of Tirana.

Swinnen, J., Gow, F. M. and Hamish, R., 1999, *Agricaltural credit problems and policies during the transition to a market economic in Central and Eastern Europe*, London, Pergamon.

The Microfinance Information Exchange, 2008, *Mix Global 100 Composite Rankings 2008*, available at: http://www.themix.org/publications/2008-mix-global-100-composite-rankings-tables (Accessed 6 September 2010).

Tripp, R., 2006, *Self-Sufficient Agriculture*, London, Earthscan.

Application of the Rural Tour Methodology for Advertising and Promoting Rural Areas in Eastern Europe

Evgenia Bitsani and Androniki Kavoura

Introduction

Society has realised the problems that could be created by the prevalent model of mass tourism and the emphasis has shifted towards alternative forms of tourism (ecotourism, rural tourism, cultural tourism, historic tourism). These forms respect the local community and its visitors and, at the same time, the cultural heritage and the environment. The Rural Tour (RT) methodology for marketing plan is a complete methodology for the promotion and tourist development of rural or disadvantaged areas, and of tourist and farm holiday's enterprises, which operate in such regions. The RT marketing plan provided the promotion and the exploitation of the tourism resources present in the area, for the purpose of obtaining a rapid and considerable increase in the capacity to attract those tourists who are interested in discovering the landscape, historical, cultural and oenologic-gastronomic richness that is typical of Eastern Europe. An essential element of a region's promotion, that was both coherent and effective, was the active participation of the local "actors" (public authorities, associations and enterprises).

Throughout such an analysis, the organisation responsible for the formulation of the territorial marketing plan fills out a series of online forms using the RT Software. The data inserted in the database are used to generate, automatically or semi-automatically, material for advertising the area (including the website of the territory, online guides, brochures, etc.) and to support subsequent operational phases of the methodology. Rural areas in Eastern Europe may well benefit from the implementation of RT methodology for advertising and promoting areas for sustainable tourism development.

Nowadays, it is typical that standardised and mass tourist packages do not cater for tourists' needs. People realised the problems that could be created by the prevalent model of mass tourism and they were driven to search for alternative forms of tourism (ecotourism, rural tourism, cultural tourism, historic tourism). These forms respect the local community and its visitors and at the same time, the cultural heritage and the environment.

In that way, a place promotes its image for attracting tourists by providing a competitive advantage. Therefore, regions promote themselves and their perceived competitive advantages (Kavoura 2005; Kavoura, 2007; Deffner and Metaxas, 2006; Hall and McArthur, 1993; Pritchard and Morgan, 2001). Also, elements of marketing management are adopted for the promotion of places and in the specific case, rural areas.

According to Kotler, Haider and Rein (1993) the S.W.O.T. (where S stands for strengths, W for weaknesses, O for opportunities and T for threats) analysis of the marketing factors (infrastructure, attractions, image and quality of life and people) may be applied to the marketing of places. The success of rural tourism does not only depend on specific tourist services (hospitality, transport, dining, etc) but also on general factors, which influence the experience rural tourists gain. These include: advertising of the promotional material before visiting the area, reservations, the trip to the area, the first welcome, information about the area, accommodation and dining infrastructure, the sights to be visited, hospitality, issues of hygiene and safety, the natural environment, the farewell, the return journey but also the possibility of getting in touch and communicating with the community keeping the memories alive (European Commission, 1999; European Committee, 2000; Bitsani, 2004).

Local traditional activities, through cultural tourism. are modernised and preserved and traditional crafts revive (MacDonald and Jolliffe, 2003). When cultural tourism is developed the accessibility of an area is improved and development projects benefiting the local community are encouraged (Bitsani and Panagou, 2003; Cano and Mysyk, 2004; Smith, 2004). Meanwhile, tourism serves to preserve artefacts for promotion in place marketing (Hall and Jenkins, 1995) and also uses features of myth as collective symbols for establishing identity (Hall and Jenkins, 1995). This way, rural areas will be associated with heritage tourism existent in the area. There is a complex role of culture in rural tourism; commodification of culture for tourism purposes may exist with all the emerging challenges for rural communities (George, Mair and Reid, 2009, p. 136). If rural areas may be associated with culture and heritage then the destination area may be promoted with the combination of attractions and activities. That is why the emphasis on tourism is necessary for rural areas.

This paper examines the contribution of the Rural Tour (RT) methodology, a complete methodology for the promotion and tourist development of rural or disadvantaged areas to satisfy tourist needs, by improving the quality of what the region offers, contributing in that way to the development of areas in Eastern Europe (Bitsani, 2002).

Description of the RT project

The RT project, financed by the European programme of transnational cooperation INTERREG IIIB CADSES, began in June 2006 with the intention of promoting a model for the development (in sustainable and innovative ways) of integrated rural tourism in Central Eastern Europe (which uses the acronym area CADSES) (http://www.cadses.net/media/files/Project_Book/983_cadses_pb_225x290_www.pdf). The project aims to promote those rural tourist resources that are on the margin of mass tourism, define strategic actions that create and promote a network between activities presently in place and provide incentives that stimulate the development of new services (European Committee, 2000). Therefore, the intention of the RT project is to satisfy tourists' needs, by improving the quality of what the region offers, and at the same time, improve the growth opportunities of rural areas by affirming cultural identity and diversity, thereby valorizing the local oenological-gastronomical products, along with the human and economic resources of the respective region (Bitsani and Panagou, 2003).

The insufficient level of promotion of environmental, cultural and landscape resources, the difficulty in accessing rural areas, and the shortage of infrastructures and lodgings that are qualified to accommodate tourism, are among the main reasons why marginal regions are not influenced by the active benefits brought by the tourism in neighboring areas (Lytras, 2005). On the other hand, the success of the initiatives connected to rural tourism requires a long term financial and environmental sustainability. This long term financial sustainability can be realized if, subsequent to an initial investment, the tourist initiatives are capable of generating a positive flow of funds to ensure an enduring success of the initiative itself (Guerini and Zandonai, 2006).

Alternatively, environmental sustainability is connected with the capability of increasing the economic value of the natural and cultural patrimony, by adopting a tourism proposal that does not damage the patrimony itself (Bitsani and D' Arcangeli, 2009). High revenues can be generated both by directing a greater number of tourists to the interested regions and by protracting their presence in the low season. The RT project allows the pursuit of such an objective by first realizing a marketing plan, along with certain guide lines for a sustainable rural tourism, and second, by applying these in the pilot zones identified within the involved regions. Additionally, the project provides the possibility of creating a recognizable brand network that clearly identifies the initiatives of a sustainable rural tourism, based on rules and operating procedures that form the conditions for the attribution of the mark itself and for the subsequent certification process. The RT project involved a partnership comprising five public institutions in four State members of the European Union (Italy, Hungary, Poland, Austria) and one outside EU (Croatia). In particular, the six institutions that participated in the project were:

- Region of Veneto– the Office for Integrated Tourist Promotion (Italy)
- Region of Emilia Romagna– Tourism Service (Italy)
- Region of Opolskie (Poland)
- Federal State of Carinthia (Austria)
- Micro-Regional Development Association of Szıcsıny Area (Hungary)
- AZRRI-Agency for Rural Development of Istria Ldt. Pazin (Croazia).

Territorial marketing according to the RT methodology

Territorial marketing based on the tourist potential of an area is an effective instrument of economic development through the promotion and the evaluation of the tourist resources of the area. The goal is to achieve a quick and consistent increase in its ability to attract an influx of tourists.

The system of governance promoted by the project activities encouraged the participation of public authorities belonging to different institutional levels (Region, Province, Mountain Communities and Municipalities), in concomitance with private economic "actors" and specific associations that were present in the region. The promotion of the region required adopting an approach of implemented actions that started with the exigencies and necessities felt as more urgent by the locals (bottom–up approach). This led to an involvement and an active participation in the process of realizing the project by all the local public institutions, and by the representative associations and private enterprises. Such partnerships were developed through a series of meetings starting in June 2007. The in-depth knowledge of the region and its particularities allowed the local actors (Municipality, Companies, Wine and Typical Products Roads, products protection Consortium, tourism promotion Consortium) to play a fundamental role in creating the on-line system of research about tourism resources (Bitsani, 2004a, pp. 177-178). These participants furnished information and data that are interesting for surveying precious tourist resources and are largely unknown.

The process suggested by the RT methodology in order to carry out a territorial marketing plan, is divided into the following phases:

- Analysis of the tourist potential of the territory
- Development of an operating plan for territorial marketing
- Analysis of the obtained results and possible adjustments to the operating plan (feedback)

The first phase, i.e. the analysis of the tourist potential of the territory, includes i) an in-depth analysis of tourist demand potentially interested in the territory and subject to tourist promotion, ii) an analysis of its tourist resources and iii) of the methods of access to the territory.

In the present paper, the territory in reference is the geographical and administrative area interested in implementing a plan of tourist development and territorial marketing. The dimensional scale of such an area can range from a town (or towns) to a province (or provinces). Throughout such an analysis, the organisation responsible for the formulation of the territorial marketing plan fills out a series of online forms using the RT Software. The data which are inserted in the database are used to generate, automatically or semi-automatically, material for advertising of the area (including the website of the territory, online guides, brochures, etc.) and to support subsequent operational phases of the methodology.

The second phase, the development of the operating plan, is carried out on the basis of the results of the advertising material of the previous phase (analysis of the potentials) and constitutes: i) planning a series of activities related to advertising communication ii) territorial intervention in order to increase the quantity of information available to the visitors iii) public relation (PR) activities and finally iv) involvement of the public (local administrations) and of the private sector (trade associations) in order to involve the local communities interested in the plan. The results of the analysis of tourist potential are then used to develop a SWOT matrix, an instrument which helps identify concrete actions to be carried out during the execution of the territorial marketing plan, with the final aim of increasing tourist influx to the area. In the third phase, the operating plan is implemented in the territory in reference and the results of the actions are collected and examined on the basis of predefined indicators (Key Performance Indicators). These data are then used, in a feedback cycle, in order to improve the plan itself and its subsequent implementation. Appropriate questionnaires are distributed to visitors of the area, to evaluate the degree of satisfaction with their visit and the quality of services. Moreover, independent audits are commissioned about the structures which are responsible for the application of the plan.

Analysis of the tourist potential of the territory

The first step in order to formulate a territorial marketing plan according to the RT methodology is analyzing the tourist potential of the territory. In fact, the territorial marketing plan will be developed on the basis of the results of such an analysis.

The analysis of the tourist potential is organised in the following phases:

- Analysis of the potential tourist offer of the territory
- Analysis of the potential tourist demand
- Analysis of the conditions of access to the territory

The analysis of the tourist offer of the territory is carried out through the compilation of a series of tables related to the advertising and communication of tourist resources, in order to provide a complete and accurate survey of the existing situation.

The satisfaction is mainly focused on the simplicity and authenticity of tradition, the local character and the way of presenting local agricultural products, distributed by the agricultural businesses (Bitsani, 2002; Foutakis, 2004; Papageorgiou, 2008). The analysis of the tourist demand, performed through the technique of segmentation of the market, is carried out through direct market analysis (administration of questionnaires), or through preexisting data in literature, or through the assessment of experts and well-informed people of the sector, and allows for the profiling of the visitor who best suits the tourist features of the area or a region (or regions). The RT method can, in fact, be applied successfully to any geographical scale (spatial) or administrative (town, province, region, etc.).

Finally, the analysis of methods of access to the area completes the picture of the tourist potential a territory possesses. In detail, the phases of the analysis are as follows:

Analysis of the potential tourist offer of the territory

The analysis of the potential tourist offer of the territory is the evaluation of all the resources having tourist value, that is, all the features able to attract a potential tourist/customer. The analysis of the tourist offer of a territory can be divided into two parts: The analysis of the attractiveness, that is, the analysis of all the tourist resources, which can be i) specific "events" (exhibitions, trade fairs, conventions, concerts, sport events, etc.) ii) natural "structures" (beaches, lakes, mountains, woods, streets, paths, etc.) or artificial structures (monuments, museums, sport courts, etc.) present in the area. This phase also includes the advertising of the potential tourist offer of the territory; that is, whether the promotional material guides, internet web pages include: analysis of the attractiveness, that is of the potential interest of visitors (be they potential or habitual) providing in that way, evaluated tourism websites (Bitsani, Kavoura and Kalomenidis, 2008, p. 300).

We also need to take into account whether the internet databases that will be created comply with intellectual property regulations and laws regarding the information provided for the specific geographical area; this is applied with respect to the legislation of each area (Bottis, 2004a; Bottis, 2004b).

Analysis of attractiveness

In order to analyse territorial attractiveness, the tourist resources of an area can be conveniently organised in the following parts:

- Natural resources (nature)
- Artistic, architectural and archaeological resources (history)

- Leisure resources (leisure)
- Resources linked to the presence of typical products (products), either from the food industry or crafts trade fair and convention resources (business)

Accessibility (to the visiting public)

Resource accessibility to the public (yes/no) needs to be stated and the methods of access need to be described. Resources which are not easily accessible or not accessible at all (forbidden access) should be entered.

Resources equipped with structures disposed towards receiving visitors (benches, tables, bus shelters, resting areas, hygienic services along the itinerary, updated maps, clear and well-kept signs) should be entered. As for bars and other catering services, it is suggested to point out the code of the catering resource.

Unequipped resources without any structures disposed towards receiving visitors should be listed.

Opening and closing hours. In case of resources which are open to the public, the opening and closing hours and seasons need to be mentioned.

Price (for the current year)

Accepted methods of payments

In case of resources with a fee, the accepted methods of payment, such as cash, credit card (Visa, Amex, Mastercard, etc.), etc. need to be written.

Presentation of an RT software online form

The resource has to be briefly described (60-70 words), with a possible reference to one photo which has to be available online.

Extended Description: The resource has to be described in detail (optional), with reference to one or more photos which have to be available online.

Online references (link to WebPages, photos, videos, etc.) and references to other nearby resources: Sources and bibliographic references, websites and other URL which are connected to the resource in reference need to be mentioned and listed. If there are other resources near (30-45 minutes) to the resource in reference, the relevant resource codes should also be entered (for example, the resource XYZ010 is close to resources XYZ022 and ABC030).

Analysis of the tourist demand

The main goal of the analysis of tourist demand is to understand which tourists can potentially be interested in visiting the territory in reference, the so-called prospects (Kelley and Rusty-Scheewe, 1975). The knowledge of the features (profile) of the potential clients can allow for i) a better qualification of the tourist resources, which are available in the territory in reference and ii) the improvement of the methods of access to the territory itself.

The prospect must also be informed about the tourist resources available in the territory in reference, and also about the methods of access to the territory. At the same time, the potential tourist can be offered a commercial message, conveyed through the most appropriate channels of communication, on the basis of the indications obtained from the analysis of the tourist demand, in order to induce them to visit the territory. The analysis of the tourist demand of a certain territory, either potential or effective, is carried out either through the distribution of questionnaires to the visitors, using well known survey techniques, or through an analysis of the existing literature about the features of the tourist demand regarding a specific basin in reference, or through information provided by experts in the field.

In order to appropriate the tourist resources available in the territory to the clients, the market segmentation technique can be used, on the basis of a series of geographic, demographic, socio-economic, psychological and behavioural variables (Kiriakidis, 2008). Analysis of the potential clients coming from poles of tourist attraction the visitors who live relatively close to the territory in reference; the visitors who pass by the territory in reference.

Poles of attraction (Tourist resources)

The pole of attraction is a tourist resource, which is available at a distance of at most 60/90 minutes from the territory in reference and which is already a consolidated target of tourist influx at a local, national or international level. The pole of attraction, therefore, represents a basin of opportunity in order to draw the consolidated tourist influx towards a territory, at least during specific seasons or occasions. Typical poles of attraction, for example, are the art cities, archaeological sites, beach/ski/spa resorts, regional or national parks, significant cultural, folklore related or wine-gastronomic events. To sum up, any relevant tourist resort which is traditionally a hub of tourist influx, has to be considered as a pole of tourist attraction.

It is important to observe that the pole of attraction is not necessarily active all year from the point of view of its attractiveness to tourists, but it could be active only on certain occasions, such as specific feasts. For example, one could think of the Christmas market in a city which normally does not enjoy a big tourist influx, or of religious ceremonies (the processions at Easter, of the "battenti" in the Neapolitan area), folklore related events (the challenge of Barletta, the Palio of Siena, etc.), gastronomic events (the festival of rice in Isola della Scala, the gnocchi festival on the Euganei hills, etc.). All of these events attract a great number of visitors only in certain times of the year, just as ski or beach resorts which are largely attended only during particular times of the year.

These features help the segmentation of the market, as they also define the typology of the visitor who attends the poles of attraction: religious tourism, sport tourism, gastronomic tourism, etc. (Kavoura, 2001).

Analysis of the demand related to the poles

The analysis of the tourist demand, which is present in such neighboring poles of attraction, allows for the qualification or re-qualification of the territory's tourist offer, in order to orient that part of the tourist influx attracted to the pole of attraction which could also be interested in the tourist resources offered by the territory in reference.

Such analysis consists of a study of the profile of the client-type, based on parameters such as age, origin, reasons for the trip and the length of stay and level of family income, in order to carry out segmentation and apply to each segment the most suitable tourist offer. For example, knowing that a pole of attraction is mostly attended by young people means that a part of the tourist offer of the specific territory could be made more attractive to that typology of prospect clients.

Analysis of the clients who visit the territory in reference

A step in the analysis of the existing demand is the analysis of the tourists who have already visited and stayed in the territory in reference. For example, in a case where a visitor is represented by "family with children", the offer of the territory should also include some family-oriented features (temporary babysitting facilities, equipped playrooms, events for children (clown shows, etc.).

In the case of young couples with no children, it could be more helpful to focus on other youth related features, such as snack bars, takeaway food, fast food, B&B, agro-tourism, hostels. The average income of the potential visitors also needs to be considered; this factor which can significantly determine the diverse tourist offers of the area. The combination of the available products and services must then be related to the prospect and made effective, on the basis of the main features of such a prospect, which can range from the safeguarding of environment to religion, entertainment, art and culture. That way, a development of an exchange of loyalty with customers may be created, depending on the way services are promoted (Maurouleas, 2006).

Analysis of the access to the territory

Access to the territory by potential visitors and their movements inside the area is a key factor for the success of any kind of territorial marketing plan based on tourism. The quicker and the more convenient it is to reach the area and the simpler it is to retrieve information about the available means of transport, the better is the experience of the tourist and potentially the higher is the number of visitors coming to the area. Moreover, the possibility of convenient tourist movement inside the territory allows the distribution of the revenues from tourism in the different areas of the territory.

The access must then be analysed with regard to i) the methods of transport and the availability of information outside the territory, ii) the methods of transport and the availability of information inside the territory. The analysis of the conditions of access to a territory consists, firstly, of a classification of the methods of transport available to prospective tourists. The analysis must not be limited only to existing infrastructures, such as streets, motorways or railways, but also to linking services, public and private, such as buses, and, in the case of a subsequent action of collective marketing, the receptivity resources under exam are those which adhere to the business network.

Analysis of the tourist accommodation capacity of the territory

The services are also important for the attraction of tourists to a territory (Pecqueur, 2001). By accommodation capacity we mean the ability to provide services related to tourist hosting, accommodation and catering, aimed at keeping the clients in the territory, and possibly offering a service with high qualitative standards, equivalent if not superior to their expectations. In the analysis of the accommodation capacity of a territory, all the receptive resources related to accommodation (hotels, hostels, farm holidays accommodation, B&B, camping sites, tourist resorts, alpine lodges, etc.) and to catering (restaurants, inns, wine bars, etc.) need to be identified. For each receptive resource, identified in the field of the marketing plan, a series of variables need to be assessed, including the receptive capability at disposal of the visitors (number of sleeping facilities, eating facilities, seats, etc.).

Formulating the operational plan

The development and formulation of the operational plan consists of the planning of a series of activities of commercial communication (marketing), public relations, with the possible involvement of the public sector (local administrations) and the private sector (trade associations) of the territory. These activities have to be put in place on the basis of the results, which emerged from the previous phase of analysis of the potential.

After the analysis follows the operating phase of the territorial marketing plan, where the following elements must be organised:

- Activities or tasks to perform;
- Human and financial resources, already available or to be acquired;

- Time required to perform such activities on the basis of the availability and the productivity of the involved resources.

The activities to be performed define the actions of territorial marketing, on the basis of the previous analysis of the potential. Each activity should then be organised in micro-activities to allow for more control of the whole operating plan. Associating a cost to each resource, it is also possible to calculate and control the overall costs of the execution of the proposed operating plan of territorial marketing. Several project management software applications, either locally or online, are available in the market.

Compilations of SWOT analysis and rural tourism

In order to draw up a territorial marketing plan for the area, a simple conceptual pattern represented by the SWOT analysis (Strengths, Weaknesses, Opportunities, Threats) should be used. Such analysis will take into account the results of the analysis of the tourist demand and offer of the area and of the existing characteristics of access to the rural territory (Kotler, Haider and Rein, 1993).

It is a decision-making instrument to be used in the initial phase of the development of the territorial marketing plan and helps focusing on the key aspects of tourist development of a territory. The aim of the SWOT analysis is the identification of the actions to be included in a strategic plan of territorial marketing.

The first thing to do is to identify the single points of the SWOT matrix as has also been employed in other cases (Kotler, Haider and Rein, 1993; Bitsani and Kavoura, in press). Then, steps can be taken for the diffusion of the plan. It can be noted that the strengths and the weaknesses often arise from internal (endogenous) factors of a territory, while opportunities and threats often are related to external (exogenous) factors of a territory.

The tourist product cannot simply be a destination; instead the whole range of the activities performed and the range of the opportunities offered to the tourist need to be considered. The actions to be performed in the territory must be carefully evaluated (analysis of the investments).

From the SWOT matrix to actions and plan diffusion

The identified SWOT points must be used as elements in the building of marketing strategies, answering the following four questions:

- How can we use each strength?
- How can we use each weakness?
- How can we use each opportunity?
- How can we use each threat?

A further output of the SWOT analysis, relevant to the features of the tourist segment of market (demand), is the definition of the commercial message(s) and of the channels of commercial communication (media).

The actions to perform should be illustrated and carried out in accordance with the local communities and administrators, with the broadest dissemination of the aims and the methods of the plan (Bitsani 2004b, pp. 192-193).

Implications from the analysis of the results of the operational plan

The territorial marketing plan provided the promotion and the exploitation of the tourism resources present in the area, for the purpose of obtaining a rapid and considerable increase in the capacity to attract those tourists who are interested in discovering the landscape, historical, cultural and oenologic-gastronomic richness that is typical of Eastern Europe.

The operating plan is implemented in the territory in reference and the results of the performed actions are collected and evaluated on the basis of predefined indicators (Key Performance Indicators), in order to be used inside a feedback cycle to improve the plan itself and its subsequent implementation. Appropriate questionnaires will be distributed to the visitors of the area to evaluate the level of satisfaction of their visit and of the quality of the received services. Moreover, independent audits will be performed, after input from the authority, about the structures which are in charge of the application of the plan. Rural areas in Eastern Europe may well benefit from the implementation of RT methodology for advertising and promoting areas for sustainable tourism development.

The specialised formative activity that the RT started in the Eastern Europe regions, made it possible for the regional administration to achieve the important objective of responding, in a concrete and targeted way, to the needs of the region and the local stakeholders.

In fact, the pilot tourist enterprises involved in the RT project benefited from a specialised formative programme that allowed them to sharpen their professionalism and to gather important instruments with which to improve both their tourist offer and that of the region. The RT methodology also is based on the philosophy to create a social local network among public administrations (at different levels: regional, provincial and municipal), the entrepreneurial world, and specific associations. Such a network presupposes a shared strategic planning concerning rural tourism.

References

Bitsani, E., and D' Arcangeli, M., 2009, The influence of Greek communities in the development of cultural identity and intercultural dialogue in European cities. The Example of Trieste, Italy, in the International Quadrennial Conference Hellenic Dimension: Studies in Language, *Literature and Culture*, 27-28 April, 2009, Riga, Latvia.

Bitsani, E., 2004a, *Culture Management and Regional Development. Culture Policy Planning and Cultural Product Planning*, Athens, Dionicos, pp.177-178 (in Greek).

—. 2004b, *Culture Management and Regional Development. Culture Policy Planning and Cultural Product Planning*, Athens, Dionicos, pp. 192-193 (in Greek).

Bitsani, E., Panagou V., 2003, Culture and Europe: Culture policies in E.U., *Applied Research Review*, IV, pp. 45-70 (in Greek).

Bitsani, E., 2002, *Local Society and Culture: The role of local authorities in cultural development and the European experience*, Phd Thesis. University of Athens, Athens Greece.

Bitsani, E. and Kavoura, A., in press, Alternative Tourism in the Mountainous Area of Nafpaktia, Greece. Implications for an advertising communication programme, *In Management Sciences and Practices Journal.*

Bitsani, E., Kavoura, A. and Kalomenidis, P., 2008, A field study of the exploration of the factors influencing visitors' preferences in the mountainous area of Nafpaktia, Greece. Implications for an advertising communication programme, *in Proceedings of the International*

Conference on Marketing and Management, Athens, Greece, pp. 296-301.

Bottis, M., 2004a, A Different Kind of War: Internet Databases and Legal Protection or how the Intellectual Property Laws of the West Threaten the Developing Countries' Information Commons, *International Journal of Information Ethics*, 2, http://papers.ssm.com/sol3/papers.cfm?abstract_id=952882 (accessed 10.04.2010).

—. 2004b, *Legislation of Information-Issues of Intellectual Property, Patent, Librarianship and Advertising*, Athens, Nomiki Bibliothhiki.

Cano, L. and Mysyk, A., 2004, Cultural tourism, the State and Day of the Dead, *Annals of Tourism Research*, 31, 4, pp. 879-898.

Deffner, A. and Metaxas, T., 2006. The Tourism Focus of Place Marketing in the Mediterranean: Evidence from Nea Ionia, Magnesia, Greece and Pafos, Cyprus, in *proceedings of the International Conference of Trends, Impacts and Policies on Tourism Development*, Crete, Greece.

European Committee, 2000, Committee's Announcementc to the member states on the 14th of April 2000 for the determination of the general directions for European Initiative in regard to rural development (Leader+), *Official Newspaper of the European Commmunities*.

European Commission, 1999, Towards quality rural tourism. Integrated Quality Management (IQM) of rural tourist destinations, Brussels, *Enterprise Directorate–General Tourism Unit*.

Wanda, G., Mair, H. and Reid, D., 2009, *Rural Tourism Development, Localism and Cultural Change, Multilingual Matters*, Channel View Publications.

Foutakis, D., 2004, Area, *Competitiveness and Social Capital: A Critical Review*, in Kaukalas, G. (ed.) Spatial Development Issues, Athens, Kritiki, pp. 39-72 (in Greek).

Guerini, G., Zandonai, F., 2006, Imprese sociali e politiche di sviluppo locale, in Taraschi S., Zandonai F. Impresa Sociale. *Dalla gestione strategica agli strumenti operativi*, Roma, Carocci, pp. 123-125.

Hall, M. C. and McArthur, S. (eds), 1993, *The Marketing of Heritage. In Heritage Management in New Zealand and Australia: Visitor Management, Interpretation and Marketing*, pp. 40-47, Auckland, NZ, Oxford University Press.

Joint Technical Secretariat, (ed), 2007, Interreg IIIB CADSES. Project Book, Advancing Transnational Cooperation, http://www.cadses.net/media/files/Project_Book/983_cadses_pb_225x290_www.pdf (accessed 02.11.2010).

Kavoura, A., 2001, *State policy for the presentation of Greek National*

Heritgae: the case of the Cultural World Heritage Sites, Phd Thesis, University of Stirling, Stirling, UK http://www.is.stir.ac.uk/research/theses/digitisation.php.

—. 2007, Advertising of National Identity and Tourism Bureaucracy, *Current Issues in Tourism*, 10, 3, pp. 399-414.

—. 2005, Approaching 'Cultural Assets' from an Economic Perspective, *Review of Social Sciences*,7, pp. 55-78 (in Greek).

Kelley, E., Rusty-Scheewe, L., 1975, Buyer Behavior in a Stagflation / Shortages Economy, *Journal of Marketing*, 39, pp. 44-50.

Kiriakidis, S., 2008, Application of the theory of planned behaviour to recidivism: the role of personal norm in predicting behavioural intentions of re-offending, *Journal of Applied Social Psychology*, 38, 9, pp. 2210-2221.

Kotler, P., Haider, D. H. and Rein, I., 1993. *Marketing Places: Attracting Investment, Industry, and Tourism to Cities, States, and Nations*, Free Press, New York.

Lytras, P., 2005, Investigation of Development of alternative Forms of Tourism in the islands of Greece through related education, *Management and Economy*, 3, pp. 255-258 (in Greek).

Maurouleas, N., 2006, *Organisation and Management of Sales*, Athens, Stamouli (in Greek).

Papageorgiou, A., 2008, Agricultural Competitiveness and local Products, *Journal of Competitiveness in Agriculture and Food Industry*: US and EU Perspectives, Bononia University Press con la collaborazione di USDA prima edizione : giugno 2008.

Pecqueur, B., 2001, Qualité et dévelopement territorial: l'hypothèse du panier de biens et de services territorialisés, *Economie rurale*, 261, pp. 37-49.

Pritchard, A. and Morgan, N., 2001, Culture, identity and tourism representation: marketing Cymru or Wales?, *Tourism Management*, 22, 1, pp. 167-179.

Smith, M., 2004. Seeing a new side to seasides: culturally regenerating the English seaside town, *International Journal of Tourism Research*, 6, 1, pp. 17-28.

PART FIVE:

SUPREME AUDIT INSTITUTION AND IFRS

REPORTING OF SUPREME AUDIT INSTITUTION (SAI) AS A DETERMINANT OF FISCAL POLICY DEVELOPING FUNCTION

LJILJANA BONIC AND IGOR MLADENOVIC

Abstract

Fiscal policy is a significant determinant of economic development. This paper focuses on research that examines the control of government expenditure caused by the realization of the development targets of fiscal policy. SAI has to control some government departments, users of budget funds, and give recommendations on more rational spending of budget funds. Also, SAI has to investigate, control and evaluate financial reports and financial transactions of governmental sector units, local self-government or administration. Thus, SAI must report on financial audit. Performance audit must include the economy, efficiency, effectiveness and effects of the government's decisions, intentions and projects. The special role of SAI is to report on compliance with laws and government regulations. According to this SAI report, it is very important to establish fiscal stability, combat inflation, stimulate investment and spending on public finances and promote economic development through growth of production and employment.

Introduction

During the last two decades, empirical examinations showed that fiscal policy has become a key element of economic growth. Triggering economic growth is the basis for the reduction of poverty and realization of social targets. Good fiscal policy is supposed to maintain low budget deficit and public debt, which contribute to macroeconomic stability and absence of crisis in national framework with many benefits (higher rate of investment, economic growth and achievement in education). Today fiscal policy is a significant determinant of economic development. Models of economic growth, traditional or modern (endogenous), provide paths for adequate tax rate that enables a balanced rate of economic development.

However, economic literature has not extensively examined the effect of controling government expenditure that has been caused by the realization of the development targets of fiscal policy. SAI is primarily concerned with the control of government expenditure, which is in jurisdiction of government agencies and institutions. The duty of SAI is to provide suggestions and recommendations for improving financial control in some government departments, and allow for the increase of efficiency in public finance. If it would be possible for SAI to accomplish this in accordance with SAI standards, SAI should report on auditing of budget and financial statements of government bodies (financial audit), economy, efficiency, effectiveness and effects of the government's decisions and intentions (performance audit) and compliance with laws and regulations.

The subject of this paper is to explain the scopes and limitations of SAI, examine the reasons for the need of SAI and show how the results of SAI can contribute to the effective management of the developing function of fiscal policy.

Development role of fiscal policy

Governments around the world must create and implement policies for government revenue and spending. According to development literature, these policies can have major impacts on economic growth, poverty, and income distribution and, thus, they tend to be at the centre of economic and daily discussions. Additionally, since 1990, the countries of West Balkans have gone through two transitions: a political transition, from totalitarianism to democracy, and an economic transition from socialism toward market economy. These transitions required an essential change in the role of the government, from controlling all economic assets to providing public goods and promoting a free competitive economy characterized by private ownership. This change in the role of the government required a major downsizing of state spending and a complete overhaul of fiscal policy. These circumstances emphasize the importance of the development role of fiscal policy.

Traditional development theories suggest ways through which fiscal policy affects economic development. Those are infrastructure, education and health. On the other hand, there are empirical studies with results that are congruent with and discrepant from development theories. Each of these ways is the object of our analysis.

Infrastructure. Throughout the last decade, there is a lot of discussion in literature about the relationship between infrastructure development and economic outcomes (Estache, 2006). However, on the whole, these researches -especially studies focusing on countries in transition- confirm that infrastructure contributes positively to economic output, growth, or productivity (or all three). The most robust studies among them (Calderon and Serven, 2004) use a large global panel data set covering 40 years that takes in account both quantitative and qualitative measures and controls for potential endogeneity of infrastructure. They argue that growth is positively affected by the level of infrastructure assets, and that higher infrastructure quality also reduces income inequality distribution. The positive effects of infrastructure seem to be stronger in low or lower-middle income countries than in more highly developed economies (Canning and Bennathan, 2000). In short, based on the available research evidence, there is every reason to believe that infrastructure has positive effects on growth in many countries. On the other side, it is reasonable that several methodological errors exist in the analyses of different researches. Impacts of infrastructure to economic growth and development depend on the efficiency with which state investments are used, and the quality and reliability of the services that are actually delivered by infrastructure.

According to what is mentioned above, better management of public investment in infrastructure is important. We argue that design and management of state investment programs in infrastructure can be an important factor that determines the impact of public investment on economy performance.

Education. Providing educational opportunities to the people is a crucial goal for all governments and it is essential for economic prosperity. The education process is the one category of government spending that is approved by all empirical studies to be positively associated with economic growth rates. "However, more spending is not the answer by itself- the efficiency of spending is as important as the amount of spending. While research is clear that a more educated population leads to rapid economic growth, higher levels of public spending are not always associated with better educational outcomes. The efficiency and effectiveness of education spending varies widely among countries. Some of the Europe and Central Asia (ECA) region and non-ECA comparator countries covered in different studies have better educational outcomes (whether enrollment rates, average years of schooling, or learning scores) than would be expected given their levels of per capita income or public spending on education, while others have worse outcomes than would be expected" (Gray, Lane and Varoudakis, 2007, p.148).

A link between education outcomes and economic growth (how to achieve better education outcomes and the role of public education expenditures) becomes important. This stems from the fact that public education expenditures constitute a significant outlay on the part of governments, averaging 5.5 percent of GDP and 13.3 percent of total public spending in OECD countries in 2003 (OECD, 2006). Additionally, governments of developing and transition countries typically spend resources equivalent to between 15 and 40 percent of GDP. Hence, small changes in the efficiency of public spending could have a significant impact on GDP and the attainment of the government objectives. Based on these results, we argue that enhancing the efficiency of spending in education is very important for all countries.

Health. Modern literature on economic development emphasizes the fact that human capital influences the pace and character of economic growth and development. However, human capital is usually broadly defined (some of which perceive human capital in terms of worker skill and knowledge, but most in terms of level of education). According to this, the relationship between health and economic growth has recently received both theoretical and empirical attention.

As a proof for this statement, Bloom, Canning and Sevilla's (2001) propose a model in which economic growth is driven by knowledge accumulation and labor services by healthy people. They showed that the proportion of healthy people in the population determines the extent to which potential labor services embodied in the population can be used effectively, and healthy hours spent for knowledge accumulation lead to economic growth. Also, based on the Schumpeterian growth theory, other research offers different channels through which an improvement in the health of a country's population will affect its long-run growth (Howitt, 2005). Research shows that health increases productive efficiency, life expectancy, learning capacity, creativity, and coping skills, which all contribute to productivity improvement. More specifically, this study underscores the beneficial effects of childhood health and maternal health on various dimensions of human capital, such as learning capacity, creativity, and coping skills. Of course, there is also likely to be some degree of reverse causation, because economic growth provides more resources to be spent on health care and other factors that affect the health status of a population.

Because the amount of money spent by a government on health is at best as important as how that money is spent, the “transmission mechanisms” from funding to health service delivery are essential for determining the effectiveness of health services provision. The organization of service delivery, monitoring, and accountability mechanisms are crucial in determining the quality of health care and accessibility of health services.

From all the above a question arises in respect to the development role of control of government spending. We argue that Reporting Supreme Audit Institution plays an important role in this process.

Scope of activities and conceptual framework of SAI

Scope of SAI activities

The Supreme Audit Institution, as one of the most important independent institutions, deals primarily with monitoring the budget funds expenditure, inspecting the level of compliance of the operations of the governmental 'bodies and institutions' with legal provisions and testing the reliability of financial statements of business entities in the public sector. A supreme state institution is obliged to submit respective information to the Parliament. However, it has to operate independently of the Parliament, as its founder, and of the Government, as the executive authority.

The role of the supreme state audit and its scope of activities differ from country to country. In France, it is defined as assistance to the Parliament and Government in supervising the state budget execution, while in Greece its role is to implement preventive control of state expenditures. Some state audit institutions have a very wide scope of activities, like in the Netherlands, where the state audit is responsible for auditing all the state revenues and expenditures, or in Spain, in which the Court of Audit carries out ex-ante and ex-post financial audits of business activities in the public sector. The activity scope of most of them also includes the audits of performance. Thus, for example, beside the financial audit, German State Audit encompasses inspection of effectiveness and correctness of financial management. The United Kingdom 1983 Law and the 1993 Law in Ireland contain specific provisions related to the performance audit of activities of governmental agencies and institutions. The State Audit in Norway includes financial audit, performance audit and the audit of environmental protection.

In general, the activity scope of a supreme state audit consists of: financial audit, performance audit and environmental protection audit. The **financial audit** includes investigation, control and evaluation of financial statements and financial transactions of governmental sector units, local self-government and administration units, and legal entities that are wholly or majority state-owned or local self-government or administrations. The primary task of a state audit institution is to audit the so-called public expenditures and collective consumption that play a significant part in the GDP, that is, to audit the activities of the Government and its institutions, as well as the use of budget funds. Furthermore, the financial audit also includes reviewing the compliance with contracts, subventions and regulations and auditing the legality of operations of budget users, as well as determining frauds in the performance of activities of state bodies and institutions. The final product of a supreme state audit is to present a report on accomplished financial audit and issuance of opinions and recommendations related to more rational expenditure of budget funds.

The **performance audit** deals with examining whether the public sector fulfills the goals set in an efficient, effective and economical manner. It encompasses the so-called 3E audit (economy, efficiency and effectiveness) of the execution of activities by state bodies and institutions on one hand, and a program audit, i.e., the audit of success in implementing the goals of a specific program, on the other hand. The 3E audit determines whether the budget users spend financial means economically, efficiently and effectively, as well as identifies possible causes of their inadequate usage. The program audit is used to determine the extent to which desired results and set goals of certain governmental programs are accomplished, define factors that possibly hinder the program realization and identify new ways for more successful program implementation. In the framework of performance audit, the state auditor also submits a report with summarizing audit results.

The **environmental protection audit** was founded in 1992, at the International Congress of INTOSAI in Washington. Based on the model of INTOSAI, a similar body was also founded in Europe at the IV Congress of EUROSAI in 1999. Its range of activities is rather limited, due to specific characteristics of environmental protection. It is necessary to develop specific skills and procedures related to this type of audit, including the education of auditors for environmental protection, and define the role and status of experts in this field.

The subject of state audits, in the broadest sense, is the investigation and evaluation of compliance of audited entities, operations and financial statements with preset criteria. There are many business entities to be audited. Various bodies are in charge of performing public functions and rendering services within every state; alongside governmental bodies, regional agencies and local authorities, there are also the enterprises fully or partially owned by the state, as well as other types of public bodies. There are also bodies that receive grants of public funds and are funded by statutory levies or have their debts underwritten by the state. Table 1 presents the review of entities audited by SAIs in EU member countries.

The activity scope of European Union SAIs covers hundreds, and in some cases even thousands, of bodies. In the United Kingdom, the state audit examines and reports on nearly 520 different governmental bodies. In Portugal, the Tribunal's remit covers 11,000 bodies, although certain entities are exempt from audit, so some 3,000 are examined in practice (State Audit in European Union, 2005, p. 217). In Spain the Audit Tribunal relies on the work of local authority internal auditors in the process of auditing 8,000 local authorities.

By definition, all SAIs examine the financial statements of central government bodies. In most countries this includes ministries and government departments. In Sweden, where agencies carry out most government executive functions, the SAI audits these agencies but not the ministries themselves. Since all ministries are small and deal mainly with policy making, they have little or no involvement in administrative matters.

In some countries the SAI also carries out the audit of regional and local government. In Italy, there are complex arrangements, according to which regional chambers of the Audit Court perform auditing of regional and local authorities and report the results to the Parliament. In other countries, such as the United Kingdom, France, Denmark and Germany, there are separate audit organizations that cover local and regional government. In the United Kingdom, local government is audited by the auditors appointed by the Audit Commission, a body established by statute for that purpose. In Denmark, most of the local government is audited by the Local Government Auditing Department, while in France regional accounting chambers were established in 1980, although appeals against their decisions can be made to the Audit Court.

Table 1. Entities subject to state audit in EU member countries

	Central governm-ent	Regional administr-ation	Lokal administr-ation	State-owned enterprise	Public bodies	Commune	Other subjects
Austria	✓	✓	✓	✓	✓	✓	✓
Belgium	✓	✓	✓	✓	✓	-	-
Cipar	✓	-	✓	✓	✓	✓	✓
R. Czech	✓	-	-	✓	✓	-	✓
Denmark	✓	-	-	✓	✓	-	✓
Estonia	✓	✓	✓	✓	✓	✓	✓
Finland	✓	-	-	✓	✓	-	✓
France	✓	-	-	✓	✓	-	✓
Greece	✓	-	✓	✓	✓	✓	✓
Ireland	✓	-	-	-	✓	-	✓
Italy	✓	✓	✓	✓	✓	✓	✓
Latvia	✓	-	✓	✓	✓	✓	✓
Litvanija	✓	-	✓	✓	✓	✓	✓
Luksemg	✓	-	-	✓	✓	-	✓
Hungary	✓	-	✓	✓	✓	✓	✓
Malta	✓	-	✓	✓	✓	-	✓
Germany	✓	-	-	✓	✓	-	✓
Poland	✓	✓	✓	✓	✓	✓	✓
Portugal	✓	✓	✓	✓	✓	✓	✓
Slovakia	✓	✓	✓	✓	✓	✓	✓
Slovenia	✓	-	✓	✓	✓	✓	✓
Spain	✓	✓	✓	✓	✓	✓	✓
Sweden	✓	-	-	✓	✓	-	✓
UK	✓	-	-	-	✓	-	-
ERS	✓	✓	✓	✓	✓	✓	✓
Netherland	✓	-	-	✓	✓	-	✓

Source: State Audit in European Union, 2005, p. 9.

Conceptual framework for supreme state audit

A supreme state institution has to respect auditing standards in organizing, planning, executing and reporting on its activities. The most significant world-wide accepted state audit standards are INTOSAI and GAGAS.

INTOSAI (International Organization of Supreme Audit Institutions) was formed in 1984 by the Auditing Standards Committee. The Committee proposed a Draft of Government Auditing Standards, and the standards were adopted in 1992 at the Congress in Washington and amended in 1995 at the Cairo Congress. As emphasized in the introduction, the adopted standards stand as a synonym for "guidelines" that should protect the interests of every supreme state audit institution. These standards provide a framework for establishing procedures that are conducted during the process of auditing. Together with the state audit postulates and premises, as well as with the Code of Ethics, the Auditing Standards make a conceptual framework for supreme state audit, determined by the INTOSAI.

Basic **postulates** of state audit are:

1. The SAI should comply with the INTOSAI auditing standards in all matters that are deemed material;
2. The SAI should apply its own judgment to the diverse situations that arise in the course of Government auditing;
3. With increased public consciousness, the demand for public accountability of persons or entities managing public resources has become increasingly evident so that there is a need for the accountability process to be in place and operating effectively;
4. Development of adequate information system within the Government will facilitate the accountability process. Management is responsible for the correctness and sufficiency of the form and content of the financial reports;
5. Consistent application of acceptable accounting standards should result in the fair presentation of the financial position and the results of operations;
6. The existence of an adequate system of internal control minimizes the risk of errors and irregularities;
7. All audit activities should be within the SAI's audit mandate;
8. SAIs should work towards improving techniques for auditing the validity of performance measures;
9. SAIs should avoid conflict of interest between the auditor and the entity under audit.

In developing government auditing standards, the following **premises** were considered:

- The term "audit" includes both financial and performance audits;
- Public officials are responsible for applying the resources efficiently, economically, and effectively to achieve the purposes for which the resources were furnished;
- Public officials should provide appropriate reports to the bodies to whom they are accountable for, for their expenditures;
- Public officials are responsible for establishing and maintaining effective internal control systems to ensure that appropriate goals and objectives are met, laws and regulations are followed and reliable data are obtained;
- Public officials are responsible for complying with applicable laws and regulations;
- Financial auditing and compliance with laws and regulations should provide independent reports on whether an entity's financial information fairly presented the results of its financial affairs;
- Performance auditing provides an independent assessment of the level of efficiency and effectiveness in performing duties by public officials;
- SAIs should make audit reports available to the public, unless legal restrictions or ethical considerations prevent it;
- When government bodies of different levels participate in a program (performance audit), the audit should be carried out in a manner that every level can clearly see its part in the collective responsibility.

INTOSAI Government Auditing Standards are categorized into three groups: general standards, field work standards and reporting standards.

GAGAS (Generally Accepted Government Auditing Standards) are the American national standards. These standards were published by the United States General Accounting Office of the AICPA in 1998 and they are often referred to in literature as the "Yellow Book". They are classified into five groups: general standards, field work standards for financial audits, reporting standards for financial audits, field work standards for performance audits and reporting standards for performance audits.

Supreme state audit institutions carry out international cooperation through INTOSAI. In keeping with its motto, "Mutual Experience Benefits All", INTOSAI issued a great number of documents, on which supreme state audit institutions base their work worldwide, as well as documents that are aimed for the improvement of public administration activities. In its strategic plan for the period of 2005-2010, INTOSAI set the goal of establishing a comprehensive framework of professional standards. For that very reason, the Professional Standards Committee decided to combine all the documents, existing and new standards and new guidelines into one document, the so-called common framework, under the new title "International Standards of Supreme Auditing Institution - ISSAI".

This common framework was formally approved in November 2007, at the 19th INTOSAI Congress held in Mexico City. The adoption of this framework had no repercussions on the contents of already existing documents (Lima Declaration, INTOSAI Standards, Code of Ethics and other documents). A systematic classification of all the existing documents was made in this framework, with the aim of general improvement of standards and guidelines, as well as their implementation in the member-countries. ISSAI was accepted as the joint name for numerous documents. INTOSAI GOV (INTOSAI Guidance for Good Governance) includes the documents containing guidelines and instructions for the public administration that issued the INTOSAI (e. g. guidelines for internal controls, accounting guidelines).

INTOSAI documents are structured in four levels:

- Level 1: Founding principles laid down in the Lima Declaration
- Level 2: Prerequisites for the functioning of supreme audit institutions based on the founding principles*. INTOSAI Code of Ethics also belongs to this level.
- Level 3: The documents of this level are based on the previous level documents, and they include documents related to fundamental state auditing principles. INTOSAI standards fall into this level.
- Level 4: INTOSAI Auditing Guidelines for implementation include details on various practical state audit problems.

Approaches to the state audit improvement

There is a dilemma related to the approach to independent state audit improvement in Europe: whether or not to focus the attention on a reform of auditing regulations, as it was done in the USA by passing the first

---

* The Declaration of Independence, so-called Mexican Declaration, adopted in the 19th INTOSAI Congress in Mexico, was registered as ISSAI 10. The development is underway of the principles of transparency and accountability, which should be adopted at the 20th INTOSAI Congress to be held in 2010 in South Africa.

federal law on corporate and auditing accountability and responsibility, the US Sarbanes-Oxley Act of 2002. The reforms of audit regulations performed in the EU and the USA point out the need for a unified and precise definition of the qualifications to be possessed by independent state auditors, as well as the obligatory activities aimed at independent audit quality assurance. This was the result of a growing network of audit organizations, but special attention is devoted to strengthening the independence of markets on both sides of the Atlantic.

Nevertheless, certain differences may be observed in the process of international audit regulations improvement. In the USA, the reform of audit regulations is mainly based on strengthening the legislative manner of conducting regulations, while the concept of audit policies and principles still exists in the EU. Another difference reflects in simultaneous retention of both national and international audit standards. These differences necessarily impose a need for greater cooperation among the public regulatory and legislative audit bodies. One of the most common measures aimed at strengthening the auditing regulations is the reestablishment of public confidence in the independent audit of financial statements in the capital market. In order to facilitate efficient capital allocation, a necessary condition is to provide confidence in the audit of the capital market. A substantial factor of independent audit quality weakening is also the auditor's compensation, the amount of which is correlated with the quality of audit.

Some professional organizations around the world, particularly in the United Kingdom, Australia and Canada, are the promoters of further improvement of private self-regulation by improving audit standards and intensifying personal responsibility of independent auditors, as well as by implementing the changes in the Auditors' Code of Professional Ethics. Constant increase of accounting and auditing scandals world-wide has proved that modest fines and disciplinary measures are not enough. Moreover, the enactment of new EU regulations represents a minimum level of audit regulations harmonization among the EU members.

The government audit contribution to the growing function of fiscal policy

The role of SAI in realizing the growing function of fiscal policy is very important. In that sense, the **duties of the SAI** are:

- auditing the central government accounts and all accounts submitted by central government agencies and other authorities, which are obliged to submit accounts to the central government, including government corporations, public administrative bodies that have been granted special powers, government funds and other bodies or undertakings where this is stipulated in separate legislation (financial auditing),
- carrying out systematic analysis of the economy, efficiency and effectiveness of the government administration (performance auditing),
- monitoring the management of the state's proprietary interests in companies etc. (corporate control),
- contributing through auditing to the prevention and detection of irregularities and errors,
- advising the government administration in order to prevent future errors and omissions,
- initiate special investigationst.

The SAI has to introduce a Parliament whereby a standard overall risk assessment is carried out annually for each ministry and its subordinate agencies. The risk assessments are reviewed at meetings with the ministries.

The SAI's **financial auditing** is intended to ensure that the accounts provide a correct picture of the financial activities, including:

a) confirming that the accounts do not contain material errors and omissions, and
b) checking whether the transactions, on which the accounts are based, are in accordance with the decisions and intentions of the Parliament and with applicable regulations, and whether the transactions can be deemed to be acceptable on the basis of norms and standards for government financial management.

Through systematic analysis of **economy, efficiency, effectiveness and effects** of the government's decisions and intentions, the SAI shall furnish the Parliament with relevant information about the implementation and effectiveness of government measures etc., including whether:

a) the government administration uses resources to perform tasks in accordance with the decisions and intentions of the Parliament;

b) the government administration's use of resources and policy instruments is effective in relation to the goals that the Parliament has set in this area;
c) regulations issued by the Parliament are complied with;
d) the government administration's management tools, policy instruments and regulations are effective and expedient in relation to following up the decisions and intentions of the Parliament;
e) the basis on which the Parliament based its decisions (i.e. the documents provided by the Government) was adequate, and
f) the government administration implements adopted environmental policies in a manner that ensures compliance with the principle of sustainable development and good management of natural resources.

Among other things, **corporate control activities** include the SAI's assessment of whether the state's interests in companies etc. have been managed in accordance with the decisions and intentions of the Parliament. The control activities are intended to shed light on matters of major importance to society and matters of principle on the basis of the SAI's assessment of risk and materiality. The control activities are performed on the basis of the following control perspectives:

- compliance with the decisions and intentions of the Parliament
- fulfilment of social responsibilities and sector policy goals
- efficient and effective operations that are financially sound
- correct information being submitted to the Parliament and the SAI.

SAI has to control government expenditure caused by the realization of development targets of fiscal policy. SAI is primarily concerned with the control of government expenditure. Also, the duty of SAI is that of delivering suggestions and recommendations for improving financial control in some government departments and allowing the boosting of efficiency in public finance. SAI must report on it in Government Audit Report. SAI's performance audit reports focus on the economy, efficiency and effectiveness of the government administration, in order to map and assess the reason(s) why the regulations are not complied with in so many cases.

Contribution of SAI to the realization of fiscal policy developing function consists of the following:

- SAI carries out the control of public expenditure and regularity of operations of the users of budget funds and gives recommendations on more rational spending of budget funds, aimed at long-term economic growth and development improvement;
- SAI performs investigation, control and evaluation of financial reports and financial transactions of governmental sector units, local self-government and administration units, and legal entities that are wholly or majority state-owned or local self-government or administration. This information may affect the regional development direction and reduction of regional disparities;
- Performance auditing enables monitoring and evaluation of governmental programs accomplishment, insight into factors that possibly hinder the program realization and identification of new ways for more successful program implementation. Its goal is to improve the effects to be achieved by budgetary investment. Public expenditure absorbs a great part of GDP and, therefore, exerts great influence on the total economy efficiency;
- Investigation within the performance auditing refers to the government activities in the fields of importance for economic growth achievement, efficient functioning of economy and welfare of the population. Performance auditing offers concrete recommendations for the implementation of conclusion adopted in relation to specific projects carried out by the government, ministries, local self-governments and even by non-profit organizations;
- The analysis of reports on performance audit conducted in certain ministries shall provide answers to the following questions:
  - to which extent the objectives of a development finance program are realized,
  - whether the procedures of funds provision are correct,
  - which results are achieved by applying special programs of employment,
  - whether satisfactory results have been achieved in the development of electronic data exchange and in the development of services rendered by the public sector,
  - what is the extent of efficiency achieved through investing into innovations and industrial development,
  - how to provide economic development through the growth of production and employment,
  - how to realize fiscal stabilization,
  - how to stimulate investment and economical spending of public funds,

- what is the level of specialist health services' facilities for adults with mental health problems,
- investigation of business development in the agricultural sector,
- to which extent the efficiency of education spending is accomplished,
- which mechanisms are critical in determining quality of care and accessibility of health services.

Finally, it should be emphasized that the outburst of another big crisis also proved the indispensability of SAI's role in overcoming this problem at the level of national economies. SAI facilitates the monitoring of the realization of a package of measures taken to avoid the crisis at the national level and enables the creation of suggestions for their efficient improvement in future.

Conclusion

Reporting of SAI is an important determinant of the development function of fiscal policy. The duties of the SAI are:

- auditing the central government accounts and all accounts submitted by central government agencies and other authorities that are obliged to submit accounts to the central government, including government corporations, public administrative bodies that have been granted special powers, government funds and other bodies or undertakings where this is stipulated in separate legislation (financial auditing),
- carrying out systematic analysis of the economy, efficiency and effectiveness of the government administration (performance auditing),
- monitoring the management of the state's proprietary interests in companies etc. (corporate control),
- contributing through auditing to the prevention and detection of irregularities and errors,
- advising the government administration in order to prevent future errors and omissions,
- initiate special investigationst.

Contribution of SAI to the realization of the development function of fiscal policy consists of the following:

- SAI carries out the control of public expenditure and regularity of operations of the users of budget funds and gives recommendations on more rational spending of budget funds, aimed at long-term economic growth and development improvement;
- SAI performs investigation, control and evaluation of financial reports and financial transactions of governmental sector units, local self-government and administration units, and legal entities that are wholly or majority state-owned or local self-government or administration. This information may affect the regional development direction and reduction of regional disparities;
- Performance auditing enables monitoring and evaluation of governmental programs accomplishment, insight into factors that possibly hinder the program realization and identification of new ways for more successful program implementation. Its goal is to improve the effects to be achieved by budgetary investment. Public expenditure absorbs a great part of GDP and, therefore, exerts great influence on the total economy efficiency;
- Investigation within the performance auditing refers to the government activities targeting for economic growth achievement, efficient functioning of economy and welfare of the population. Performance auditing offers concrete recommendations for the implementation of adopted conclusions related to specific projects carried out by the government, ministries, local self-governments and even by non-profit organizations;
- The analysis of reports on performance audit can make possible certain ministries to realize about economy, efficiency, effectiveness and effects of the government's decisions, intentions and projects (programs of employment, investments into innovations and industrial development, development in the agricultural sector, health services, development infrastructure, a package of measures taken to avoid the crisis, etc.).

References

Bloom, D., Canning, D. and Sevilla, J., 2001, *The Effects of Health on Economic Growth: Theory and Evidence*, NBER Working Paper No. 8587, Cambridge, MA, National Bureau of Economic Research.

Calderon, C. and Serven, L. 2004, *The Effects of Infrastructure Development on Growth and Income Distribution*, Working Paper No. 270, Santiago, Central Bank of Chile.

Canning, D. and Bennathan, E., 2000, *The Social Rate of Return on Infrastructure Investment*, Policy Research Working Paper No. 2390, Washington, DC, World Bank.

Estache, A., 2006, *Infrastructure: A Survey of Recent and Upcoming Issues*, PREM and INF Vice Presidencies, Washington, DC, World Bank.

Gray, C., Lane, T. and Varoudakis, A., 2007, *Fiscal Policy and Economic Growth*- Lessons for Eastern Europe and Central Asia, Washington DC, World Bank.

Howitt, P., 2005, *Health, Human Capital and Economic Growth: A Schumpeterian Perspective*, in Health and Economic Growth: Findings and Policy Implications, ed. Lopez-Casasnovas, G., Rivera, B. and Currais, L., pp. 19–40, Cambridge, MA, MIT Press.

OECD, 2006, *Education at a Glance*: OECD Indicators 2006, Paris, OECD.

Official Gazette of the Republic of Serbia, No. 101/2005 and 54/2007, Belgrade, Official Gazette.

State Audit in European Union, 2005, London, National Audit Office.

TRANSPARENCY IN FAIR VALUE ACCOUNTING UNDER IFRS: AN EXAMINATION OF GREEK LISTED COMPANIES' LEVEL OF COMPLIANCE WITH IFRS GOODWILL DISCLOSURE REQUIREMENTS

DIOGENIS E. BABOUKARDOS

Abstract

The mandatory adoption of IFRS in 2005 by publicly held companies in the European Union is viewed as another step toward establishing a high quality and transparent business language for European companies. Currently many voices warn that it is meaningless to talk about high quality and transparent financial reporting unless the effective and consistent implementation of IFRS is ensured; especially in issues that involve fair value accounting. Despite the importance of disclosures in issues where fair value accounting is involved, there is little evidence about companies' level of compliance with IFRS disclosure requirements in a mandatory environment. This study focuses on IFRS goodwill disclosures due to the fact that goodwill accounting under IFRS is heavily influenced by fair value accounting. Specifically it examines compliance with IFRS 3 and IAS 36 for companies listed on the Athens Stock Exchange during the first four years of mandatory use of IFRS with the use of a content analysis method. Findings show some potentially serious deficiencies in the implementation of IFRS disclosures for goodwill and mainly with those that are closely related to fair value accounting. Moreover, a particularly alarming finding of this study is that even after four years of IFRS introduction, Greek companies have not increased the volume of information that IAS 36 mandates. The findings of this study could be valuable for standard setters as well as for local enforcement mechanisms.

Introduction - Research Motives

The mandatory adoption of IFRS in 2005 by all listed companies in the European Union (EU) is intended to be a step toward establishing a common, high quality business language for European companies. Among the main objectives of IFRS is to ensure a high degree of transparency (EC Regulation 1606/2002, Article 1; IASCF Constitution, Article 2) by mandating the publication of extensive disclosures as an integral part of companies' general purpose financial reports. IFRS mandate a minimum level of acceptable disclosures that exceeds those of many European domestic accounting standards (Jermakowicz and Tomaszewski, 2006; Ernst & Young, 2006) and consequently it potentially narrows the information gap between informed and uninformed investors (Healy and Palepu, 2001).

Disclosures play a crucial role on issues in which fair value accounting is involved because fair value accounting is based, to a large extent, on management assumptions that may lack objectivity (Hoogendoom, 2006; Ball, 2006; Jermakowicz and Tomaszewski, 2006; Penman, 2007). Consequently, it is more likely that information asymmetry problems occur (Daske et al., 2008). Specifically, fair value accounting is based on a binding sale agreement between two independent parties or alternatively on current or recent prices in an active market. In many cases, though, such information is not available. In such cases fair values are determined with so called "mark to model" calculations using sometimes arbitrary management estimates (Ball, 2006), which may lead to intended or inadvertent failures of asset valuations and consequently to low quality information.

Goodwill is a characteristic example of an accounting item heavily influenced by fair value accounting under IFRS. Many studies argue that the wide use of fair values in the accounting treatment of goodwill creates many opportunities for management manipulation. Sevin and Schroeder (2005) argue that goodwill's impairment test allows companies to apply "big bath" techniques for managing their earnings. Wines et al. (2007) stress out that the new accounting treatment of goodwill "*is fraught with subjectivity and ambiguity for financial report preparers and auditors, and potentially has serious impacts on financial reports*" (Wines et al., 2007, p. 863) and also that "*it provides many avenues for preparers to be creative*" (Wines et al., 2007, p. 865). Ramanna (2008) argues that goodwill impairment test is based on unverifiable fair values (i.e. not actively traded market prices) and, hence, can increase opportunistic disclosures. Mandating extensive disclosures about the valuation models used and about the assumptions made enables users to assess the objectivity and accuracy of adopted evaluations and, hence, maintains the information value of financial reports (IASB Conceptual Framework, paragraph 21).

It is meaningless, however, to talk about high quality financial reporting and transparency unless the effective and consistent implementation of IFRS is ensured (Whittington, 2005; Daske et al., 2008). Positive economic consequences of IFRS adoption have been found only in countries with strict enforcement regimes (Daske et al., 2008), indicating that the level of compliance with accounting standards is as important as the standards themselves (Hodgdon et al., 2009). Today, IFRS implementation is considered as the "*Achilles Heel of IFRS*" (Ball, 2006) because partial compliance with IFRS may lead to uncertainty about the real economic condition of an entity. Therefore, a question that arises is whether companies have adapted to IFRS and maintain a high level of compliance with IFRS disclosure requirements.

Taking into consideration the importance of disclosures in issues where fair value accounting is involved, the present study examines the extent of compliance with IFRS disclosure requirements for goodwill of listed companies on the Athens Stock Exchange (ASE) during the first four years (2005-2008) of mandatory IFRS implementation. Specifically, using a comprehensive index, this study examines the extent of compliance with IFRS 3 and IAS 36 disclosure requirements for goodwill of almost all companies (91% of the population) listed on the ASE that have recognized goodwill during these four years.

Most prior studies in a mandatory environment (Paananen, 2008; Fekete, 2008; Tsalavoutas, 2010; Ballas and Tzovas, 2010) were not focused on the content of financial reports and hence they did not reveal potential problematic issues of IFRS implementation by locating which disclosures companies do not report. Instead, they calculated a compliance ratio, which was used as independent variable for the examination of its value relevance (Tsalavoutas, 2010) and other accounting figures' value relevance (Paananen, 2008), as well as a dependent variable for the examination of the determinants that drive the level of compliance (Fekete, 2008; Ballas and Tzovas, 2010). The calculation of an index score is a measure of the extent of compliance but it does not necessarily provide any evidence for the quality of disclosures (Marston and Shrives,

1991). This study adds to the research literature about compliance with IFRS disclosure requirements, attempting to give some more insights on the issue of quality. It attempts an in-depth examination of goodwill disclosures by scrutinizing the extent of compliance with all disclosure items for goodwill during the first four years of mandatory adoption of IFRS. Moreover, this study is the first that examines the level of compliance for four consecutive years, taking advantage of the fact that during the period under examination (2005-2008) no amendments to the two standards occurred and no company adopted optionally the amendments of IFRS 3 and IAS 36 before their mandatory adoption on January 1st, 2009. Consequently, annual results are perfectly comparable and allow an assessment of the progress of compliance levels over time.

The examination of goodwill disclosures under IFRS in a typical European code law country like Greece that it is an interesting setting because, similar to other European countries (see for example, Ernst and Young, 2005), under Greek GAAP fair value accounting is "limited and underdeveloped" (Ntzanatos, 2008a, p. 499) and explanatory notes are also limited (Apostolou and Nanopoulos, 2008). In addition, prior studies (Jermakowicz and Tomaszewski, 2006; Hoogendoorn, 2006) have concluded that IFRS 3 and IAS 36 are among the most difficult standards to implement; hence, their examination provides a reliable indicator of the overall level of compliance with IFRS disclosure requirements (Sevin et al., 2007).

The findings of this study are expected to shed light upon problematic issues of IFRS implementation and to locate which specific disclosures are not reported by companies. In addition, since the extent to which companies comply with legal and regulatory requirements depends on the strictness or laxity of the government, professional and other regulatory bodies (Marston and Shrives, 1991), the findings are expected to detect (although indirectly), whether there is a need for enhancing the existing enforcement mechanisms which have been characterized as "*toothless watchdogs*" (Ball, 2006). Such findings could be valuable for standard setters as well as for local enforcement mechanisms.

The remainder of this study is organized as follows: The second section reviews prior studies of the level of compliance with IFRS disclosure requirements. The third section gives a brief review of disclosure requirements relating to goodwill under IFRS. The fourth section presents the methodology and the company selection procedure.

The fifth section presents the empirical results. The sixth discusses the conclusions and limitations of the study and makes suggestions for further research.

Prior Studies

The studies for the level of compliance with IFRS disclosure requirements can be classified in two broad categories: Those conducted in a voluntary environment (Street et al., 1999; Street and Bryant, 2000; Street and Gray, 2002; Glaum and Street, 2003; Hodgdon et al., 2009) and those conducted in a mandatory one. Regarding the first group of studies, their results are not comparable with that of the present study due to the dramatic changes IFRS have undergone during the last few years. In addition, these studies were conducted in voluntary adoption environments and may present sample selection bias issues because their samples necessarily consisted only of companies that chose to adopt IFRS voluntarily and hence may have innate characteristics that affected their adoption decision (Soderstrom and Sun, 2007). Nevertheless, it is worth mentioning that in two studies specific references in goodwill disclosures are found. Street et al. (1999) and Street and Gray (2002) both found extensive non-compliance with goodwill disclosures for goodwill amortization under the IAS 22 "*Business Combinations*".

After the mandatory adoption of IFRS, most studies examining companies' level of compliance involved the calculation of a compliance ratio for statistical analysis without, however, focusing on the disclosures and their deficiencies. Moreover, all studies were focused on only one year, making it impossible to drawn conclusions regarding the progress of compliance levels over time. Specifically, six studies are found to provide information relevant to the present study; that is the level of compliance with IFRS disclosure requirements for goodwill.

Paananen (2008) identified 13 items for the measurement of the volume of information companies in Germany, France and the UK provide about the fair value estimation of goodwill in their 2005 annual reports. The results of her study showed that the level of provided information was particularly low. Specifically, by calculating a ratio which represented the number of disclosed items to the number of applicable disclosure items, she found that in a scale from 0 (non-compliance) to 13 (full compliance), the average level of compliance of her sample was 4.

Fekete et al. (2008) examined the level of compliance of 18 listed companies on the Budapest Stock Exchange with IFRS disclosure requirements for consolidation; that are IFRS 3, IAS 27, IAS 28 and IAS 31. Similar to the present study, the compliance ratio was calculated by dividing the actual disclosed items by the maximum score possible for each company and standard. Their results showed that the average Hungarian company disclosed nearly the 62% of the applicable disclosure items in 2006 annual reports. Specifically regarding IFRS 3, which has particular relevance to the current study, the overall level of compliance was 0.58.

Tsalavoutas (2010) examined the level of compliance of a sample of 153 Greek companies with all IFRS mandatory disclosure requirements in 2005. Similarly to the present study, he used an index with all disclosure requirements IFRS mandate and calculated a compliance ratio dividing the number of disclosed items by the number of applicable disclosure items. His results showed a low level of compliance with IFRS 3 disclosure requirements and an even lower with IAS 36. Specifically, he found that Greek companies disclosed two out of three applicable disclosure items of IFRS 3 and half of IAS 36. It should be also mentioned that the level of compliance for both standards presented an extremely high variation among companies.

Ballas and Tzovas (2010) examined the level of compliance with disclosure requirements of all IFRS in a sample of 16 listed and 16 non-listed Greek companies that have adopted IFRS in 2006. In their study they used a disclosure index based on IFRS for small and medium sized entities (SMEs), even though in 2006 IFRS for SMEs had not been released yet. For the computation of the compliance ratio, they used the same method as Paananen (2008), Fekete et al (2008) and Tsalavoutas (2010) described previously. They concluded that the overall compliance ratio for their sample was relatively low (0.63). Similarly to the previous discussed studies, they found that the level of compliance with disclosure requirements for goodwill was even lower (0.49).

As discussed earlier, most prior studies did not focus on the content of financial reports and their scope was not to reveal problematic issues of IFRS implementation. Carlin et al. (2009) applied a content analysis method in 36 Malaysian listed companies for the examination of the disclosures mandated by FRS 136 for goodwill, which is the Malaysian equivalent of IAS 36 "*Impairment of Assets*", in the first year of IFRS adoption in Malaysia (2006). The results showed a substantial non-compliance with disclosure requirements (directly or indirectly) related with fair value accounting. These disclosures related to the allocation of goodwill to CGUs (42% of the sample), the method used in determining the recoverable amount of CGUs (25% of the sample) and the discount and growth rates applied (40% and 60% respectively).

Lastly, the only study which is found to examine in depth goodwill disclosures in Europe is that of the Financial Reporting Council (2008). It examined the disclosures about goodwill impairment testing in a small sample of 32 UK listed companies in their 2007 annual reports. Disclosures of half of the examined companies were characterized as "boiler plate" and rather uninformative. Most companies estimated the recoverable amount of their CGUs' goodwill based on value in use. However, incomplete and generalized information was detected about disclosures for the methods and assumptions employed for the impairment tests. In addition, the information provided was at an aggregate level and not by CGU regardless of the amount of goodwill allocated to each CGU.

Studies regarding goodwill disclosures have also been conducted under US GAAP. Sevin et al. (2007) examined whether 120 US listed companies that recognized goodwill impairment losses in 2002 complied with SFAS 142 "*Goodwill and Other Intangible Assets*" disclosure requirements. For the examination of the level of compliance they set six questions that reflected the main provisions of the standard. Their results indicated that compliance was sporadic and unpredictable. Specifically, they found a relatively low compliance with disclosures about the method used for determining the fair value of companies' reporting units and an even lower compliance with requirements about the facts and circumstances that led to recognition of impairment losses. Shalev (2009) examined the level of compliance with disclosure requirements for business combinations under SFAS 141 "*Business Combinations*" of listed companies in the S&P 500 index in the US. He found that the average company discloses only half of the mandatory disclosure items. Specifically, he found considerable low compliance with disclosure requirements about the reasons that drove business combinations and about purchase price allocation to acquiree's assets, liabilities and contingent liabilities.

Goodwill Disclosures under IFRS

Goodwill is one of the most controversial issues of accounting. Currently, a major element of the debate about goodwill is the use of fair value accounting. Under IFRS 3, goodwill recognized and reported on financial statements is calculated as the difference between the total cost of the business combination and the net fair value of the identifiable assets, liabilities and contingent liabilities of the acquired entity. In addition, IAS 36 prescribes that in goodwill impairment tests, the valuation of cash generating units (CGUs) that contain goodwill shall be based on fair values. Due to the wide use of fair value accounting, both IFRS 3 and IAS 36 mandate extensive disclosures about the valuation methods used and assumptions made in order to enhance the information content of goodwill reported on the balance sheet. The following paragraphs review briefly IFRS disclosure requirements that are related directly or indirectly to goodwill. The method employed to examine the extent and compliance with IFRS disclosure requirements for goodwill involves the segregation of disclosure into five categories based on their general scope. This is fully discussed in the methodology section that follows.

***General disclosures about the carrying amount of goodwill*:** Most disclosures about the carrying amount of goodwill are prescribed in IFRS 3 paragraph 75 that mandates a detailed reconciliation of the carrying amount of goodwill at the beginning and end of the reported period. Moreover, IAS 36 paragraphs 126a and 129a require disclosure of the amount of impairment losses recognized in the statement of comprehensive income during the period and the specific line item(s) in which the impairment losses are included.

***Estimates used to measure recoverable amounts of cash-generating units containing goodwill*:** IAS 36 paragraphs 134 and 135 mandate disclosure requirements about the methods and assumptions on which management bases its estimates of CGUs' impairment tests. Additionally, IAS 36 paragraph 36 mandates disclosing evidence that supports the tenability and consistency of estimates used to measure CGU's recoverable amount through sensitivity tests that examine whether a reasonably possible change in a key assumption would cause the unit's carrying amount to exceed its recoverable amount.

Business combinations effected during the period**:** IFRS 3 mandates information about the identity of the combination, the details of the method of consolidation, i.e. purchase method, a description of the factors that contributed to a cost that results in the recognition of goodwill (or the amount of negative goodwill) and information about the effect of the combination on the acquirer's income statement.

Goodwill not yet allocated to a cash-generating unit**:** IAS 36 paragraph 84 prescribes that if the allocation of goodwill to CGUs cannot be completed before the end of the annual period in which the business combination is affected, the entity shall disclose the portion of goodwill that remains unallocated as well as the reasons why that amount remains unallocated.

Adjustment of comparative information where the initial accounting was determined provisionally: For cases in which the initial accounting for a business combination is determined only provisionally, IFRS 3 prescribes that if the acquirer makes any adjustments in the initial amounts, it should disclose the amounts and explanations of adjustments to the provisional values recognized during the reported period.

Methodology

This study uses a content analysis method for examining the level of compliance with IFRS disclosure requirements for goodwill using a five-point comprehensive disclosure index. Content analysis is useful for this study because it is systematic, covering all aspects of the issue uniformly and objectively, considering all content (in this case disclosure items) in a similar manner, and impartially collected (for a detailed discussion see Krippendorff, 1980 and Steenkamp, 2007). The used index includes all disclosure requirements of IFRS 3 (38 disclosure items) because all of these disclosures are associated with goodwill, at least indirectly, as well as the disclosure requirements of IAS 36 that are associated with goodwill impairment testing (20 disclosure items). The use of this index enables the quantification of the level of compliance through a *compliance ratio,* with values 0 (no compliance) and 1 (full compliance). The quantification of the results is critical for drawing a conclusion in the present study due to the relatively large number of observations (185 annual reports). Specifically, in order to calculate company score the *dichotomous approach* is used (Cooke, 1989; Street and Bryant, 2000; Glaum and Street, 2003; Fekete et al., 2008; Tsalavoutas, 2010; Ballas and Tzovas,

2010) in which, if a required item is found to be disclosed, it is scored as 1, otherwise it is scored 0, while if an item is not applicable for a company, it is characterized as "NA". Then, the level of compliance for each company is calculated as the ratio of the total items disclosed to the total number of applicable disclosure items as follows:

$$LC_{i,t} = \frac{D_{i,t} = \sum_{j=1}^{n} d_j}{A_{i,t} = \sum_{j=1}^{m} a_j}$$

Where,
$LC_{i,t}$ = The total Level of Compliance score for firm i in year t $0 \leq L.C. \leq 1$
$D_{i,t}$ = The total number n (0, m) of disclosed items d for firm i in year t
$A_{i,t}$ = The total number m (3, 58) of applicable disclosure items a for firm i in year t

This approach is also known as *unweighted* because it treats every disclosure item as being of equal importance. The selection of this approach is not only made for the sake of comparability with prior studies and also because any effort for encapsulating subjective weights "*would be unwieldy and probably futile*" (Cooke, 1989, p. 182), since it is virtually certain that every user attaches different weights to a disclosure item.

Following Glaum and Street (2003) and Fekete (2008), the construction of the disclosure index is based on a checklist issued by the audit firm Deloitte (2008). In order to ensure the completeness of the index, items are compared with similar checklists of the other three major audit firms and with Ntzanatos (2008b). During the period under examination (2005-2008) no amendments to the two standards occurred and no company adopted optionally the amendments of IFRS 3 and IAS 36, before their mandatory adoption on 1 January 2009. Last but not least, in order to ensure that the examined companies will not be penalized for non-compliance with disclosures that are not applicable, the complete annual report of every company is reviewed. The index is divided into five categories, each of which is applicable only under specific conditions as it is discussed in the third section. These categories are:

Category Nº 1: General disclosures about the carrying amount of goodwill.
Category Nº 2: Estimates used to measure recoverable amounts of cash-generating units containing goodwill.
Category Nº 3: Business combinations effected during the period.
Category Nº 4: Goodwill not yet allocated to a cash-generating unit.
Category Nº 5: Adjustment of comparative information where the initial accounting was determined provisionally.

Company selection

During the company selection procedure, the first important query is the *materiality* of the carrying amount of goodwill, because this characteristic is closely related with the volume of disclosures mandated by IFRS 3 and IAS 36. The issue of materiality is particularly broad and uncertain because there is not an objective method of measuring it (Hoogendoorn, 2006). As a consequence, in many cases both preparers and users of financial statements use "*rules of thumb*" in order to determine whether an item or event is material or not (Shalev, 2009). In this study the materiality of the balance sheet item of goodwill is based on the following assumption of IAS 1, Paragraph 29 which specifies:

> "An entity shall present separately each material class of similar items. An entity shall present separately items of a dissimilar nature or function unless they are immaterial"

Consequently it can be inferred that if companies recognize goodwill as a separate line item on their balance sheets, they indirectly recognize its materiality and, hence, they are subject to all of IFRS 3 and IAS 36 disclosure requirements. Using the above assumption, the study includes all companies listed on the ASE that have recognized goodwill as a separate line item on their balance sheets during the period 2005-2008. In order to identify which companies have recognized goodwill in their balance sheets the iMentor database of Hellastat is used. From a population of 1412 annual reports, 204 annual reports have goodwill as a separate line item on the balance sheet. From the initial group of 66 companies and 204 firm-year observations, three observations from the banking sector, three with fiscal years ended on June 30, and 11 that were under suspicion or under supervision by the Greek Capital Market Commission were excluded. Moreover, for one company annual reports could not be retrieved. The final group consists of 60 companies and 185 firm-year observations (Table 1).

Table 1. Company selection

Company Selection	Companies	Firm – Year Obs.
Initial Group	66	204
Bank Sector	1	3
Fiscal Year End June 30	3	3
Under Suspicion	-	1
Under Supervision	1	10
Not Found	1	2
Final Number of Companies	**60**	**185**

Findings

Greek listed companies' average level of compliance with disclosure requirements for goodwill for the first four years of IFRS implementation is not encouraging. As Table 2 shows, the mean of the compliance ratio for the four years is 0.49. An encouraging observation for the future, though, is the considerable increase of items disclosed in 2008. The mean of compliance ratio in this year is 12.50% higher than in 2005 and 2007 and 17.4% higher than in 2006.

Table 2. Descriptive statistics of total and annual compliance ratio

Level of Compliance	Total	2005	2006	2007	2008
Mean	0.49	0.48	0.46	0.48	0.54
Median	0.45	0.33	0.42	0.46	0.52
St. Dev.	0.23	0.29	0.22	0.21	0.22
N	185	35	46	53	51

Another positive indication is inferred by the fact that the median of compliance ratio presents a substantial year by year increase, which indicates that every year more and more companies tend to comply with more and more disclosure requirements. Nevertheless, despite the positive observations, a considerable negative inference is drawn from the high value of standard deviation of companies' compliance ratios, which implies a high variation of the level of compliance by company.

Further, examining companies' level of compliance by standard reveals that the total low compliance ratio, discussed above, originates mainly from extensive non-compliance with IAS 36 requirements. Table 3 shows that the Greek companies disclose, on average, one out of three items that IAS 36 mandates. At the same time, companies are much more transparent in IFRS 3 disclosures; the average ratio in this case reaches 0.75.

Table 3. Average level of compliance by standard and year

Standard	Total	2005	2006	2007	2008
IFRS 3	0.75	0.78	0.69	0.73	0.80
IAS 36	0.32	0.32	0.29	0.31	0.34

In addition, compliance ratios by year show that within the last three years a constant improvement in transparency is observed. Nevertheless, taking into account that 2005 was the first year of IFRS implementation, IFRS 3 higher disclosure ratio in 2005, compared to 2006 and 2007, is puzzling. In 2005, companies were less prepared and experienced, and therefore, a lower ratio than those of the following years would be expected. A more detailed view of the results shows that in 2005 only 31% of the companies engaged in a new business combination. In the three following years the percentage climbs to 61%, 59% and 57%, respectively. This means that in 2005 most of companies were subject to basic quantitative disclosures for previously recognized goodwill. The following results indicate that companies comply with these requirements, while they present a lower level of compliance with disclosure requirements about new business combinations.

Moreover, based on the categories of disclosures discussed in the second section above, Table 4 reveals substantial differences in the level of compliance by disclosure category. Specifically, the examination of companies' annual reports reveals the following:

General disclosures about the carrying amount of goodwill. In the first category the highest compliance ratio among the five categories is observed (0.91). This is not a surprising finding because this category comprises mainly quantitative disclosure items, such as the gross amount and the accumulated impairment losses at the beginning and the end of the reported period. It should be mentioned, though, that one disclosure item negatively influences the overall scoring of this category. Only in three, out of thirty applicable cases, companies disclose the line item of the statement of comprehensive income, in which the impairment losses are included (IAS 36, par. 126).

Table 4. Average level of compliance by disclosure category

Category	Level of Compliance
General disclosures for the carrying amount of goodwill	0.91
Estimates used to measure recoverable amounts of cash-generating units containing goodwill	0.34
Business combinations effected during the period	0.51
Goodwill not yet allocated to a cash-generating unit	0.25
Adjustment of comparative information where the initial accounting was determined provisionally	0.67

Estimates used to measure recoverable amounts of cash-generating units containing goodwill. In the second category an extensive non-compliance with IAS 36 disclosure requirements is observed. Table 5 shows that only 40% of companies directly state the basis on which CGUs' recoverable amount is determined (i.e. value in use or fair value less costs to sell). Indirectly, it can be inferred that Greek companies mostly select the "*value in use*" method as the basis for calculating CGU's recoverable amounts (95% of the applicable cases) without, though, disclosing the assumptions and projections on which they base their calculations. Specifically, the number of cases in which companies comply with these disclosure items varies from 18% to 30% of the number of companies that should do so (Table 6). Additionally, only 1 of the 185 annual reports has a disclosure about whether a reasonably possible change in a key assumption would cause CGUs' carrying amounts to exceed their recoverable amounts. Further, no disclosure is found justifying the low level as a result of the "immateriality" of goodwill's carrying amount.

Table 5. Basis used for CGUs recoverable amount calculation

Basis	Number of Companies
Value in Use (directly stated)	73 (40%)
Value in Use (indirectly inferred)	101 (55%)
Fair Value less Cost to Sell	10 (5%)

Table 6. Number of companies complied with disclosure requirements for the calculation of the *value in use*

Disclosure Item	Complied	Not Complied
Description of each key assumption on which management has based its cash flow projections for the period covered by the most recent budgets/forecasts.	52 (30%)	122 (70%)
Description of management's approach to determining the value(s) assigned to each key assumption.	31 (18%)	143 (82%)
The period over which management has projected cash flows based on financial budgets/forecasts. When a period greater than five years is used, an explanation of why that longer period is justified.	41 (23%)	133 (77%)
The growth rate used to extrapolate cash flow projections beyond the period covered by the most recent budgets/forecasts, and the justification for using any growth rate that exceeds the long-term average growth rate.	46 (26%)	128 (74%)
The discount rate(s) applied to the cash flow projections.	51 (29%)	123 (71%)

Business combinations effected during the period. In the third category substantial differences are found in the level of compliance among different disclosure items. Although companies comply highly with disclosure requirements about the identity of business combinations (e.g. names and descriptions of the combining entities, acquisition dates, percentage of voting equity instruments acquired, cost of combinations), they present a low level of compliance with disclosure requirements about goodwill. It is indicative that in 78% of the cases to which disclosures of the third category are applicable, companies avoid disclosing a detailed description of the factors that contributed to a cost that results in recognition of goodwill but they vaguely report that "*goodwill results from intangible assets that cannot be recognized and measured separately*". Even lower compliance is detected in explaining why intangible assets' fair value could not be measured reliably. Only 8 out of the 89 cases that this disclosure item is applicable to actually disclose it (Table 7).

Table 7. Number of companies complying with disclosure requirements for unrecognized intangible assets that contribute to goodwill recognition

Disclosure Item	Complied	Not Complied
Description of each intangible asset that was not recognized separately from goodwill	20 (22%)	69 (78%)
Explanation of why the intangible assets' fair value could not be measured reliably	8 (9%)	81 (92%)

Moreover, companies present a relatively low level of compliance with disclosure requirements about the carrying amounts and the fair values of acquired entities' liabilities and contingent liabilities, immediately before the combination. Specifically, in 60% of the cases that disclosures of the third category apply disclose in detail the carrying amounts and the total acquisition cost and in 55% they disclose separately the fair values determined immediately before the combination (Table 8). It is also worth mentioning that companies that do not disclose the aforementioned information also do not disclose any explanation of the reasons for not disclosing it.

Lastly, Greek companies present a substantial non-compliance with disclosure requirements about acquired companies' financial performance in the acquisition year (Table 9). Only in the 56% of applicable cases companies disclose the amount of acquired companies' profit or loss since the acquisition date that included in their income statement. Even lower is the percentage of applicable cases in which companies disclose the revenue (28%) and profit or loss (29%) of acquired companies as though the acquisition date was the beginning of the period.

Table 8. Number of companies complying with disclosure requirements for the carrying amounts and fair values of recognized assets, liabilities and contingent liabilities

Disclosure Item	Complied	Not Complied
The amounts recognized at the acquisition date for each class of the acquiree's assets, liabilities and contingent liabilities	59 (60%)	40 (40%)
The carrying amounts of each class of the acquiree's assets, liabilities and contingent liabilities, determined in accordance with IFRSs, immediately before the combination	55 (55%)	44 (45%)
If disclosure of such carrying amounts immediately before combination is impracticable, that fact, together with an explanation of why this is the case	3 (7%)	41 (93%)

Goodwill not yet allocated to a cash-generating unit. In the fourth category only in 3 out of 12 cases, to which these disclosures are applicable, do companies disclose the amount of goodwill that is not allocated to a CGU and the reasons why that amount remains unallocated.

Adjustment of comparative information where the initial accounting was determined provisionally. In the fifth category the companies comply at a relatively higher level. In 70% of the cases in which companies are required to disclose information about the adjustments they make to the provisional values of the initial accounting of a business combination, do they make the required disclosures.

Additionally, Table 10 shows the historical progress of levels of compliance by category. Greek companies present a stable high compliance with the first disclosure category "*General disclosures about the carrying amount of goodwill*" which is near and above 0.90. In the second category "*Estimates used to measure recoverable amounts of cash-generating units containing goodwill*", the extensive non-compliance discussed above is confirmed. Greek companies not only present a substantial low level of compliance but also they do not improve over the first four years of IFRS implementation.

Table 9. Number of companies complying with disclosure requirements for acquired company's financial performance

Disclosure Item	Complied	Not Complied
The amount of the acquiree's profit or loss since the acquisition date included in the acquirer's profit or loss for the period	55 (56%)	44 (44%)
If it is impracticable to disclose the amount of the acquiree's profit or loss since the acquisition date included in the acquirer's profit or loss for the period that fact; and an explanation	5 (11%)	39 (89%)
The revenue of the combined entity for the period as though the acquisition date for all business combinations effected during the period had been the beginning of the period	28 (28%)	71 (72%)
The profit or loss of the combined entity for the period as though the acquisition date for all business combinations effected during the period had been the beginning of the period	29 (29%)	70 (71%)
If disclosure of the information required by the two above paragraphs would be impracticable, the entity shall disclose that fact and an explanation of why this is the case	8 (11%)	63 (89%)

For the third category "*Business combinations effected during the period*", a considerable increase of the compliance ratio is detected throughout the period examined. It is indicative that the level of compliance in this category has almost doubled from 2005 to 2008 (0.33 to 0.64). It seems that the increase in the overall compliance ratio comes from increased compliance in this category.

In the fourth category "*Goodwill not yet allocated to a cash-generating unit*" a steep increase in the level of compliance is also detected. Nevertheless, this improvement does not affect substantially the overall compliance ratio because of the small number of cases to which these disclosures are applicable (only 12 out of 185).

Lastly, in the fifth category companies present a considerably high level of compliance, but again the number of cases to which these disclosures are applicable are relatively small and do not affect substantially the overall compliance ratio (23 out of 185). It should be also mentioned that the zero level of compliance in 2006 is of little importance because only two companies would have been acquired to disclose these items that year.

Table 10. Historical progress of the average level of compliance by disclosure category

Category	2005	2006	2007	2008
General disclosures for the carrying amount of goodwill	0.90	0.96	0.89	0.90
Estimates used to measure recoverable amounts of cash-generating units containing goodwill	0.35	0.30	0.33	0.36
Business combinations effected during the period	0.33	0.43	0.52	0.64
Goodwill not yet allocated to a cash-generating unit	0.00	0.25	0.20	0.33
Adjustment of comparative information where the initial accounting was determined provisionally	1.00	0.00	0.56	0.83

In conclusion, it can be stated that, throughout the first four years of IFRS implementation, Greek companies' level of compliance presents a substantial improvement in all categories, apart from the second: "*Estimates used to measure recoverable amounts of cash-generating units containing goodwill*", i.e. disclosures prescribed by IAS 36.

In summary, the five disclosure items that are detected more frequently in companies' annual reports are:

- The gross amount and accumulated impairment losses at the beginning and at the end of the period, as well as the additional goodwill recognized during the period (IFRS 3, paragraph 75, Disclosure Category 2)

- Basic information for each business combination effected during the period: 1) The names and descriptions of the combining entities or businesses 2) The acquisition date 3) The percentage of voting equity instruments acquired (IFRS 3, paragraph. 67, Disclosure Category 2)
- The cost of the business combination, and a description of the components of that cost, including any costs directly attributable to the combination (IFRS 3, paragraph 67, Disclosure Category 2)
- Where the initial accounting is determined provisionally, comparative information for the periods before the initial accounting for the combination is complete as if the initial accounting had been completed from the acquisition date (IFRS 3, paragraph 62, Disclosure Category 2)
- The carrying amount of goodwill allocated to each (group of) cash generating unit(s) (IAS 36, paragraph 134 Disclosure Category 3)

On the contrary, the five disclosure items that are detected more rarely in companies' annual reports are:

- The line item(s) of the statement of comprehensive income in which the impairment losses are included (IAS 36, paragraph 129, Disclosure Category 1)
- The key assumptions and projections on which the unit's (group of units') recoverable amount has been determined (IAS 36, paragraph 134, Disclosure Category 2)
- A description of the factors that contributed to a cost that results in the recognition of goodwill (IFRS 3, paragraph 67, Disclosure Category 3)
- The revenue and the profit or loss of the combined entity for the period as though the acquisition date for all business combinations effected during the period had been the beginning of the period (IFRS 3, paragraph 70, Disclosure Category 3)
- An explanation of why the information required above about the revenue and the profit or loss of the combined entity is impracticable to be disclosed (IFRS 3, paragraph 70, Disclosure Category 3)

Concluding Discussion

The scope of this study is to examine the extent of compliance with IFRS disclosure requirements for goodwill of Greek listed companies during the first four years of IFRS mandatory implementation. Goodwill disclosures is an interesting setting because accounting for goodwill under IFRS is heavily influenced by fair value accounting which is based, to a large extent, on management assumptions that may lack objectivity (Hoogendoom, 2006; Ball, 2006; Jermakowicz and Tomaszewski, 2006; Penman, 2007). Mandating extensive disclosures about accounting figures, that are "fair value driven" potentially, secures the information value of financial reports, because it enables users to assess the objectivity of management's assumptions.

Nevertheless, the results reveal some potentially serious deficiencies in the implementation of IFRS disclosures for goodwill and mainly with those that are closely related to fair value accounting. Similar to Financial Reporting Council (2008), Paananen (2008) and Tsalavoutas (2010) in Europe, Carlin et al (2009) in Malaysia and Sevin et al (2007) in the US, the results show that there is an extensive non-compliance with disclosure requirements about goodwill impairment test under IAS 36. Greek companies select mostly the "*value in use*" method as the basis for calculating CGU's recoverable amounts, without disclosing adequately the details of the adopted method such as management assumptions about cash flow projections, discount and growth rates. Additionally, although companies present a much higher compliance ratio with IFRS 3 disclosure requirements, they do not comply with those requirements that are related to fair value accounting. Specifically the results show that Greek listed companies do not comply with requirements about disclosing information for the initial recognition and measurement of goodwill, while they also present a relatively low level of compliance with requirements about disclosing the carrying and fair values of acquired companies' assets, liabilities and contingent liabilities.

Comparing the results of this study with those of Tsalavoutas (2010) for 2005 annual reports, although both studies find a similar level of compliance with IFRS 3 disclosure requirements, this is not the case for IAS 36. The detected difference may be addressed to the different indices used for the calculation of the level of compliance with IAS 36 requirements. Thus, while this study includes in its index only disclosure items related with goodwill, Tsalavoutas (2010) examined the whole of IAS 36 requirements. The results of this study cannot be compared with those of Ballas and Tzovas (2010) because the latter used a different disclosure index based on IFRS for SMEs.

A particularly alarming finding of this study is that even after four years of IFRS introduction, Greek companies have not increased the volume of information that IAS 36 mandates. On the contrary, a positive indication for the future is the substantial improvement of the volume of information IFRS 3 mandates. Even though this study does not examine the significance of these misstatements, it is clear that companies do not disclose important information related to fair value accounting. The high levels of non-compliance that Greek companies present may not enable users to draw clear inferences about the correctness of the adopted assumptions and, consequently, may undermine the information value of the accounting figure of goodwill. The results of this study also indicate (although indirectly), that there is a need for enhancing the existing enforcement mechanisms which have been characterized as "*toothless watchdogs*" (Ball, 2006).

Lastly, this study has a number of limitations. It assumes, but not examines, that the volume of information provided by the financial reports affects the relevance of the accounting number of goodwill. This research question is still open for further examination.

Acknowledgments

I would like to special thank Professor Gary Cunningham, Dr Louise Macniven, Berit Hartmann and all the participants of the accounting stream of the EBEEC 2010 Conference for their valuable comments and suggestions and Professor Spyros Vasiliadis for his unreserved support.

References

Apostolou, A. and Nanopoulos, K., 2008, IFRS Voluntary Compliance: The Case of Greece, *7th International Conference of the Hellenic Finance and Accounting Association*, Chania, Greece

Ball, R., 2006, International Financial Reporting Standards: Pros and Cons for Investors, *Accounting and Business Research, International Accounting Policy Forum*, pp. 5-27.

Ballas, A.A. and Tzovas, C., 2010, An Empirical Investigation of Greek Firms' Compliance to IFRS Disclosure Requirements, *International Journal of Managerial and Financial Accounting*, 2, 1, pp. 40-62.

Bellas, A., Toudas, K. and Papadatos, K., 2007, The Consequences of Applying International Accounting Standards to the Financial Statements of Greek Companies, *30th Annual Congress of the European Accounting Association*, Lisbon, Portugal

Carlin, M.T., Finch, N. and Laili, H.N., 2009, Goodwill Accounting in Malaysia and the Transition to IFRS – A Compliance Assessment of

Large First Year Adopters, *Journal of Financial Reporting & Accounting*, 7, 1, pp 75-104

Committee of European Securities Regulators – CESR, 2003, *Standard No. 1 on financial information: enforcement of standards on financial information in Europe*, Ref: CESR/03-073.

Cooke, T.E., 1989, Voluntary Corporate Disclosure by Swedish Companies, *Journal of International Financial Management and Accounting*, 1, 2, pp. 171-195.

Daske, H., Hail, L., Leuz, C. and Verdi, R., 2008, Mandatory IFRS Reporting Around the World: Early Evidence on the Economic Consequences, *Journal of Accounting Research*¸ 46, 5, pp. 1085-1142.

Deloitte Touche Tohmatsu, 2008, *International Financial Reporting Standards – Presentation and Disclosure Checklist*, retrieved from http://www.iasplus.com /fs/2008checklist.pdf in 30/6/09,

Epstein, J.B., Jermakowicz, K.E., 2008, Wiley IFRS 2008: Interpretation and Application of International Accounting and Financial Reporting Standards 2008, USA, John Willey & Sons Inc. Publications,

Ernst & Young, 2005, *How fair is fair value? IFRS stakeholders' series*, London.

—. 2006, *Observations on the Implementation of IFRS*, London.

—. 2008, International GAAP 2008 - Volume 1, USA, John Willey & Sons Inc. Publications.

—. 2008, *International GAAP Disclosure Checklist*, retrieved from http://www.ey.com/Publication/vwLUAssets/ IFRS_GAAP_Disclosure_checklist_2008/$FILE/IFRS_Disclosure_Checklist_2008.pdf (in 30/8/09).

Fekete, S., Matis, D. and Lukacs, J., 2008, Factors Influencing the Extent of Corporate Compliance with IFRS. The Case of Hungarian Listed Companies, Working Paper published in *Social Science Research Network* website http://papers.ssrn.com/sol3/papers.cfm?abstract_id=1295722

Financial Reporting Council, 2008, *Review of Goodwill Impairment Disclosures*, London.

Glaum, M. and Street, L.D., 2003, Compliance with the Disclosure Requirements of Germany's New Market: IAS Versus US GAAP, *Journal of International Financial Management and Accounting*, 14, 1, pp. 64-100.

Healy, M.P. and Palepu, G.K., 2001, Information Asymmetry, Corporate Disclosure and the Capital Markets: A Review of the Empirical Disclosure Literature, *Journal of Accounting and Economics*, 31, pp. 405-440.

Hodgdon, C., Tondkar, H.R., Harless, W.D. and Adhikari, A., 2009, Compliance with International Financial Reporting Standards and Auditor Choice: New Evidence on the Importance of the Statutory Audit, *The International Journal of Accounting*, 44, pp. 33-35.

Hoogendoorn, M., 2006, International Accounting Regulation and IFRS Implementation in Europe and Beyond – Experiences with First Time Adoption in Europe, *Accounting in Europe*, 3, pp. 23-26.

International Accounting Standards Board, 2008, *International Financial Reporting Standards 2008*, UK, IASCF Publications.

International Accounting Standards Committee Foundation, *Revised Constitution* March 2010, London, IASCF

Jermakowicz, K.E. and Gornik-Tomaszewski, S., 2006, Implementing IFRS from the perspective of EU publicly traded companies, *Journal of International Accounting Auditing and Taxation*, 15, pp. 170-196.

Krippendorff, K., 1980, *Content Analysis: An Introduction to its Methodology*, London, Sage Publications.

KPMG, 2008, *Disclosure Checklist International Financial Reporting Standards*, retrieved from http://www.ey.com/Publication/vwLUAs sets/IFRS_GAAP_Disclosure_checklist_2008/$FILE/IFRS_Disclosure _Checklist_2008.pdf in 30/8/09

Mirza, A.A., Orrell, M. and Holt, J.G., 2008, "*IFRS Practical Implementation Guide and Workbook, Second Edition*, USA, John Willey & Sons Inc. Publications.

Marston, L.C. and Shrives, J.P., 1991, The Use of Disclosure Indices in Accounting Research: A Review Article, *British Accounting Review*, 23, pp. 195-210.

Ntzanatos, D., 2008a, *International Accounting Standards and their Differences with Greek GAAP*, Athens, Kastanioti Publications.

—. 2008b, *Preparation of Financial Statements Notes and Control of their Completeness – Volumes A & B,* Athens, Kastanioti Publications.

Paananen, M., 2008, Fair Value Accounting for Goodwill under IFRS: An Exploratory Study of the Comparability in France, Germany and the United Kingdom, Working Paper published in *Social Science Research Network* website http://www.papers.ssrn.com/sol3/papers.cfm?abstract _id=1275803

Penman, H.S., 2007, Financial Reporting Quality: Is Fair Value a Plus or a Minus?, *Accounting and Business Research* Special Issue, International Accounting Policy Forum, pp. 33-44.

Pricewaterhouse Coopers, 2008, *IFRS Disclosure Checklist 2008*, retrieved from http://www.pwc.com/en_GX/gx/ifrs-reporting/pdf/ifrs _disclchlist08.pdf in 30/8/09

Ramanna, K., 2008, The Implications of Unverifiable Fair-Value Accounting: Evidence from the Political Economy of Goodwill Accounting, *Journal of Accounting and Economics*, 45, pp. 253-281.

Regulation (EC) 1606/2002, *On the Application of International Accounting Standards*, Official Journal of the European Communities, L 243/1/11.9.2002.

Sevin, S. and Schroeder, R., 2005, Earnings Management: Evidence from SFAS No. 142 Reporting, *Managerial Auditing Journal*, 20, 1, pp. 47-54.

Sevin, S., Schroeder, R. and Bhamornsiri, S., 2007, Transparent Financial Disclosure and SFAS No. 142, *Managerial Auditing Journal*, 22, 7, pp. 674-687.

Shalev, R., 2009, The Information Level of Business Combination Level, *The Accounting Review*, 84, 1, pp. 239-270.

Soderstrom, S.N. and Sun, J.K., 2007, IFRS Adoption and Accounting Quality: A Review, *European Accounting Review*, 16, 4, pp. 675-702.

Steenkamp, N., 2007, Content Analysis in Accounting Research: The Practical Challenges, *Australian Accounting Review*, November, pp. 12-26.

Street, L.D., Gray, J.S. and Bryant, M.S., 1999, Acceptance and Observance of International Accounting Standards: An Empirical Study of Companies Claiming to Comply with IASs, *The International Journal of Accounting*, 34, 1, pp. 11-48.

Street, L.D. and Bryant, M.S., 2000, Disclosure Level and Compliance with IASs: A Comparison of Companies with and without U.S. Listings and Fillings, *The International Journal of Accounting*, 35, 3, pp. 305-329.

Street, L.D. and Gray, J.S., 2002, Factors Influencing the Extent of Corporate Compliance with International Accounting Standards: Summary of a Research Monograph, *Journal of International Accounting Auditing and Taxation*, 11, pp. 51-76.

Tsalavoutas, I., 2010, *IFRS mandatory disclosures and value relevance*, British Accounting Association Conference, Cardiff, UK.

Wines, G., Dagwell, R., Windsor, C., 2007, Implications of the IFRS Goodwill Accounting Treatment, *Managerial Auditing Journal*, 22,9, pp. 862-880.

Whittington G. (2005) "The Adoption of International Accounting Standards in the European Union", *European Accounting Review*, 14, 1, pp 127-153.

PART SIX:

LABOR MARKET, ENTERPRISES AND ENTREPRENEURSHIP

LABOR MARKET SEGMENTATION AND GENDER WAGE GAP IN UKRAINE

NORBERTO PIGNATTI

Abstract

Ukrainian women are on average much more educated than women in developing countries and they also tend to show higher participation rates, albeit smaller than men's. They are also at least as educated as Ukrainian men. Both men and women show higher propensity to go from the informal sector to the formal one than vice versa. However, contrary to what is predicted by segmented labour market theories a higher concentration of women in the formal sector is found.

On average, Ukrainian women do earn less than men and this is true both in the formal and in the informal sector. However, when the gender is earnings differential is decomposed evidence of two very different patterns between the two sectors it found. In the formal sector the earnings differential is entirely due to the unexplained component. In the informal sector, on the contrary, when the earnings differential is significantly different from zero it is entirely due to differences in the explained component (personal, household and job characteristics).

Overall, these results can be interpreted as the evidence that the Ukrainian labour market is indeed segmented and that women suffer some sort of discrimination. This discrimination is not taking place through the segregation of women in the informal sector but, more likely, through different remuneration of characteristics in the formal sector, with different career opportunities and the exclusion of women from the better remunerated jobs at the top of the hierarchy. This may also explain why women in the upper tier of the wage distribution experience higher earnings when they are self-employed compared to when they are salaried, both in the formal and in the informal sector.

Introduction

Labour market segmentation can be characterized as a situation in which people working in some jobs or in some sectors experience differences in earnings and enjoy different levels of protection and sets of opportunities with respect to others with similar productivity and are at the same time facing significant obstacles to move to the "good" jobs or segments of the market.

Past research suggests us that women tend to have a more vulnerable position than men in the labour market, showing lower participation rates, lower earnings and a tendency to advance more slowly in their career. A possible explanation for the existence and the persistence of the gender wage gap might be the different impact of labour market segmentation on the two genders.

It follows that, if we are to fully understand the nature and the reasons of the persistence of the gender wage gap, we also have to take into account the impact that the existence of different sectors in the labour market (formal and informal) has on this measure.

Research on informal employment in transition countries has been very limited, mainly because of the lack of appropriate data. Instead, there have been several works studying the extent of the gender gap in earnings, both at the beginning and in the subsequent phases of transition. This paper is probably the first attempt to analyze jointly labour market segmentation and the gender wage gap in the context of a country in transition. Using the data of the two available waves of the ULMS (2003 and 2004) the patterns characterizing male and female employment will be identified, both in terms of mobility across labour market states and earnings. This will help us understand to what extent the evidence is in line with the predictions given by the theory about labour market segmentation in developing countries and how labour market segmentation, if it exists in Ukraine, contributes to the gender wage differential. This appears to be particularly relevant as, in the years under analysis, the growth in the Ukrainian employment rate is driven mainly by the growth of the informal sector.

This paper begins with a brief introduction to the debate about the nature of the informal labour market and a short description of how economic theory envisions the relationship between women and the informal sector. In section 3 the data used will be introduced. In section 4 the main characteristics and patterns of mobility in the Ukrainian labour markets will be described. In section 5 the links between earnings, employment status and gender differentials will be explored. Finally, section 6 concludes.

The debate about the informal labour market under a gender perspective

Traditionally, the formal sector has been characterized as the "good" sector, in which jobs provide higher pay, more security, better working conditions and better opportunities for advancement. The primary/formal sector coexists, according to the "traditional" school, with a secondary/informal one providing no benefits, protections or guarantees, little or no chances of promotion, poor working conditions and low pay. In this traditional view, people in the secondary/informal sector find it extremely difficult to move to the formal sector. It is this separation that justifies different remuneration of factors in the two sectors.

More recently, however, two main "revisionist schools" have been developed, which challenge this characterization of the labour market. According to the first "revisionist school" (e.g. Maloney 1999; 2004), SLM would not exist, and individuals would choose freely to move between formal and informal sectors on the basis of their preferences. The second "revisionist" school argues instead that the freedom of movement between different segments of the labour market is still limited and the share of individuals forced to stay in "bad" jobs despite their personal characteristics and preferences is not negligible. However, even for this school of thought, informal jobs are not necessarily "bad" jobs. The informal sector itself is characterized as segmented, with the simultaneous presence of "upper tier" (restricted access) jobs and "lower tier" (free entry) jobs. Upper tier informal jobs in terms of utility are now almost indistinguishable from formal ones, while lower tier informal jobs constitute the "truly disadvantaged" segment (Fields, 1990; 2005).

If labour markets are segmented and men and women have different propensity to enter one or the other segment of the labour market, they might be hit differently by labour market segmentation. Several possible explanations have been offered about why women might be more present in the informal sector than men.

For instance, women may actually prefer working in the informal sector because it offers the flexibility they need (in terms of working time, work location, seasonal patterns, etc.) to be able to combine paid work and homework and nurturing activities (Maloney, 2004).

There might also be demand-side motivations for a concentration of women in the informal sector. For example, employers' "taste for discrimination" (Becker, 1957) or "statistical discrimination" (Phelps, 1972).

Women could also be forced to accept informal jobs because of legislation making it more costly for employers to hire them formally (for example, mandatory leave legislation) (World Bank, 2001; Paci, 2002).

Finally, women can also be forced into the informal sector because of limited physical mobility caused by social norms (Chen, 2001).

Horizontal segregation, which we have been examining so far, is not the only one possible. The most recent literature identifies a second type of segregation: vertical segregation. Vertical segregation refers to the hierarchy or status of women within each occupation or sector, in particular to the fact that men are more likely to be in supervision/ managerial positions within each occupation or sector (Hakim, 1992; Blackburn, et al., 2001).

It might be, then, that gender segmentation exists also within each sector of the labour market.

This view is compatible with the "overcrowding" theory (Zellner, 1972; Bergmann 1971 and 1974), according to which women tend to be more concentrated in relatively few "female" occupations mostly in the secondary segment of the market. This would explain the existence of gender wage differentials in the informal and in the formal sector with the different degrees of competition men and women have to face.

The theories exposed so far have been essentially carried out for developed or developing countries. There are, however, several reasons to believe that the results obtained for developing countries might not hold necessarily in the case of transition countries. The economic structure of the economy in transition countries has always been very different from that of developing countries, with a much larger emphasis on the role of the industrial sector and large firms. In transition countries individuals enjoyed secure, life-long employment and (especially in the former Soviet Union) no possibility to engage independently in entrepreneurial activity existed. This was certainly not the case in most developing countries. Moreover, the labour force in socialist countries had much higher levels of human capital than in developing countries.

In transition countries women were "encouraged" to participate to the labour force offering a "guarantee" of equal pay[1], generous maternity benefits and other incentives all aimed at this purpose. Even if this was only partially true in practice (there is evidence in the literature on transition countries that women tended to be segregated in some sectors of the economy and in certain types of occupation, see, Brainerd (2000); Newell and Reilly (1996)), this led to participation rates much higher than those in developing, and developed countries. Even nowadays, generous maternity leave rules and protective legislation in general are still in place in several countries, together with anti-discriminatory legislation[2] and, despite the reduction in female participation rates following the transition, levels of participation in ex-socialist countries remain relatively high. One might well argue that in the presence of the existing incentive structure and of a relatively small informal sector women might prefer a formal sector job rather than a job in the informal sector and that only those whose opportunities in the formal sector are extremely scarce might decide to move to the informal sector.

Data and data issues

This work is based on the Ukrainian Longitudinal Monitoring Survey (ULMS), a household panel established to monitor Ukraine's path of transition from Communism to a market-oriented economy. The target of the household survey is the working age population, spanning years of age 15 to 70. The central data used in this paper are those from the individual questionnaire for the two reference weeks in 2003 (around 4,000 households and approximately 8,500 individuals) and 2004 (3,397 households and 7,200 individuals).

The household questionnaire contains items on the demographic structure of the household, its income and expenditure patterns together

---

[1] In reality, also under state socialism female-male wage differentials existed. However, women in socialist countries were performing certainly better than their counterparts in developing countries.

[2] Among which we also find Ukraine, where gender discrimination is prohibited by article 24 of the constitution as documented in Ganguli and Terrell (2005).

with living conditions. From the individual questionnaire we obtain information on earnings[3], labour market status, job characteristics and nature of the employment relationship. In the present analysis there is a focus on informal employment relationships (job not registered in either informal or formal sector firms) rather than to employment in the informal sector (individuals working in informal sector firms).

Like in all CIS countries, salaried workers in Ukraine have been confronted with wage arrears. This also can be seen in ULMS data. In order to take into account the effects of these "disturbances", a dummy variable is included for those cases in the wage regressions where last wage exceeds the contractual wage and a dummy variable for those in which last wage is less.

Another issue is represented by the non-normality of log hourly earnings. Jarque-Bera (1980) tests of normality reject the null hypothesis in both years, both for trimmed and untrimmed log hourly earnings. Consequently, in the wage regressions that are performed the untrimmed log hourly earnings are still being used. To check whether the problem connected to non-normality is likely to affect significantly the results of the analysis. Eearnings functions using robust and quantile regressions are also estimated. The main patterns remain broadly the same.

Informality and mobility between labour market states: differences across genders

In the Ukrainian working age population, women are more numerous than men (Table 1), yet participate to the labour force significantly less than men (51% against 65 %) in both periods. The level of participation for both genders remains a bit higher than that for developing countries and more in line with participation rates of transition countries. When employment rates are compared, it cannot be identified a clear difference between men and women[4]. In this case the pattern is clearly different from

[3] Salaried employees are asked in the two reference weeks to give their last monthly net salary in Hryvnia. The self-employed are asked to give an estimate of net income for the last month preceding the reference week. Since in the ULMS is not available a measure of the capital used by the self-employed, I cannot include returns to capital in net monthly income. However, as suggested in Lehmann and Pignatti (2007) this component is not likely to be substantial in the Ukrainian context.

[4] 2003 and 2004 were years of a vigorous growth for Ukraine. This growth started

the one found in developing countries, where women tend also to have lower employment rates.

Ukrainian women show a greater Formal/Informal ratio than men in both the years under analysis and seem to move towards informality at roughly the same speed as men. This does not indicate, at first sight, any preference for informality for women. This issue will be investigated further in the section on movements between labour market states.

From Table 2 it can be seen that the age of women in the sample is slightly higher than that of men and their educational attainments appear to be almost always better than those of men[5]. The same is also true for tenure. If we look at how many men and women choose an informal employment (both as salaried and as self-employed) it emerges that women do choose to go informal less than men in both periods, with a larger preference for self-employment. The fraction of voluntarily informal is pretty low in both years (especially among the salaried).

Women and men appear to behave differently when their work choices are compared with their level of education. The share of women with university degree or higher is much higher among the informal salaried who voluntarily chose to become informal than among the informally self-employed, especially in 2004. The opposite is true for men and it becomes also more evident when one looks at what happens in the second period.

In Table 3 the mean and median earnings for males and females are reported at the aggregate level as well as disaggregated by sector (formal/informal) for 2003 and 2004. Women appear to experience negative wage differentials with respect to men in both the formal and the informal sector, with the wage gap being larger in the formal sector in 2003 and in the informal sector in 2004.

Men and women are distributed across sectors and occupations (Tables 4 and 5), consistently with what has been described by the literature analyzing labour markets of transition countries after the fall of the Soviet Union (Fong and Paul, 1992; Brainerd, 2000). Employed women are concentrated in Services (which include Health and Education sectors) in

---

already in 1998 but resulted in a reduction in unemployment only in 2004 (see Lehmann, Kupets and Pignatti, 2005).

[5] This is certainly a consequence of the investment in public education that has taken place in this country and of the large exit from the workforce of less skilled women as reported by Ganguli and Terrell (2005).

both sectors, while men are more evenly distributed. The second largest sectors in terms of concentration of women are industry in the formal sector and agriculture in the informal sector. In almost all sectors women experience a negative wage differential.

There are differences in the distribution of men and women between the formal and the informal sector even when we look at occupations. In the formal sector women tend to be significantly more concentrated in the occupations classified as "highly skilled" (ISCO categories 1 to 3) than men (45% against 28% in the first period and 46% against 27% in the second period). However, they are always less concentrated than men to the top (managerial positions) and more in the categories of professionals and technicians. Men are instead more concentrated in the occupational category classified as "craft and related trades workers" (ISCO category 7). If we look at the informal sector, women appear to be more concentrated in categories 5 and 9 (service workers and shop and market sales and elementary occupation). It is worth noting that the share of women in managerial positions in the informal sector is larger than men's. In any case, women in managerial position still earn less than men. Men's distribution among the different occupations inside the informal sector does not differ significantly from that in the formal one.

From this descriptive analysis some interesting patterns already emerge. Ukrainian women are not disproportionately found in the informal sector and their human capital (as measured by the variables we have considered) is not considerably lower than that of men. However, there seem to be clearly different patterns in the distribution of both groups among different occupations and sectors and also evidence of the existence of unconditional wage differences among men and women across occupational groups and sectors. Causes for these differences might be several. Among them, it might be the presence of different risk-aversion between the two gender groups or the existence of different sets of opportunities available to them.

The analysis of patterns of mobility across labour market states follows. This is particularly important in an analysis of labour market segmentation, as one of the characteristics of a SLM is limited mobility, especially from the secondary sector of the economy to the primary one.

Table 1. Labour market status, participation rate and employment rate by gender

	Formal	Informal	Unemployed	OLF	Participation rate	Employment rate	Sample		Ratio F/I	% Δ from previous year of F/I ratio
							Share	N		
2003										
Women	0.383	0.038	0.084	0.495	0.505	0.833	0.579	4739	10.197	
Men	0.483	0.057	0.111	0.350	0.650	0.830	0.421	3446	8.442	
2004										
Women	0.378	0.055	0.074	0.492	0.508	0.853	0.584	3974	6.863	-0.327
Men	0.469	0.084	0.095	0.352	0.648	0.854	0.416	2826	5.571	-0.340

Source:ULMS

Table 2. Distribution of characteristics among the employed in the sample

	2003					2004				
	Total	Formal		Informal		Total	Formal		Informal	
		Females	Males	Females	Males		Females	Males	Females	Males
All										
N. obs.	3853	1815	1663	178	197	3392	1537	1356	242	257
age	40.18	40.68	40.66	36.79	34.65	39.96	40.71	40.65	37.80	33.81
secondary	0.61	0.61	0.60	0.72	0.54	0.63	0.61	0.65	0.64	0.60
university	0.21	0.26	0.18	0.09	0.12	0.21	0.27	0.19	0.10	0.06
tenure	9.76	11.23	9.61	2.99	3.34	8.98	11.16	8.78	2.99	2.09
choice	0.02			0.22	0.20	0.03			0.17	0.20
self	0.07	0.03	0.05	0.34	0.43	0.09	0.03	0.06	0.38	0.39

Choice of being informal										
nobs	79			40	39	94			42	52
age	32.90			33.85	31.92	33.33			35.29	31.75
secondary	0.66			0.75	0.56	0.66			0.62	0.69
university	0.10			0.10	0.10	0.11			0.21	0.02
tenure	2.25			1.99	2.52	1.29			1.71	0.93
Self-employed										
nobs	282	50	88	60	84	318	46	80	92	100
age	38.26	38.36	37.73	40.18	37.39	39.51	39.61	38.95	42.91	36.79
secondary	0.63	0.68	0.53	0.82	0.57	0.63	0.54	0.68	0.65	0.61
university	0.18	0.22	0.27	0.08	0.14	0.17	0.35	0.30	0.07	0.08
tenure	4.73	4.76	5.05	4.64	4.44	4.81	5.03	5.01	4.21	3.51

Source: ULMS

Table 3. Mean and median earning differentials

2003									
	Total			Formal			Informal		
	Females	Males	% earnings differential[b]	Females	Males	% earnings differential[b]	Females	Males	% earnings differential[b]
Mean earnings[a]	1.684	2.257	-25.4%	1.681	2.261	-25.7%	1.722	2.215	-22.2%
Median earnings[a]	1.333	1.875	-28.9%	1.333	1.875	-28.9%	1.250	1.708	-26.8%
N. Obs.	1746	1498		1609	1362		137	136	
2004									
	Females	Males	% earnings differential[b]	Females	Males	% earnings differential[b]	Females	Males	% earnings differential[b]
Mean earnings[a]	2.166	2.889	-25.0%	2.213	2.891	-23.5%	1.840	2.878	-36.0%
Median earnings[a]	1.634	2.294	-28.7%	1.720	2.294	-25.0%	1.318	1.946	-32.3%
N. Obs.	1568	1344		1371	1160		197	184	

Source:ULMS

[a] Real hourly earnings.

[b]The % earnings differential is calculated as follows: (wf-wm)/wm. A negative number indicates that women earn less than men.

Table 4. Distribution of employed by sector (within gender) and gender differentials between median earnings[a] by sector

	2003				2004			
	Formal		Informal		Formal		Informal	
	Females	Males	Females	Males	Females	Males	Females	Males
Agrriculture	0.08	0.15	0.24	0.25	0.08	0.14	0.34	0.21
Industry	0.22	0.38	0.08	0.12	0.23	0.40	0.08	0.16
Construction	0.02	0.07	0.01	0.23	0.02	0.06	0.02	0.28
Services	0.59	0.34	0.55	0.29	0.59	0.33	0.47	0.25
Other services and activities	0.09	0.07	0.12	0.11	0.08	0.07	0.09	0.10

	Females	Males	% earnings differential[b]	Females	Males	% earnings differential[b]	Females	Males	% earnings differential[b]	Females	Males	% earnings differential[b]
Agrriculture	1.13	0.90	0.25	0.63	0.92	-0.31	1.38	1.38	0.00	0.76	0.94	-0.18
Industry	1.56	2.19	-0.29	1.88	2.34	-0.20	1.91	2.68	-0.29	1.67	2.29	-0.27
Construction	1.77	2.00	-0.11	3.22	2.06	0.57	2.61	2.87	-0.09	2.87	2.39	0.20
Services	1.28	1.75	-0.27	1.36	1.79	-0.24	1.59	2.29	-0.31	1.41	1.91	-0.26
Other services and activities	1.30	1.56	-0.17	1.61	1.15	0.41	1.61	1.86	-0.14	1.94	1.92	0.01

Source:ULMS

[a] Real hourly earnings.

[b]The % earnings differential is calculated as follows: (wf-wm)/wm. A negative number indicates that women earn less than men.

Table 5. Distribution of employed by occupation (within gender) and gender differentials between median earningsa by sector

	2003				2004			
	Formal		Informal		Formal		Informal	
	Females	Males	Females	Males	Females	Males	Females	Males
Managers	0.03	0.06	0.16	0.13	0.05	0.08	0.14	0.12
Professionals	0.21	0.11	0.02	0.04	0.20	0.11	0.01	0.01
Technicians	0.21	0.11	0.01	0.03	0.21	0.08	0.00	0.02
Clerks	0.11	0.03	0.03	0.03	0.11	0.03	0.03	0.01
Service workers and shop and market sales	0.10	0.04	0.36	0.12	0.10	0.03	0.38	0.06
Skilled agricultural, forestry, and fishery	0.01	0.04	0.03	0.03	0.01	0.04	0.01	0.01
Craft and related trades workers	0.10	0.32	0.04	0.21	0.10	0.31	0.06	0.27
Plant and machine operators and assemblers	0.03	0.11	0.00	0.04	0.03	0.15	0.00	0.06
Elementary occupations	0.20	0.18	0.35	0.38	0.20	0.16	0.37	0.44

	Females	Males	Diff.	Females	Males	Diff.	Females	Males	Diff.	Females	Males	Diff.
Managers	1.88	2.44	-0.23	1.48	2.82	-0.47	2.80	3.44	-0.19	0.49	2.25	-0.78
Professionals	1.89	2.20	-0.14	6.39	1.29	3.97	2.76	2.87	-0.04	2.87	5.10	-0.44
Technicians	1.25	2.00	-0.38	1.72	2.42	-0.29	1.51	2.24	-0.33		5.73	
Clerks	1.38	1.50	-0.08	1.82	1.91	-0.05	1.81	2.09	-0.13	2.68	4.25	-0.37
Service workers and shop and market sales	1.13	1.56	-0.28	1.25	1.15	0.09	1.27	1.72	-0.26	1.37	1.72	-0.20
Skilled agricultural, forestry, and fishery	1.13	0.94	0.20	0.59	1.58	-0.62	1.26	1.15	0.10	0.84	1.15	-0.27
Craft and related trades workers	1.37	2.03	-0.32	2.44	2.00	0.22	1.72	2.68	-0.36	2.46	2.87	-0.14
Plant and machine operators and assemblers	1.81	1.88	-0.03		3.00		1.90	2.18	-0.13	0.82	2.87	-0.71
Elementary occupations	1.10	1.25	-0.12	1.07	1.14	-0.06	1.18	1.43	-0.18	1.06	1.37	-0.23

Source:ULMS

[a] Real hourly earnings.

[b]The % earnings differential is calculated as follows: (wf-wm)/wm. A negative number indicates that women earn less than men.

Exploiting the panel structure of the ULMS these patterns using the same set of matrices used by Maloney (1999) and Lehmann and Pignatti (2007) will be examined, with reference to the Mexican and Ukrainian labour markets. In this case, however, the sample will be split in two in order to test whether there are diverging patterns between males and females.

In the upper panel of Table 6 the raw transition probabilities across four states are reported (formal employment, informal employment, unemployment, out of the labour force) for females and males in the period 2003-2004. These probabilities assume that movements between states are governed by a Markov process[1] and are calculated as the ratio of the outflows from the origin state in 2003 to the destination state in 2004 over the total stock in the origin state in 2003[2].

Contrary to the expectations held, women in Ukraine show higher probability to remain in the formal sector and lower to remain in the informal sector. This reflects a lower share of women moving from formal to informal jobs, even more so if we consider that a higher percentage of women leaving formal employment move out of the labour force compared to men. A lower share of women leaving informal employment moves to formal employment relative to men. Women instead move more than men towards unemployment and out of the labour force, indicating perhaps higher barriers to entry into the formal segment for women coming from informality. Looking at transitions from unemployment, another diverging pattern between men and women can be identified. Most men (about two thirds) flowing out of unemployment tend to enter either the formal or the informal sector. Women flowing out of unemployment instead tend to go back to work only in about half of the cases while the remaining half moves out of the labour force. Indeed, this is just another confirmation of the worldwide tendency of women's participation rates to be lower than those of men. What is striking however is that most of the

---

[1] As argued in Bellmann et al. (1995), the assumption that movements between states are governed by a Markov process seems appropriate for an economy subject to sudden structural shocks, where individual work histories become of lesser importance. This is indeed the case for Ukraine, which, despite having started the transition process almost a decade ago is still in an early phase of transition in the period under exam

[2] One potential problem with these estimated probabilities might rise if "round tripping" problems were relevant. However, as discussed in Lehmann and Pignatti (2007) in this dataset round tripping is minimal.

difference between men and women appears to be due to a much lower fraction of women going back to work in the informal sector (9.4%) with respect to men (17.4%) while the fractions of the two groups of unemployed flowing back to work in the formal sector is very similar (25.3% for men against 24.8% for women).

The raw probabilities that have just been seen do not take into account the fact that departure and destination states may differ very much in terms of relative size and that labour market states' shares might grow and shrink at different paces in the period under exam (within the same group and/or between the two groups). In this case, for example, the size of the formal sector remains much larger in both periods for both males and females, but the relative importance of these sectors is different for the two groups, with formal employment being the state where more men can be found in both periods while out of the labour force is the state with the highest number of women in both periods. Informal employment's share is growing faster for men than for women. To take into account these effects in the analysis, the raw probabilities are standardized by the share of the destination state at the end of the period (P.j) obtaining the Q matrices (Maloney, 1999).

Even adjusting for the size of the terminal state, men show a higher probability to move from formal to informal employment and a higher probability to move from informality to formality. Women show instead a much higher probability to move from informality to unemployment rather than to go formal.

If we want to compare the results obtained and attempt to identify the "disposition" of individuals to move across sectors, we need to take into account how likely is an individual to leave the state he comes from and how difficult it can be finding an "opening" in a different state. This is the intuition behind the V matrix that we find at the bottom panel of the table. In practice, the values of the Q matrix are multiplied by the reciprocal of the outflow rate from the origin and destination states[3].

Both Ukrainian men and women show a higher disposition to move from the informal sector to the formal sector than vice versa. However, this effect appears to be stronger for women than for men. If we look at the

[3] Under Markovian assumptions, this corresponds to the duration of state occupancy (exponentially distributed). For a more detailed description of Q and V matrices, please see Lehmann and Pignatti (2007) or Maloney (1999).

unemployed, again men seem more likely to move to informality than formality, while for women the result is the opposite. Only when we look at individuals flowing back from out of the labour force, we see a common pattern (much stronger for females than for males, this time), that is, a higher propensity to enter in the informal sector rather than in the formal one. This result might indicate that individuals (especially women) with lower attachment to the labour force, when they decide to go back to work might prefer informal employment to formal employment (arguably for the same reasons that cause their low attachment).

Table 6. P, Q and V matrices built using observed transition probabilities

MALES					
TRANSITION PROBABILITIES : Pij					
	F	I	U	NLF	**Pi.**
Formal	**0.855**	0.042	0.035	0.067	0.492
Informal	0.271	**0.583**	0.069	0.076	0.054
Unem-ployed	0.253	0.174	0.368	0.205	0.107
Not in labor force	0.072	0.037	0.097	0.795	0.347
P.j	0.488	0.083	0.094	0.335	
Q MATRIX: Pij/P.j - "Probability standardized by size of the destination state at the end of the period"					
	F	I	U	NLF	
Formal		**0.508**	0.371	0.201	
Informal	**0.555**		0.739	0.228	
Unemployed	0.520	2.079		0.612	
Not in labor force	0.148	0.438	1.030		
V MATRIX: Pij / (P.j*(1-Pii)*(1-Pjj)) - "Disposition to move to a sector"					
	F	I	U	NLF	
Formal		**8.428**	4.058	6.779	
Informal	**9.214**		2.808	2.667	
Unemployed	5.686	7.897		4.716	
Not in labor force	4.973	5.117	7.939		

FEMALES					
TRANSITION PROBABILITIES : Pij					
	F	I	U	NLF	**Pi.**
Formal	**0.865**	0.022	0.036	0.077	0.384
Informal	0.200	**0.572**	0.117	0.110	0.038
Unem-ployed	0.248	0.094	0.313	0.345	0.080
Not in labor force	0.055	0.038	0.061	0.846	0.498
P.j	0.387	0.056	0.074	0.483	
Q MATRIX: Pij/P.j - "Probability standardized by size of the destination state at the end of the period"					
	F	I	U	NLF	
Formal		**0.382**	0.493	0.159	
Informal	**0.517**		1.589	0.229	
Unem-ployed	0.642	1.657		0.715	
Not in labor force	0.141	0.682	0.824		
V MATRIX: Pij / (P.j*(1-Pii)*(1-Pjj)) - "Disposition to move to a sector"					
	F	I	U	NLF	
Formal		**6.629**	5.325	7.672	
Informal	**8.966**		5.408	3.474	
Unem-ployed	6.929	6.133		6.762	
Not in labor force	6.799	10.358	7.795		

Source:ULMS

Note: **Pi.** is the relative size of a sector at the beginning of the period; **P.j** is the relative size of a sector at the end of a period.

Wages, employment status and gender differentials

After analysing labour market mobility, there is a focus on the way in which labour is remunerated in the formal and informal sectors, checking if the same mechanisms seem to hold for both men and women. In their study about labour market segmentation in Ukraine, Lehmann and Pignatti (2007) find that female workers in the formal sector are disadvantaged in both years with respect to men. This is also true for the informal sector, but only for the first period.

Their results, however, do not reveal anything about the determinants of this differential. In their model, in fact, coefficients for men and women are forced to be the same. It might be that coefficients for men and women are indeed the same, or that, instead, similar characteristics are remunerated differently according to the gender of the worker (this could be true, for example, if one of the two groups was discriminated against).

In this section two hypotheses are tested: whether this wage differential is due to a different remuneration of similar characteristics (coefficients) or to a difference in endowments (characteristics). There will also be an effort to will also try to identify the determinants of the log earnings in the two periods and in the two sectors of the labour market for men and for men and women, looking for additional evidence for or against labour market segmentation.

To decompose the wage differential, a twofold Oaxaca decomposition (Oaxaca, 1973) of the difference in mean predicted wages is performed, choosing males as the "non-discriminated group". This is the usual assumption in literature studying the gender wage differential. This procedure decomposes the difference in the mean predicted wages in an explained component (due in our case to differences in endowments between men and women) and an unexplained one (due to differences in coefficients and to the interaction of coefficients and endowments). To account for the possible presence of selection the Oaxaca decomposition correcting is also performed for selection as suggested in the literature (see for example Neuman and Oaxaca, 2004). The results of the OLS regressions (with and without correcting for selection) are reported in Tables 7 to 10.

The simple OLS regressions performed show the existence of some common trends, but also some differences across genders. Both in 2003 and 2004, for example, the formal sector remunerates more individuals (men and women) with higher human capital, while in the informal sector this does not seem to happen. In one case, (Table10), to higher age (my proxy for experience) is associated with a wage penalty. Another interesting result is represented by the dummy for the self employed in the informal sector that becomes significant and positive for both men and women in 2004. For women, also having chosen to work informally in

2004 leads to an increase in the expected wage. Unfortunately, however, when we look at median and robust regressions (Tables 11 to 18), the effect for women becomes insignificant. Suspecting that this, coherently with the most recent versions of the theory on market segmentation, might hide radically different behaviours in the top of the distribution with respect to the bottom, in addition to robust and median regressions two sets of quantile regressions calculated at the 10th percentile and at the 90th percentile were performed. The results of these regressions, at least for 2004, indeed show different patterns not only between genders but also within the genders themselves[4].

The first difference is related to the significance of the variables choice to be informal and self-employed. In the regression for males the coefficient remains significant at the median but it is not significant anymore in the tails of the distribution (10th and 90th percentile). For women the effect of these variables at the 10th percentile and at the median is insignificant. Women who choose the option to be informal salaried or self-employed provides them with a significant increase in the expected wage. This is a very interesting result, in line with what segmentation theories suggest: informal sector seems segmented in informal in the upper tier of the wage distribution appear to reap the (monetary) benefits of being informal, while those in the lower tiers do not. It is interesting to note that also in the formal sector the variable relative to self-employment is significantly positive only for the women in the upper tier of the distribution, while it is not so for men.

Going back to OLS, gender differences emerge also in other cases. For example, women working part-time experience in most cases (except in the formal sector in 2004), *ceteris paribus*, earn higher hourly salaries than women working full time, while this is not true for men[5]. Again, women seem to gain more from having university degree or higher.

[4] This does not happen for 2003. For completeness, even thought they will not be discussed here, I also add the tables for median and robust regressions relative to 2003

[5] This is confirmed by robust regressions, but it does not appear to be significant in quantile regressions.

Table 7. Log hourly earnings – Females – 2003

	OLS Without Selection		OLS With Selection	
	Informal	Formal	Informal	Formal
Age	-0.021	0.014	-0.072	-0.007
	(0.046)	(0.007)*	(0.071)	(0.015)
Age^2	0.000	-0.000	0.001	0.000
	(0.001)	(0.000)**	(0.001)	(0.000)
Secondary	-0.103	0.090	-0.137	0.059
	(0.145)	(0.041)**	(0.158)	(0.045)
University	0.246	0.408	0.488	0.334
	(0.276)	(0.049)***	(0.372)	(0.068)***
Tenure	0.036	0.006	0.020	0.006
	(0.060)	(0.004)	(0.069)	(0.004)
Tenure^2/100	-0.314	-0.008	-0.173	-0.007
	(0.413)	(0.011)	(0.446)	(0.011)
Positive Δ[a]	0.620	0.428	0.660	0.426
	(0.180)***	(0.112)***	(0.179)***	(0.111)***
Negative Δ[b]	-0.710	-0.604	-0.662	-0.611
	(0.464)	(0.069)***	(0.459)	(0.069)***
Choice Informality	0.061		0.108	
	(0.132)		(0.135)	
Self Employed	0.062	0.202	0.084	0.197
	(0.219)	(0.164)	(0.225)	(0.163)
Part time	0.446	0.147	0.435	0.144
	(0.211)**	(0.057)**	(0.210)**	(0.057)**
occupation4	-0.087	-0.054	-0.020	-0.056
	(0.381)	(0.040)	(0.367)	(0.040)
occupation5	-0.362	-0.215	-0.315	-0.212
	(0.245)	(0.048)***	(0.236)	(0.048)***
occupation6	-0.386	-0.102	-0.363	-0.103
	(0.605)	(0.154)	(0.605)	(0.153)
occupation7	0.171	-0.068	0.440	-0.070
	(0.391)	(0.055)	(0.415)	(0.055)
occupation8		0.040		0.041
		(0.082)		(0.082)
occupation9	-0.350	-0.181	-0.284	-0.179
	(0.300)	(0.037)***	(0.286)	(0.037)***
Industry	0.944	0.291	0.969	0.288
	(0.308)***	(0.060)***	(0.313)***	(0.060)***
Construction	1.493	0.264	1.276	0.256
	(0.266)***	(0.111)**	(0.297)***	(0.111)**

Services	0.786	0.081	0.815	0.079
	(0.260)***	(0.051)	(0.258)***	(0.051)
Other services and activities	0.731	0.113	0.698	0.111
	(0.298)**	(0.066)*	(0.310)**	(0.066)*
State	0.739	-0.196	0.847	-0.195
	(0.317)**	(0.043)***	(0.327)**	(0.043)***
Privatized	-0.355	-0.148	-0.439	-0.148
	(0.235)	(0.058)**	(0.239)*	(0.059)**
Cooperative		-0.643	-0.779	-0.635
		(0.142)***	(0.329)**	(0.139)***
lambda021			-0.698	
			(0.665)	
lambda011				-0.132
				(0.081)
Constant	0.301	0.316	2.430	0.825
	(0.956)	(0.163)*	(2.561)	(0.360)**
Observations	131	1573	131	1572
R-squared	0.34	0.29	0.35	0.29

Source:ULMS
Robust standard errors in parentheses
* significant at 10%; ** significant at 5%; *** significant at 1%
Default categories are: Elementary and less, highly skilled (ISCO 1 to 3), agriculture, hunting and fishing, newly established enterprises. Regional controls have been included in the regression but their coefficients have not been reported

Table 8. Log hourly earnings – Females – 2004

	OLS Without Selection		OLS With Selection	
	Informal	Formal	Informal	Formal
Age	0.031	0.001	-0.002	-0.019
	(0.032)	(0.008)	(0.048)	(0.019)
Age^2	-0.001	-0.000	-0.000	0.000
	(0.000)	(0.000)	(0.001)	(0.000)
Secondary	0.051	0.120	0.143	0.082
	(0.145)	(0.050)**	(0.155)	(0.058)
University	0.148	0.536	0.370	0.458
	(0.191)	(0.068)***	(0.258)	(0.092)***
Tenure	-0.022	0.012	-0.026	0.012
	(0.035)	(0.004)***	(0.034)	(0.004)***
$Tenure^2/100$	0.006	-0.022	0.024	-0.021
	(0.125)	(0.009)**	(0.121)	(0.009)**
Positive Δ^a		0.599		0.593
		(0.130)***		(0.128)***
Negative Δ^b	-0.814	-0.559	-0.725	-0.559
	(0.469)*	(0.133)***	(0.539)	(0.132)***
Choice Informality	0.266		0.280	
	(0.150)*		(0.151)*	
Self Employed	0.435	0.277	0.446	0.267
	(0.260)*	(0.253)	(0.266)*	(0.250)
Part time	0.511	0.054	0.515	0.066
	(0.243)**	(0.079)	(0.244)**	(0.081)
occupation4	0.542	-0.094	0.566	-0.103
	(0.418)	(0.051)*	(0.420)	(0.052)**
occupation5	0.216	-0.277	0.261	-0.274
	(0.352)	(0.067)***	(0.349)	(0.068)***
occupation6		-0.222		-0.220
		(0.139)		(0.138)
occupation7	0.956	-0.018	1.030	-0.019
	(0.363)***	(0.058)	(0.354)***	(0.058)
occupation8		0.069		0.071
		(0.095)		(0.095)
occupation9	0.275	-0.260	0.314	-0.260
	(0.302)	(0.048)***	(0.296)	(0.048)***
Industry	0.467	0.193	0.486	0.191
	(0.313)	(0.057)***	(0.321)	(0.057)***
Construction	0.614	0.199	0.654	0.218
	(0.412)	(0.100)**	(0.420)	(0.103)**

Services	0.393	0.151	0.395	0.149
	(0.282)	(0.050)***	(0.281)	(0.050)***
Other services and activities	0.825	0.102	0.833	0.106
	(0.340)**	(0.072)	(0.342)**	(0.072)
State	-0.584	-0.057	-0.483	-0.050
	(0.248)**	(0.049)	(0.294)	(0.049)
Privatized	-0.081	0.030	-0.096	0.032
	(0.180)	(0.056)	(0.184)	(0.056)
Cooperative		0.106		0.111
		(0.301)		(0.294)
lambda021			-0.445	
			(0.386)	
lambda011				-0.127
				(0.103)
Constant	-0.425	0.479	0.830	0.989
	(0.649)	(0.191)**	(1.411)	(0.470)**
Observations	162	1222	161	1213
R-squared	0.38	0.27	0.36	0.27

Source:ULMS

Robust standard errors in parentheses

* significant at 10%; ** significant at 5%; *** significant at 1%

Default categories are: Elementary and less, highly skilled (ISCO 1 to 3), agriculture, hunting and fishing, newly established enterprises. Regional controls have been included in the regression but their coefficients have not been reported.

Table 9. Log hourly earnings – Males – 2003

	OLS Without Selection		OLS With Selection	
	Informal	Formal	Informal	Formal
Age	-0.017	0.007	0.018	-0.021
	(0.037)	(0.010)	(0.052)	(0.017)
Age^2	0.000	-0.000	-0.000	0.000
	(0.000)	(0.000)	(0.001)	(0.000)
Secondary	0.142	0.086	0.031	0.052
	(0.201)	(0.043)**	(0.215)	(0.046)
University	0.267	0.238	0.156	0.156
	(0.277)	(0.073)***	(0.276)	(0.083)*
Tenure	0.066	0.013	0.070	0.013
	(0.059)	(0.006)**	(0.060)	(0.006)**
$Tenure^2/100$	-0.699	-0.028	-0.730	-0.028
	(0.384)*	(0.016)*	(0.388)*	(0.016)*
Positive Δ[a]		0.487		0.483
		(0.141)***		(0.142)***
Negative Δ[b]	-0.523	-0.674	-0.551	-0.679
	(0.440)	(0.088)***	(0.435)	(0.088)***
Choice Informality	-0.002		0.040	
	(0.191)		(0.199)	
Self Employed	0.145	0.185	0.159	0.192
	(0.198)	(0.155)	(0.204)	(0.155)
Part time	0.220	0.097	0.173	0.097
	(0.290)	(0.113)	(0.291)	(0.114)
occupation4	-0.353	-0.280	-0.253	-0.270
	(0.457)	(0.100)***	(0.466)	(0.100)***
occupation5	-0.926	-0.170	-0.845	-0.166
	(0.314)***	(0.111)	(0.335)**	(0.110)
occupation6	-0.086	-0.422	-0.090	-0.424
	(0.681)	(0.128)***	(0.672)	(0.128)***
occupation7	-0.383	-0.088	-0.393	-0.089
	(0.325)	(0.059)	(0.319)	(0.059)
occupation8	-0.084	-0.085	-0.097	-0.089
	(0.279)	(0.069)	(0.282)	(0.069)
occupation9	-0.262	-0.319	-0.285	-0.316
	(0.270)	(0.067)***	(0.265)	(0.067)***
Industry	0.887	0.615	0.883	0.619
	(0.283)***	(0.067)***	(0.286)***	(0.067)***
Construction	0.512	0.473	0.502	0.480
	(0.309)	(0.093)***	(0.303)	(0.092)***

Services	0.781	0.418	0.754	0.417
	(0.292)***	(0.068)***	(0.292)**	(0.067)***
Other services and activities	0.545	0.400	0.542	0.401
	(0.337)	(0.093)***	(0.332)	(0.092)***
State	-0.599	0.032	-0.752	0.031
	(0.416)	(0.056)	(0.378)**	(0.056)
Privatized	-0.615	0.000	-0.566	-0.004
	(0.253)**	(0.065)	(0.260)**	(0.064)
Cooperative		-0.492	-0.402	-0.476
		(0.176)***	(0.471)	(0.176)***
lambda021			0.686	
			(0.669)	
lambda011				-0.238
				(0.117)**
Constant	0.969	0.370	-0.712	1.066
	(0.891)	(0.198)*	(1.943)	(0.396)***
Observations	131	1312	131	1311
R-squared	0.34	0.31	0.34	0.31

Source:ULMS
Robust standard errors in parentheses
* significant at 10%; ** significant at 5%; *** significant at 1%
Default categories are: Elementary and less, highly skilled (ISCO 1 to 3), agriculture, hunting and fishing, newly established enterprises. Regional controls have been included in the regression but their coefficients have not been reported.

Table 10. Log hourly earnings – Males – 2004

	OLS Without Selection		OLS With Selection	
	Informal	Formal	Informal	Formal
Age	-0.075	0.025	-0.096	0.011
	(0.034)**	(0.010)**	(0.046)**	(0.017)
Age^2	0.001	-0.000	0.001	-0.000
	(0.000)*	(0.000)***	(0.001)*	(0.000)
Secondary	0.202	0.147	0.186	0.129
	(0.135)	(0.051)***	(0.191)	(0.056)**
University	0.066	0.341	0.130	0.297
	(0.287)	(0.076)***	(0.389)	(0.092)***
Tenure	-0.027	0.009	-0.020	0.009
	(0.045)	(0.006)	(0.047)	(0.006)
$Tenure^2/100$	0.168	-0.011	0.135	-0.012
	(0.183)	(0.015)	(0.189)	(0.015)
Positive Δ[a]		0.119		0.115
		(0.209)		(0.211)
Negative Δ[b]	-0.942	-0.767	-0.858	-0.721
	(0.289)***	(0.134)***	(0.294)***	(0.132)***
Choice Informality	0.100		0.141	
	(0.153)		(0.163)	
Self Employed	0.366	0.010	0.424	0.010
	(0.173)**	(0.148)	(0.178)**	(0.148)
Part time	0.055	-0.044	-0.001	-0.049
	(0.325)	(0.141)	(0.335)	(0.148)
occupation4	0.250	-0.136	0.882	-0.152
	(0.472)	(0.091)	(0.315)***	(0.095)
occupation5	-0.138	-0.189	-0.187	-0.187
	(0.315)	(0.115)	(0.315)	(0.116)
occupation6	0.437	-0.583	0.473	-0.597
	(0.336)	(0.148)***	(0.343)	(0.150)***
occupation7	0.004	-0.099	0.015	-0.105
	(0.251)	(0.056)*	(0.251)	(0.056)*
occupation8	0.064	-0.142	0.068	-0.137
	(0.343)	(0.070)**	(0.350)	(0.071)*
occupation9	-0.566	-0.427	-0.563	-0.434
	(0.232)**	(0.078)***	(0.237)**	(0.078)***
Industry	0.237	0.464	0.255	0.478
	(0.267)	(0.074)***	(0.272)	(0.074)***
Construction	0.252	0.419	0.263	0.437
	(0.273)	(0.092)***	(0.278)	(0.094)***

Services	0.184	0.223	0.174	0.246
	(0.266)	(0.070)***	(0.266)	(0.070)***
Other services and activities	0.041	0.156	0.263	0.157
	(0.311)	(0.094)*	(0.349)	(0.092)*
State	0.044	0.106	0.077	0.101
	(0.264)	(0.062)*	(0.259)	(0.062)
Privatized	0.264	0.005	0.292	0.005
	(0.178)	(0.066)	(0.192)	(0.066)
Cooperative	0.800	-0.157	0.725	-0.207
	(0.282)***	(0.212)	(0.310)**	(0.246)
lambda021			-0.077	
			(0.410)	
lambda011				-0.130
				(0.115)
Constant	2.524	0.500	2.978	0.848
	(0.761)***	(0.224)**	(1.285)**	(0.416)**
Observations	164	1020	156	1004
R-squared	0.30	0.29	0.33	0.29

Source:ULMS
Robust standard errors in parentheses
* significant at 10%; ** significant at 5%; *** significant at 1%
Default categories are: Elementary and less, highly skilled (ISCO 1 to 3), agriculture, hunting and fishing, newly established enterprises. Regional controls have been included in the regression but their coefficients have not been reported.

Table 11. Quantile regressions 10th , median and 90th percentile – Females – 2003

	Informal			Formal		
	P10	Median	P90	P10	Median	P90
Age	0.003	0.025	-0.019	0.011	0.013	0.015
	(0.058)	(0.060)	(0.072)	(0.010)	(0.010)	(0.014)
Age^2	-0.000	-0.000	0.000	-0.000	-0.000	-0.000
	(0.001)	(0.001)	(0.001)	(0.000)	(0.000)	(0.000)
Secondary	0.140	0.001	-0.182	0.013	0.097	0.125
	(0.254)	(0.228)	(0.325)	(0.046)	(0.040)**	(0.077)
University	0.244	0.179	0.143	0.188	0.432	0.454
	(0.335)	(0.336)	(0.591)	(0.051)***	(0.055)***	(0.097)***
Tenure	-0.006	-0.000	0.047	0.007	0.004	0.014
	(0.092)	(0.080)	(0.112)	(0.006)	(0.005)	(0.007)**
Tenure^2/100	0.030	0.159	-0.741	-0.014	-0.003	-0.022
	(0.841)	(0.759)	(1.409)	(0.018)	(0.013)	(0.019)
Positive Δ[a]	0.678	0.619	0.101	0.337	0.406	0.602
	(0.480)	(0.299)**	(0.234)	(0.129)***	(0.148)***	(0.339)*
Negative Δ[b]	-0.834	-0.775	-1.345	-0.956	-0.507	-0.496
	(0.813)	(0.749)	(0.791)*	(0.127)***	(0.077)***	(0.105)***
Choice Informality	-0.088	0.125	0.173			
	(0.211)	(0.209)	(0.279)			
Self Employed	-0.151	-0.018	0.326	-0.015	0.131	1.170
	(0.350)	(0.276)	(0.419)	(0.312)	(0.176)	(0.387)***
Part time	1.089	0.621	0.018	0.009	0.097	0.214
	(0.429)**	(0.273)**	(0.375)	(0.061)	(0.081)	(0.095)**
occupation4	0.782	-0.030	-0.962	-0.027	-0.074	-0.056
	(0.563)	(0.573)	(0.725)	(0.059)	(0.050)	(0.082)
occupation5	0.428	-0.220	-1.203	-0.251	-0.202	-0.257
	(0.455)	(0.375)	(0.568)**	(0.073)***	(0.059)***	(0.092)***
occupation6	-0.037	0.135	-0.906	-0.781	-0.073	-0.202
	(0.668)	(0.997)	(1.016)	(0.601)	(0.102)	(0.277)
occupation7	1.024	0.387	-0.503	-0.210	-0.075	0.145
	(0.695)	(0.679)	(0.974)	(0.070)***	(0.069)	(0.093)
occupation8		-0.065		-0.124	-0.238	-0.015
		(0.442)		(0.111)	(0.075)***	(0.224)
occupation9	0.297		-1.148	-0.163	0.092	-0.211
	(0.444)		(0.554)**	(0.045)***	(0.133)	(0.091)**
Industry	0.445	-0.202	0.555	0.438	-0.181	0.167
	(0.575)	(0.418)	(0.591)	(0.128)***	(0.039)***	(0.087)*

Construction	1.538	0.914	0.760	0.482	0.206	0.157
	(0.832)*	(0.480)*	(0.749)	(0.216)**	(0.061)***	(0.155)
Services	0.685	1.491	0.696	0.242	0.220	-0.002
	(0.391)*	(0.696)**	(0.401)*	(0.123)**	(0.124)*	(0.074)
Other services and activities	-0.044	0.735	0.586	0.296	-0.015	-0.004
	(0.617)	(0.351)**	(0.487)	(0.141)**	(0.040)	(0.094)
State	1.133	0.609	-0.298	-0.047	0.019	-0.259
	(0.774)	(0.463)	(0.654)	(0.076)	(0.068)	(0.077)***
Privatized	-1.053	0.985	-0.820	-0.025	-0.221	-0.035
	(0.515)**	(0.537)*	(0.556)	(0.096)	(0.069)***	(0.119)
Cooperative		-0.227		-0.016	-0.226	-0.735
		(0.349)		(0.155)	(0.076)***	(0.287)**
Constant	-0.732	-0.603	1.901	-0.420	0.392	0.966
	(1.332)	(1.332)	(1.346)	(0.247)*	(0.231)*	(0.301)***
Observations	131	131	131	1573	1573	1573

Source:ULMS

Robust standard errors in parentheses

* significant at 10%; ** significant at 5%; *** significant at 1%

Default categories are: Elementary and less, highly skilled (ISCO 1 to 3), agriculture, hunting and fishing, newly established enterprises. Regional controls have been included in the regression but their coefficients have not been reported.

Table 12. Quantile regressions 10th , median and 90th percentile – Females – 2004

	Informal			Formal		
	P10	Median	P90	P10	Median	P90
Age	-0.000	0.032	0.048	-0.001	0.008	0.011
	(0.048)	(0.037)	(0.050)	(0.009)	(0.009)	(0.018)
Age^2	0.000	-0.000	-0.001	0.000	-0.000	-0.000
	(0.001)	(0.001)	(0.001)	(0.000)	(0.000)	(0.000)
Secondary	-0.168	-0.078	0.097	0.192	0.071	0.062
	(0.206)	(0.161)	(0.223)	(0.113)*	(0.045)	(0.125)
University	-0.184	-0.052	-0.420	0.440	0.454	0.663
	(0.327)	(0.257)	(0.364)	(0.131)***	(0.058)***	(0.173)***
Tenure	-0.067	-0.014	-0.084	0.007	0.008	0.015
	(0.059)	(0.056)	(0.072)	(0.005)	(0.004)**	(0.009)*
$Tenure^2/100$	0.149	-0.053	0.203	-0.007	-0.017	-0.032
	(0.244)	(0.207)	(0.301)	(0.011)	(0.009)*	(0.022)
Positive Δ[a]				0.528	0.802	0.246
				(0.194)***	(0.265)***	(0.135)*
Negative Δ[b]	-1.932	-1.476	-0.078	-1.217	-0.520	-0.009
	(0.791)**	(0.798)*	(0.721)	(0.247)***	(0.115)***	(0.324)
Choice Informality	0.137	0.266	0.605			
	(0.216)	(0.192)	(0.255)**			
Self Employed	-0.441	0.169	1.479	-0.487	0.310	1.228
	(0.449)	(0.321)	(0.611)**	(0.325)	(0.266)	(0.723)*
Part time	-0.295	0.497	0.279	-0.074	0.099	0.081
	(0.456)	(0.393)	(0.512)	(0.081)	(0.095)	(0.160)
occupation4	1.183	0.809	0.631	-0.194	-0.103	-0.003
	(0.789)	(0.644)	(0.908)	(0.056)***	(0.057)*	(0.158)
occupation5	0.995	0.162	0.472	-0.325	-0.283	-0.376
	(0.626)	(0.490)	(0.735)	(0.121)***	(0.059)***	(0.113)***
occupation6				-0.361	-0.246	-0.230
				(0.199)*	(0.170)	(0.384)
occupation7	1.688	0.803	0.596	-0.072	-0.088	0.008
	(0.690)**	(0.544)	(0.686)	(0.076)	(0.062)	(0.108)
occupation8				-0.025	-0.043	0.164
				(0.152)	(0.112)	(0.233)
occupation9	0.465	0.223	0.358	-0.238	-0.259	-0.293
	(0.591)	(0.433)	(0.670)	(0.064)***	(0.041)***	(0.106)***
Industry	0.009	0.296	1.252	0.066	0.275	0.264
	(0.600)	(0.423)	(0.663)*	(0.077)	(0.056)***	(0.132)**

Construction	-0.424	0.660	1.361	0.232	0.240	0.144
	(0.755)	(0.620)	(0.928)	(0.146)	(0.127)*	(0.184)
Services	-0.426	0.275	0.485	0.016	0.131	0.278
	(0.537)	(0.367)	(0.552)	(0.058)	(0.047)***	(0.114)**
Other services and activities	-1.068	0.394	1.321	0.007	0.116	0.207
	(0.643)*	(0.556)	(0.591)**	(0.097)	(0.073)	(0.158)
State	-0.041	-0.464	-0.419	0.041	-0.082	-0.063
	(0.687)	(0.537)	(0.824)	(0.086)	(0.052)	(0.106)
Privatized	-0.014	-0.194	0.349	0.046	0.050	0.002
	(0.305)	(0.249)	(0.381)	(0.114)	(0.058)	(0.101)
Cooperative				-0.295	0.375	0.043
				(0.627)	(0.322)	(0.233)
Constant	-0.274	-0.078	-0.724	0.020	0.291	0.831
	(0.961)	(0.828)	(1.202)	(0.230)	(0.225)	(0.388)**
Observations	162	162	162	1222	1222	1222

Source:ULMS
Robust standard errors in parentheses
* significant at 10%; ** significant at 5%; *** significant at 1%
Default categories are: Elementary and less, highly skilled (ISCO 1 to 3), agriculture, hunting and fishing, newly established enterprises. Regional controls have been included in the regression but their coefficients have not been reported.

Table 13. Quantile regressions 10th , median and 90th percentile – Males – 2003

	Informal			Formal		
	P10	Median	P90	P10	Median	P90
Age	-0.041	-0.044	0.005	-0.008	0.024	0.034
	(0.077)	(0.055)	(0.066)	(0.013)	(0.011)**	(0.015)**
Age^2	0.001	0.000	-0.000	0.000	-0.000	-0.000
	(0.001)	(0.001)	(0.001)	(0.000)	(0.000)***	(0.000)***
Secondary	0.165	-0.029	-0.013	0.017	0.109	0.047
	(0.363)	(0.278)	(0.221)	(0.071)	(0.043)**	(0.077)
University	0.262	0.016	-0.008	0.117	0.241	0.193
	(0.551)	(0.403)	(0.394)	(0.073)	(0.071)***	(0.122)
Tenure	0.006	0.040	0.120	0.016	0.009	0.000
	(0.137)	(0.098)	(0.093)	(0.010)	(0.007)	(0.007)
$Tenure^2/100$	0.014	-0.555	-0.979	-0.036	-0.008	-0.002
	(1.009)	(0.716)	(0.806)	(0.032)	(0.019)	(0.019)
Positive Δ[a]				0.512	0.447	0.725
				(0.208)**	(0.176)**	(0.359)**
Negative Δ[b]	-1.219	-0.427	0.644	-1.048	-0.650	-0.419
	(0.848)	(0.726)	(0.871)	(0.193)***	(0.102)***	(0.110)***
Choice Informality	-0.241	0.027	-0.124			
	(0.358)	(0.313)	(0.290)			
Self Employed	-0.096	0.247	0.378	-0.371	0.119	0.602
	(0.375)	(0.286)	(0.334)	(0.210)*	(0.199)	(0.359)*
Part time	-0.109	0.140	0.422	0.111	-0.057	0.400
	(0.570)	(0.425)	(0.420)	(0.133)	(0.078)	(0.342)
occupation4	-0.811	0.302	-0.659	-0.319	-0.277	-0.208
	(0.917)	(0.803)	(0.688)	(0.100)***	(0.114)**	(0.163)
occupation5	-0.888	-0.843	-1.426	-0.060	-0.130	-0.296
	(0.551)	(0.544)	(0.553)**	(0.176)	(0.147)	(0.196)
occupation6	-0.929	-0.100	-0.270	-0.562	-0.420	-0.427
	(1.268)	(1.060)	(0.656)	(0.262)**	(0.106)***	(0.237)*
occupation7	-0.310	-0.163	-0.461	-0.154	-0.073	-0.102
	(0.661)	(0.474)	(0.407)	(0.077)**	(0.056)	(0.092)
occupation8	0.278	0.095	-0.573	-0.200	-0.055	-0.092
	(0.513)	(0.466)	(0.463)	(0.106)*	(0.075)	(0.113)
occupation9	-0.512	-0.352	-0.487	-0.415	-0.335	-0.367
	(0.562)	(0.432)	(0.344)	(0.083)***	(0.064)***	(0.114)***
Industry	1.247	0.496	0.421	0.749	0.510	0.555
	(0.686)*	(0.426)	(0.395)	(0.108)***	(0.060)***	(0.118)***

Construction	0.565	0.413	0.660	0.580	0.319	0.453
	(0.666)	(0.442)	(0.329)**	(0.125)***	(0.146)**	(0.137)***
Services	1.359	0.550	1.085	0.528	0.278	0.409
	(0.570)**	(0.445)	(0.285)***	(0.111)***	(0.063)***	(0.125)***
Other services and activities	0.480	0.606	0.759	0.477	0.212	0.485
	(0.661)	(0.490)	(0.573)	(0.148)***	(0.101)**	(0.197)**
State	-0.154	-0.678	-0.916	0.095	-0.056	0.028
	(0.985)	(0.704)	(1.084)	(0.091)	(0.072)	(0.102)
Privatized	-0.642	-0.494	-0.860	0.154	-0.052	-0.068
	(0.623)	(0.406)	(0.374)**	(0.084)*	(0.079)	(0.113)
Cooperative		-0.788		-0.164	-0.372	-0.771
		(0.555)		(0.285)	(0.073)***	(0.288)***
Constant	0.283	1.717	1.584	-0.228	0.225	0.667
	(1.750)	(1.390)	(1.382)	(0.269)	(0.231)	(0.373)*
Observations	131	131	131	1312	1312	1312

Source:ULMS
Robust standard errors in parentheses
* significant at 10%; ** significant at 5%; *** significant at 1%
Default categories are: Elementary and less, highly skilled (ISCO 1 to 3), agriculture, hunting and fishing, newly established enterprises. Regional controls have been included in the regression but their coefficients have not been reported.

Table 14. Quantile regressions 10th , median and 90th percentile – Males – 2004

	Informal			Formal		
	P10	Median	P90	P10	Median	P90
Age	-0.093	-0.102	0.020	0.019	0.029	0.036
	(0.071)	(0.044)**	(0.062)	(0.016)	(0.011)***	(0.019)*
Age^2	0.001	0.001	-0.000	-0.000	-0.000	-0.001
	(0.001)	(0.001)**	(0.001)	(0.000)	(0.000)***	(0.000)**
Secondary	-0.094	0.247	0.483	0.189	0.131	0.248
	(0.257)	(0.180)	(0.272)*	(0.090)**	(0.055)**	(0.123)**
University	0.474	0.137	-0.052	0.313	0.313	0.599
	(0.626)	(1.436)	(1.337)	(0.116)***	(0.078)***	(0.173)***
Tenure	0.067	-0.035	-0.001	0.008	0.016	0.015
	(0.114)	(0.105)	(0.127)	(0.010)	(0.006)***	(0.015)
Tenure^2/100	-0.200	0.176	-0.003	-0.014	-0.022	-0.026
	(0.832)	(0.998)	(1.034)	(0.024)	(0.018)	(0.036)
Positive Δ^a				-0.145	0.180	-0.252
				(0.433)	(0.368)	(0.229)
Negative Δ^b	-0.352	-0.376	-2.190	-1.151	-0.749	-0.273
	(0.420)	(0.549)	(0.864)**	(0.170)***	(0.204)***	(0.183)
Choice Informality	0.085	0.046	-0.171			
	(0.353)	(0.204)	(0.295)			
Self Employed	0.104	0.393	0.325	-0.294	0.126	0.157
	(0.441)	(0.230)*	(0.240)	(0.372)	(0.127)	(0.313)
Part time	0.308	0.134	-0.177	-0.188	-0.020	0.578
	(0.844)	(0.489)	(0.518)	(0.152)	(0.225)	(0.425)
occupation4	0.276	0.612	-0.570	-0.143	-0.123	-0.299
	(0.691)	(0.611)	(0.606)	(0.134)	(0.105)	(0.284)
occupation5	0.412	-0.469	0.327	-0.187	-0.283	-0.076
	(0.471)	(0.535)	(0.806)	(0.293)	(0.135)**	(0.217)
occupation6	1.415	0.807	-0.607	-0.806	-0.437	-0.737
	(0.800)*	(0.478)*	(0.634)	(0.299)***	(0.175)**	(0.270)***
occupation7	0.101	0.082	-0.138	-0.107	-0.042	-0.227
	(0.557)	(0.388)	(0.437)	(0.086)	(0.063)	(0.103)**
occupation8	-0.032	0.133	0.253	-0.203	-0.168	-0.037
	(0.675)	(0.501)	(0.633)	(0.098)**	(0.073)**	(0.156)
occupation9	-0.310	-0.457	-0.661	-0.530	-0.400	-0.419
	(0.403)	(0.352)	(0.442)	(0.122)***	(0.077)***	(0.127)***
Industry	0.516	0.485	0.016	0.528	0.446	0.442
	(0.445)	(0.387)	(0.431)	(0.124)***	(0.072)***	(0.170)***

Construction	0.244	0.511	-0.334	0.320	0.399	0.374
	(0.396)	(0.390)	(0.473)	(0.183)*	(0.098)***	(0.198)*
Services	0.314	0.489	0.049	0.173	0.291	0.156
	(0.432)	(0.417)	(0.452)	(0.121)	(0.072)***	(0.156)
Other services and activities	-0.117	0.408	-0.736	0.179	0.089	0.214
	(0.586)	(0.485)	(0.571)	(0.177)	(0.114)	(0.195)
State	0.474	0.343	0.303	0.089	0.027	0.097
	(0.592)	(0.427)	(0.637)	(0.101)	(0.060)	(0.130)
Privatized	0.450	0.243	-0.033	0.026	-0.014	-0.044
	(0.423)	(0.265)	(0.315)	(0.111)	(0.068)	(0.127)
Cooperative	1.422	1.100	-0.130	0.194	-0.193	0.241
	(0.786)*	(0.499)**	(0.414)	(0.300)	(0.297)	(0.545)
Constant	2.156	2.573	1.686	-0.119	0.493	0.796
	(1.634)	(1.109)**	(1.127)	(0.426)	(0.240)**	(0.486)
Observations	164	164	164	1020	1020	1020

Source:ULMS
Robust standard errors in parentheses
* significant at 10%; ** significant at 5%; *** significant at 1%
Default categories are: Elementary and less, highly skilled (ISCO 1 to 3), agriculture, hunting and fishing, newly established enterprises. Regional controls have been included in the regression but their coefficients have not been reported.

Table 15. Robust regression – Females – 2003

	Informal	Formal
Age	-0.001	0.012
	(0.042)	(0.007)*
Age^2	-0.000	-0.000
	(0.001)	(0.000)**
Secondary	-0.068	0.095
	(0.181)	(0.037)***
University	0.074	0.399
	(0.277)	(0.045)***
Tenure	0.006	0.006
	(0.058)	(0.004)
$Tenure^2/100$	0.019	-0.008
	(0.447)	(0.010)
Positive Δ^a		0.357
		(0.082)***
Negative Δ^b	-0.669	-0.515
	(0.442)	(0.048)***
Choice Informality	0.023	
	(0.178)	
Self Employed	-0.089	0.008
	(0.204)	(0.084)
Part time	0.605	0.080
	(0.229)***	(0.046)*
occupation4	-0.114	-0.073
	(0.444)	(0.039)*
occupation5	-0.247	-0.245
	(0.253)	(0.043)***
occupation6	-0.692	-0.041
	(0.400)*	(0.111)
occupation7	0.161	-0.044
	(0.446)	(0.045)
occupation8	0.000	0.084
	(0.000)	(0.076)
occupation9	-0.298	-0.198
	(0.236)	(0.036)***
Industry	0.896	0.190
	(0.326)***	(0.049)***
Construction	1.459	0.264
	(0.557)**	(0.088)***
Services	0.722	0.006
	(0.207)***	(0.043)

Other services and activities	0.705	0.026
	(0.277)**	(0.056)
State	0.822	-0.201
	(0.547)	(0.040)***
Privatized	-0.245	-0.138
	(0.296)	(0.053)***
Cooperative		-0.669
		(0.184)***
Center North	-0.411	-0.288
	(0.310)	(0.045)***
Constant	0.207	0.389
	(0.808)	(0.149)***
Observations	131	1573
R-squared	0.38	0.29

Source:ULMS
Robust standard errors in parentheses
* significant at 10%; ** significant at 5%; *** significant at 1%
Default categories are: Elementary and less, highly skilled (ISCO 1 to 3), agriculture, hunting and fishing, newly established enterprises. Regional controls have been included in the regression but their coefficients have not been reported.

Table 16. Robust regression – Females – 2004

	Informal	Formal
Age	0.006	0.005
	(0.029)	(0.008)
Age^2	-0.000	-0.000
	(0.000)	(0.000)
Secondary	0.026	0.117
	(0.137)	(0.046)**
University	0.148	0.487
	(0.220)	(0.055)***
Tenure	0.008	0.010
	(0.031)	(0.004)**
$Tenure^2/100$	-0.096	-0.019
	(0.122)	(0.010)*
Positive Δ[a]	0.000	0.647
	(0.000)	(0.156)***
Negative Δ[b]	-1.014	-0.558
	(0.330)***	(0.081)***
Choice Informality	0.177	
	(0.142)	
Self Employed	0.212	0.093
	(0.217)	(0.113)
Part time	0.415	0.046
	(0.208)**	(0.060)
occupation4	0.532	-0.086
	(0.348)	(0.046)*
occupation5	0.145	-0.278
	(0.240)	(0.053)***
occupation6	0.000	-0.222
	(0.000)	(0.137)
occupation7	0.960	-0.012
	(0.310)***	(0.054)
occupation8	0.000	0.015
	(0.000)	(0.088)
occupation9	0.173	-0.259
	(0.222)	(0.043)***
Industry	0.304	0.241
	(0.278)	(0.055)***
Construction	0.466	0.240
	(0.420)	(0.111)**
Services	0.301	0.149
	(0.234)	(0.048)***

Other services and activities	0.745	0.146
	(0.246)***	(0.068)**
State	-0.592	-0.084
	(0.337)*	(0.045)*
Privatized	0.000	0.440
	(0.000)	(0.200)**
Cooperative	-0.140	0.019
	(0.183)	(0.052)
Constant	0.238	0.371
	(0.646)	(0.180)**
Observations	162	1222
R-squared	0.39	0.30

Source:ULMS

Robust standard errors in parentheses

* significant at 10%; ** significant at 5%; *** significant at 1%

Default categories are: Elementary and less, highly skilled (ISCO 1 to 3), agriculture, hunting and fishing, newly established enterprises. Regional controls have been included in the regression but their coefficients have not been reported.

Table 17. Robust regression – Males – 2003

	Informal	Formal
Age	-0.047	0.015
	(0.038)	(0.009)*
Age^2	0.000	-0.000
	(0.001)	(0.000)**
Secondary	-0.111	0.098
	(0.170)	(0.040)**
University	0.014	0.229
	(0.259)	(0.060)***
Tenure	0.105	0.009
	(0.057)*	(0.005)*
$Tenure^2/100$	-0.742	-0.014
	(0.435)*	(0.014)
Positive Δ[a]		0.396
		(0.117)***
Negative Δ[b]	-0.222	-0.616
	(0.352)	(0.059)***
Choice Informality	0.003	
	(0.208)	
Self Employed	0.261	0.045
	(0.202)	(0.103)
Part time	0.228	-0.030
	(0.295)	(0.089)
occupation4	-0.357	-0.322
	(0.451)	(0.088)***
occupation5	-0.912	-0.138
	(0.330)***	(0.101)
occupation6	0.186	-0.390
	(0.472)	(0.105)***
occupation7	-0.531	-0.083
	(0.282)*	(0.050)*
occupation8	0.003	-0.073
	(0.389)	(0.063)
occupation9	-0.384	-0.320
	(0.244)	(0.056)***
Industry	0.702	0.570
	(0.319)**	(0.056)***
Construction	0.649	0.415
	(0.255)**	(0.082)***
Services	0.702	0.350
	(0.254)***	(0.056)***

Other services and activities	0.550	0.307
	(0.298)*	(0.079)***
State	-0.787	-0.019
	(0.651)	(0.049)
Privatized	-0.386	-0.053
	(0.334)	(0.060)
Cooperative		-0.467
		(0.239)*
Constant	1.967	0.329
	(0.817)**	(0.185)*
Observations	131	1312
R-squared	0.37	0.30

Source:ULMS
Robust standard errors in parentheses
* significant at 10%; ** significant at 5%; *** significant at 1%
Default categories are: Elementary and less, highly skilled (ISCO 1 to 3), agriculture, hunting and fishing, newly established enterprises. Regional controls have been included in the regression but their coefficients have not been reported.

Table 18. Robust regression – Males – 2004

	Informal	Formal
Age	-0.086	0.023
	(0.035)**	(0.009)**
Age^2	0.001	-0.000
	(0.000)**	(0.000)***
Secondary	0.230	0.166
	(0.147)	(0.051)***
University	0.030	0.336
	(0.421)	(0.073)***
Tenure	-0.029	0.012
	(0.044)	(0.006)**
$Tenure^2/100$	0.181	-0.015
	(0.219)	(0.016)
Positive Δ[a]	0.000	0.161
	(0.000)	(0.232)
Negative Δ[b]	-0.801	-0.818
	(0.588)	(0.095)***
Choice Informality	0.124	
	(0.173)	
Self Employed	0.395	0.006
	(0.168)**	(0.102)
Part time	0.389	-0.148
	(0.252)	(0.107)
occupation4	0.289	-0.159
	(0.600)	(0.098)
occupation5	-0.240	-0.223
	(0.318)	(0.109)**
occupation6	0.582	-0.500
	(0.838)	(0.126)***
occupation7	0.013	-0.082
	(0.239)	(0.058)
occupation8	0.015	-0.142
	(0.336)	(0.066)**
occupation9	-0.516	-0.368
	(0.208)**	(0.069)***
Industry	0.519	0.462
	(0.246)**	(0.063)***
Construction	0.541	0.448
	(0.227)**	(0.088)***
Services	0.409	0.244
	(0.240)*	(0.062)***

Other services and activities	0.125	0.180
	(0.308)	(0.090)**
State	0.057	0.025
	(0.408)	(0.054)
Privatized	0.240	-0.053
	(0.278)	(0.058)
Cooperative	0.809	-0.221
	(0.814)	(0.222)
Constant	2.377	0.514
	(0.761)***	(0.210)**
Observations	164	1020
R-squared	0.35	0.31

Source:ULMS
Robust standard errors in parentheses
* significant at 10%; ** significant at 5%; *** significant at 1%

Default categories are: Elementary and less, highly skilled (ISCO 1 to 3), agriculture, hunting and fishing, newly established enterprises. Regional controls have been included in the regression but their coefficients have not been reported.

Looking at quantile regressions it can be seen that these gains are larger for those at the top of the distribution and lower for those at the bottom[6].

To control for selection a second set of OLS regressions is also run, where the selection equation was estimated with a multinomial logit model, following the methodology suggested by Lee (1983). The results in columns 3 and 4 of Tables 7 to 10, however, do not differ significantly from those of the OLS regressions without selection. Only in one case does the selection term become significant, in the case of men working in the formal sector in 2004.

After estimating wage equations, the Oaxaca decomposition of the earning differential between men and women can be implemented. As there is an effort to test if earnings dynamics differ, not only between genders in general, but also within the different sectors, the Oaxaca decomposition separately is appled to the two sectors. The results of the Oaxaca decomposition (adjusted and not adjusted for selection) are in

[6] In 2004 most sectorial coefficients turn out to be insignificant in the informal sector, except the coefficient for Other services and activities for women, showing a significant and positive effect on wages

Table 19[7].

Looking at the decomposition not adjusted for selection it can be seen that in both sectors the difference in the mean predicted earnings is fairly similar (slightly higher in the formal sector in 2003 and in the informal sector in 2004). However, when one looks at the decomposition of the differential, a big difference emerges. While in the informal sector the positive differential of men is almost entirely due to differences in characteristics (personal characteristics, job characteristics or sector characteristics), in the formal sector the differential appears to be due to unexplained factors. When one adjusts for selection, the main conclusions do not change for the formal sector, with an increase in the predicted differential in 2003 and a reduction in the predicted differential for 2004. For the informal sector, instead, the estimated gender differential becomes insignificant. However, given the loss of precision of the predicted differential due to the introduction of the selection term in the regression and taking into account that the selection term is never significant in the present regressions for the informal sector, the possibility that the correct decomposition results are unadjusted ones cannot be excluded.

Overall, these results seem to confirm the existence of gender "discrimination" in the formal sector. For the informal sector instead, maybe because of stronger competition between employers, earnings differentials appear to be in line with the different characteristics associated with the individual and with the type of job. Therefore, if discriminatory behaviours take place, they might be in the form of vertical segregation that is allowing men to have a faster career progression with respect to women and segregating women at the lower levels of the hierarchy. This however might also be simply the consequence of the greater desire of flexibility by women, self selecting themselves in positions characterized by lower responsibilities.

[7] The standard errors are calculated using the procedure developed by Jann (2005) for STATA.

Table 19. Gender wage gap – Oaxaca decomposition not adjusted and adjusted for selection – 2003 and 2004

	2003			
	Formal		Informal	
	Not adjusted	Adjusted	Not adjusted	Adjusted
Difference	0.234***	0.298***	0.195*	-2.540
Explained[a]	-0.003	0.013	0.221**	0.222*
Unexplained[b]	0.236***	0.285***	-0.027	-2.762
	2004			
	Formal		Informal	
	Not adjusted	Adjusted	Not adjusted	Adjusted
Difference	0.238***	0.228**	0.280***	-0.436
Explained	-0.005	0.011	0.286**	0.268***
Unexplained	0.243***	0.218*	-0.006	-0.704

Source:ULMS
Notes:
Reference (non-discriminated) group is males.
[a] Endowments
[b] Coefficients and interaction between coefficients and endowments
* significant at 10%; ** significant at 5%; *** significant at 1%

Conclusions

In this paper several differences in the patterns characterizing the participation of men and women to the labour market have been identified. These results show a picture of the labour market that is very different from the one that characterizes labour markets of developing countries and from what is predicted by labour market theories.

Ukrainian women are on average much more educated than women in developing countries and they also tend to show higher participation rates, albeit smaller than men's. They are also at least as educated as Ukrainian men.

Both men and women show higher propensity to go to the formal sector from the informal one than vice versa. However, this effect is much stronger for women than for men. This result is surprising, as segmented labour market theories predict a higher concentration of women in the informal sector, both for demand side and supply side reasons.

On average, Ukrainian women do earn less than men and this is true both in the formal and in the informal sector. However, when the gender earnings differential is decomposed evidence of very different patterns in the two sectors is found. In the formal sector the earnings differential is entirely due to the unexplained component, usually taken as an indicator of wage discrimination. In the informal sector, on the contrary, when the earnings differential is significantly different from zero it is entirely due to differences in the explained component (personal, household and job characteristics). This can be interpreted as an indication that, probably because of the greater competition in the informal sector, it might be more difficult to discriminate women paying them less than men doing the same job and having the same characteristics.

There is also evidence for the fact that women actually choosing to be informal in the "upper tier" of the wage distribution (either as salaried or as self employed) earn more than those involuntarily informal, suggesting that informal labour market for women might be segmented in an "upper tier and a lower tier".

Overall, these results can be interpreted as the evidence that the Ukrainian labour market is indeed segmented and that women suffer some sort of discrimination. This discrimination is not taking place through the segregation of women in the informal sector but, more likely, through different remuneration of characteristics in the formal sector and different career opportunities and the exclusion of women from the better remunerated jobs at the top of the hierarchy. This might also explain why women in the upper tier of the wage distribution experience higher earnings when they are self-employed compared to when they are salaried, both in the formal and in the informal sector.

If this is true, the increasing competition for workers with higher skills, or the possibility to become self-employed seem to constitute the two best opportunities for Ukrainian women to see a reduction in the earnings gap.

Acknowledgement

Financial support from the European Commission within the framework 6 project "Economic and Social Consequences of Industrial Restructuring in Russia and Ukraine (ESCIRRU)" is acknowledged. I would like to thank Hartmut Lehmann for the precious comments and suggestions.

References

Becker, G.S., 1957, *The Economics of Discrimination*, Chicago, University of Chicago Press.

Bellman, L., Estrin, S., Lehmann, H. and Wadsworth, J., 1995, The East German Labor Market in Transition: Gross Flows Estimates from Panel Data, *Journal of Comparative Economics*, 20, pp. 139-170.

Bera, A.K., Jarque, C.M., 1980, Efficient tests for normality, homoscedasticity and serial independence of regression residuals, *Economics Letters*, 6 3, pp. 255–259.

Bergmann, B., 1971, The Effect on White Incomes of Discrimination in Employment, *Journal of Political Economy*, 79, pp. 103-110.

Bergmann, B.R., 1974, Occupational segregation, wages and profits when employers discriminate by race and sex, *Eastern Economic Journal*, 1, 1-2, pp. 103-110.

Blackburn, R.M., Bradley B. and Jarman, J., 2001, Occupational Stratification: The Vertical Dimension of Occupational Segregation, *Work, Employment and Society*, 15, 3, pp. 511-38.

Brainerd, E., 2000, Women in Transition: Changes in Gender Wage Differentials in Eastern Europe and the Former Union, *Industrial and Labor Relations Review*, 54, pp. 138-162.

Cain, G., 1976, The Challenge of Segmented Labor Market Theories to Orthodox Theory: A Survey, *Journal of Economic Literature*, 14, pp. 1215-1257.

Chen, M. and Snodgrass, D., 2001, *Managing Resources, Activities, and Risk in Urban India: The Impact of SEWA Bank*, Washington, D.C., Agency for International Development USAID AIMS Project.

Fields, G.S., 1990, Labour Market Modeling and the Urban Informal Sector: Theory and Evidence, David Turnham, Bernard Salomé, and Antoine Schwarz, eds., *The Informal Sector Revisited*. Paris, Development Centre of the Organisation for Economic Co-Operation and Development.

—. 2005, A Guide to Multisector Labor Market Models, *World Bank Discussion Paper*.

—. 2007, Modeling Labor Market Policy in Developing Countries: A Selective Review of the Literature and Needs for the Future, *World Bank Policy Research Working Paper No. 4362*.

Fong, M.S. and Paul, G., 1992, The Changing Role of Women in Employment in Eastern Europe, *World Bank Population and Human Resources Division, Report No. 8213.*

Ganguli, I. and Terrell, K., 2005, Wage Ceilings and Floors: The Gender Gap in Ukraine's Transition. *IZA DP No. 1776.*

Hakim, C., 1992, Explaining Trends in Occupational Segregation: The Measurement, Causes and Consequences of the Sexual Division of Labour, *European Sociological Review*, 8, 2, pp. 127-152.

ILO, 2007, Global Employment Trends for Women Brief 2007, Geneva, International Labour Office.

Jann, B., 2005, Standard Errors for the Blinder–Oaxaca Decomposition, http://repec.org/dsug2005/oaxaca_se_handout.pdf.

Lee, L., 1983, Generalized Econometric Models with Selectivity, *Econometrica*, 51, pp. 507-512.

Lehmann, H., Kupets, O. and Pignatti, N., 2005, Labor Market Adjustment in Ukraine: An Overview, Background Paper prepared for the World Bank Study on the Ukrainian Labor Market, Bologna and Kiev, mimeo.

Lehmann, H. and Pignatti, N., 2007, Informal Employment Relationships and Labor Market Segmentation in Transition Economies: Evidence from Ukraine. *IZA DP. N. 3269.*

Maloney, W.F., 1999, Does Informality Imply Segmentation in Urban Labor Markets? Evidence from Sectoral Transitions in Mexico, *The World Bank Economic Review*, 13 2, pp. 275-302.

Maloney, W.F., 2004, Informality Revisited, *World Development,* 32 7, pp. 1159-1178.

Neuman, S. and Oaxaca, R.L., 2004, Wage decompositions with selectivity-corrected wage equations: a methodological note, *Journal of Economic Inequality,* 2, pp. 3–10.

Newell, A. and Reilly, B., 1996, The Gender Wage Gap in Russia: Some Empirical Evidence, *Labour Economics*, 3, pp. 337-356.

Oaxaca, R. 1973, Male-Female Wage Differentials in Urban Labor Markets, *International Economic Review*, 14, 3, pp. 693-709.

Paci, P., 2002, *Gender in Transition*, Washington D.C., The World Bank.

Phelps, E.S., 1972, The Statistical Theory of Racism and Sexism, *American* Economic *Review*, 62, 4, pp.659-661.

World Bank, 2001, *Engendering Development: Through Gender Equality in Rights, Resources, and Voice*, World Bank Policy Research Report, Washington D.C. and New York City, The World Bank and Oxford University Press.

Zellner, H., 1972, Discrimination against Women, Occupational Segregation, and the Relative Wage, *American Economic Review*, 62, 2, pp. 157-60.

STANDARD AND NON-STANDARD EMPLOYMENT IN RUSSIA: HOW LARGE IS THE WAGE GAP

TATIANA KARABCHUK

Abstract

The paper deals with the phenomenon of non-standard employment in Russia. In particular, the author tries to answer the question of how large the wage gap between standard and non-standard workers is. Two types of non-standard employment are highlighted; part-time and temporary employment. The main result of the paper is that part-timers have premiums in hourly wages while temporary employees suffer a loss in their hourly wage rates. Furthermore, it was revealed that the wage gap is diminished when econometric models are used from simple to more sophisticated ones step by step. It was shown that the theory of compensation differences is true for part-time employees while the labour costs' theory comes true for temporary employment.

In the XX century the most part of employees in all industrially developed countries worked on so called standard labour contracts, that means that employees were dependant workers on permanent contracts and worked full-time. In case a person worked part-time or was hired only for a certain amount of time then he/she could be described as a non-standard worker. Part-time employment, fixed-term contracts, self-employment, casual work and daily workers comprise non-standard employment. Now the tendency is that more and more people are working on part-time base or hired temporarily and it is becoming a norm.

On the one hand, a high proportion of non-standard workers is the indicator of the labour market flexibility which allows enterprises to adapt quickly to different market changes and economic shocks. On the other hand, it implies high social risks, wage shortages and loses of employees' human capital. The main task for social policy here is the optimal balance between flexibility and security on the labour market.

During the last thirty years the percentage of non-standard employed has grown substantially (for example temporary contracts dominate in education). Nevertheless, Russia has about 50 million people (that is about 80% of all employed) working on full-time basis with unlimited contract in time. So, we could still talk about the predominance of the standard working arrangements in this country.

Non-standard employment existed in the Soviet Union but the percentage was extremely small. Up to 1990-s the temporary and part-time employment was highly restricted and unpopular in the Russian labour market. After 1994 the non-standard employment began to grow. Firstly, partial liberalization of the labour legislation allowed using different types of contracts. Secondly, there was a big growth of the self-employment and employment out of enterprises. The new Labour Code taken in 2002 pushed the increase of temporary employment considerably. As a result, about 8 million people are working on temporary basis by 2007.

There is a serious gap in the literature on the issue of non-standard employment in transitional countries. Though there are papers which address the peculiarities and the scope of non-standard employment in Russia (Gimpelson and Kapelyushnikov, 2006), they do not discuss wages. For instance, it is not clear whether non-standard workers win or lose in terms of wage as compared with standard workers and if their wages do really differ regarding the size of the wage gap.

On the one hand, the theory of segmented labour markets (Doeringer and Piore, 1971) implies that if non-standard jobs are occupied by workers with weaker positions and worse personal characteristics then their wage should be lower than that of those who are on standard jobs. The same negative effect of non-standard employment is predicted by human capital theory. On the other hand, the theory of compensation differences says that all disadvantages of such precarious work should be compensated in terms of wages (Rosen, 1986).

The paper is aimed to show what the effect of being a non-standard worker in Russia is and tries to answer the question of how large is the wage between standard and non-standard workers. Two major types of non-standard employment which seemed to be more widespread in Russia are in the focus of the paper. They are temporary employment and part-time employment.

There could be made a comparison between the observed average wages of standard and non-standard employees but it is not enough to assert that these differences are due to their status on the labour market. Firstly, the composition of standard and non-standard workforce might differ substantially in terms of education, occupation, work experience, residence and many other important aspects. Secondly, there is nonrandom selection into these types of employment depending on observed and unobserved characteristics of employees and employers. The choice of employment contract and of corresponding wage could be done simultaneously. Therefore, in order to talk about wage differences the alternative wage for each non-standard employee which he or she would have in the case of standard employment should be estimated. It should also be kept in mind that the causality between wages and types of job is not so simple, the situation of endogenity could arise when type of contract and the level of wages are determined at the same time. So, the main contribution of the paper is to add in the methodological issues on assessing the wage gap between standard and non-standard employees and to throw some light on Russian case comparing it with other countries.

The structure of the paper is the following: after reviewing the existing literature the data and methodology are discussed. The wage differentials between full-time/part time and permanent/temporary employees are discussed in the fourth part of the paper. The final section contains the main conclusions and policy implications.

Literature review

The literature review provides at least three main theories which could explain the differences in payment of standard and non-standard workers. 1) In the case of very strict labour legislation the firing costs might be very high so that employers would prefer the fixed-term contractors. On the one hand, the strong bargaining power of insiders might push the wages of permanent workers upward (see the insider-outsider theory of Lindbeck and Snower, 1988). As a result, we could see the wage premium for standard workers compared to the earnings of non-standard workers with similar characteristics.

2) On the other hand, temporary employees bare more risks of unemployment and uncertainty in the future so they could claim for higher payment as compensation for less job security (Graaf-Zijl, 2005). Temporary employment could also be used as probationary period for

screening and choosing the best applicants to take them into permanent staff. Then, lower payments in temporary positions could be compensated later when an employee is given a permanent job. The research showed that in European countries temporary employment serves usually as a step to permanent employment rather than a trap to prolonged temporary work (Booth, et al., 2002; Engellandt and Riphahn, 2005). Unfortunately, such assumption cannot be tested on Russian data as there are not any long panel data sets with detailed work histories.

3) According to the theory of human capital, the impact of non-standard employment can only be negative. There is no use and interest for employers to invest in temporary staff. As for part-timers, they spend less time while working and learning so they accumulate less knowledge and specific human capital than full-timers do. These differences in accumulated human capital will affect their wages. It is worth mentioning that the standard indicator for measuring specific human capital – tenure – does not grasp these differences. A full-time permanent employee working for the same calendar period of time as temporary employee or part-time employee will have larger stock of human capital than those engaged in non-standard working arrangements.

To sum up this theoretical part it should be mentioned that temporary and part-time employment definitely refers to precarious jobs, at least in the discussion of "bad" and "good" jobs (Tucker, 2002). So, the employees working on such conditions are considered to be the victims of labour market flexibilization. They usually have no bargaining power to negotiate with employers, so the insiders maximize their benefits at the expense of outsiders (Lindbeck and Snower, 1988). The wage gap is increasing while barriers between outsiders and insiders are strengthening. Firstly, since the employees occupy the "bad" segment of jobs due to self-selection, part-time or temporary employment would comprise of workers with low competitive power. Secondly, workers who occupy such jobs accumulate human capital more slowly than standard workers.

However, there are theoretical arguments relevant to the premium of nonstandard employees compared to the wages of standard workers. According to the theory of compensating differentials, adverse characteristics of work places (like high risk of unemployment and uncertainty in the future) should be compensated in terms of higher wages. Such quick glance on the possible theoretical explanations of the wage gaps between standard and non-standard employees shows that various factors could influence earnings of non-standard workers in both ways. So, the question who gets the benefits: standard or non-standard workers? - is an empirical one.

Despite the fact that the theoretical discussion on good and bad jobs has been taking place during the last dozens of years there is not so much empirical research on wage differences between standard and non-standard workers. One of the obvious reasons is the lack of necessary micro- data. The most part of the existing studies shows that non-standard workers earn less than standard ones. Unfortunately, these studies usually ignore the heterogeneity of workers and jobs. But when these observed and unobserved characteristics are taken into account the observed wage gap is narrowing or even disappearing.

The initial research on women engaged in part-time employment demonstrated that hourly wage rates of part-time employees are considerably lower than that of full-time employees (Ermisch and Wright, 1993; Simpson, 1986). However, later studies argue that part-timers do not suffer from the wage losses or even benefit compared to full-timers.

Such results are much more evident for the countries with high proportions of part-time workers in the labour force. It is worth pointing our that Australia and Netherland are those countries with the highest rates of part-time employment. The studies for the Australian labour market which consider the individual characteristics of employees (both observed and unobserved) demonstrate that the hourly wage is higher for the part-timers. This is true both for men and women. For those part-time employees who at the same time are casually employed the size of the benefit is even higher. The authors give at least two explanations of the fact. According to the first explanation the part-time employees have better hourly payment due to the Australian tax-system which punishes the second and the third workers in the family. In order to attract such workers the employers have to pay more. The second explanation stems from the theory of effective hours: despite that part-timers work less hours per week, their productivitity per hour is higher (Booth and Wood, 2008).

Barry T. Hirsch analyzed the differences in hourly wages of full-time and part-time workers in the USA on the basis of panel data of Current Population Survey. Crude assessments revealed the big observed gap which was higher for men than for women and was growing along with tenure. The control for the individual characteristics diminishes this wage gap. However, the part-time employees of older age still earn less due to the fact that the longer tenure the larger the difference in stocks of human capital acquired by permanent and non-permanent workers. Actually Barry T. Hirsch explained the differences in wages between standard and non-standard employees with similar individual characteristics by different qualifications and skills (Hirsch, 2004).

Manning and Petrongolo came to the same conclusions while analyzing the gap in women's payment engaged in part-time or full-time work in Britain. Part-time employed women on average earn 25% less than full-time employed women. Moreover, this gap rose greatly during the last 30 years. Its significant part could be explained by individual characteristics. When authors account for the demographic characteristics the disparity halves and when they take into consideration the differences in occupational composition of these groups the wage gap disappears. As the paper concludes the main reason for the observed difference in earnings is the professional segmentation (Manning and Petrongolo, 2006).

The part-time employment has female features and the majority of empirical research papers are devoted to women. However, analysis of the men's employment provides the same results. According to the recent studies the observed average wage gap between part-time and full-time employees is 16% in Spain, 24% in Belgium, 28% in Denmark and Italy, 67% in Great Britain and 149% in Ireland. This gap began to shrink as soon as researchers started studying the individual and work place characteristics (such as occupation, industry, enterprise size, trade union coverage and etc.) (O'Dorchai, et al., 2007).

The empirical literature on wages of permanent and temporary workers is not so rich. However, all the existing papers argue that temporary employees earn usually less than permanent workers (Segal and Sullivan, 1998; Booth, et al., 2002; Hagen, 2002, Addison and Surfield, 2005). For instance, the same methodology was applied for calculating differences of part-time/full-time wages and temporary/permanent wages in Netherlands and they identified benefits for part-timers and losses for temps (Graaf-Zijl, 2005).

The researchers from Tinbergen Institute found out that temporary workers in Germany earn one third less than permanent workers. Lesser wage differences but still significant were marked in the UK, Netherlands and Sweden. Yet, the authors did not allow for possible self selection effect which could have led to the biased estimations (Gustafsson, et al., 2001).

Taking into account only the observed workers' characteristics T.Hagen assessed the wage gap of temporary/permanent employees as 6-10%, while controlling for unobserved characteristics he received the results of 23% (Hagen, 2002). Addison and Surfild argue that temporary workers suffer from 7-12% loss in wages which is determined by observed differences between workers. In case they take unobserved characteristics into account the losses changed into wage benefits for temporary employees compensating the lack of job security.

To sum up the theoretical and empirical literature review it is worth emphasising that the reality is more complex than a pure theory. Both negative and positive effects of non-standard employment were shown in the previous empirical studies. What theoretical approaches are more consistent with realities of the Russian labour market? Do Russian non-standard workers lose or win in wages? Using available data sets these questions are answered in the next part of the paper.

Data and methodology

This research is based on the micro level data, NOBUS, the household survey representative for Russia which was held by the World Bank and Rosstat in spring of 2003. Unfortunately, the well-known RLMS data didn't allow to identify temporary workers since there is no question about the contract type. The most reliable and long-ran Russian data on the labour market issues – Labour Force Survey (produced by Rosstat) – is not appropriate either, as it doesn't contain any information on wages.

Table 1 shows the number and the level of part-time and temporary employment according to LFS and NOBUS data. Both data sets draw very similar picture: approximately 10-11% of all employed have temporary jobs and around 5% of all employed work part-time.

Table 1. Temporary and part-time employment according to NOBUS and LFS data, (% of all employed)

	NOBUS data, 2003			LFS data, 2003		
	Total	Among men	Among women	Total	Among men	Among women
Level of part-time employment	4,5	2,6	6,3	5,3	3,5	7,3
Level of temporary employment	10,0	11,4	8,7	11,0	12,5	9,5

It is very important to classify standard and non-standard workers in the data set correctly. Firstly, dependant workers are identified (according to ILO definition). Then they are divided into those who usually work less than 30 hours per week and those who usually work 30 hours per week and more, so part-time and full-time employees are separated. Permanent workers are determined as those who declare that they were hired on the contract unlimited in time. Temporary employees are those who report that they were hired on fixed-term contracts, contracts for particular tasks or unwritten agreements.

NOBUS sample by the age of 15-65 years old was restricted and only those who were dependant workers were taken. Self-employed and army were also excluded. Self-employed do not get wages as they have entrepreneurial incomes which are determined by different mechanisms. Earnings of the military personnel are determined mainly by non-market forces. Moreover, information on incomes of these two groups was not collected in the NOBUS data.

Answering the question about wages the respondents have to point out the size of wage for the last month subtracting tax payments. It is needed to underline that the wage is accounted for from the primary work place only (as it was reported by the individual) even in case a person has two or three jobs. To sum up, the final sample consists of 46 thousand of respondents who declare their earnings for the last month in the survey. All non-standard jobs vary greatly in working hours so wage data on differences in working time are adjusted. The respondents are to answer the question about the number of hours worked usually per week, so the hourly wages are computed according to these two questions assuming that one month consists of 4 weeks. The natural logarithm of hourly wage rates is employed into the regression models.

It is worth to emphasize that actual observed wage of non-standard worker is compared with actual observed wage of standard worker who has similar observed characteristics. It was not possible to have the exact estimations here as one person could not be in standard and non-standard employment at the same time, and it was neither possible to control all the characteristics when such alternative was constructed for him/her. It should also be kept in mind that very often the alternative earning for non-standard worker is not the higher wage in standard employment but unemployment with only unemployment benefit or without any income at all. There is one more restriction here – it is not possible to account for differences in job security between standard and non-standard workers, so, only the differences in wages between them are analysed.

The logic of the analysis is the following: the differences in wages of full-time/part-time and permanent/temporary employees are assessed moving step by step from crude to more correct econometric estimations (from simple means analysis to OLS regression, OLS plus Heckman correction and Propensity Score Matching) aiming at getting close the real figures.

The wage equation for the OLS regression is the following:

$$Ln(w_i) = a + bT_i + \sum_j \beta_j X_{ji} + \varepsilon_i .$$

a, b, β_j - coefficients;

Ln ($wage_i$) – natural logarithm of hourly wage;

T_i – dummy for temporary or part-time employment (1 – temporary, 0- permanent or 1- part-time, 0- full-time);

X_j – the list of personal and workplace characteristics explaining the wage rate (gender, age, educational level, marital status, number of children, occupation, industry, ownership, type of settlement, regional dummies);

ε - unexplained residual.

B-coefficients show the corresponding return for personal and work-place characteristics, b-coefficient equals the average wage gap of the individuals with similar characteristics but working by different type of contract (temporary/permanent) or regime (part-time/full-time). As the natural logarithm of wage is estimated the effect of dummy variable is calculated as follows: $(e^{D} - 1) \cdot 100\%$, where D – dummy coefficient (Halvorsen and Palmquist, 1980). We assume that unexplained residual $[E_i]$ distributes normally $[E_i \sim NID\ [0, \sigma^2]]$.

After the OLS regression the regression with Heckman correction is estimated. The main regression has the same list of independent variables. The selection equation contains the following list of variables:

- gender
- 5 age groups
- marital status
- 4 dummies for educational level
- number of children of 0-1 years old
- number of children of 1-3 years old
- number of children of 4-6 years old
- getting pension
- having studies
- having a flat/house

Finally, the last model of estimating the wage gap is presented, which is the Propensity Score Matching. The method and its practical use were discussed in details by Caliendo, Kopeinig (2005). The approach has become a very popular one to estimate casual treatment effects and widely applied when evaluating labour market policies. Lately, it is widely used to evaluate the wage differences according to the effect of union membership, foreign firms, public sector etc. (Bryson, 2002; Pedro and Martins, 2004; Glinskaya and Lokshin, 2005). This method is used here to evaluate the effect of part-time and temporary employment. So, the treated groups are those who engaged in part-time or temporary work and untreated individuals are those who work full-time or on permanent basis. The observed wage of treated people (part-time and temporary workers) is compared to the unobserved wage of untreated individuals (full-time and permanent workers) the characteristics of which are highly comparable to treated individuals. The effect is calculated as the difference between what a person really earns as part-time or temporary worker and what he/she could earn in case he was a full-time or permanent employee:

$$\Delta Wage_i^b = Wage_{1i}^b - Wage_{0i}^b$$

There is an estimation of the average treatment effect on treated as we cannot afford too strict assumptions about the form of combined distribution of observed and non-observed wages:

$$\Delta Wage^{b} = ATT = E\{Wage_1 \mid D=1, X\} - E\{Wage_0 \mid D=1, X\}$$

where D=1 for part-timers and temps, D=0 for full-timers and permanent workers, X – the list of control individual characteristics (the same one as it was given above in OLS model). Then, $Wage_1 \mid D=1, X$ - is the observed wage of the treated people (part-time or temporary employees), and $Wage_0 \mid D=1, X$ - is the average wage of untreated persons with comparable (the same X) characteristics (full-time or permanent workers).

As the alternative wages cannot be observed the task is to select the untreated control group with the characteristics maximum similar to those of the treated group. The basis of the propensity score matching model is the index of *propensity score* which is specially constructed according to the probability of being a part of the treated group depending on many observed person's characteristics. The meanings of the index lie between 0 and 1 (as it is calculated with the help of probit or logit model) and describe the differences of individual characteristics among people. Individuals with similar characteristics have very close values of these indexes (no matter if they were treated or not). So, the *propensity scores* let us sort out a very similar control group and eliminate the bias due to the self-selection. The main advantage of the method is that it does not require any preliminary assumptions about function form of selection equation and wage equation and form of error's distribution in these equations.

Special module for STATA is used in order to apply PSM regression to the data (Leuven and Sianesi, 2004). The individuals were selected by the nearest neighbour method to sort out the control group. What follows is the analysis of the results.

Results - Discussion

The wage analysis starts with comparing simple average monthly wages of standard and non-standard workers. The relative monthly wages and relative working hours of non-standard workers are placed in the Table 2. It shows that in 2003 temporary employees got about 6% less than permanent workers, and part-time employees earned half less than full-time employees (per month). Regarding working hours the picture is changing. Permanent and full time employees work 40,7 and 42,7 hours per day respectively, while temporary and part-time employees work 43,3 and 21,9. Comparing the average hourly wage rates we see that temporary workers got even lesser per one hour (by about 12%) however they work longer (by 6%). Part-time workers are another case: although they work half less their hourly wage rate is 32% more than that of the full-time workers. These results from the comparison of simple means are more or less the same for males and females. It follows from this that in terms of hourly wages temporary workers suffer from their non-standard status while part-time employees benefit from it.

Table 2. Relative monthly wage and relative working hours of temporary and part-time employees, 2003, NOBUS data, % (wages and working hours of permanent workers and full-time employees = 100%)

	Monthly wage	Working hours per month	Hourly wage rate
All employed			
Temporary/permanent	94,4	106,5	87,9
Part-time/full-time	61,2	51,3	133,3
Women			
Temporary/permanent	87,8	105,5	86,7
Part-time/full-time	70,5	53,3	142,2
Men			
Temporary/permanent	94,2	106	85,8
Part-time/full-time	59,3	48,5	145,1

Comparisons of the average wage differences for various socio-demographic groups provide another interesting finding. Looking at the wage differences between part-time and full-time employees (Table 3) one could conclude that hourly wage rate is always higher for part-timers. The gap is positive for every social-demographic group and on the average is about +30-40%. It is worth mentioning that the lowest difference is observed for professionals (+9%) and employees with tertiary education (+11,8%), the highest one for persons engaged in agriculture (+85,5%), electricity (+82,3%) and senior managers (+72,1%). Such great variation could be explained by the fact that there are small numbers of part-time workers in the sample and the further subdivisions increase standard errors. For that reason it seems more reasonable to discuss the sign of the gap and overall tendency but not the values of particular gaps.

The first column of Table 4 (see below) reflects differences in the average hourly wages of temporary and permanent workers by socio-demographic groups. Men have larger wage difference between temporary and permanent workers than women (-14,2% and -13,3% respectively). It is interesting that married temporary and permanent workers have lesser wage gap (-6,7%) than not married employees (16,4%). The average wages of temporary and permanent workers differ greatly depending on age. The highest wage gap is for employees of 26-35 years old while the smallest one for workers under 25 years old and for those of 36-45 years. One possible explanation here is that the most part of young people start working on probationary period and hence on temporary contracts. They all have almost no working experience which really decreases their salaries. Temps of 26-35 years old still have small working experience and poor skills. At the same time those who occupy permanent positions need to be motivated to stay with the firm, so their wages could be much higher. Temps of 36-45 years old are usually highly qualified professionals occupying high positions. That is why their hourly wages do not differ greatly from that of permanent employees. The gap is growing for those older than 46 years because temporary workers here are usually those who have lower skills and are engaged in the second labour market.

The difference in earnings of temporary and permanent workers shrinks with the educational level: the higher the education the smaller the gap. The same is true for the occupational status - the higher the position the narrower the gap in hourly wages. A special case is the group of elementary occupations for which the gap is positive. Temporary employees with the highest rank on the occupational ladder even got benefits. The higher wages of managers, professionals and technicians reflects the importance of their social status while the premium for elementary occupations means that they have casual unstable work which costs much. There is also a large variation in hourly wages depending on the sector. Almost in every sector the permanent employees earn more except for agriculture and budget sector where the temporary employees do receive higher wages. The differentiation of wage gaps depending on occupation and sector reflects the significant heterogeneity of temporary jobs. At the same time the difference in average wages of temporary and permanent workers does not vary very much depending on the type of the settlement (it is higher by about -12-13% for urban residents).

It is worth keeping in mind that while comparing simple averages workers heterogeneity and sample selection bias is ignored. So, in order to take this into account a series of regressions is assessed to estimate the "pure" wage gaps between standard and non-standard workers. All the results (OLS, OLS+Heckman and PSM) were placed in Table 3 for part-timers and Table 4 for temporary employees. It is clear that results obtained vary considerably depending on the used model. Firstly, some light will be thrown on coefficients for temporary and part-time work in OLS wage regressions.

As it was explained earlier the dependant variable in the regressions is the logarithm of hourly wages and the independent variables are part-time and temporary employment. At the same time gender, age, education level, occupation, industry, type of ownership, type of settlement, regional rate of unemployment and region are also controlled. The results go in line with the results for some European countries: the temporary employment negatively affects wages, this is true both for men and women (see, Table 3 below).

Russian men working part-time get 50% more (per hour) than those working full-time (column 2 and 3, in Table 3). Women engaged in part-time employment earn more as well (+40%). It cannot be said that unambiguous tendency is observed for decreasing the wage gaps for different social-demographic groups when taking into account the personal and work place characteristics. For some groups it is true – the wage gap becomes smaller compared to the mean difference (women, youngest age group etc.) but in most cases it even grows. It is interesting that control for personal characteristics increases the wage premium for the most qualified workers – for those with tertiary education and occupied professional positions. It is natural to assume that while the demand for such highly skilled workers is large their supply is rather limited. These occupations could be expensive consultancies or private teachers who offer a small number of their working hours for a very high price. Either way, it should be stated that the positive effect of part-time employment is significant for all social-demographic groups and it is rather considerable.

Table 3. Wage differences between part-time and full-time workers by socio-demographic factors, %

	Means differences	OLS	OLS with Heckman correction	PSM
Total	33,3	43,6*	43,1*	59,7*
men	45,3	50,9*	50,8*	82,4*
women	42,2	40,8*	40,4*	46,6*
By age				
15-25 years old	47,1	45,8*	44,7*	71,0*
26-35 years old	42,3	52,6*	52,6*	66,9*
36-45 years old	26,5	37,0*	37,1*	48,8*
46-55 years old	23,9	40,0*	39,2*	52,3*
56-65 years old	42,6	45,1*	45,1*	52,2*
By marriage				
Married	35,0	45,4*	45,2*	63,4*
Not married	32,9	40,9*	40,1*	48,9*
By education				
Lower then secondary	40,6	44,1*	43,4*	76,3*
Secondary	34,3	46,8*	45,9*	63,4*
Tertiary	11,8	37,6*	37,9*	47,8*
By professional groups				
Managers	72,1	54,1*		135,7*
Professionals	9,0	37,7*		40,8*
Technicians	36,3	50,0*		74,7*
Clerks and service workers	58,8	44,6*		70,4*
Skilled agricultural workers, graft workers	60,2	42,9*		65,4*
Operators	40,8	45,6*		41,6*
Elementary occupations	45,9	35,2*		53,3*
By industries				
Agriculture, hunting, forestry and fishing	85,5	50,0*		108,0*
Mining, quarrying and manufacturing	43,3	38,0*		47,5*
Electricity, gas and water supply	82,3	70,1*		100,0*
Construction	51,7	41,3*		104,8*
Wholesale and retail trade; repair of motor vehicles, motorcycles and personal and household goods, hotels and restaurants	57,5	56,1*		75,2*
Transport, storage and communications	30,3	21,6*		86,8*

Financial intermediation, real estate, renting and business activities	38,2	22,5		67,7*
Public administration and defence; compulsory social security, education, health, social work, other community, social and personal service activities	41,5	40,9*		44,3*
Other activities	40,8	43,5*		65,9*
By type of settlement				
City with more than 500 thousand people	39,1	44,7*	45,5*	77,9*
City with 100-500 thousand people	27,4	43,5*	43,3*	55,3*
Town with 20-100 thousand people	27,4	39,4*	39,2*	47,9*
Country side, village	52,0	41,2*	40,6*	58,9*

**<0,05*

The temporary workers earn 3,1%-3,7% less than permanent ones and this is true both for men and women (column 2 and 3 in Table 4). The wage gap between temporary and permanent workers tends to shrink when accounting for the personal and work-place characteristics: from -14% to -3,1% for men and from -13 to -3,7% for women. Moreover, the gaps become less significant for some social-demographic groups (for age groups of 15-25 years old, 36-45 years old, 56-65 years old; for employees with lowest educational level and for those living in the countryside).

Table 4. Wage differences between temporary and permanent workers by socio-demographic factors, %

	Means differences	OLS	OLS with Heckman correction	PSM
Total	-12,1	-3,7*	-3,8*	-3,4
By gender				
men	-14,2	-3,1*	-3,1*	-2,8
women	-13,3	-3,6*	-3,7*	-2,6
By age				
15-25 years old	-5,9	-2,2	-2,5	2,4
26-35 years old	-14,6	-5,4*	-5,4*	-2,2
36-45 years old	-7,6	-2,1	-2,0	-4,2
46-55 years old	-11,0	-6,8*	-6,9*	-2,1
56-65 years old	-9,5	-2,3	-2,1	5,1
By marriage				
Married	-6,7	-3,4*	-3,5*	-4,3
Not married	-16,4	-4,7*	-4,9*	-6,7*
By education				
Lower then secondary	-12,1	-1,4	-1,6	-4,6
Secondary	-8,6	-5,6*	-5,8*	-4,2
Tertiary	3,8	-4,3	-4,3*	-0,7
By professional groups				
Managers	33,4	-2,0		37,0
Professionals	4,8	-0,6		0,9
Technicians	9,0	0,5		-7,2
Clerks and service workers	-9,8	-6,8*		-10,6*
Skilled agricultural workers, graft workers	-3,8	-5,5*		4,1
Operators	-12,0	-11,5*		-10,7
Elementary occupations	14,5	2,1		9,8
By industries				
Agriculture, hunting, forestry and fishing	36,2	24,6*		15,3
Mining, quarrying and manufacturing	-5,2	-10,2*		3,5
Electricity, gas and water supply	-22,1	-19,5*		-16,9
Construction	-14,5	-4,5		-1,1
Wholesale and retail trade; repair of motor vehicles, motorcycles and personal and household goods, hotels and restaurants	-20,5	-6,9*		-12,0*

Transport, storage and communications	-17,1	-15,4*		-13,2
Financial intermediation, real estate, renting and business activities	-20,3	-13,8*		1,4
Public administration and defence; compulsory social security, education, health, social work, other community, social and personal service activities	15,3	6,1*		13,1*
Other activities	-10,7	-11,3*		-18,3*
By type of settlement				
City with more than 500 thousand people	-13,3	-9,5*	-9,5*	-3,6
City with 100-500 thousand people	-11,2	-5,8*	-5,9*	-8,5
Town with 20-100 thousand people	-15,7	-7,7*	-7,7*	-6,5
Country side, village	-12,8	2,6	2,4	-1,5

Last, there is a presentation of the results obtained with the last method of evaluating wage gaps - *Propensity Score Matching*. It is a non-parametric regression model assuming the comparison with the control group. The estimations are placed in the last columns of the Tables 3 and 4.

The results show that the wage gaps between temporary and permanent workers are lower than the total means almost for all social-demographic groups but at the same time they are not significant in the most cases. Although in general the results of PSM regressions for temporary employment are consistent with the simple means and the results of OLS regressions. The negative effect is not universal and there is a considerable variation in the wage gaps between different social-demographic groups. There is a modest negative effect for those temporary workers who are not married, they get 6,7% less than those who have a spouse. The employees engaged in trade and hotel business and occupying clerks positions suffer a loss in terms of hourly wages equaled to 12% and 10,6%. As it was showed before the budget sector employees on temporary contracts have a significant benefit (13,1%).

The PMS results for wage gap between the part-time and full-time employees are also in line with the results obtained with other methods.

All the gaps are positive and significant but for some particular groups they are much higher than in OLS or OLS with Heckman correction models. For example, for men the gap increases from 45% to 82,4%, for workers with lowest education level from 40% to 76%, and for managers from 72% up to 135%.

To sum up the empirical part of the paper it could be concluded that temporary workers in Russia do suffer a loss in wages so the Insider-outsider theory as well as the theory of Human capital could be appropriate for the Russian Labour Market. Temporary workers in this country usually have jobs in the second segment of the labour market, have poor education and skills and almost no bargaining power. As in many Western countries like Spain, Germany, Netherlands, Great Britain, they are not compensated for the risks of uncertainty, moreover they overwork in hours as a rule. The part-timers on the contrary have bonuses in hourly wage rates compared to the full-timers in Russia. It is difficult to say whether the theory of Compensating differences or the theory of Effective hours do better explain this fact, we need more detailed research on that with better data set. Another important result of the paper is that the accounting for the observed and unobserved variables diminishes the wage gap between standard and non-standard workers.

Conclusions

The paper is addressed to the problem of the differentiation in wages between standard and non-standard workers in Russia. This is the first attempt to evaluate the wage gap between temporary and permanent, part-time and full-time employees using the large-scale survey of Russian households, conducted in 2003. The author applied several regression models to estimate the effects of temporary and part-time employment of hourly wage rate in Russia.

The main conclusion from the paper is that the part-time employees have premiums in hourly wages comparing with full-timers while temporary workers are less paid per hour comparing with permanent workers. Furthermore temporary employees tend to work more hours per month comparing with permanent workers.

The results allow us to sum up that the initial conclusion that temporary and part-time employees considerably suffer in terms of earnings is not totally true. The wage gap between standard and non-standard workers often stems from their differences in educational level, occupations personal characteristics and even work place characteristics. Moreover, the labour market tends to compensate the disadvantages associated with such jobs (for example fewer working hours) by higher hourly wage rate.

The advantage of the paper is that it covers a crucial for Russian social policy topic – non-standard employment. Not too much was written in the literature so this paper shed some light on the problem of the growing fast phenomenon of low-skilled and low-educated labour force employed on temporary contracts or working part-time. The focus of the paper was on the size of wage differentials between standard and non-standard workers in Russia but it does not provide exact explanations. In order to do that a more detailed analysis on factors of these differentials is needed, as well as the decomposition of the gaps which are the next step for future estimations.

The paper could be used by policymakers to understand the mechanisms of wage formation of permanent and temporary employees as well as of full-time and part-time workers. It should be said that temporary workers comprise low quality labour force in the second labour market sector with lower wages, so it is worth at least to think about the problem of the expansion of this sector.

Acknowledment

The paper is prepared as a part of the ESCIRRU (European and Social Consequences of Industrial Restructuring in Russia and Ukraine) project funded by the EU (the 6th Framework Program). The author thanks Vladimir Gimpelson, Rostislav Kapelyushnikov and Nina Vishenvskaya for their comments and useful advice at all stages of the paper.

References

Bentolila S., Dolado, J., 1994, Labour Market Flexibility and Wages: Lessons from Spain, *Economic Policy*, 9, 18, pp. 53-99.

Boeri, T., Del-Boca, D. and Pissarides, Ch., 2005, *Women at Work: an Economic Perspective*, Oxford University Press.

Booth, A., Francesconi, M., Frank, J., 2002, *Temporary Jobs: Stepping Stones or Dead Ends?*, *Economic Journal*, 112, 480, pp. 585-606.

Booth, A., Wood, M., 2008, Back-to-front Down-under? Part-time/Full-time Wage Differentials in Australia, *Industrial Relations: A Journal of Economy and Society*, 47, pp. 114–135.

Bryson, A., 2002, The Union Membership Wage Premium: An Analysis Using Propensity Score Matching, *Centre for Economic Performance, LSE*, Discussion paper No. 0530.

Caliendo, M., Kopeinig, S., 2005, Some Practical Guidance for the Implementation of Propensity Score Matching, *IZA Discussion paper* No.1588, May.

Doeringer, P. and Piore, M., 1971, *Segmented Labor Markets and Manpower Analysis*, Lexington, Mass.

Engellandt, A., Riphahn., R., 2005, Temporary Contracts and Employee Effort, *Labour Economics*, 12, pp. 281-299.

Ermisch, J. and Wright, R., 1993, Wage Offers and Full-Time and Part-Time Employment by British Women, *Journal of Human Resources*, 28, 1, pp. 111-113.

Gimpelson V. and Kapelyushnikov R., 2006, *Nestandartnaya zanyatost na Rossiskom rinke truda*, (Non-standard employment in Russia), Moscow, IISE.

Glinskaya, E. and Lokshin, M., 2005, Wage Differentials Between the Public and Private Sectors in India, *World Bank Policy Research Working Paper* 3574, April.

Gustafsson, S., Kenjoh, E. and Wetzels, C., 2001, Employment Choices and Pay Differences between Non-Standard and Standard Work in Britain, Germany, Netherlands and Sweden, *Tinbergen Institute Discussion Paper* No. 086/3.

Halvorsen, R. and R.Palmquist, 1980, The Interpretation of Dummy Variables in Semilogarithmic Equations, *American Economic Review*, 70, 3, pp.474-475.

Hagen, T., 2002, Do Temporary Workers Receive Risk Premiums? Assessing the Wage Effects of Fixed-Term Contracts in West Germany by a Matching Estimator Compared with Parametric Approaches, *LABOUR*, 16, 4, pp. 667-705.

Halvorsen, R. and Palmquist, R., 1980, The Interpretation of Dummy Variables in Semilogarithmic Equations, *American Economic Review*, 70, 3, pp.474-475.

Hirsch, B., 2004, Why Do Part-Time Workers Earn Less? The Role of Worker and Job Skills, *IZA Discussion paper* No. 1261.

Leuven, E. and Sianesi, B., 2004, PSMATCH2: Stata module to perform full Mahalanobis and propensity score matching, common support graphing, and covariate imbalance testing. Version 2.0.8.

Lindbeck, A. and Snower, D.J., 1988, *The insider-outsider theory of employment and unemployment*, MIT-Press, Cambridge/Mass. and London.

Manning, A. and Petrongolo, B., 2006, The Part-Time Pay Penalty for Women in Britain, *IZA Discussion paper* No 2419.

Martins, P.S., 2004, Do Foreign Firms Really Pay Higher Wages? Evidence from Different Estimators *IZA Discussion paper* 1388.

M. de Graaf-Zijl, 2005, Compensation of On-Call and Fixed-Term Employment: The Role of Uncertainty, *Tinbergen Institute Discussion Paper* 120/3.

O'Dorchai, S., Plasman, R., Rycx F., 2007, The Part-Time Wage Penalty in European Countries: How Large Is It for Men? IZA *Discussion Paper* 2591.

Rosen, S., 1986, The Theory of Equalizing Differences, in Ashenfelter, O. and Layard, R. (eds.), *Handbook of Labor Economics*, 1, pp. 641-692, North-Holland.

Segal, L. and Sullivan D., 1997, The Growth of Temporary Services Work, *Journal of Economic Perspectives*, American Economic Association, 11, 2, pp. 117-136.

Simpson, W., 1986, Analysis of Part-Time Pay in Canada, *The Canadian Journal of Economics*, 19, 4, pp. 798-807.

Tucker, D., 2002, Precarious' Non-Standard Employment – a Review of the Literature, *Working paper of Labour Market Policy Groui*, www.futureofwork.govt.nz.

ORGANISATIONAL COMMUNICATION AND ITS EFFECT ON ENTERPRISE PERFORMANCE

KATINA BOGA-KARTERI, GEORGE STALIDIS AND CONNIE PAPANICOLAS

Abstract

In this work, the organizational practices in relation to external and internal communication are studied through a survey in SMEs of Northern Greece. The aim is to identify successful communication practices and to relate them with possible contributing factors. A questionnaire-based survey has been carried out, aiming at the evaluation of the extent to which the organisations are aware and implement organisational communication as well as the procedures, methods and channels used to improve the quality of their services, customer satisfaction and internal operation. The data have been analyzed using Multivariate Correspondence Analysis, which is particularly suited to surveys with qualitative variables. The size of the data set, after preprocessing and coding, was 84 organizations and 34 variables. The analysis resulted in interesting findings regarding the way that communication may function inside an organisation and the cases where effectiveness and satisfaction are maximized. Among the conclusions is that a significant number of organisations use conventional means of external and internal communication (e.g. oral, memos), they do not consider communication as a critical parameter of their operation and they achieve medium performance at all levels of information flow, work relations and external image. On the contrary, organisations which adopt electronic forms of communication tend to spend considerable time in communication and they consider it as an important factor for their success. In these cases, high effectiveness and satisfaction is reported. As a general conclusion, the importance of organisational communication in the environment of Northern Greece has become evident and practices related to higher effectiveness have been identified.

Introduction

An organisation's communication strategy is directly related to all other organisational functions, such as management of manpower and work relations, marketing strategies and public relations, product promotion, etc. (Cushman, 2000). Effective communication strategies in an organisation consist of the development of satisfactory relations between individuals and groups who communicate with each other for the achievement of the organisation's goals (Heintzman, et al., 1993). Organizational communication is of particular importance to all enterprises active in competitive environments, but especially to those involved in demanding international activities such as inter-state transactions in the Balkan area.

In this section, the importance of communication for organisations in Northern Greece is being studied. In particular, it has been surveyed the extent to which the organisations are aware and implement organisational communication; which related procedures, methods and channels are used to improve the quality of their services; what the goals and achievements related to communication are. One of the aims of this study was also to assess the dependence between the effectiveness of communication and the overall organisation performance, as well as to identify successful communication practices and to relate them with possible contributing factors.

This study has been based on data collected through a primary survey carried out on the enterprises of Northern Greece. An initial statistical analysis of the data has depicted how organizational communication is handled and has shown the basic characteristics, attitudes and effectiveness of the surveyed sample. However, conventional statistical analysis (Hays, 1973, p. 954) was not able to reveal the different tendencies underlying in the target group, neither the complex dependencies among a large number of factors affecting communication. In order to discover more complex hidden information factorial analysis methods have been applied within this work. The applied data analysis method is particularly suited to surveys with qualitative variables and results in sets of related attributes which form behaviour patterns and tendencies. In this way, it was made possible to discern valuable information about the combined effect of a variety of factors to the effectiveness of communication and to the overall performance of enterprises.

Field survey on Organizational Communication

Background

Organisational communication is the communication of an organisation with its direct and indirect external environment, as well as the internal communication at all inter-personal and inter-departmental levels. The direct environment consists of merchandisers, customers, product delivery and competitors (Adler, 2005, p. 462). The indirect external environment consists of branches of the government, political system, technology, the community and the natural environment. To succeed in communicating with its customers, suppliers, public agencies, etc, an organisation must use the correct means and methods of communication (Boga-Karteri, 2005). The most important methods of communication which an organisation uses in order to make its products, activities, interests and opinions known to its environment, are electronic communication (public and private television and radio stations, Internet, telephone, fax, multimedia, etc.) and written communication (newspapers, magazines, letters). Other communication methods are the interviews, advertisements, brochures, leaflets, posters, movies, video, sponsors and donors, demonstrations and visits.

Survey method

A written questionnaire was the basic tool used to gather information. The questionnaire contained closed questions, which were selected to cover all aspects of communication inside an organization and also some basic data about the questioned organisations. The person responsible for answering has been a representative of the higher management and has been asked to answer in written form honestly and precisely. The questions (together with certain guidelines) followed the basic rules for designing questionnaires and particular attention has been paid to cover a wide field of information, in order to ensure a rich information source on aspects that have not been explored in depth (Paraskevopoulos, 1993, p. 191). The written questionnaires have been sent to the interviewee either by post mail, fax, e-mail or personal visit by the interviewer.

The questions contained in the questionnaire are categorized as:

- Questions regarding given facts: These questions appear to be easy to think about, understand and ask. It is also very likely that they will be answered honestly. For example, "how many people are employed in the organization".

- Questions of knowledge and opinion: With these questions the interviewer will never learn what the interviewee knows, but will learn about their opinion regarding what they believe or what they think they know. For example, "does communication take seriously into account a person's feelings and culture?".

All the questions belong to the closed type, in which all possible answers are predefined and structured. In other words, open expression was not allowed (Dimitropoulos, 1994, p. 216). In some of the questions, the interviewee was restricted to answer only one of the given answers, while in others it was possible to select more than one answer. The main advantage of closed questions is that these can be easily coded and easily categorized for the analysis stage. It is noted that the analysis method applied in this work (multiple correspondence analysis) is applicable to categorical data (Benzecri, 1992), which means that a closed questionnaire is the ideal data source for this method. Also, closed questions are less expected to be left unanswered. The formulation of the questions has been done by carefully selecting the wording and considering the number of questions, the order and the general structure and format.

The research population (Javeau, 2000) for this survey was the 705 organisations listed in the records of the Organizations of Northern Greece. It was decided to select a sample of 200 organisations (28.4% of the whole), to address. A random sample has been selected with the use of Chart of Random Numbers. The final sample size for this research was 84 completed and quality checked questionnaires. This number qualifies for the maximum statistical expectations (Sachs, 1984).

The questions fell into 2 categories: questions where rating was required on a scale of 5 levels and questions which require the selection of one or more from a closed set of answers (i.e. which are the main obstacles in communication) (Heintzman, et al, 1993). The organizations were categorized according to the number of employees (European Standards 2003/362/EK), the activity sector and the existence of quality certification.

Factorial Analysis

Methodology

The survey data that were collected through questionnaires from 84 organisations have been analyzed using Multiple Correspondence Analysis (Benzecri, 1973; Benzecri, 1992), in order to discover tendencies and practices in relation to organisational communication. The applied method belongs in the family of Factor Analysis methods and is particularly suited to surveys with qualitative variables. The strength of Multiple Correspondence Analysis is that it is able to relate together all the questions of the survey and extract patterns of dependencies, without any limitation to the number of variables and without the need for any a priori assumptions on an underlying model (Karapistolis, 2008).

Each question of the questionnaire is treated as one categorical or ordinal variable and all possible answers are seen as classifications which correspond to attributes of the population under survey. Multiple Correspondence Analysis is able to detect sets of attributes which seem to be related and form specific behaviour patterns and tendencies. The method is also effective in breaking down the collected information into individual phenomena, each one of which corresponds to a specific percentage of the total information and can be interpreted qualitatively.

Coding and preprocessing of survey data

The survey questionnaire has been coded for analysis by defining one variable for each of the 34 questions and adding 3 more variables for representing the activity sector, the number of employees and the possession of quality certification, respectively. All variables are defined as qualitative, the 22 being categorical and the 12 scale variables. For the questions where more than one answers are acceptable (for example to determine which are the goals of communication), one secondary variable has been used for each possible answer with allowed values Yes / No.

The number of parameters that resulted for the entire survey was 38 and the number of classifications was 178. Since the number of classifications was high in relation to the sample size, the analysis has been applied on subsets of the survey variables. More specifically, 2 subsets of the variables have been defined, which were partially overlapping, and the correspondence analysis has been applied to each one separately. Particular attention has been paid in ensuring a significant overlap among the subsets, in order to minimize the possibility of missing an existing dependence among classifications. In addition, several experiments with different variable groupings have been performed and it has been verified that the analysis does not result in any more patterns.

Analysis

The analysis has been performed using the data analysis software MAD (Méthodes d'Analyses des Donées). This software has been developed in the division of Information Technology and Documentation of the Department of Marketing, Alexandrian Technological Educational Institute of Thessaloniki and is being used for qualitative and statistical survey data analysis, for both teaching and research purposes. The data of the entire survey on organizational communication have been entered from the collected questionnaires to the analysis programme, after suitable coding and preprocessing. Two separate initial data tables were created, corresponding to 2 partially overlapping subsets of variables.

The first step of the analysis was to calculate the Burt table for each data set and then to apply multiple correspondence analysis (Greenacre, 2007). The factorial axes with most significant percentage of information (measured as percentage of inertia) were produced graphically, after applying the typical property selection criteria (COR>200, CTR>1000/number of classifications). Each axis corresponded to a specific fraction of the total information and depicted sets of properties (classifications) that characterised specific groups of the surveyed enterprises. The resulting sets of properties were interpreted qualitatively as profiles representative of different groups of organizations. As a second phase of interpretation, the most significant factorial axes were used in pairs to form factorial planes. Groups of properties were again identified graphically on the planes and interpreted qualitatively. In order to conclude with the final results, the property profiles found on factorial planes were consolidated with the ones found on single axes, eliminating any possible overlap.

Results

The factorial axes and planes produced by the analysis depicted several profiles regarding the way organisational communication is dealt by enterprises of Northern Greece and led to interesting conclusions about the factors which contribute to improved performance, customer and employee satisfaction, as well as organisation efficiency. It is noted, however, that a number of axes did not produce useful results, as they corresponded to obvious response patterns without any information value (i.e. the obvious distinction between all positive and all negative answers to the secondary Yes / No variables). The results with the highest interpretation value are presented in the following figures.

The notation used to refer to a factorial axis is Fi.j, where i indicates to which of the two sub-surveys it corresponds and j is the index of the axis, as this resulted from the analysis in descending order regarding the percentage of inertia.

Figure 1. Factorial axis F1.2

The factorial axis F1.2 shows the opposition between bilateral communication with very good performance at most organisation levels against one-way communication with reduced effectiveness and satisfaction.

In the second factorial axis of the first subset of variables F1.2, corresponding to the 7,94% of the information, it is observed (Figure 1) the opposition between 2 groups with the following characteristics: In the first group, it is stated that communication between the actors involved is bidirectional or interpersonal, the effectiveness of bilateral communication is excellent, while the information flow top-down and bottom-up is satisfactory. The satisfaction from personal communication is also good and the reliability of the channel used is excellent. At the same time, respondents state that they know very well the person with whom they are communicating, the information flow system is effective, they spend up to 75% of their time for communication and the external communication is very effective. On the contrary, in the second group, the communication used is one-way and the information flow top-down is not satisfactory. The satisfaction from personal communication is just good, as well as the reliability of the channel. It is stated that respondents fairly know the person with whom they are communicating, the information flow system is not efficient, external communication is not effective and responds fairly to the needs/wishes of customers. To the question whether communication reflects the organization's social responsibility, the answer is "fairly" and to whether it considers people's emotions and culture, the answer is "much". The result drawn is that there can be found a population of enterprises that use bilateral communication and achieve good effectiveness, information flow and reliability and a group that uses one-way communication with medium satisfaction and reliability in internal and external communication, as well as reduced effectiveness in information flow. It has also been noted that the two groups are not differentiated according to their size, area of activity or existence of quality certification.

Figure 2. The factorial axis F1.3, showing the opposition between organizations that adopted electronic forms of communications and those that have not.

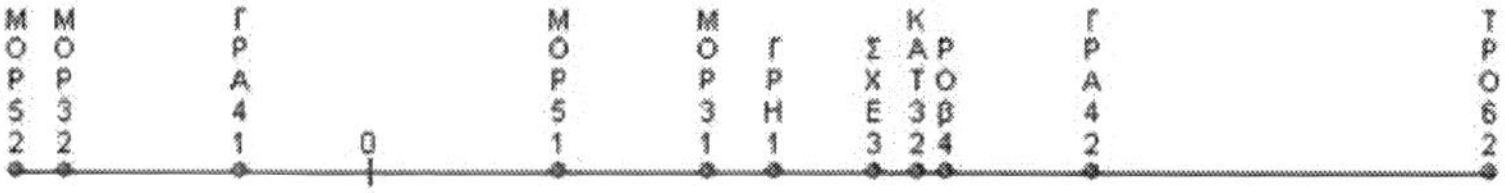

The factorial axis F1.3 shows the opposition between organisations that adopted electronic forms of communications and those that have not.

In axis F1.3, corresponding to 6,4% of the information, it is observed (Figure 2) that in relation to the adopted forms of communication, one can identify a group that does not use visual and electronic communication and that in internal communication uses memos, as opposed to a group of organisations that use visual and electronic communication. In the second case, the speed of information transfer is "immediate", the flow from top to bottom is satisfactory, while the use of phone in external communication is limited. In axis F1.4 with 3,8% of the information, there is an opposition found again between organizations that use electronic communication and those who do not, with additional information that in cases where electronic means are not used, the purpose of communication is mainly for discussing problems and complaints, while the information flow is characterised but is not effective.

Figure 3. Factorial plane 1.2 x 1.3. We identify 3 groups with different attitude in relation to communication.

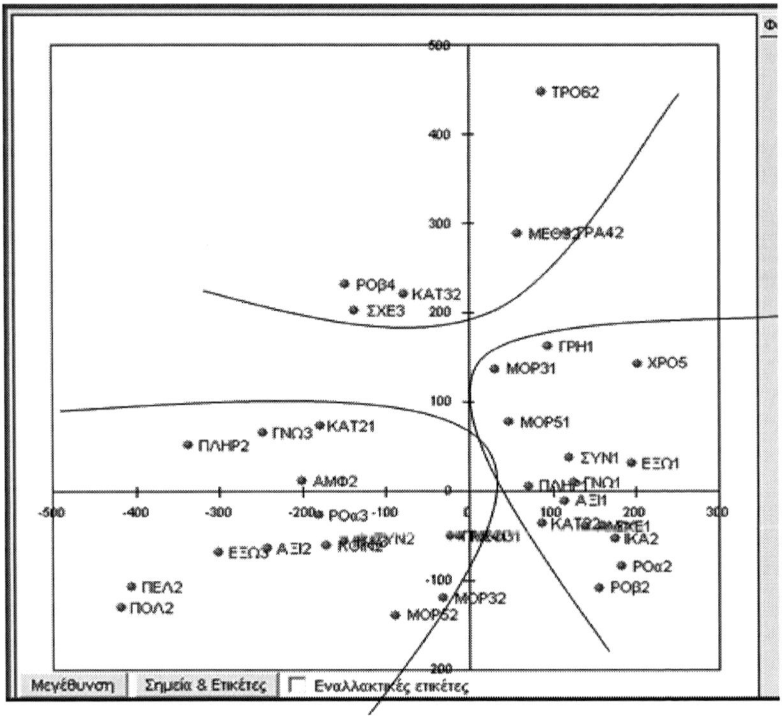

In the factorial plane 1.2 x 1.3 3 groups with different attitude are identified in relation to communication.

The factorial plane 1.1 x 1.2 confirms the findings of F1.2 and does not add new information, while the plane 1.2 x 1.3 concentrates the 14,4% of information and identifies 3 groups of organizations regarding the applied forms of communication, as shown in Figure 3. Comparing the characteristics of the groups in this plane, it is concluded that organizations that mostly use conventional means of communication do not seem to consider communication as a serious parameter and they achieve medium effectiveness at all levels of internal and external communication. On the other hand, enterprises that spend more time in communication and seem to consider it as important part of their operation, tend to adopt electronic forms of communication and achieve high effectiveness and satisfaction. Finally, there exist a number of enterprises where the role of communication is seriously degraded and for them, lack of satisfaction on behalf of the employees is reported.

On the factorial plane 2.2 X 2.4 (Figure 4), the combination of two phenomena is observed, the first one being related to the channels used and the second to the existence of a devoted department for communication in the organisation's structure. The use of letters in internal communication, e-mail and telephone are correlated with the statement that the main purposes of communication are the collection of information and decision making and not the organization's reputation. The existence of a dedicated department for the planning and implementation of communication is closely related to increased satisfaction from personal communication within the organization and excellent effectiveness of bidirectional communication and information flow both top-down and bottom-up.

Figure 4. The plane 2.2 x 2.4

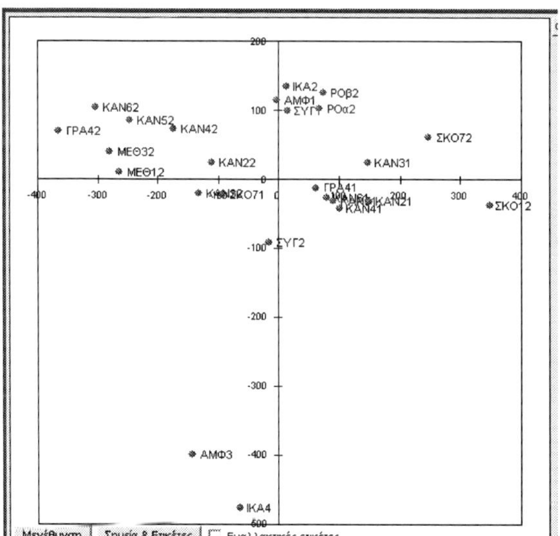

Finally, an additional finding, resulting from axis F2.3, is that "satisfactory" information flow, reduced satisfaction from personal communication and "fair" effectiveness of bi-directional communication are related to the statement that "age" is the main obstacle in the process of communication.

Conclusions

The survey reported in this paper showed the importance of organisational communication in the environment of Northern Greece, although a significant part of the surveyed sample seems to underestimate communication as a success factor. The 95% of the organisations answered that they apply communication processes, but only 46% reported that a specific department responsible for communication exists in the structure of the organisation. One of the results of the applied analysis was to verify that the existence of a specific department for the planning and application of communication is closely related to excellent information flow and satisfaction on behalf of the employees.

By applying multiple correspondence analysis on the data collected from the questionnaire-based primary survey, characteristics and practices affecting the performance of organisation at internal and external aspects have been identified. The analysis resulted in interesting findings regarding the way that communication may function inside an organization and the cases where effectiveness and satisfaction are maximized.

According to the analysis, a significant number of organisations use conventional means of external and internal communication (e.g. oral, memos), they do not consider communication as a critical parameter of heir operation and they achieve medium performance at all levels of information flow, work relations and external image. This group is distinguished from organizations which adopt electronic forms of communication, they spend considerable time in communication and they consider it as an important factor for their success. In these cases, high effectiveness and satisfaction is reported, which is an indication that the overall performance can be affected by the forms and degree of adoption of internal and external communication. The analysis also showed that the above categorisations are independent from the organisation size, its sector of activity or the possession of quality certification. Additionally, the issue of age has been identified as a potential problem in the process of communication and is related to considerable deterioration of the performance in information flow, interactive communication and reliability of the used channels.

References

Adler, R.B. and Elmhorst, J.M., 2005, *Communicating at work:principles and practices for business and professions*, 8th ed. New York, MC Graw Hill.

Benzécri, J.P., 1973, L'analyse des correspondances, Paris, Dunod.

—. 1992, *Correspondence Analysis Handbook*, New-York, Dekker, P.

Boga-Karteri, K., 2005, *Communication human / organizational. Theory and Applications*, Thessaloniki, University Studio Press.

Cushman, D.P., 2000, Stimulating and integrating the development of organizational communication: High speed management theory. *Management Communication Quarterly*, 13, pp. 486-501.

Dimitropoulos, E., 1994, *Introduction to the Methodology of Scientific Research*, Athens, Publisher ELLIN.

Greenacre, M., 2007, *Correspondence Analysis in Practice*, Chapman & Hall.

Hays, W.L.,1973, *Statistics for the Social Sciences*, 2nd Edition, New York, Holt, Rinehart and Winston, Inc.

Heintzman, M., Leathers, D.G., Parrott, R.L. and Cairns, A.B., 1993, Nonverbal rapport-building behaviors' effects on perceptions of a supervisor, *Management Communication Quarterly*, 7, pp. 181-208.

Javeau, C., 2000, *Survey using questionnaires, The manual of the good researcher*, Athens, Tipothito (in Greek).

Karapistolis, D., 2008, *Data Analysis – Statistics without models, Vol I*, Thessaloniki, Anikoula (in Greek).

Paraskevopoulos, I., 1993, *Methodology of Scientific Research*. Volume B, Athens.

Sachs, L., 1984, *Angewandte Statistik: Anwendung statistischer Methoden*, Springer-Verlag Berlin Heidelberg New York Tokyo.

THE IMPACT OF THE CURRENT FINANCIAL CRISIS ON BANK FINANCING OF SMES IN SELECTED COUNTRIES OF CENTRAL AND EASTERN EUROPE

ANGELA ROMAN
AND VALENTINA DIANA IGNATESCU

Abstract

This paper aims to make a comparative analysis on the impact of the global economic crisis on bank financing of small and medium sized enterprises (SMEs) in some countries of Central and Eastern Europe.

In the present study we will consider SMEs because they represent more than 90% of all enterprises operating on the markets of Central and Eastern European countries.

The SMEs, in terms of size and the specifics of their activities, face difficulties in procuring external financing resources, in conditions of normal operation of the economy. Moreover, in the context of the current international crisis, the SMEs access to financial resources is more difficult due to the deterioration of the economic environment and due to the increasing of the uncertainties about its progress.

In the first part of the study the aim is to highlight the place of the bank loans within the financing resources of the SMEs activity, in recent years, because, after the internal financing, this type of financing plays the most important role in getting the necessary resources of the enterprises.

In the context of the global financial and economic crisis, the dynamics of the bank loans granted to SMEs was interrupted both due to the decrease of the supply of bank loans and the demand. Thus, the second part of the study aims to highlight the impact of crisis on financing the activity of SMEs through bank loans.

The negative economic outlook, the deteriorating ability to pay off the bank customers (especially the SMEs) and the increase of the cost of financing led the credit institutions in most countries considered in the study to significantly tighten the lending standards.

Given the economic reality, which shows that the SME sector is a pillar of the national economies, the national authorities, but also some European institutions have taken significant measures to support the SME sector, in particular to facilitate the access to finance. In this respect, in the last part of the study it is planned to highlight, in particular, the measures taken by the authorities from the analyzed countries to reduce the impact of the current crisis on bank financing of SMEs.

Introduction

SMEs constitute the dominant form of business organization, holding a share of about 99% of all enterprises on the market in European Union countries.

According to the economic literature and practice there is not a universally accepted definition of the concept of small and medium enterprise. The definition of SMEs varies according to the international organisation that aims through its mission to support SMEs in the Member States, to the country itself or even the industry.

In the European Union the single market without internal barriers and the interaction between national measures and those imposed by the European Union to support SMEs, required to establish a common definition for these companies. Thus, on April 3, 1996, the European Commission adopted a Recommendation (Commission Recommendation 96/280/EC of 3 April 1996), which established the first definition of SMEs applied throughout the European Union. On May 6, 2003, the European Commission adopted a new definition of SMEs, taking into account the economic development of EU countries since 1996. This definition came into force on January 1, 2005 (see, Table 1) and is applied to all policies, programs and measures for SMEs launched by the European Commission.

Table 1. European definition of SMEs

Type of SME	Number of employees	Turnover (in EUR)	Or	Balance sheet total (in EUR)
Medium-sized	< 250	≤ 50 million (40 million in 1996)		≤ 43 million (27 million in 1996)
Small	< 50	≤ 10 million		≤ 10 million
Micro	< 10	≤ 2 million		≤ 2 million

Source: European Commission (2004).

The SME sector has an important role in a national economy by contributing significantly to its economic and social development. The important role of SMEs results from the fact that they generate most of the GDP of each country, usually between 55% - 95%; provide jobs for most occupied population; present the largest dynamism (demonstrated by the growth of their number, the volume of their turnover and the size of their employment); they have a high degree of adaptability to market requirements due to their smaller size and the direct involvement of the entrepreneur in the current activities; offer professional and social fulfillment of a significant proportion of the population.

In the European Union there are 23 million SMEs, which have a share of 99.8% in the total number of enterprises. Micro-enterprises hold an overwhelming share of 90% in the total number of enterprises.

The place and the role of small and medium enterprises in the economies of selected countries for the present research can be observed using data from Table 2.

Based on data from Table 2, one can observe that the importance of the SME sector varies considerably from country to country. For example, in terms of occupancy of labour it can be sees that the SME sector uses over 60% of the workforce in all five countries under review, accounting the largest share in Bulgaria (72.6%) and the lowest share in Romania (60.8%). Analyzing the contribution to the added value, it can be noted that all five countries of Central and Eastern Europe under review recorded lower values than the average of EU-27, Czech has the greatest contribution to the added value (56.7%), while the smallest contribution was registered in Romania and Poland (48.4%). Regarding the density of

SMEs, it is observed that this indicator recorded the highest values in the Czech Republic (86.0, well above the EU-27 average), while in Romania it recorded the lowest values (18.9).

Table 2. Key indicators for SMEs in the selected countries from Central and Eastern Europe, 2005

	% share of SMEs in national total			Density of SMEs
	Number of enterprises	Number of persons Employed	Value added	Number of SME /1.000 inhabitants
EU-27	**99.8**	**67.1**	**57.6**	**39.9**
Bulgaria	99.7	72.6	53.2	30.9
Czech Republic	99.8	68.9	56.7	86.0
Hungary	99.8	70.9	50.2	55.1
Poland	99.8	69.8	48.4	36.8
Romania	99.5	60.8	48.4	18.9

Source: Eurostat (2008).

Traditionally, internal financing is the most important source of financing the SME activities. But often, since this method of funding is insufficient, SMEs are forced to resort to external financing. Analyzing the utilisation of external funding, we observe that most SMEs turn to financial resources from banks. But the banking products and services needs of SMEs are different depending on their size and the legal form of organisation.

Figure 1 consolidates several views on SMEs and their segmentation, starting with the most typical turnover thresholds, and indicating also behavioural and product need specifics. Starting from the definition of SMEs and the classification of enterprises in the European Union countries on size categories it can be highlighted a separation of the behaviour of these companies in dealing with banks, their needs and of how these needs are met through the banking products offered by banks.

Figure 1. Segmentation of business clients

Segment limits (European Commission)	Segment limits (turnover)	Segments and share of clients	Behavioural specifics	Client product needs	Driver of client satisfaction
Turnover: EUR 10 - 50m Employees: 50 – 240	Average turnover: EUR 24.6 m Turnover range: EUR 1.2 – 50 m	Medium 5%	- pure corporate attitude - complex product requirements	- investment credit - working capital loan - FX and trade finance	- specialized advisory service - flexibility - depth of products /service portfolio
Turnover: EUR 2 – 10m Employees: 10 – 49	Average turnover: EUR 3.6 m Turnover range: EUR 0.5 – 11 m	Small 15%	- clear separation between business and private financial needs - "plain vanilla" products	- working capital loan - overdraft - car loan	- personal relationship -speed/ flexibility/ transparency
Turnover: EUR < 2 m Employees: 0 – 9	Average turnover: EUR 0.65 m Turnover range: EUR 50 k – 2 m	Micro 80%	- business and private financial needs often mixed - standardized products	- credit card - overdraft - consumer loan - mortgage - car loan	- customer service - proximity -speed/ flexibility - pricing - online resources

Source: processed data after Central and Eastern European Banking Study- SME Banking in CEE (2009), p.14.

Thus, Figure 1 presents the main banking products required by SMEs according to the size category that they fit. So, it can be seen that micro-enterprises request standardized banking products: credit cards, overdrafts, consumer loan, mortgage and car loan, unlike most small businesses that use: working capital loan, overdraft and car loan. In the case of these companies there is a clear separation between private financial needs and the needs of the business. The medium enterprises, which have the lowest percentage (5%) prefer more complex products such as investment credit, working capital loan and trade finance.

The paper is structured as follows: section two analyzes the particularities of the access to finance for SMEs in the analyzed countries, focusing on the financing possibilities for these companies on markets in those countries but also highlighting the main barriers faced by SMEs when they attempt to procure the resources necessary to conduct their business. In the third section the role of the bank credit in financing the activities of SMEs is presented, but also the impact of the financial crisis on bank financing of SMEs, making a comparative analysis between the analyzed countries. Section four highlights the measures taken by public authorities in the five states to support bank financing of SMEs. The study ends with the general conclusions.

Particularities of the access to finance of SMEs in the analyzed countries

The problems of the financing of companies have vital importance, because their solution ensures the survival of the company, its development prospects, its present and future performance, its autonomy and ownership of its leaders. Lack of capital in the opportune moment and in appropriate size can lead, not only to loss of business opportunities, but also to endangering the company's market position or even to bankruptcy.

To highlight the ways of SMEs financing in the selected countries, will be considered the results of the study made by Flash Eurobarometer, no. 271. This study, initiated by the European Commission and the European Central Bank, has sought the access to finance of SMEs in the European Union but also in other European countries. Interviews were conducted during June-July 2009 and the sample in each country was divided into size classes of enterprises: 50% - micro enterprises (1-9 employees), 30% - small (10-49 employees), 10% - medium enterprises (50-249 employees) and 10% - large enterprises (with 250 employees and over).

The survey excluded firms from the following sectors: agriculture, fishing, public administration, financial services, activities of households, extra-territorial organization and bodies as well as holding companies. The targeted number of main interviews varies by the size of the country. The target sample distribution for the countries considered in this research is presented below:

Table 3. The number of firms, on size classes, chosen for every country

Country	SME	LSE	The share of SME in total number of firms
Bulgaria	200	20	90.9%
Romania	200	20	90.9%
Czech Republic	200	20	90.9%
Hungary	200	20	90.9%
Poland	450	50	90%

Source: processed data after Flash Eurobarometer (2009), p. 274.

As it can be seen from Table 3, SMEs have an overwhelming share of 90% of the companies of the sample. Therefore, the results obtained by this survey can be considered as relevant to the present research.

Compared with large firms, SMEs face a number of difficulties when they are trying to procure financial resources. Such difficulties are related, in particular, to insufficient guarantees offered to creditors and even to their incomplete information about the situation and the development prospects of SMEs.

The firms' access to finance is one of their main concerns, as shown in the Flash Eurobarometer survey (Flash Eurobarometer, 2009), realised from June 17 to July 23, 2009, on a sample of 9.063 companies from EU countries, Croatia, Iceland and Norway. More specifically, to the question "What is currently the most pressing issue your firm is facing?", 29% of companies surveyed identified the most pressing problem finding customers, and the access to finance was regarded as the second pressing issue, being identified by 16% of respondents (see Figure 2).

The competition, the availability of skilled staff and experienced managers, the cost of production or labour, and regulations were the most pressing issues for more than 13% of the respondents.

It is important to keep in mind that this study was conducted during the time that the financial crisis occurred, so the results obtained by looking at the most pressing issues faced by SMEs are actually the problems that these companies feel at the time of the financial crisis.

Regarding the answers to the question of the managers in different countries, the survey results show significant differentiation between countries (see Figure 3). The access to finance was identified as the most pressing problem by 19% of interviewed enterprises in Romania and Hungary and by less than 16% (the EU-27 average) of companies surveyed in Czech Republic, Bulgaria and Poland.

Figure 2. Companies' most pressing problem

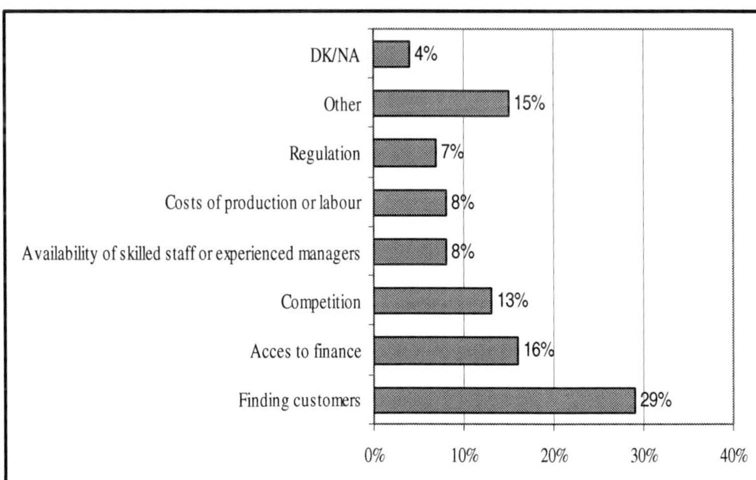

Source: processed data after Flash Eurobarometer (2009), p. 27.

Figure 3. Companies identifying access to finance as the most pressing problem

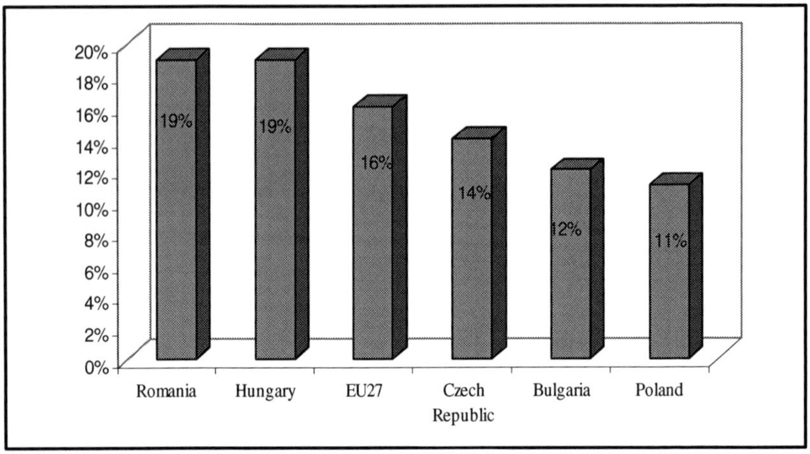

Source: processed data after Flash Eurobarometer (2009), p. 28.

Companies can use internal resources or external resources to finance their activities or investments. The economic business practices indicate that functioning of a business without adequate capital is one of the most common causes of business failure. In addition to sufficient capital, the company must have an appropriate capital structure, namely an optimal mix between own funds and borrowed capital. To select the optimal capital structure several factors are analyzed, one is chosen and after that every financing decision is made in accordance with that capital structure. So, as it is highlighted by the Flash Eurobarometer study, firms in different countries have different financial structures (see, Figure 4).

Figure 4. The financial structure of firms in the analysed countries (using internal resources or external financing resources) (% of firms)

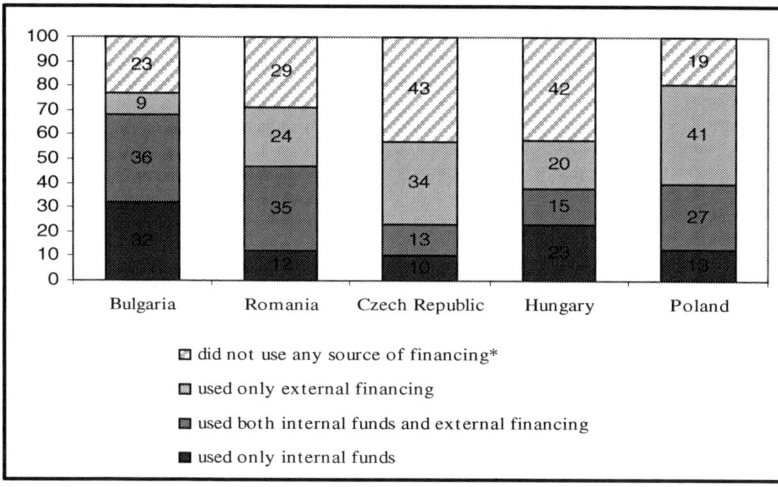

* - firms that could not answer to this question
Source: processed data after Flash Eurobarometer (2009), p. 29.

From the presented figure it can be observed that the financing of SMEs in the five analyzed countries is quite different. Companies from Bulgaria and Romania have preferred a larger proportion using a combination of internal funds and external funds to finance their activities (36%, respectively 35% of firms analyzed), while firms in the Czech Republic and Poland have preferred funding from external resources (34%, 41%). In Hungary there was a small difference between the percentage of firms that have preferred internal funds to finance their activity and the one that preferred external resources (23% and 20%).

These differences arise primarily because of the economic situation of each country but also due to different access to external financing resources. For example, regarding acccss to bank loans (financing resource on which we focus) large differences are observed in the reasons given by firms from considered countries to have determined not to use the resource of financing (see, Figure 5).

Figure 5. Firms that applied for a bank loan (new or renewal)

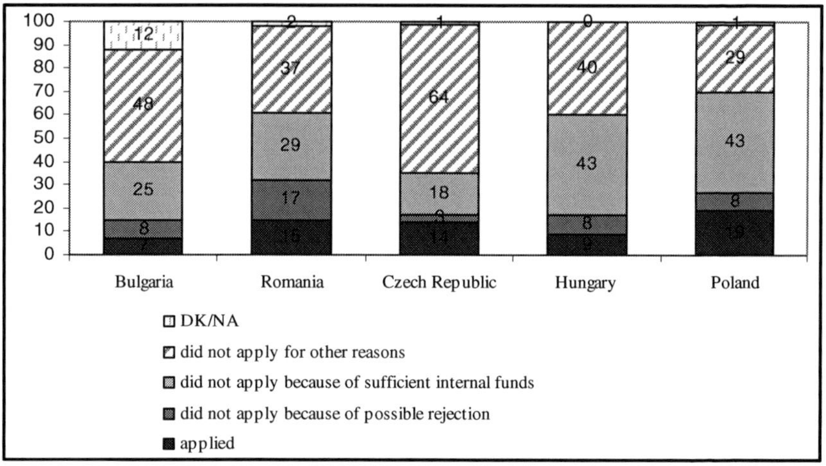

Source: processed data after Flash Eurobarometer (2009), p. 34.

From the figure it can be seen that the percentage of the managers who have applied for a bank loan in the six months preceding the study is less than 20% in all five countries analysed. Also, analysing the reasons of those who did not apply for a bank credit in the analysed countries, it is observed that the highest percentage of managers who did not use bank loans due to a possible rejection was recorded in Romania (17%), followed by Bulgaria, Hungary and Poland (8%). Most companies in the five countries have not applied to bank loans for other reasons, including excessive cost of these funding resources. However, the percentage of firms that have sufficient internal funds and did not apply to bank loans is quite high especially in Hungary and Poland (43%), followed by Romania (29%), Bulgaria (25%) and Czech Republic (18%). This demonstrates an already known fact that companies in the context of the financial crisis prefer to use internal funds to finance their activities because these are the most reliable sources of funding.

The role of bank loan in financing SMEs activity and implications of the current global crisis

As it was observed from the data presented above, SMEs prefer to finance their activity from their own resources. Yet, when they are forced to seek external financing resources, either due to the lack of own funds, either because they need additional resources to expand, they prefer some specific resources. The aim of this paper is to emphasise the external resources that are most used by SMEs and highlight the place of the bank credit within these resources.

In order to do so, there should be made a reference back to the analysis of the data obtained from Flash Eurobarometer (2009). This study shows that banks were the most popular provider of loans in the EU; they were mentioned by 89% of companies that had obtained a loan in the past two years. Also, one in 20 managers of the companies of the sample had received a loan from a private individual, such as a family member or a friend. Other sources (micro-finance institutions, or government-related sources) were mentioned by 6% of interviewees as the provider of their most recent loan.

When one looks at the situation on countries, they see that in most countries, banks were the most popular provider of loans for over 87% of SMEs. On the other hand, Czech banks were the most popular provider of loans for only 68% of the analyzed companies (see Figure 6). The leading role that the bank loan plays in financing the activities of SMEs is observed in all the countries of the sample.

Figure 6. The role of bank loan in SMEs financing

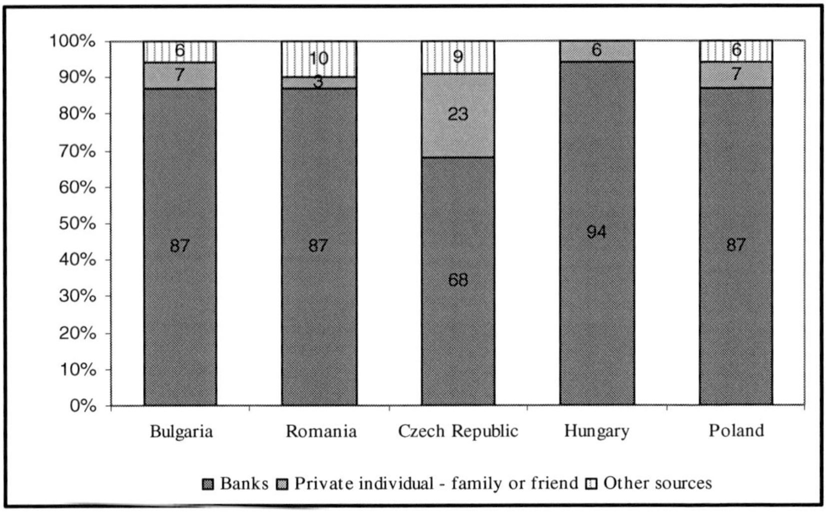

Source: processed data after Flash Eurobarometer (2009), p. 42.

Despite the different definitions and approaches of the concept of SME, most banks focus on loan products offered to these types of businesses. As in any other market segment, the most popular approach of the banks was to grow rapidly and gain market share from the sale of an existing product (bank loans) to new customers. Income potential seemed to be quite good, while the risk appeared to be relatively low due to rapid growth of national economies. Thus, gradually, banks began to significantly increase their lending to SMEs. As it can be seen in Figure 6, the bank loans held the first position in bank products and services required by SMEs in the European Union.

As firm size increases, the demand for banking products and services changes becomes more complex. So, banks must meet these growing needs by providing a range of products and services as appropriate to the firms. For example, a small enterprise which has grown in recent years might be interested in getting upgraded from the current account to the cash management solution.

To highlight the differences between the main banking products required by small enterprises and the medium ones, there can be an analysis of the results obtained by the study realised in 2009 in collaboration between zeb, EFMA and ERSTE Group regarding SME Banking in CEE. These results can be observed in the figure presented below (Figure 7).

Figure 7. Banking products required by small and medium enterprises in Central and Eastern Europe countries

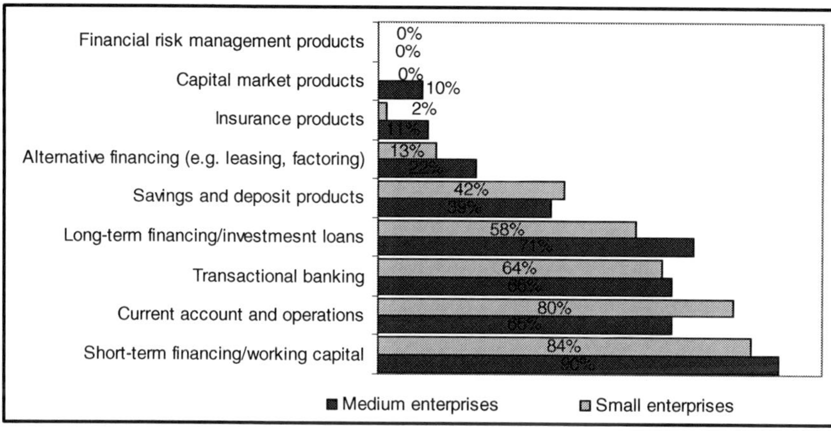

Source: Central and Eastern European Banking (2009), p. 30.

In the context of the current economic and financial crisis, the access to credit for SMEs and, in general, for individuals and businesses has become extremely difficult because of the increase of the bank interest rates, tightening lending standards by banks and even the suspension of lending by some banks (Raiffeisen Research, 2009, p.11).

The global economic crisis has dramatically changed the market conditions in which businesses operate. The redemption of debts by financial institutions increased capital costs and reduced credit availability, while the exchange rate adjustments have increased the price of imported inputs and exports made them become more competitive. While the financial shock that hit the emerging Europe in the fourth quarter of 2008 and at the beginning of 2009 was large and damaging, it was nonetheless moderate compared to shocks suffered by other emerging market regions and advanced financial markets (Berglöf, et al., 2009).

Even in "normal" economic conditions the governments have recognized that in order to survive and grow, SMEs need specific policies and programs, hence the full range of measures for SMEs in force in most countries of the world. However, now SMEs were particularly hard hit by the global crisis. These companies are now vulnerable for several reasons: in addition to traditional challenges regarding access to finance, which continues to apply, new capital supply difficulties appear.

It is important to note that SMEs are generally more vulnerable in times of crisis for several reasons, among which are the following: it is harder for them to reduce their activities since they are already small; they are less diversified individual within their business; they have a weaker financial structure (e.g. lower capitalisation); they have a lower credit rating; they are strongly dependent on credit and have fewer financing options.

Analyzing the results of Flash Eurobarometer (2009) on the offer of bank loans for SMEs in the European Union, it can be observed that almost half of the SMEs surveyed (46%) claimed that the supply of bank credit has declined (see Figure 8), while 34% of them claimed that it was unchanged, and 8% claimed that there was registered an improvement in the bank credit offer.

Figure 8. Changes in the availability of bank loans (% firms)

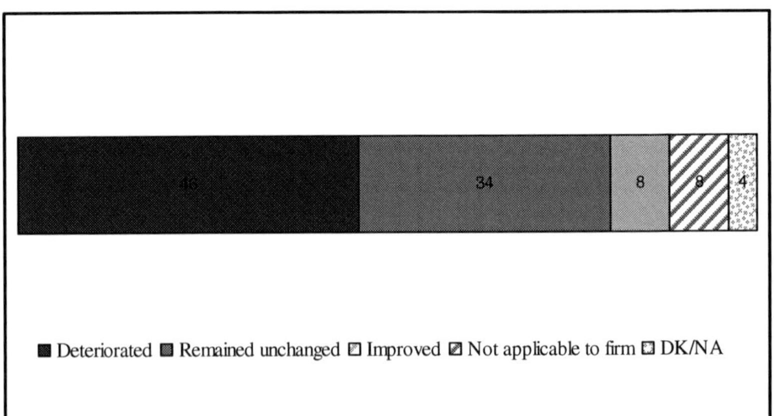

Source: processed data after Flash Eurobarometer (2009), p. 55.

In order to see how the current economic situation (the financial crisis) affects the activities of the banking sector in Central and Eastern European countries and in particular SME banking, the figure presented below can be examined (Figure 9).

Figure 9. The biggest threats to SME Banking in Central and Eastern European countries

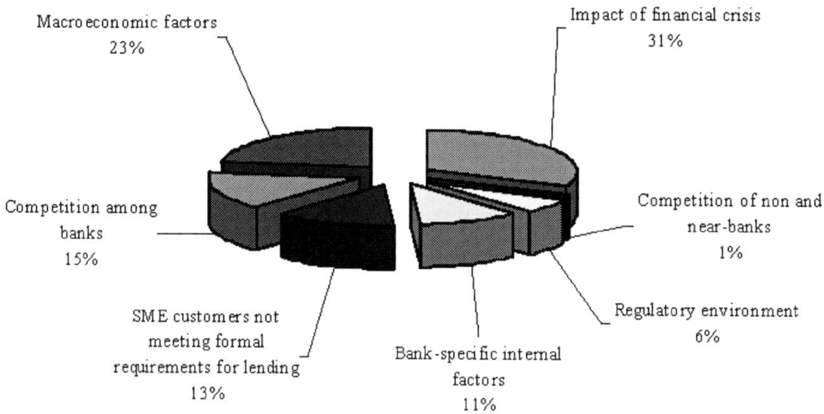

Source: Central and Eastern European Banking Study-SME Banking in CEE (2009), p. 10.

As we can see, the current financial crisis is the threat with the largest share (31%) on SME banking in Central and Eastern Europe, followed by macroeconomic factors with a share of 23%, competition among banks (15%) and SME customers that do not meet the formal requirements for obtaining a bank loan (13%). Internal factors are a low threat (11%) as well as the regulatory environment (6%) and competition with non-banking financial institutions (1%).

Regarding the impact of the financial crisis on the banking business in SMEs area, 69% of the bankers participating in the study saw a worsened quality of the loan portfolio as an issue. Under current conditions of global financial crisis, many banks have tightened credit conditions and have initiated activities to improve early warning system and collection procedures. Another concern for most banks is the sharp decrease in sales of banking products, which appeared due to the fact that SMEs do not meet banks' increased need for approval of funding, and declining demand from the customers of banks, which expected future development (seen as a problem for 65% of bankers surveyed).

Moreover, SMEs do not want to increase indebtedness despite lower sales and increased late payments. Currently, many SMEs do not even try to obtain a loan, even if the financial situation of these companies is almost healthy. Faced with an uncertain future, this reaction is fully rational especially when these enterprises are confronted with tightened credit conditions imposed by banks and other creditors. In all countries the tightening of SME credit conditions by banks is clearly visible for all the banks' clients. This happens because banks operating in CEE are confronted with limited sources of funds as the bond markets look quite flat (Raiffeisen Research, 2008, p. 56)

The current financial crisis reveals a number of changes in the relations between banks and SMEs, such as:

- SMEs (and businesses generally) have postponed their investment projects financed by loans;
- Application of credit for working capital for SMEs and short-term loans decreased in some countries but not as strong as that for investment;
- Banks have tightened lending standards in terms of security guarantees and amounts, but not exclusively towards SMEs;
- In some countries, banks and other financial intermediaries have increased substantially the cost (and extent) of credit to all their customers, which might seem paradoxical in relation to the relaxed monetary policies applied by the central banks of countries considered (by lowering interest monetary policy rate, bank reserve requirements).

Banks and other financial intermediaries are under pressure and have tried to maintain or strengthen their capital base. As part of this strategy they are looking fully secured transactions and minimize the use of their economic capital.

In some countries, banks have reduced lending, not only because of increased risk, but also because they face difficulties in securing financial resources, both from outside the country and the inter-banking market. The cost of these resources is high, especially that due to significant deterioration of bank loan portfolio.

The OECD study on the impact of the financial crisis on the financing of SMEs revealed some effects of the crisis on SMEs business but also on their demand for credit in the OECD member countries (see Table 4).

Table 4. Experienced or expected impacts of the crisis on SME and entrepreneurship financing in the analyzed countries

	Impact on SMEs			SME demand for credit		
	Demand	Working capital & payment delays	Exits (insolvencies and bankruptcies)	Total	Short-term	Long-term
Ungaria			+		+	-
Cehia			=			
Polonia	-			+		

"+" indicates that there has been registered or it is expected an increase in the impact of the indicators in each column;
"=" does not indicates any change in the indicators;
"-" indicates a registered or an expected decrease in the impact of the indicators in each column.
Source: OECD, 2009, p. 23.

As it can be seen from Table 4, SMEs in the countries of the sample have experienced different effects of the financial crisis. Hungary has registered increased rates of insolvency and bankruptcy of SMEs, but also an increase in the demand for short-term loans from SMEs, compared to a decrease in the demand for long-term loans from these enterprises.

SMEs in Poland have registered a decrease in demand but also a growing need for capital, for which the total demand for credit has been increased. In the Czech Republic there was no change in the rates of insolvency and bankruptcy of the SMEs.

Measures taken by public authorities from the analyzed countries to support bank financing of SME

The ability of countries to deal with the current financial crisis depends to a large extent on their fiscal and monetary policies. . The study realised by OECD (2009) highlights the fact that many countries have now put up some anti-crisis packages combining in different proportions three lines of action: stimulating demand (consumer packages, infrastructure programs, tax policies), measures to improve the lending activity, including recapitalization of banks, which in some cases, include explicit provisions or mechanisms to maintain or develop the capacity of banks to finance

SMEs, such as public credit guarantees, and labour market measures (reduction of taxes on employment or social taxes and social unemployment programs temporarily enlarged).

The anti-crisis packages and accompanying measures address, in many countries, more specifically the financing problem of SMEs. According to the preceding analysis, the measures put in place by countries can be classified in three different groups depending on the aspect of the SME financing problem to which they are geared. Three main groups of measures can be distinguished:

- measures supporting sales, cash flows, and working capital;
- measures to enhance SMEs access to liquidity, mainly to bank lending;
- measures aimed at helping SMEs to maintain their investment level and more generally to build their capacity to respond in the near future to a possible surge in demand.

SMEs have significant gaps in information which would enable them to know their environment better. In particular, a lack of clear, transparent information tends to harm their financial relationships with lenders. A policy that is focused on improving the transparency of the position of individual SMEs could lead to less tightened conditions for achieving capital during recessions (European Commsion, 2009, p. 63).

With regard to the support of bank financing it is important to emphasize that banks should promote a separate credit system for SMEs. This process should permit the incorporation of the specificity of these companies in business lending and avoid increasing complexity of banking products and services offered at a level that is not necessary. This approach would not only have a positive impact on the banking business conducted in SMEs sector but, more, should meet those customer needs and expectations. Some banks have already started the process of specialization, by implementing specific banking products to SMEs, but the benefits will be seen when the process will extend to the entire banking sector in the analysed countries (Central and Eastern European Banking Study, 2009).

One of the measures used by the public authorities from the analyzed countries involves the expansion and diversification of public security systems, or in some cases even direct lending by public institutions. These policy measures are addressing one of the key reasons that might explain the reluctance of banks lending to SMEs, which represents their constraint regarding the capital requirements ratio (OECD, 2009, p.32).

In order to alleviate the effects on SMEs of the twin shock of falling sales and more difficult access to funding, governments are using two different approaches to increase availability of credit to SMEs:

- on the incentive side, the creation and extension of guarantee schemes for loans to SMEs, or when that fails direct public lending;
- on the discipline or sanction side, setting targets for SME lending for banks that have been recapitalized by public monies, putting them under administrative monitoring or putting in place specific procedures to solve problems between individual SMEs and banks.

Public credit guarantee schemes for SMEs are expected to be an incentive for bank loans for this segment of customers. Loan guarantee schemes can improve access to finance for SMEs, as an incentive for banks. For EU countries, the potential leverage of public guarantees on bank loans to SMEs has been extended by the European Commission decision to allow member states temporarily to facilitate access to finance for companies, through subsidized guarantees and loan subsidies for investments. Moreover, some countries have resorted to measures of discipline, which in some cases complement incentives in order to press the banks to continue lending to businesses (OECD, 2009, p. 10).

To prevent loss by SMEs of their competitive advantage in the medium term and to help them be prepared to revive economic activity, some governments have implemented measures to strengthen capital base and to develop their capacity or both. These measures are either tax incentives or provide specific funding opportunities such as grants or loans guaranteed (Czech Republic, Hungary). In addition, the existence of structural funds within the European Union new member states gives the flexibility to support investment projects of SMEs in specific technologies, sectors or regions (Romania and Czech Republic). The main policy measures enhancing SMEs' access to liquidity can be observed in Table 5.

Table 5. Policy measures enhancing SMEs' access to liquidity, especially to bank lending

Country	Creation and extension of loans and guarantee schemes for SMEs
Czech Republic	In late 2008, the Ministry of Industry and Commerce has transferred one billion Czech crowns (the equivalent of 37.2 million euros) turnover to the bottom of the Czech-Moravian Guarantee and Development Bank as collateral for loans from commercial banks. In February 2009, Ministry of Trade and Industry announced another section of the Guarantee Program, which allows the entrepreneurs to obtain guarantees for loans from commercial banks. In total, the Ministry of Industry and Trade contributes with 1.650 billion (EUR 61.4 million) to the guarantee program.
Hungary	In Hungary, the New Hungary Portfolio Guarantee Programme was established after the apparition of the financial crisis. The portfolio guarantee program, Venture Finance Hungary Plc. provides direct guarantees to financial claims (supporting credit for SMEs) of the financial intermediaries (mostly commercial banks), pre-determined based on risk sharing, and thereby improving bank financing options for SMEs. For a given loan, the security to be provided by Venture Finance Hungary Plc is up 80% of bank debt - the rest is bank's own risk. Guarantee Program provides loans worth a maximum of 100 million Hungarian forints (equivalent to 344,000 euros). Resources invested for this purpose require a total of 28.2 billion Hungarian forints (97 million). In Hungary the total public security, which is provided by credit guarantee Garantiqa Credit guarantee Co. Ltd. banks for lending to SMEs has been increased from 450 million Hungarian forints (1.5 million) to 900 million Hungarians forints (3 million).
Romania	Now tax benefits were granted to companies, having allocated an amount of about 2.900 million for 2009-2011. These benefits include: - Tax exemption for contracts to increase the labour productivity; - Deduction of 10% of regional tax from the income tax and personal income tax; - VAT payment at the moment of actual receipt of sale payment; - in March 2009 was established up the Romanian Fund for Credit Contragarantation, whose mission is to improve the access to finance for SMEs through the acquisition of part of risk assumed by guarantee funds.

Source: OECD, 2009.

Conclusion

The significant contribution of the SME sector to economic and social development of countries permits the assessment that the functionality and the performance of economies are largely conditioned by the development of this sector.

In order for SMEs to operate significant financial resources are required. As it has been seen over this paper the companies prefer to use, first, the own resources being the most secure and without risk. Yet, their resources are often insufficient so that SMEs have to rely on external financial resources. Within this context, there is a preference of SMEs for loans from banks, which seems normal if one considers that the financial systems of the analyzed countries focus on banks. In the study significant differences were observed related to the modalities of financing of SMEs in each of the five countries examined, but also the important role of bank credit in financing these companies.

In the context of the current financial crisis, a significant part of the SME sector in most of the world is strongly affected. The effects of the current crisis on SMEs business is primarily significant decrease of the revenue, reduced opportunities to enter on new markets, reduced access to finance and thus reduced opportunities to develop and even to survive.

Even when the economy is operating normally SMEs have difficulties in terms of obtaining bank loans. In the context of the financial crisis these problems are more acute, especially given that banks have restricted lending activity and imposed more stringent conditions on loans by tightening lending standards and increasing the demands for guarantees as well as the request guarantees even for short-term loans.

To improve the situation and make bank loans more affordable for SMEs public authorities in the countries considered a series of measures were adopted: public guarantee schemes, disciplinary measures designed to support business loans filled with resources from EU structural funds.

Revival of bank lending in general, and the one oriented to SMEs in particular depend on real economic recovery and the improvement of economic and financial situation of the enterprises. For this purpose, given the current crisis event, a decisive role has been developed by the national public authorities and the European Commission for appropriate economic policy measures, which are meant to revive the business environment and induce the co-interested banks to finance SMEs.

References

Berglöf, E., Korniyenko, Y., Plekhanov, A. and Zettelmeyer, J., 2009, *Understanding the crisis in emerging Europe*, European Bank for Reconstruction and Development, http://www.mof.go.jp/english/pp_review/ppr012/ppr012d.pdf (accessed in 19.11.2010).

European Central Bank, 2009, *Survey on the access to finance of small and medium sized enterprises in the euro area*, http://www.ecb.int/stats/money/surveys/sme/html/index.en.html, (accessed in 18.11.2010).

European Commision, 2004, SME Definition.

—. 2009, *Cyclicality of SME finance- Literature survey, data analysis and econometric analysis*, Zoetermeer, Netherland, http://ec.europa.eu/enterprise/newsroom/cf/_getdocument.cfm?doc_id =3127 (accessed in 20.11.2010).

Eurostat, 2008, *Enterprise by size class – overview of SMEs in the EU*, 31, http://epp.eurostat.ec.europa.eu/cache/ITY_OFFPUB/KS-SF-08-031/EN/KS-SF-08-031-EN.PDF (accessed in 20.11.2010).

Flash Eurobarometer, 2009, *Access to finance*, Analytical Report, 271, http://ec.europa.eu/public_opinion/flash/fl_271_en.pdf (accessed in 20.11.2010).

—. 2009, *Access to finance-Annex*, Issue no. 271, http://ec.europa.eu/public_opinion/flash/fl_271_annex_en.pdf (accessed in 20.11.2010).

—. 2009, *Observatory of European SMEs*, Analytical Report, Summary, 196, http://ec.europa.eu/public_opinion/flash/fl196_en.pdf (accessed in 20.11.2010).

OECD, 2009, *The Impact of the Global Crisis on SME and Entrepreneurship Financing and Policy Responses*, Centre for Entrepreneurship, SMEs and Local Development, http://www.oecd.org/dataoecd/40/34/43183090.pdf (accessed in 20.11.2010).

OECD-Eurostat Entrepreneurship Indicators Programme, 2009, Measuring Entrepreneurship. A Collection of Indicators, http://www.oecd.org/dataoecd/43/50/44068449.pdf (accessed in 20.11.2010).

Raiffeisen Research, 2008, *CEE Banking sector report - Size matters as deposits move into the spotlight*, http://www.rzb.at/eBusiness/services/resources/media/1026359884948-1026359885014_1026067974202-511396645989197153-1-NA-EN.pdf (accessed in 19.11.2010).

—. 2009, *CEE Banking sector report, Rough playing field committed players*, http://www.rzb.at/eBusiness/services/resources/media/1026359884948-1026359885014_1026067924320_1026689962565-574060325146557957-1-38-EN.pdf (accessed in 19.11.2010).

zeb, EFMA, ERSTE Group, *Central and Eastern European Banking Study*, 2009, SME Banking in CEE.

GEO no. 23 of 11 March 2009 about establishing the Romanian Fund for Credit Contragarantation, published in Official Gazette of Romania No. 190 of March 26, 2009.

CONTRIBUTORS

Part One: European Union and Economic Developments in the Balkan and Eastern European Countries

Ljubomir Kekenovski
Professor, Faculty of Economics, University of Ss. Cyril and Methodius, F.Y.R.O.M.

Violeta Cvetkoska
Teaching Assistant, Faculty of Economics, University of Ss. Cyril and Methodius, F.Y.R.O.M.

Marietta Fessel Harsányi
Assistant Professor, College for Modern Business Studies, Hungary

Theofanis Malkidis
Lecturer, Democritus University of Thrace, Greece

Silvia Trifonova
Associate Professor, University of National and World Economy, Bulgaria

Peter Pochaleev
PhD student, University of Agriculture, Bulgaria

Stela Todorova
Associate Professor, University of Agriculture, Bulgaria

Part Two: Regional Development

Alketa Bejko
Lecturer, Economic Department, Eqrem Çabej University, Albania

Kristaq Çombi
Lecturer, Economic Department, Eqrem Çabej University, Albania

Daniela Qiqi
Lecturer, Economic Department, Eqrem Çabej University, Albania

Anestis D. Mantatzis
PhD student, Department in Economic Studies, University of Macedonia, Greece

Lindita Rova
Lecturer, Economic Department, Eqrem Çabej University, Albania

Ilirjana Zyberi
Senior Lecturer, Economic Department, Eqrem Çabej University, Albania

Michael Nikolaidis
Associate Professor, Department of Accountancy, Kavala Institute of Technology, Greece

Christos Batzios
Professor, Faculty of Veterinary Medicine, Aristotle University of Thessaloniki, Greece

Athanasios Mandilas
Assistant Professor, Department of Accountancy, Kavala Institute of Technology, Greece

Athanasios Nikolaidis
MSc, Department of Accountancy, Kavala Institute of Technology, Greece

Persefoni Polychronidou
Adjoined Assistant Professor, Department of Accountancy, Kavala Institute of Technology, Greece

Part Three: FDI, Enterprise Finance and Banking

Dimitrios Maditinos
Assistant Professor, Department of Business Administration, Kavala Institute of Technology, Greece

Dimitrios Kousenidis
Assistant Professor, Department of Economic Sciences, Aristotle University of Thessaloniki, Greece

Dimitrios Chatzoudes
Adjoined Lecturer, Department of Accountancy, Kavala Institute of Technology, Greece

Makogon Yuriy
Professor, Donetsk National University, Ukraine

Orekhova Tatyana
Professor, Donetsk National University, Ukraine

Oleksiy Ryabchyn
Associate Professor, Donetsk National University, Ukraine

Maria-Eleni Voutsa
PhD Candidate, Department of Economics, University of Thessaly, Greece

Persefoni Polychronidou
Adjoined Assistant Professor, Department of Accountancy, Kavala Institute of Technology, Greece

Ioannis Kazanidis
Adjoined Assistant Professor, Department of Accountancy, Kavala Institute of Technology, Greece

Gesthimani Eleftheriadou
Lecturer, Department of Accountancy, Kavala Institute of Technology, Greece

Stavros Valsamidis
Lecturer, Department of Accountancy, Kavala Institute of Technology, Greece

Part Four: Rural Developments in Specific Countries

Matteo Belletti
SAIFET Department, Polytechnic University of Marche, Italy

Elvira Leksinaj
Faculty of Economics and Agribusiness, Agricultural University of Tirana, Albania

Eugenia Bitsani
Associate Professor, Department of Management of Health and Welfare Unit, Kalamata Institute of Technology, Greece

Androniki Kavoura
Assistant Professor, Department of Marketing, Athens Institute of Technology, Greece

Part Five: Supreme Audit Institution and IFRS

Ljiljana Bonic
Assistant Professor, Faculty of Economics, University of Nis, Serbia

Igor Mladenovic
Assistant Professor, Faculty of Economics, University of Nis, Serbia

Diogenis Baboukardos
PhD Candidate, Jonkoping International Business School, Department of Accounting & Finance, Sweden

Part Six: Labour Market, Enterprises and Entrepreneurship

Norberto Pignatti
Research Fellow, International School of Economics at Tbilisi State University, Georgia,

Tatiana Karabchuk
Researcher, Centre for Labour Market Studies, The Higher School of Economics, Russia

Katina Boga-Karteri
Associate Professor, Department of Marketing, Thessaloniki Institute of Technology, Greece

George Stalidis
Lecturer, Department of Marketing, Thessaloniki Institute of Technology, Greece

Connie Papanicolas
Department of Marketing, Thessaloniki Institute of Technology, Greece

Angela Roman
Assistant Professor, Al. I. Cuza University of Iasi, Faculty of Economics and Business Administration, Romania

Valentina Diana Ignatescu
PhD Candidate, Al. I. Cuza University of Iasi, Faculty of Economics and Business Administration, Romania